J31-22

The Prehistory of Eastern Zambia

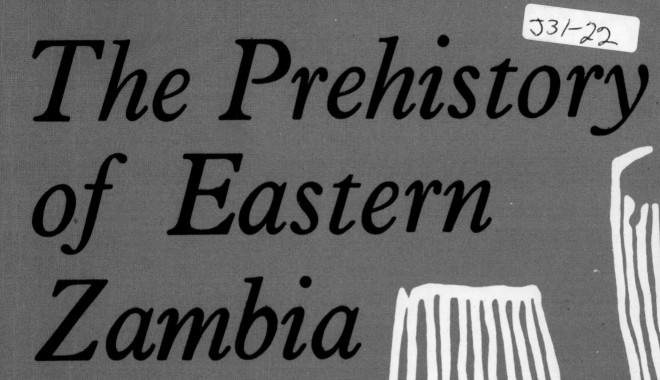

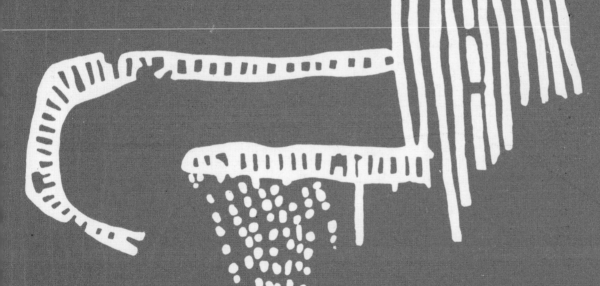

by
D. W. Phillipson

THE PREHISTORY OF
EASTERN ZAMBIA

British Institute in Eastern Africa
P.O. Box 30710, Nairobi, Kenya

London Address: c/o Royal Geographical Society,
1 Kensington Gore, London SW 7

Printed by Kenya Litho Limited, Changamwe Road, P.O. Box 40775, Nairobi, Kenya.

MEMOIR NUMBER SIX
OF THE BRITISH INSTITUTE IN EASTERN AFRICA

The Prehistory of Eastern Zambia

by

D. W. Phillipson

NAIROBI
BRITISH INSTITUTE IN EASTERN AFRICA
1976

Contents

Q.916.894
P54p

CONTENTS

Preface

This book presents detailed reports on archaeological excavations conducted in eastern Zambia in 1966, 1970 and 1971, and on prehistoric sites visited but less intensively investigated during the same period. The data collected are used as the basis for a reconstruction of the prehistory of the region during the past forty thousand years. In later chapters this local succession is reviewed in the context of a re-evaluation of contemporaneous developments over a wide area of sub-Saharan Africa.

The fieldwork here described was undertaken, and the text of much of this book completed in draft, while I held the post of Secretary/Inspector to the National Monuments Commission of Zambia from 1964 until 1973. Almost all the fieldwork costs and other expenses of this work were met from Commission funds; I am grateful to the members of the Commission, and particularly to its Chairman, Mr Spedio Tembo, for their constant support and encouragement. Educational Expeditions International provided funds and participants which made possible a second season of excavation at Kalemba rock-shelter in 1971. The final preparation of this book in its present form has been undertaken at the British Institute in Eastern Africa where, since 1973, I have been Assistant Director. I wish to thank the Institute's Director and Governing Council for providing facilities for the completion of this work, and for consenting to its publication in the Institute's series of Memoirs. Publication has been subsidised by a generous grant from the Anglo American Corporation (Central Africa) Ltd., and by a substantial order for copies from the Zambia National Monuments Commission.

NOTE ON ILLUSTRATIONS

To facilitate comparisons, all illustrations of artefacts contained in this book are reproduced at a constant series of scales. Drawings of chipped stone artefacts and those of bone and shell are printed full size; all other artefacts are shown at half their original size, with the sole exception of tracings of rock-paintings which are presented at a scale of 0.06.

NOTE ON CHRONOLOGY

The now widespread convention is here followed whereby uncorrected radiocarbon dates, and age-estimates based on such dates, are quoted in (radiocarbon) years bc or ad: BC and AD signify dates expressed in calendar years.

ACKNOWLEDGEMENTS

This book contains valuable contributions by Professor Brian M. Fagan, Dr Ian Hodder and Dr Hertha de Villiers. Analyses and identifications have been made by Mr G. Bell-Cross, Dr D. H. S. Davis, the Geological Survey Department in Lusaka, Dr J. B. Gillett, Dr John M. Harris, Miss C. H. S. Kabuye, Professor J. H. Langenheim, the Mount Makulu Research Station at Chilanga, the late Dewan Mohinder Nath Nair, Dr Laurel Phillipson, and the Royal Botanical Gardens at Kew. I thank them all for their co-operation and expertise.

In the field, volunteer assistance on excavations was provided by Mr N. T. Filmer, Mr E. A. C. Mills and Miss Olive Wilks. A team of participants took part in the fieldwork season which was sponsored by Educational Expeditions International. The help of Mr Michael Bisson at Kalemba is also gratefully acknowledged. Perhaps my greatest debt is to Mr Benson Mutema, who acted as foreman and general assistant on all the excavations here described. Dr H. W. Langworthy was a frequent visitor and companion in the field, and I thank him for his discussions and explanations of eastern Zambian history.

Last, but by no means least, I owe much to the scores of residents in eastern Zambia, from all walks of life, who have assisted me in elucidating the prehistory of their homeland. They have helped in ways too many to mention: by labouring on excavations, directing me to sites, explaining traditions, and (although—as one visitor to my excavation said—she had never before seen a white man so dirty) extending to me a welcome which was invariably friendly and courteous.

The drawings here reproduced I owe to the skill of Mrs Marjorie Bradshaw, Mrs Joan Musgrave, Mr John Nyakure Ochieng' and Dr Laurel Phillipson: to ensure uniformity of style they have all been prepared for the printer by Mr Ochieng'. I thank Mrs Margaret Sharman for her help in preparing the manuscript and in seeing the book through the press.

The name of my wife, Laurel, has been mentioned twice in these acknowledgements already, but it is fitting to include it once more. She has helped, advised and encouraged me throughout the ten years' of work here described.

Nairobi,   D. W. Phillipson
7th July 1976.

List of Text Figures

List of Plates

Chapter I

Introduction

I. THE AIMS AND SCOPE OF THE INVESTIGATION

The archaeological research described in this volume was undertaken in an attempt to establish, in general terms, the succession of prehistoric cultures in the plateau region of eastern central Africa which now forms the southern part of the Eastern Province of the Republic of Zambia (fig.1). Attention has been concentrated on those cultural stages conventionally known as the 'Middle Stone Age', the 'Late Stone Age' and the Iron Age. Although the presence of several promising sites had been reported, no intensive research into the prehistory of the region had previously been undertaken. It was my aim, through selective and usually small-scale excavation, to illustrate the technological and economic development of the prehistoric populations of this area; to tie this developmental sequence to the most detailed radiocarbon chronology which it proved possible to establish from the limited number of sites investigated; to compare the results obtained with the data available for contemporary societies elsewhere in sub-Saharan Africa; and to interpret the conclusions reached in terms of the prehistory of the sub-continent as a whole.

The research, involving three major rock-shelter excavations and the investigation of numerous minor sites, has revealed an archaeological sequence covering at least the past thirty-five thousand years. The greater part of this period covers the later phases of the local 'Middle Stone Age' and the whole of the inception and development of the 'Late Stone Age'. A detailed picture was obtained of the technology and economy of the region's inhabitants through this long period of development: this is here discussed in relation both to the changing environmental conditions of eastern Zambia, and to contemporary events in other regions of sub-Saharan Africa. One of the most important results of the work here described has been the demonstration that the 'Late Stone Age' industries of eastern Zambia and, by implication, those of a much wider area of south-central and eastern Africa, were an essentially local development which owed little to inspiration or cultural contact from the inhabitants of more distant regions.

Also investigated were the Early and later Iron Ages of eastern Zambia, which mark the arrival of agricultural societies in the region. The long period of chronological overlap between these peoples and the stone-tool-using hunter/gatherers is here discussed in detail, and the extent of contact and acculturation between the two groups is evaluated. Both the Early and later Iron Age societies are considered with regard to their place in the general picture which is now emerging, from both archaeological and linguistic studies, of the spread of Bantu-speaking agriculturalists into sub-equatorial Africa. In the case of the later Iron Age, comparison is also made between the archaeological record and the historical evidence provided by the oral traditions of the present inhabitants of eastern Zambia.

Finally, a detailed description is presented of the over forty rock-painting sites which have now been discovered in the region. A stylistic sequence is established which may be correlated with the archaeological succession. Within the chronological framework thus provided, it has proved possible to ascertain the probable significance which the rock-paintings held in the lives of the artists.

One of the major problems faced by the prehistorian in Africa is the scarcity of the basic archaeological data and its uneven distribution. Many areas, sometimes even whole countries, remain virtually blank on the archaeological map. The framework for synthesis is thus far from complete; and the prehistorian must frequently rely on what is sometimes little more than inspired guesswork based on isolated occurrences or sequences which may or may not be typical. As the work here described was conducted in a part of Zambia where very little archaeological research had previously been undertaken, priority was given to the establishment of the basic sequence. No attempt was made to conduct a complete survey of sites in any part of the research area; and no doubt many substantial and important sites remain to be discovered. Similarly, no studies were made of prehistoric settlement-patterns either within individual sites or over wider territories, although the potential of eastern Zambia for studies of both types is considerable.

Particular attention was paid to the analysis of aggregates from the smallest cultural-stratigraphic units which it proved practicable to isolate. This was done in order to evaluate the degree of continuity through the cultural succession—that is, the extent to which technological and economic innovations represent indigenous developments within the area investigated, rather than introductions from or by the populations of neighbouring areas. This approach has resulted in a view of the local prehistoric sequence as a developmental continuum in which innovation progressed at some times more rapidly than at others. Such a view contrasts with the more rigid and sometimes arbitrary compartmentalisation into cultures, industries or phases which remains the vogue in many studies of African prehistory. The concept of the developmental continuum presents numerous terminological difficulties which have not yet been fully resolved. However, in the present writer's view, it offers a more meaningful model for the interpretation of the archaeological data in that it provides a reasonably objective test of the justification for any compartmentalised nomenclature which may subsequently be proposed.

The contents of the present volume are put forward in the hope that they will provide the framework for an understanding of the prehistoric succession in south-eastern Zambia, and will be relevant to the continuing re-assessment of African prehistory over a wide area. Further fieldwork, on a more substantial scale, will be required both to fill in the gaps and to provide a more detailed local picture.

* * * * *

The research began with a four-week reconnaissance in the winter of 1965, particular attention being paid to locating caves and rock-shelters showing evidence of prolonged occupation, excavation of which might be expected to reveal a succession of prehistoric industries, as well as evidence for the date of the many rock-paintings of the region. Several previously unreported rock-paintings were located and recorded at this time. Of the sites investigated, that most suitable for excavation appeared to be the Makwe rock-shelter (fig. 2, p. 8), located near the Moçambique border south-west of Katete.

Excavations were conducted at Makwe during a six-week period in April and May, 1966. The deposits in the northern half of the rock-shelter were completely removed and found to attain a maximum depth of 2.08 m. Nine stratigraphical horizons were recognised and the abundant 'Late Stone Age' aggregates which they yielded were regarded as successive developing phases of a single industry. No material suitable for radiocarbon dating was recovered from the lowest horizon; but the one immediately overlying it was shown to date from approximately 3000 bc. Further radiocarbon dates suggested that there may have been a hiatus in the occupation of the site covering approximately the last two millennia bc; but no break in the succession of deposits which could correspond with such a hiatus was observed. The later levels yielded evidence for contact between 'Late Stone Age' and Early Iron Age peoples; and the occupation of the shelter from the beginning of the Christian era until comparatively recent times was well attested.

Concurrently with the excavation at Makwe, an investigation was made into traditional Chewa iron-smelting methods in the Katete region. The results of this work have already been published (D. W. Phillipson, 1968b). During further reconnaissance of rock-painting sites the presence of a large rock-shelter at Thandwe, in Chief Nzomane's area of the Chipata District, was reported by the Reverend Father M. Zimmermann. The site was visited in May 1966, and its varied rock-painting series was recorded.

During the three years following 1966, detailed analysis of the prehistoric aggregates recovered from Makwe was undertaken, but research priorities dictated that fieldwork be undertaken elsewhere; and it was not until 1970 that I was able to resume operations in the Eastern Province itself. In that year two sites were excavated. At Thandwe rock-shelter a small excavation indicated that the archaeological deposits attained a maximum depth of 1.6 m. It was clear from the typology of the associated artefacts, as well as from the three radiocarbon dates, that the occupation of this site may

all be attributed to the last 2000 years. It apparently began during the period that Makwe was unoccupied and continued into extremely recent times. Two elaborate graves unearthed in the lower levels were dated to the first few centuries ad, immediately prior to the arrival of the first Early Iron Age immigrants in the Thandwe area.

The Thandwe excavations thus filled several gaps in our knowledge of the Eastern Province sequence as revealed at Makwe; but they did not succeed in carrying the known industrial succession further back than the approximately fourth millennium bc date of the initial occupation of the latter site. Following the completion of the Thandwe excavations, therefore, in June 1970, further reconnaissance was conducted, principally in the Chipata and Chadiza Districts, for a site the excavation of which could be expected to reveal the earlier stages of the local 'Late Stone Age'.

While this search was being conducted, in the area adjacent to the Zambia/Malawi border some 25 km to the north of Chipata, an extensive Early Iron Age village site at Kamnama was located and briefly investigated. Trial trenches indicated that only one phase of Early Iron Age occupation had occurred; and this was dated by radiocarbon to about the fourth century ad.

Subsequently, a survey was conducted in Chief Mwangala's area of the Chadiza District to investigate rock-painting sites reported to the then Rhodes-Livingstone Museum by Mr R. A. Hamilton in 1955. One of these sites, Kalemba rock-shelter, was relocated 3 km north-east of Mbangombe village. Kalemba was recognised as one of the largest rock-shelters known in Zambia containing deep, apparently undisturbed, archaeological deposits; artefacts of 'Middle Stone Age' as well as 'Late Stone Age' type were visible on the talus.

Excavations were conducted at Kalemba for a total of ten weeks in May-July and August-September, 1971. By the end of the second period a maximum depth of 4.30 m had been reached without encountering bedrock or, indeed, any indication that the base of the archaeological deposits was being approached. At this depth an area less than 1.0 m square remained available for excavation because of the presence of large fallen rocks and the necessity to step the sections inwards to prevent collapse. Thus far, the excavations have yielded a stratified succession of industries, extending back to an apparently late phase of the 'Middle Stone Age'. Radiocarbon dates indicate that the lowest level reached in the excavations has an antiquity in excess of 37,000 radiocarbon years.

It is hoped that it will prove possible in the future to return to Kalemba to investigate the lower levels of the site, which may be expected to illustrate the earlier developmental stages of the local 'Middle Stone Age'. Meanwhile, the three rock-shelters so far investigated, Makwe, Thandwe and Kalemba, provide between them an outline succession of prehistoric industrial development covering most of the last four hundred centuries.

II. METHODOLOGICAL CONSIDERATIONS

Our knowledge concerning any prehistoric archae-ological sequence is a function of the available evidence

and of the methodology of the investigations which have been conducted. Brief consideration of these factors

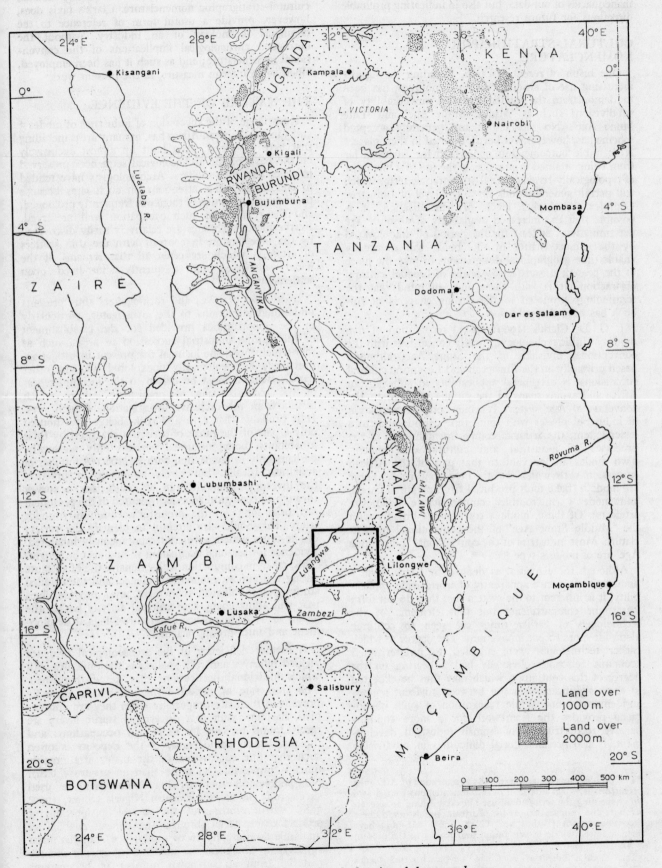

Fig. 1. Eastern Africa, showing the location of the research area.

will be of value not only in explaining the prevailing inadequacies of our data, but also in indicating profitable directions for future research.

CULTURAL-STRATIGRAPHIC NOMENCLATURE

One result of recent research, including the rapidly increasing use of absolute dating techniques, has been to demonstrate the inadequacy and unworkability of subdivisions such as 'Middle Stone Age' and 'Late Stone Age'. No satisfactory and generally accepted scheme has, however, yet been proposed in their place.* A desirable outcome, but one which for Africa is far from being attained in practice, is the use of a hierarchy of typologically-based cultural-stratigraphic terms which will permit generalisations up to the level of Industrial Complex. At higher levels of generalisation, it is possible that the increased availability of absolute age determinations, at least for the period of time covered by the subject matter of this book, will eventually enable time-geographical designations to take the place of the present unsatisfactory terms of broader cultural abstraction. It is with these aims in mind that the terminology proposed in the closing chapters of this book has been devised.

J. G. D. Clark's (1969: 29-31) recognition of five modes of lithic technology, broadly concordant with the conventional divisions of the Stone Age, although based primarily on the European and Levantine cultural successions, is of general applicability in sub-Saharan Africa and avoids many of the pitfalls inherent to the conventional 'Age' system. It avoids both the correlation of industrial phases with finite time-periods and, to a lesser extent, the artificial compartmentalisation of the processes of industrial and cultural development. Two modes are relevant to that part of the African succession with which we are here concerned. These are mode 3 (flake tools produced from prepared cores), and mode 5 (microlithic components of composite artefacts). Of these, mode 3 corresponds broadly with the 'Middle Stone Age' of the conventional nomenclature. Most industries of the conventional 'Late Stone Age' are of mode 5 type.†

Although these modes, as defined by Clark, form a homotaxial sequence apparently of world-wide applicability, it is inherent to the system that they do not form watertight compartments but that elements of the technologies of earlier times are seen to continue alongside more recent innovations. The degree to which earlier technologies were adapted to uninterrupted economic functions obviously had a bearing on the degree of this continuity, which may thus be expected to show significant variation between adjacent regions and environments. While recognition of such phenomena provides the framework for a more comprehensive reconstruction of human industrial development, it also presents initial difficulties in subdivision

and in the establishment of an adequately defined cultural-stratigraphic nomenclature. Clark's taxis does, however, provide a useful form of reference to the dominant technology of an industry, without the outmoded chronological implications of the conventional nomenclature; and as such it has been employed, albeit as an interim measure, in the present work.

THE NATURE OF THE EVIDENCE

Knowledge of the succession of industries of modes 3 and 5 in sub-Saharan Africa has, in many areas including that here described, been built up almost exclusively on the basis of the archaeological sequences preserved in caves and rock-shelters. Archaeologists have tended to concentrate their attentions on such sites because prehistoric occupation of them was frequently prolonged, and the remains of such occupation well preserved. Furthermore, such sites are relatively easily discovered by the investigator, in contrast with the thin scatters of artefacts which are often all that remains of the widely dispersed and frequently short-lived open settlements.

Excavation of caves and rock-shelters thus presents undoubted attractions to the investigator, particularly in the opportunities provided for the establishment of the outline industrial succession in areas, such as that which forms the locus of the present investigation, previously archaeologically unexplored. On the other hand, attention must be drawn to the incompleteness of the reconstruction of prehistoric culture which results from the exclusive investigation of such sites. It is probable that cave and rock-shelter sites housed only a part of the range of activities practised by their inhabitants, being occupied perhaps only seasonally, perhaps only in connection with a restricted number of activities. Ideally, but rarely attainable in practice, the investigator should aim at conducting a survey through all ecological zones represented in the presumed territorial range of the prehistoric community under study. He should also attempt to identify the variety of site-types which were contemporaneously inhabited. Evidence for seasonal occupation should also be sought. This, taken in conjunction with extensive use of absolute dating techniques, economic evidence, and the detailed study of technological refinement, may provide clues that will allow changes in cultural activity within the group to be distinguished from chronological development and inter-group variability.

A further deficiency of the archaeological evidence yielded by caves and rock-shelters is the difficulty with which individual occupations may be distinguished. The slow rate of deposit-formation which generally prevails in such sites, especially when they are unoccupied, has the result that discernible sterile layers are rarely found to separate individual occupations; and the pedological homogeneity of the deposits is often such that fine subdivision of the major stratigraphic units is impossible on other than an arbitrary basis. Non-pedological methods may sometimes be used successfully (as at Iwo Eleru in Nigeria (Shaw, 1969: 368), where plotting of the variable proportions of artefact raw-material through the deposit enabled an 'invisible stratigraphy' to be established), but the finest subdivision which can be made must usually include material from an unknown number of occupations spread, perhaps intermittently, over a period of time which may be better measured in centuries than in decades.

---

*The problem was discussed in 1965 at a meeting of Africanist prehistorians, when a number of recommendations were drawn up concerning the terms to be used in establishing a cultural-stratigraphic nomenclature for African prehistory. These recommendations (Bishop and Clark, 1967: 861-901) have been followed, as far as was found practicable, in the present work.

†True mode 4 industries (dominated by punch-struck blades with steep retouch) are found only rarely in sub-Saharan Africa, being restricted, so far as is at present known, to the Horn and adjacent regions of East Africa, although they have recently also been recognised in the southern Sahara.

The concentration of occupation in the restricted areas provided by most rock-shelters, on accumulated deposits which are frequently loose and unconsolidated, must also mean that artefact mixture is to be expected to such an extent that even the most meticulous excavator may not always be able to differentiate successive aggregates. As in many other types of site, use of separate activity-areas may have resulted in differential horizontal distribution of artefact types (e.g. Leakey, 1931: 106; Shaw, 1969: 369), which may perhaps vary from time to time through the period of occupation. In rock-shelters and caves the high density of artefactual material, combined with physical obstructions such as rock-falls, frequently means that total excavation is impracticable or impossible, even were it desirable; the distorted picture of artefact aggregates which can arise from these complications must always be recognised.

One of the more urgent priorities of Stone Age archaeology in sub-Saharan Africa is the extension to open settlement sites of later periods of the techniques of large-scale stripping and planning which have so successfully been applied to very early sites. The application of such techniques on sites which yield principally microlithic artefacts will, of course, present practical difficulties, but these will not be unsurmountable; and the results of such studies on selected single-phase settlement sites of the 'Late Stone Age' may be expected greatly to amplify our knowledge of the societies responsible, and to aid the interpretation of sites already excavated.

INTERPRETATION OF STONE ARTEFACT AGGREGATES

Further difficulties arise in dealing with the frequently enormous numbers of mode 5 artefacts which are recovered from many sites. Artefact yields well in excess of 50,000 pieces per cubic metre of deposit are by no means unusual at cave and rock-shelter sites. However, the number of artefacts bearing intentional secondary retouch is often less than one per cent of the total. For the majority of sites detailed analysis has been restricted to the pieces bearing such retouch and, sometimes, to the cores; yet there are indications that, at least in some assemblages, a high proportion of the pieces utilised as tools did not bear intentional secondary retouch but were of the class frequently characterised as 'waste' and excluded from detailed analysis.

The only sub-Saharan African site known to the present writer where the total mode 5 chipped-stone-artefact aggregate has been subjected to microscopic examination and analysis of the edge-damage resulting from use is Chiwemupula on the Zambian Copperbelt (Phillipson and Phillipson, 1970). Here, it was found that over seventy per cent of the 'waste' flakes and blades showed signs of utilisation. Among the utilised pieces such 'waste' flakes outnumbered 'tools' bearing intentional secondary retouch by a factor of 15:1. In addition, some thirty per cent of the cores showed signs of utilisation subsequent to having been struck. Analysis of the edge-damage on intentionally retouched tools showed that there was a tendency for the morphological types conventionally recognised to be used in mutually distinctive ways, but such conformity was by no means invariable. Typologically identical tools could be used in different ways and single specimens

had evidently often been put to more than one use. Identical wear-patterns were found on many 'waste' pieces and on the intentionally retouched 'tools'. It is thus clear that, at this site at any rate, conventional tool typology can give only a very approximate indication of function, and that analysis restricted to intentionally retouched 'tools' may cover only a small proportion of the pieces so used. Such analysis can thus be expected to give only a very incomplete picture of the total site activity.

It is commonly realised that many microlithic artefacts were used hafted, but only rarely have specimens been recovered which clearly illustrate this practice. A number of demonstrably or presumed final 'Late Stone Age' sites in South Africa have yielded hafted specimens, and similar objects have been recorded ethnographically (Goodwin, 1945). Examples from the Cape Province, described by J. D. Clark (1958a; 1959a: 232-4) and H. Deacon (1966) confirm that pieces lacking intentional secondary retouch were frequently used as tools. Particular interest thus attaches to the recovery from Makwe rock-shelter, described below, of over fifty mode 5 artefacts to which adhered a hard resinous substance. The fact that this was preserved almost exclusively on the backed areas of microliths, and that in nine instances it formed a cast of a neatly cut groove into which the microlith had evidently been hafted, demonstrated that this substance was the remains of a mastic used for cementing the microliths to their hafts. On many specimens sufficient mastic was preserved to allow reconstruction of the hafting methods employed; and significant differences were observed in the manner in which different types of microlith were mounted. These interpretations show frequent agreement with the implications of the edge-damage patterns observed on the Chiwemupula material. There is as yet no evidence that the specific results of this research are of other than local applicability, but they do indicate the directions in which future investigations could profitably be conducted.

It will be apparent from the foregoing that there is little reason to believe that the conventional analyses of stone artefact aggregates, which are largely restricted to the intentionally retouched tools, will reflect at all accurately the various functions of all components of the aggregate. Only in comparatively few cases do we have any indication of the function of any particular artefact type, information on this topic being largely restricted to the inconclusive implications of ethnographic observations and of experimental production of edge-wear patterns which may be paralleled on selected artefacts. Even those types which are conventionally known by a functional designation, such as 'scraper,' 'projectile point', etc., can only rarely be shown actually to have served the function thus attributed to them. In realisation of this uncertainty, archaeologists in sub-Saharan Africa now tend to describe artefacts of modes 3 and 5 in primarily morphological terms; and there have recently been concerted efforts to achieve uniformity of nomenclature between workers in different areas. While these efforts will undoubtedly reduce confusion in cases where identical artefact-types do indeed occur in different areas, there are clear dangers of obscuring important features through the adoption of a too-rigid classification which does not adequately comprehend the idiosyncracies of individual aggregates, whether these be due to cultural factors or to the nature of the raw material employed. In many areas of sub-Saharan Africa, study of the Stone Age industries is at such a preliminary stage that attempts are surely premature to ensure uniformity of classification and nomenclature over artefact variability which, both in itself and in its causes, is so imperfectly understood. What is needed, and is now rapidly being achieved, is an improved standard of definition of artefact classes and descriptive terms which can then be rigorously applied by the investigator and readily and clearly understood by his readers.

Attention has been drawn above to our almost total ignorance of the uses to which many prehistoric artefacts were put. Studies of utilisation patterns indicate that artefacts morphologically indistinguishable from one another may have been put to quite disparate uses, though the precise nature of these uses can be determined only rarely. While gross differences between assemblages in the relative frequency of various artefact classes may reflect activity differences at the respective sites, this cannot be demonstrated convincingly. Despite this uncertainty, the tacit assumption is often made that long-distance correlations and comparisons between industries can be made on the basis of such percentage frequencies of gross artefact categories, even between aggregates from sites of different types situated in areas of greatly contrasting environments. If the archaeologist is to attempt the differentiation of cultural groupings on the basis of his typological analyses, he must direct his attention to stylistic and technological details which may reflect the idiosyncratic cultural traditions of a particular group.

The policy which has been followed in the present work has been to devise an analytical system primarily on the basis of the eastern Zambian material itself. This applies equally to the pottery collections and to the chipped stone artefact aggregates. The classes involved have been defined in sufficiently broad terms that they may be applied in a uniform manner to all the aggregates investigated, thus facilitating inter-site comparisons. These definitions are set out in chapter 4. The aim has been to propose a series of artefact classes, each member of which resembles the other members of the same class more closely than it resembles any member of any other class. The intuitive division into classes has been made on morphological grounds only. Wherever possible, arbitrary dividing lines between classes have been avoided: where this has proved impracticable, the position has been stated clearly. When generally accepted or previously used terms and definitions could be fitted in without violation of these principles, they have been adopted. Metrical and stylistic data are recorded separately for each horizon at each site.

Wherever possible, the definitions chosen allow direct comparisons to be made with other central African material which has been analysed by the present writer and others. Minor and stylistic differences apart, it appears that the classifications here proposed are of wide central African applicability.

It is believed that the course here followed has several advantages over the more elaborate methods of classification which have frequently been applied to mode 3 and 5 stone industries and, on occasion, to pottery assemblages. It is impossible for the modern archaeologist to know how the makers of a prehistoric industry may have classified their products. A classification such as that here presented, based on the morphology of the particular material under study, clearly has greater relevance than one originally devised in a far-distant region for material which is probably not genetically related. Such an attempt must necessarily involve approximations and the attribution of whole classes on a 'best fit' principle. It is the present writer's belief that qualitative and stylistic features have considerable relevance to the adequate description and comparison of prehistoric artefact aggregates.

Chapter 2

The Research Area

I. THE GEOGRAPHICAL SETTING

The area of Zambia covered by the present investigation lies in the southern part of the tongue of high ground which extends southwards from the Tanganyika Plateau between the Lake Malawi rift on the east and the Luangwa valley on the west. To the south, the high ground is curtailed by the valley of the Zambezi into which both Lake Malawi and the Luangwa drain. The region (fig. 2) lies well within the tropics, at latitude 13° to 15° south, longitude 31° to 34° east. Politically, the plateau is divided between three countries: the Republics of Zambia, Malawi and Moçambique. Malawi comprises all the territory draining to the homonymous lake, while the border separating Zambia from Moçambique follows an almost straight line, unrelated to topographical features or to the territory of indigenous population units, somewhat to the south of the Luangwa-Zambezi watershed. For practical reasons, fieldwork was restricted to the Zambian part of the plateau, which forms a roughly triangular area some 25,000 sq. km in extent, delineated on the south and east respectively by the borders of Moçambique and Malawi, and on the north-west by the eastern escarpment of the Luangwa valley. Administratively it is part of the Eastern Province of Zambia, incorporating the whole of the Chadiza and Katete Districts, together with substantial portions of the Districts of Chipata and Petauke.

The plateau is formed of extremely variable sedimentary rocks belonging to the pre-Cambrian Basement Complex; there are frequent intrusions of granites, seyenites and other igneous rocks forming the frequent massive rocky outcrops, or *kopjes*, which provide relief to the flat monotony of the plateau landscape around Chipata and Chadiza, becoming progressively rarer as one moves westwards into the Katete and Petauke Districts. Detailed and up-to-date geological mapping has recently been conducted or is under way in much of the area, but it is only for the Petauke region, west of longitude 32° east, that the results are so far available in published form (Phillips, 1960; 1963; 1965; Barr and Drysdall, 1972).

The geomorphology of the region is basically monotonous. The Luangwa-Zambezi watershed lies at a general altitude of 1050 to 1100 m above sea level, rising gently to meet the Luangwa/Lake Malawi watershed at about 1300 m near Chipata. On the Luangwa/Zambezi watershed immediately east of Katete the isolated massif of the Mphangwe Hills, the highest point in the area, reaches an altitude of 1660 m. Elsewhere, the rocky *kopjes* rarely rise more than 200 to 300 m above the plateau. To the south of the watershed, the Kapoche and other Zambezi tributaries rise in open grassy plains or *dambos* which form almost imperceptible depressions in the plateau surface, sloping very gently downwards to the south. The major exception is the Mwangazi which, rising in more rugged hilly country between Chadiza and the Malawi border, has cut more

deeply into the plateau producing the most broken terrain encountered in the area investigated. On the northern, Luangwa, side of the watershed the drop is more rapid and the major rivers, Lutembwe, Mvuvye and Nyimba, occupy broad mature valleys eroded 100 to 120 m below the main plateau surface. Dixey (1944: 40) ascribes these valleys, which are many kilometres in width, to the lower Pleistocene and notes the presence of several low-level terraces.

The main plateau is regarded by Dixey as part of an end-Tertiary peneplain of wide central African extent, locally inclined gently north-westwards. Along the Malawi border north and east of Chipata are what Dixey considers to be remnants of a Miocene peneplain at about 1300 m above sea level: residuals of this surface also occur in the west of our area, around Petauke and Sasare. The end-Tertiary surface slopes gently down to the low shoulder of the Luangwa valley at approximately 880 m above sea level. Here, the well defined escarpment, 150 to 200 m in height, has been taken as the north-western limit of the research area. Below the escarpment is a post-Tertiary surface, probably lower Pleistocene, at 600 m and a resurrected early Cretaceous surface at 550 m above sea level. To the west, the gorge of the Luangwa, 200 m deep at the Great East Road bridge, is eroded through and postdates the lower Pleistocene surface (Dixey, 1939; 1944: 27).

The dominant vegetation-type of the sandy plateau soils is *Brachystegia-Julbernardia* woodland (with some *Isoberlinia* in the north) which extends into the escarpment hill soils of the Luangwa valley and into the hills around the Mwangazi. Patches of predominantly *Isoberlinia paniculata*, with some *Brachystegia*, are found near the watersheds. High-grass woodlands with *Combretum-Afrormosia* and *Pterocarpus-Combretum* occur on upper valley soils and on the allied brown loams in the valleys of the Lutembwe, Mlozi, Rukuzye, Kapoche and other major rivers of both the Luangwa and the Zambezi systems. *Copaifera mopani*–grassland mixtures are found on grey alluvial clays on the southern side of the watershed west of Katete. Further details of vegetation and soil types are given by Trapnell (1943; 1962) and by the Zambia Survey Department (1967), while a useful summary of the soils of the region and their distribution is provided by Kay (1965: 101-2).

Eastern Zambia lies within the central African summer rainfall area. June and July are the coolest months, with mean daily temperatures on the plateau in the region of 18° centigrade: mornings are cool and crisp, but frost is virtually unknown. The dry season continues with steadily increasing heat into late October or early November. Mean temperatures then approximate to 26°; and daily maxima in excess of 35° are not uncommon. The advent of the rains, usually about the beginning of November, is sudden, bringing immediate relief; but high temperatures may return if there is

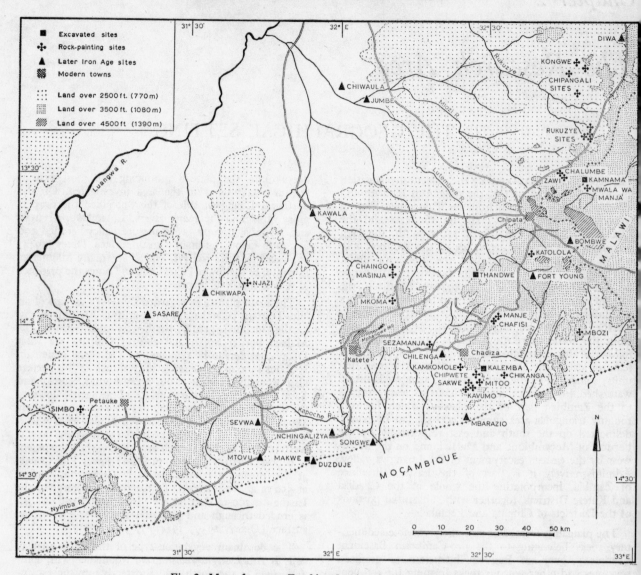

Fig. 2. Map of eastern Zambia, showing the sites investigated.

any prolonged hiatus in the rains, as frequently occurs in January or February. The annual rainfall on the plateau is variable but generally within the range 65 to 140 cm, with long-term means of 101 cm at Chipata and 97 cm at Petauke. Ninety-five per cent of the annual rainfall comes during the five-month period from November to March, mainly in short but violent storms. In late March or early April the rainfall peters out and dry weather returns, with moderate but steadily falling temperatures. Towards the Luangwa valley, with reduced altitude, rainfall tends to decrease and temperature, at all seasons, to increase.

Wildlife, other than small species, is now rare over much of the plateau except in the rugged country around the Mwangazi river; but it is still plentiful in and below the Luangwa escarpment. There are abundant records of the species present in the Luangwa Valley Game Reserve, but for the plateau the best summary is that of Wilson (1975: 347-51) for the Chipangali Tsetse Control Area, situated in the north of the study area, on the right bank of the Rukuzye river. It is probable that the rich and varied fauna recorded for this sparsely settled tract is representative of that which formerly roamed over much of the Eastern Province

plateau. Species recorded include elephant, black rhinoceros, zebra, buffalo, eland, kudu, bushbuck, wildebeest, Lichtenstein's hartebeest, roan and sable antelope, waterbuck, reedbuck, klipspringer, oribi, Sharpe's grysbok, duiker, wart-hog, lion, leopard, cheetah, wild dog, yellow baboon and vervet monkey.

Tsetse flies are now almost entirely absent from the plateau areas, but are common in the Luangwa valley and in the escarpment, where large-scale control measures are in progress (Wilson, 1975). The retreat of tsetse from the western areas of the plateau is a comparatively recent phenomenon, and has been brought about largely by increased density of human settlement and the attendant clearance of vegetation and destruction of wildlife.

The main artery of present-day communication is the tarred Great East Road from Lusaka to Chipata and on into Malawi. The road crosses the Luangwa only 2 km upstream of the Moçambique border, climbs the escarpment to Nyimba and follows the approximate line of the Luangwa-Zambezi watershed past the administrative posts of Petauke and Katete, reaching Chipata at a distance of 360 km from the Luangwa bridge. From Chipata, main roads lead southwards to Chadiza and northwards, roughly following the Zambian side of the Luangwa/Lake Malawi watershed, to Lundazi. There is an excellent network of secondary roads in the Katete-Chadiza-Chipata region; but the rugged and more sparsely populated regions lying near and east of the Mwangazi, and those to the north of the Great East Road near the escarpment, are less well served. Many parts of the Luangwa escarpment are almost uninhabited and access, other than on foot, is extremely difficult.

II. THE PRESENT POPULATION

The plateau country in the southern part of the Eastern Province is one of the most densely populated regions of rural Zambia. In the 'reserve' areas (see below, p. 13) lying south of the Great East Road and north of the Moçambique border, average population density is now in the order of twenty persons per square kilometre. To the north, however, densities rarely exceed one fifth of this figure, while the Luangwa escarpment country is virtually uninhabited. The rural population practises a mixed farming economy and, particularly in the neighbourhood of Chipata and the 'reserves' south of the Great East Road, subsistence farming is accompanied by a significant degree of cash-cropping.

Maize is the staple cereal crop, although sorghum and finger millet are also grown, particularly on the poorer soils (Allan, 1965: 99-102). Groundnuts and burley tobacco are important cash-crops. Pumpkin and water-melon are grown in well watered areas. Cattle, formerly largely restricted to the plateau areas of the Chipata District, are now spreading further west following the retreat of the tsetse fly belts. Eastern Zambia has the densest stock of traditionally maintained cattle of any region in Zambia with the exception of the Kafue Flats and the Barotse Plain (Kay, 1967: 54). Oxen are widely used as draught animals. Chickens, goats and pigs are common; the last named are attributed to recent introduction from Portuguese sources, but are much interbred with wild swine. Sheep are rarely encountered. To the north, in the Luangwa valley and the almost uninhabited escarpment country, finger millet replaces maize as the staple crop, cattle are absent because of tsetse fly, and other domestic animals are rare.

Away from the townships, most people live in substantial villages of rectangular houses built of puddled clay (daga) applied over a substantial frame of wooden poles linked by interwoven laths. Most of these houses are surrounded by a narrow raised platform or verandah over which the thatched roof extends supported on wooden poles. In some remoter areas, particularly in the north and west, an older, circular type of house is still encountered. Villages are large, particularly in the more easterly country occupied by the Chewa and Ngoni, where a single village may have several hundreds of inhabitants. Isolated farmsteads are now becoming more common, particularly in areas devoted to cash-cropping.

The uneven distribution and varying patterns of rural settlement may be attributed largely to historical causes. As is explained below (p. 13), during the early years of the present century much of the area, particularly that along the Moçambique border, was designated 'Native Reserve' and population was moved thither from other areas which then remained largely uninhabited, although theoretically available for European settlement (Kay, 1965). The 'reserve' areas soon become severely overpopulated, with villages spread along all available watercourses; and the natural vegetation was largely destroyed over wide areas through intensive cultivation and overgrazing. Subsequently, resettlement schemes were instituted in the formerly depopulated areas (Fraser, 1945; Kay, 1965: 25-9; Wilson, 1975: 351-8). Here, the land has been divided into rectangular blocks, and small villages and farmsteads are regularly spaced in clearings in the forest; water is drawn mainly from wells.

In socio-political terms, the population falls basically into three groups (fig. 3). In the west, in the Petauke District, the Nsenga predominate, while elsewhere the most numerous inhabitants are Chewa. Ngoni are also represented, particularly between Chipata and Chadiza and in watershed areas north of Chipata. Peripheral to our area are the Ambo of the lower Luangwa valley and a small group of Swahili in the Luangwa escarpment of the Petauke District (Brelsford, 1965:113). The histories of these 'tribes' will be discussed briefly in the following section.

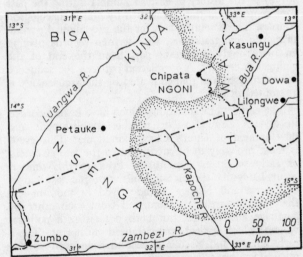

Fig. 3. *Modern peoples of eastern Zambia and adjacent areas (after Ntara, 1973).*

The Nsenga and Chewa languages (ChiNsenga and ChiNyanja) are distinct but closely related: the latter, having received governmental recognition as an 'official' language, is now gaining ground and is widely understood in Nsenga areas. The old ChiNgoni language is now rarely heard, being remembered only by a very few old people. Its use also survives in ceremonial contexts. In everyday situations, most Ngoni speak ChiNsenga, a relic of their previous residence among that people, although their territory is now completely encircled by Chewa. Here too, however, the use of ChiNyanja is rapidly spreading.

It is not proposed here to discuss the rapidly changing social and traditional political organization of the Eastern Province people, since these topics are beyond the present writer's expertise and are not directly relevant to the present work. General accounts are provided by Coxhead (1914), Lane-Poole (1938) and, for closely related people in Malawi, by Hodgson (1933) and Werner (1906). More recent detailed studies are those of the Ngoni by Barnes (1951; 1954), of the Chewa by Marwick (1965) and of the Ambo by Stefaniszyn (1964a).

Material culture is of more direct relevance to archaeology and the account by Barnes (1948) of Ngoni material culture may be regarded as giving a general picture of that in most plateau areas as it was a quarter of a century ago. Since then, the practice of most traditional crafts has declined, and it may be assumed that, with improved communications, this trend will continue to accelerate. Of the traditional items still manufactured, pottery is of paramount interest to the archaeologist. Potting among all the peoples of the region is the work of women. It is remarkably uniform in style, being attributed to the Luangwa tradition (D. W. Phillipson, 1974:7-10). Characteristic vessels (plate Ia) are necked pots and shallow bowls, the former almost always having an everted rim. Rims on all vessels are usually tapered, undifferentiated forms being rare and thickened ones completely absent. Decoration is generally banded, the most common technique

being comb-stamping applied diagonally to form horizontal bands which are often associated with pendant chordate blocks, also of diagonally-applied comb-stamping. Diagonal or criss-cross incision often takes the place of the comb-stamping. Applied decoration is encountered rarely and, so far as I know, only in the more northerly Chewa areas. Pottery vessels in this area are characteristically coated externally with graphite and finished by burnishing with a pebble. Potters are specialists, there being rarely more than one or two such women even in the largest villages; and today pottery is usually made to order, rather than as stock for subsequent sale. Traditional pottery is mainly used for the storage of drinking water, for cooking, and for heating beer—brewing being generally done in large metal drums.

The use of bored stones (*chimtunga*) as pot-boilers for heating beer is of interest (plate Ib). Basketry and woodwork are tasks reserved for men as, formerly, was the weaving of cloth from locally grown cotton. Such are the items of material culture of chief concern to the archaeologist; for a more detailed account the reader is referred to the works of Brelsford (1938), Barnes (1948) and Stefaniszyn (1964a).

III. HISTORY OF EASTERN ZAMBIA

In this section it is proposed to present an outline survey of the history of eastern Zambia during the past four centuries, as this is revealed by non-archaeological sources. These sources are, for the pre-colonial period, primarily oral traditions, with written records playing an increasingly important part from the end of the eighteenth century. A correlation between the sequence here discussed and that indicated by the archaeology is attempted in chapter 20.

The earliest oral traditions which have been recorded in eastern Zambia relate to the establishment and development of Undi's Chewa kingdom.* This event is most probably to be attributed to the late sixteenth or early seventeenth centuries. Prior to this time it seems likely that the ancestors of the people now known as Chewa and Nsenga already lived in more-or-less their present areas, differentiated from each other by language and culture, but both possessing a political system which lacked a centralised authority. These early Chewa and Nsenga appear to have been settled, mixed-farming villagers who, at least in the hilly country of the Luangwa/Lake Malawi watershed, were in occasional contact with a distinct people, known by such names as Akafula, Arungu or Abatwa. These latter people are described as wandering hunters who differed markedly from the Chewa and Nsenga in language, culture and physical appearance, timidity and vanity being their most memorable characteristics (J. D. Clark, 1950a: 82-3; see also Rangeley, 1963). Some of them may have been the last surviving remnants of the 'Late Stone Age' population.

Sometime before the beginning of the sixteenth century, the first Malawi kingdom was established near the southern end of Lake Malawi by one Kalonga, of the Phiri (Hill) clan, who is said to have come thither from

the Luba area of Shaba in Zaire. Establishment of a chronology for this and related events is hampered by the fact that the name Kalonga, like many chiefly names, was hereditary, so the deeds of several successive Kalongas are recalled in oral tradition as those of a single individual. It is possible, therefore, that Kalonga's Malawi kingdom may have a rather greater antiquity than is frequently supposed (for a comparable situation in another area, see J. C. Miller, 1972). Be that as it may, it was probably during the late sixteenth century that a succession dispute arose between the Kalonga of the day and his younger brother, Undi.† As a result of this the latter is said to have left Kalonga's kingdom and departed to the west, where he established his own kingdom in the Kapoche valley area known as Mano in Moçambique, south of the modern Katete. It is stated that, since virtually all Kalonga's kinsmen accompanied Undi, the latter had, in subsequent generations, to supply successors to the Kalongaship.

At about the same time as Undi's defection, several other members of the Phiri and other clans appear to have established their own breakaway kingdoms, including those of Mwaze Lundazi among the northern Chewa in the modern Lundazi District, and of Mkanda, north of the present Chipata. Undi established his authority over surrounding areas by leaving Phiri kinsmen as chiefs in areas through which he passed en route to Mano. He also retained control of the Chewa religious centre, the rain-shrine of Makewane at Msinja in the modern Lilongwe District. In due course Undi and his successors built up a three-tier hierarchy of rulers beneath themselves as king: their position was maintained "more by religious and ritual services which Undi performed than by a well-organized bureaucracy or military establishment" (Langworthy,

---

*The account of Chewa oral history here presented is based largely on the work of Dr H. W. Langworthy (1971; 1972a: 21-35, 55-60, 88-95; 1972b and personal communications), whose help is gratefully acknowledged.

†It is doubtful whether this account should be taken literally; more probably it is an allegorical version developed to explain in personal terms the inter-relationship between the kingdoms of Undi and Kalonga.

1972a: 31). These subsidiary rulers were Undi's kinsmen; and their successors retained this nominative relationship to succeeding Undis in perpetual descent.

During the seventeeth century Undi's kingdom expanded until it reached the maximum extent shown in fig. 4, covering substantial areas of what are now eastern Zambia and adjacent parts of Malawi and Moçambique. Its major expansion was to the north and west of Mano, taking in the Nsenga who had previously not possessed a chiefly hierarchy, being ruled by headmen holding sway only over single or a few adjacent villages, but united by bonds of culture and language (Apthorpe, 1960). It seems probable, as has been noted above, that such an uncentralised system had formerly been common to the Chewa and other neighbouring peoples before the establishment of chiefly dynasties by immigrants of Luba origin. In some Nsenga areas Phiri chiefs were installed: elsewhere Nsenga, such as the Mwanza Kalindawalo, were appointed chiefs and linked through marriage alliances to the royal family of Undi. Later, perhaps about 1700, Undi also gained control of Mkanda's previously independent Chewa kingdom; but this area, perhaps partly due to its peripheral position, was never fully integrated. At no time did Undi's authority extend as far north as the northern Chewa kingdoms of the present Lundazi District. By the eighteenth century, Kalonga's Malawi kingdom had shrunk to insignificance by comparison with the large empire controlled by Undi.

To the south, Undi's kingdom bordered upon an area of the Zambezi valley which had been under partial Portuguese control since the first half of the sixteenth century. The garrison town of Tete, just below the Cabora Bassa rapids, had been founded in about 1540. It is doubtful, however, whether there was any intensive contact between the Chewa and the Portuguese much before the eighteenth century, since the latter's interests were concentrated south of the Zambezi in the gold-rich empire of Monomotapa (Alpers, 1968). In the closing decades of the seventeenth century, the Monomotapa, who had by this time become little more than a puppet of the Portuguese, lost control of much of his territory to the Changamire dynasty, based on Guruhuswa (Butua) in the far south of what is now Rhodesia. The Portuguese were then to a large extent debarred from direct trading on the Mashonaland plateau and they turned their attention to the north, where their previous trading activities had been restricted to sporadic purchases of ivory. A Portuguese settlement at Zumbo, at the confluence of the Zambezi and Luangwa rivers, was established by at least 1720, with a trading post (Feira) on the opposite side of the Luangwa in what is now Zambian territory (J. D. Clark, 1965). An account of Zumbo's trade, principally for copper and ivory, has been given by Sutherland-Harris (1970); one area with which this trade was conducted has been identified as the modern Petauke District, where small quantities of gold were also available. In more easterly regions, closer to the heart of Undi's empire, gold was also discovered around the middle of the eighteenth century to the south of the Chadiza District. The increased Portuguese presence, together with the large amount of imported trade-goods which Undi was now able to obtain by maintaining control of this lucrative commerce, greatly strengthened his position; and Undi's empire probably achieved its greatest power and extent around the middle of the eighteenth century.

Undi's monopoly of trade and tribute soon led, however, to the disintegration of his empire, as tributary chiefs from its outlying areas attempted to open trade routes on their own account. They were no doubt aided in this by the activities of Bisa traders who, by the second half of the eighteenth century, had penetrated Undi's empire while forging a trade link between Tete and the Lunda kingdom of Kazembe on the Luapula, far to the north-east. By the end of the eighteenth century, tributary rulers in the southern part of Undi's empire had begun to alienate land to the Portuguese for the formation of crown estates or *prazos*. Despite these processes, which continued for several decades, Undi's state retained a considerable degree of strength and cohesion well into the nineteenth century.

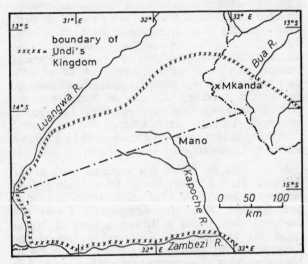

Fig. 4. Undi's kingdom at its greatest extent (after Langworthy, 1972b: 105).

In 1798 the first documented European expedition to traverse Undi's empire passed through what is now eastern Zambia. This, under the leadership of Dr Francisco José Maria de Lacerda e Almeida, Governor of the Rios de Sena, was instructed to open a direct Portuguese-controlled trade-route from Tete to the town of Kazembe who, at that time, controlled the Shaba copper mines and who was also in trade-contact with the lands under Portuguese hegemony on the west coast of Africa. De Lacerda has left the first written account of the people and country of eastern Zambia through which he passed. The expedition met many hardships and de Lacerda himself died shortly before Kazembe's town was reached (Burton, 1873: 55-164). The following year the remnants of the expedition struggled back to Tete having achieved little of lasting value to the Portuguese. It is significant that this, the first Portuguese attempt to link up their possessions on the east and west coasts of the continent, took place only three years after the British had displaced the Dutch and established themselves at the Cape of Good Hope.

About a decade later, land contact between Angola and Moçambique was finally established when two half-caste *pombeiros*, Battista and José, arrived in Tete from Angola *via* Kazembe's town, where they had been detained by that potentate for four years. Unfortunately, Battista's diary, particularly the section which refers to the last stage of their journey through Undi's country, consists of little more than a record of marches, rivers crossed and halting places, and it tells us little about the people whom the *pombeiros* encountered (Burton, 1873: 167-244). A Portuguese military post was occupied for two years from 1827 at Marambo on the east bank of the Luangwa near de Lacerda's crossing, on land formally ceded to the Portuguese crown by the Chewa Chief Mwase wa Minga (Mwanya) (Lane-Poole, 1931).

A further Portuguese expedition from Tete to Kazembe was dispatched in 1831 under Major José Monteiro and Captain Antonio Gamitto. The latter has left a remarkably detailed diary of his travels (Gamitto, 1854; English translation by I. Cunnison, 1960). David Livingstone followed approximately the same route in 1866 (Livingstone, 1874, I: 111-58). These two authors provide much valuable information concerning the Chewa, Bisa and other peoples through whose territory their expeditions passed. It is clear that by this time Undi's empire was rapidly disintegrating, a process which Langworthy (1972a: 55) would attribute both to the decentralised nature of the state itself with its lack of a powerful internal bureaucracy, and to the increasing activities of Portuguese and Chikunda traders seeking slaves and ivory. Later in the nineteenth century, slave trading was intensified (Langworthy, 1971) and was accompanied by a further decline in Chewa cohesion and prosperity.

At this time the Ngoni first appeared north of the Zambezi. Having broken away from Shaka's Zulu kingdom in Natal about 1818, settled briefly in what is now Rhodesia where they defeated the Rozwi and destroyed their capital at Khami, a band of Ngoni under the leadership of Zwangendaba crossed the Zambezi a short distance downstream of Zumbo in November 1835 (Lancaster, 1937). They established themselves for a short while in Nsenga territory, in the modern Petauke District of Zambia. Many Nsenga chiefs were raided and defeated, but the central part of Undi's kingdom appears to have escaped major molestation. By about 1840, the majority of the Ngoni left Nsenga country and proceeded northwards, where they raided over extensive areas of Zambia and northern Malawi, finally settling in Fipa country in south-western Tanzania. Here Zwangendaba died and a succession dispute arose which resulted in the break-up of the kingdom. One group, under Mbelwa, raided extensively in the Bemba country of northern Zambia before settling, about 1855, in northern Malawi whence for the next thirty or forty years they raided the northern Chewa, Senga and Tumbuka of the Lundazi District. A second group, led by Mpezeni, left Mbelwa while the latter was raiding the Bemba and eventually, about 1870, returned southwards to the Nsenga country around Petauke.

During the previous Ngoni settlement of this area, some thirty years before, Undi's kingdom had been strong enough to discourage Ngoni attacks upon the central Chewa area, but by now the process of disintegration had proceded so far that little organised resistance could be offered. Within a few years Mpezeni's Ngoni established themselves in the fertile grazing land around the headwaters of the Lutembwe river, south of the modern Chipata (Omer-Cooper, 1966: 79). From there they raided many Chewa areas, obtaining large herds of cattle and assimilating many Chewa women into Ngoni society. During this process they brought about the final destruction of Undi's empire; and a virtually uninhabited 'no-man's land' encircled the Ngoni country itself where, as one Scottish visitor wrote, "village after village surrounded by waving cornfields, and green plains dotted with herds of cattle, stretched away into the distance" (Angus, 1899: 78).

Mpezeni's supremacy was, however, short-lived. While he was consolidating his position during the late 1880's, British influence was being established along the shores of Lake Malawi and in the Shire highlands to the south. Church of Scotland missions, inspired largely by the work of David Livingstone, had been founded to the south of the lake in 1875/6; and within a decade they were exercising a powerful influence over the Yao and Chewa in that area (Oliver, 1952). In 1878 the missions were instrumental in setting up the African Lakes Company which built up wide trading interests and which operated a steamship on Lake Malawi. On the northern shores of the lake, the Company came into conflict with Arab traders and slavers; and pressure came to be exerted on the British Government to take steps to protect British interests in the area and also to prevent any further expansion by the Portuguese. As there was great reluctance in official circles to incur the necessary expenditure, it was not until 1889, when Cecil Rhodes undertook that his British South Africa Company would finance the administration of territories north of the Zambezi as well as in Southern Rhodesia, that action was taken. Later that same year a British Protectorate was declared over the Shire Highlands. In 1891 (Sir) Harry Johnston was appointed Commissioner and Consul-General, and he energetically set about expanding the British Central Africa Protectorate and organising its administration (Johnston, 1897: 80-154). By 1898, reasonably effective British control had been established over the whole area of the present-day Malawi (Hanna, 1956; Oliver, 1957; Baker, 1972). During the same decade British forces and those of Mpezeni came into open conflict.

European encroachment on Mpezeni's authority in fact began as early as 1885, when the latter granted a large mining concession to Carl Wiese, a German hunter and trader who travelled extensively in what is now eastern Zambia and adjacent parts of Moçambique. Wiese was working in close conjuction with Portuguese interests; and there can be little doubt that his concession would have ended up in Portuguese hands. Indeed, in April 1891 he obtained from Mpezeni a general territorial concession covering 25,000 sq. km and persuaded the chief to accept the Portuguese flag. Mpezeni cannot have appreciated what a symbolic act the Europeans held this to be, since Wiese (1891: 488) notes that he had to point out to the Ngoni ruler that the flag was not to be used as an article of clothing. Wiese's machinations were, however, forestalled later that year by an Anglo-Portuguese agreement which placed Mpezeni's territory firmly in the British sphere of influence (Barnes, 1954: 71). The Lake Malawi/Luangwa watershed had already been determined as the boundary between the territories of the British Central Africa Protectorate (under Imperial Government control) and the domain of the British South Africa Company.

The anomaly was resolved, as far as the rivalries of the European powers were concerned, when Wiese sold his concession to the newly floated North Charterland Exploration Company, in which the British South Africa Company held a controlling interest; but Mpezeni's hostility remained. Wiese gained

Mpezeni's acceptance of a North Charterland Exploration Company expedition, but the British administration resolved that the Ngonis' power should be broken by force and, as they had done in the case of Lobengula a few years previously, proceeded to tempt Mpezeni to institute hostilities. The excuse came in December 1897, and by the end of the following month Mpezeni's town was captured, the chief imprisoned and his son shot. The Chewa and Nsenga had previously been so broken by the Ngoni that they offered little or no resistance; now the Ngoni themselves were defeated and the British South Africa Company was master of the area. An administrative framework was established with a headquarters at Fort Jameson which, after several removals, was finally built at the present Chipata (Chaplin, 1961a; O'Mahoney, 1963b). From here the B.S.A. Company ruled its whole territory of North-Eastern Rhodesia until 1911 when, following the amalgamation of that territory with North-Western Rhodesia, the capital was transferred to Livingstone.

The subsequent colonial history of Northern Rhodesia (Gann, 1964; Hall, 1965) is of little relevance to the present work. A succinct summary, with particular reference to the Eastern Province, is given by Kay (1965: 3-35). It may be noted that the Chipata area, which had been the centre of Ngoni settlement, attracted at an early date a substantial number of European farming settlers—growing principally cotton, rubber and latterly tobacco—who waxed prosperous until declining producer prices in the early 1930's sharply reduced their numbers. The presence of the settlers greatly increased land-pressure in the African areas, which was only partly compensated by the excision of over a third of the North Charterland Concession to form Native Reserves in 1928, four years after the administration of the territory had been taken over from the British South Africa Company by the Imperial Government. The Reserves rapidly became overpopulated while over half of the original Concession was virtually uninhabited. This pattern, with the resultant effect upon the vegetation, has continued with relatively minor modification up to the present time, although the North Charterland Concession was taken over by the Government in 1947 and its unalienated portions redesignated as Native Trust Land. Many of the European farms remained unoccupied but in foreign hands; this injustice has only been rectified since Zambia's independence in 1964.

Chapter 3

The Archaeological Background

Although the present volume is the first major work to be devoted to the prehistoric succession in eastern Zambia, the general outline of south-central African prehistory has been known for several years (J. D. Clark, 1970b; Sampson, 1974). The distribution of research has, however, remained extremely uneven; and it was principally to fill one of the major geographical lacunae in our knowledge that the fieldwork here described was undertaken.

The earliest period with which we are here concerned is that conventionally known as the 'Middle Stone Age'. It is mainly represented in the archaeological record by stone industries based on a prepared core technique —mode 3 of J. G. D. Clark's (1969: 29-31) classification of stone-tool-making technologies. The chronology of these industries remains poorly understood. In some parts of central and southern Africa their inception may have taken place more than 70,000 years ago: generally they were replaced around 20,000-12,000 bc, but in some areas—notably the upper Zambezi valley—they continued in vogue as late as the second millennium bc (Sampson, 1974; L. Phillipson, 1975: 168-281). By around 15,000 years ago contrasting industries of 'Late Stone Age' type, characterised by backed microliths (Clark's mode 5), were present in central and northern Zambia and in adjacent regions to the north and east. For the first time numerous human settlements are attested on the plateaux, where caves and rock-shelters often shown signs of prolonged occupation by hunter/gatherers. Villages of farming peoples are not attested in the central African archaeological record until the advent of the Early Iron Age, during the first few centuries ad.

I. THE ARCHAEOLOGY OF NEIGHBOURING AREAS

ZAMBIA

Of the regions bordering on eastern Zambia, that best known archaeologically lies to the west, across the formidable Luangwa valley, and comprises the Central, Copperbelt and Northern Provinces of the same country (fig. 5). Most of the published research in this area has been conducted by Dr J. D. Clark and his associates from 1948, and by the present writer between 1964 and 1972. The succession of pre-'Middle Stone Age' industries, known mainly from Clark's excavations at Kalambo Falls near the southern end of Lake Tanganyika (J. D. Clark, 1969; 1974), need not concern us here. The mode 3 material from that site has been described as 'Lupemban'; and its affinities are clearly with more westerly regions. Apart from a probably mode 3 occurrence at Lukupa near Kasama (now housed in the Livingstone Museum), the only other significant mode 3 site which has so far been investigated in this area is that of Twin Rivers Kopje, 24 km south-west of Lusaka (J. D. Clark, 1970b: 130, 138; 1971). The artefacts, dated by radiocarbon to between 31,000 and 20,000 bc, include small scraping tools and both bifacial and unifacial points: climatological and faunal data were also recovered.

Apparently broadly contemporary with the later stages of the occupation of Twin Rivers was the initial settlement of Leopard's Hill Cave, 50 km south-east of Lusaka. The associated industry, referred to as 'proto-Late Stone Age' by J. D. Clark (1970b: 241) is discussed at length later in this book in comparison with eastern Zambian material. Subsequent levels at Leopard's Hill have yielded a succession of mode 5 'Nachikufan' industries, to a consideration of which we may now turn.

Three successive 'Nachikufan' industries were originally described on the basis of material recovered during Clark's 1948 excavations at Nachikufu Cave in the Muchinga mountains 50 km south of Mpika (J. D. Clark, 1950c). Analyses by S. F. Miller (1969; 1971; 1972) of material from Nachikufu and other sites including Leopard's Hill, have been presented as confirming the three-stage succession originally proposed, with a further subdivision of the middle stage.*

Aggregates attributed to 'Nachikufan I' appear to have a time-span of some 5000 or 6000 years beginning around the fifteenth millennium bc. They display a microlithic, bladelet-based technology and are characterised by narrow, pointed curved-backed flakes which numerically dominate the geometrics, among which deep and angle-backed forms are generally rare. Scrapers, including concave forms, are few. Bored stones are comparatively common, but the occurrence of ground stone axes remains to be proven.

In the succeeding stage, 'Nachikufan IIA', dated between the eighth and the sixth millennia bc, the curved-backed flakes of stage I give way to broader forms. Ground axes are clearly attested and the bored stones continue. In 'Nachikufan IIB' aggregates (fourth and third millennia bc), deep lunates and angle-backed microliths are the vogue. Both 'Nachikufan II' phases have a more restricted distribution than does 'Nachikufan I'.

In later times, the microlithic industries show greater regional variety. That from Kalambo Falls, dated to around 2000 bc, has been named the Kaposwa Industry (J. D. Clark, 1974: 107-52). It is characterised by large numbers of backed microliths, many of which were made by means of a well developed microburin technique. The apparent idiosyncracy of this industry is probably largely due to the fine chert of which it is

---

*Clark's and Miller's systematisation of the 'Nachikufan' industries has been criticised by Sampson and Southard (1973). It is further discussed in chapter 21, below.

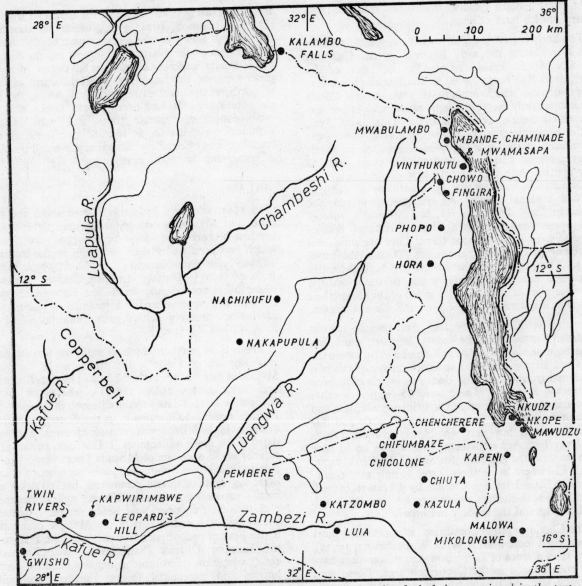

Fig. 5. Regions adjacent to eastern Zambia, showing the principal archaeological sites mentioned in the text.

made—a material which has markedly different flaking properties from those of the quartz which was generally used for microlith manufacture in other areas.* Broadly contemporary aggregates from sites further to the south as far as the Lusaka region have been generally lumped together under the heading 'Nachikufan III', but they have little typological homogeneity, and show the continuation—in varying proportions—of all the tool types recognised in the earlier phases. Many of these industries, such as that from Nakapapula (D. W. Phillipson, 1969), survived long after the advent of the Early Iron Age, in several cases until about the middle of the present millennium.

A contrast to the 'Nachikufan III' aggregates, and one which serves to emphasise their lack of unity, is provided by the mode 5 industries of the Copperbelt region (Gabel, 1967; Phillipson and Phillipson, 1970). These show a dominance of pointed lunates and

a scarcity of all types of scrapers; they appear to have more in common with the 'Wilton' industries found south of the Kafue as, for example, at Gwisho (Gabel, 1965; Fagan and van Noten, 1971). It appears probable, as will be shown in a later chapter, that microlithic industries did not spread to these more southerly regions until the last four millennia bc.

In conclusion, it should be noted that the Zambian 'Late Stone Age' industries, prior to the time of Iron Age contact, lacked all traces of pottery and of metallurgy. A hunting-gathering economy is indicated, in which all techniques of food production appear to have been unknown. Human skeletal remains are rarely encountered, except at Gwisho; here—as on contemporary sites elsewhere in central and southern Africa—they are stated for the most part to display predominantly Khoi-San physical features (Gabel, 1965: 95). Rock paintings of the naturalistic type attributed to the 'Late Stone Age' are rare, except in the Kasama area (D. W. Phillipson, 1972b). A further consideration of these problems and of the inter-relationship of the various mode 5 industries, in the

---

*Examination of 'Nachikufan' aggregates from Leopard's Hill Cave has provided clear evidence for the use of a microburin technique, not noted or commented upon by Miller (L. Phillipson, *personal communication*).

15

light of the Eastern Province discoveries, must be postponed until a later chapter.

The Early Iron Age appears to have begun throughout this area during the early centuries of the Christian era (D. W. Phillipson, 1975). The inception of the Early Iron Age is attributed to substantial movements of population which brought to south-central Africa a predominantly Negroid people whose way of life was in marked contrast with that of the 'Late Stone Age'. Both agriculture and animal domestication were introduced at this time, as were techniques of metallurgy, pottery, and house-construction using puddled clay applied over a wooden framework; together with settlement in substantial semi-permanent villages. Several regional groups are recognised within the Zambian Early Iron Age (D. W. Phillipson, 1968a), and appear to have been discrete cultural entities prior to their establishment there. They are now seen to belong to two principal streams (D. W. Phillipson, 1975). The groups with which we are here primarily concerned are the Kalambo group of the Northern Province plateau, the Chondwe group of the Copperbelt and the Kapwirimbwe group of the Lusaka region.

In the north, the Early Iron Age population was apparently sparse, and the only village site which has so far been discovered is that at Kalambo Falls, where the finds are largely restricted to characteristic potsherds, occasional iron objects, and deep pits which have been interpreted as graves. There were no copper or other imported objects. The economic evidence is sparse and difficult to interpret: bones of domestic cattle and dog were recovered but were not clearly associated with the Early Iron Age settlement. Grindstones could have been used for the grinding of cereals (J. D. Clark, 1974: 8–70). Elsewhere in northern Zambia, only rare occurrences of Early Iron Age artefacts have been recovered, often from rock-shelters where they are associated with the late stages of the mode 5 industries.

The Chondwe group population, in contrast, appears to have been more numerous (D. W. Phillipson, 1972a). More than a score of Early Iron Age village sites have now been located in the Copperbelt area. These were generally situated beside streams and appear usually to have been abandoned after only brief occupation. Iron and copper working is attested, but exploitation of the rich local deposits appears to have remained on a small scale until later Iron Age times. Around Lusaka, the Kapwirimbwe group settlements such as Twickenham Road and Kapwirimbwe itself (D. W. Phillipson, 1970; 1968c) show similar features, with particularly intensive iron working. Domestic cattle and goats are attested there. Both the Chondwe and Kapwirimbwe groups are attributed to the Early Iron Age's western stream (D. W. Phillipson, 1975).

In each of the two more northerly culture-areas here discussed (the Northern Province and the Copperbelt) there has been recognised a distinct style of schematic rock painting. These distributional data, together with other considerations, have led to a tentative attribution of this schematic art to the Early Iron Age (D. W. Phillipson, 1972b).

Throughout these areas, the Early Iron Age evidently came to an end around the eleventh century. Wherever an interface with the succeeding later Iron Age has been located, there is a clear discontinuity in the associated pottery traditions. Throughout the Zambian areas with which we are here concerned, the later

Iron Age pottery is attributed to the Luangwa tradition (D. W. Phillipson, 1974: 7–10), which has continued into recent times in the greater part of the region. The origins of the Luangwa tradition remain obscure, but it clearly indicates a considerable degree of homogeneity among the later Iron Age inhabitants of most of north, central and eastern Zambia during the past eight centuries. It has been argued (ibid.) that the establishment of separate states and 'tribal' groups within this population, as recalled in the extant oral tradition, was effected by comparatively small numbers of immigrants from the north-west.

MALAWI

In 1965, relatively little was known about the prehistory of Malawi, a country which had never had a resident archaeologist. Most of the professional work which had been undertaken had been in the hands of archaeologists from Zambia (J. D. Clark, 1956; 1959b; Inskeep, 1965). During the past decade, however, research has been greatly intensified, although many of the available reports are of a preliminary nature. An invaluable summary has recently been published by P. A. Cole-King (1973).

There is in northern Malawi evidence for the early establishment of mode 5 industries, as at the Hora Mountain rock-shelter in the Mzimba District (Robinson and Sandelowsky, 1968: 108-11), where the lowest occupation level is dated to the fifteenth millennium bc. Further north, at Chaminade in the Karonga District, a single backed flake was recovered from a deposit dated to the ninth millennium (J. D. Clark, 1970a: 344). Nearby is the open site of Mbande Court (ibid.: 344-5), dated to the last two thousand years bc, where a microlithic aggregate of quartz geometrics, backed flakes and small scrapers is associated with larger tools of basement rock including choppers and heavy scrapers. Contemporary with the earlier part of the Mbande occupation is the Fingira rock-shelter site on the Nyika Plateau of the Rumphi District (Sandelowsky and Robinson, 1968), where the microlithic aggregates included deeper lunates and trapezoidal forms. Further rock-shelter excavations in more southerly regions include those at Mwana wa Chencherere near Dedza (J. D. Clark, 1973), Malowa in the Chiradzulu District (Denbow, 1973) and Mikolongwe in the Thyolo District (Cole-King, 1968).

J. D. Clark (1972) has recognised two regional variants (or "contemporary phases") in the mode 5 industries of Malawi: a northern, lake-shore variant characterised by a high proportion of large tools made from quartzite cobbles, and a plateau variant best known from the Nyika Plateau rock-shelters of Fingira and Chowo. Trapezoidal and lunate-shaped microliths, scrapers, ground stone axes and bone arrow-points and awls are the characteristic artefacts. The data are not yet available which will enable a comparison to be made between these industries and those from more southerly rock-shelters.

Rock paintings are widely distributed notably in the Mzimba, Dedza and Lilongwe Districts (J. D. Clark, 1959b; Cole-King, 1973). No true naturalistic paintings have so far been discovered. The earliest designs are done in red paint and are exclusively schematic. They are frequently overlain by red and white bichromes and by white semi-naturalistic anthropomorphic or zoomorphic figures. At a few sites the white figures are in turn covered by crude charcoal drawings. The white paintings and their successors may be regarded as being of Iron Age date: no evidence has yet been obtained from Malawi concerning the absolute age of the earlier red schematic designs.

In the upper levels of several of these rock-shelters there is clear evidence for the contemporaneity of mode 5 industries with the manufacture of Early Iron Age pottery. Extensive research by K. R. Robinson has elucidated an outline Iron Age succession for much of the country: from the Karonga area (Robinson, 1966a), more southerly parts of the Northern Region (Robinson and Sandelowsky, 1968), and from around the southern end of the lake (Robinson, 1970). More recently, intensive fieldwork has been undertaken in southern Malawi (Cole-King et al., 1973; Robinson, 1973; Kurashina, 1973).

Considerable overlap is attested between the 'Late Stone Age' and the Early Iron Age populations in several areas of Malawi. This is most clearly shown by Clark's excavations at Chencherere rock-shelter in the Dedza District (J. D. Clark, 1973). Within the Malawi Early Iron Age two major regional variants are distinguished by Robinson on the basis of the associated pottery. That in the north is known as Mwabulambo (originally published as Mwavarambo) ware from its type-site on the Lufilya river (Robinson, 1966a; Robinson and Sandelowsky, 1968). Its earliest radiocarbon date suggests that its makers were established in Malawi by the beginning of the fourth century. Further to the south, the characteristic Early Iron Age artefact is the pottery first recognised at Nkope on the lake-shore north-west of Mangochi, which also dates back at least to early in the fourth century ad. The typology and affinities of this material are discussed in some detail later in this book (pp. 208-9). Cole-King (1973:10) has noted that "only limited Iron Age research has been carried out in the central areas of Malawi and it is not possible to say at present where lies the northern limit of Nkope ware and the southern limit of Mwabulambo ware, or whether the two merge together and represent a basic cultural unity". Both groups clearly belong to the eastern stream of the Early Iron Age (D. W. Phillipson, 1975).

Around 1000 ad Nkope ware appears to have been replaced by a distinctive pottery style, named after Kapeni Hill in the Ncheu District. Radiocarbon dates indicate an age somewhere between the early tenth and the mid-fifteenth centuries (Cole-King, 1973: 11). Kapeni ware has a restricted distribution and is markedly less common than both its predecessor and the later Mawudzu ware. The type-site of the latter ware, Mawudzu Hill, is situated close to the shore of Lake Malawi not far from Nkope. Only two radiocarbon dates are available and they cover the period from the mid-fourteenth to the mid-seventeenth centuries. Mawudzu ware has been tentatively attributed by Robinson (1970:120) and Cole King (1973:11) to the Maravi.

In the northern area, Mwabulambo ware appears to have been replaced by, or have evolved into, that known from the site of Mwamasapa on the Rukuru river near Karonga, dated between the early eleventh and early sixteenth centuries (Robinson, 1966a: 177-85). The relationship of this material with that from Kapeni and Mawudzu remains unclear. A small assemblage from Vinthukutu in the Karonga District shares affinities with both Kapeni and Mwamasapa (Robinson

and Sandelowsky, 1968: 131), but has yielded a remarkably early radiocarbon date around the ninth century. In the north of Malawi, the time-span of the more southerly Mawudzu ware is occupied by the pottery named Mbande ware. The type-site, Mbande Hill in the Karonga District, is the installation place of the Ngonde chiefs, with which people this pottery is logically to be associated. Several of these Malawian later Iron Age pottery traditions bear a marked resemblance to those broadly contemporary wares from Zambia which have been attributed to the Luangwa tradition (D. W. Phillipson, 1974: 7-10). The relationship of the archaeological material with the modern pottery traditions, here or elsewhere in Malawi, has not been adequately investigated.

MOÇAMBIQUE

In contrast to that of neighbouring countries, the archaeology of Moçambique remains very imperfectly understood (dos Santos, 1961). Especially is this true of the Tete Province, the large wedge of Moçambique territory which stretches inland along the lower Zambezi as far west as the Luangwa confluence. Research into the prehistory of this area has been largely restricted to the recording of rock paintings. Since the relevant publications are, to English-speaking readers, largely unknown and inaccessible, an attempt will be made here to summarise the sparse available data.

Investigation of prehistoric sites in this region began in 1907 when Carl Wiese, whose political exploits in Mpezeni's country we have already described (p. 12), located several rock paintings within a 2-days' march of Chifumbaze (fig. 5). Wiese's discoveries were described by Letcher (1910, quoted by Dart, 1931: 478-9). The only one of these sites which appears to have been recorded by Wiese in any detail consists of a large rock slab 3 or 4 km from Chifumbaze gold mine, whose name it has taken, and 3 km from the Vubwe river. Letcher (loc.cit.) reports that below these paintings was a cave which was excavated by Wiese "to a depth of about 15 feet ... he took with him to Germany a large quantity of bones, etc., discovered in the cave ... in the process of excavation". In 1909 the material excavated by Wiese arrived at the Museum für Völkerkunde in Berlin; some was lost during the Second World War, but Dr Angelika Rumpf of the Museum has informed me that thirteen stone artefacts and twenty-five potsherds from Chifumbaze are still preserved there (pace dos Santos, 1955: 749). Three of the sherds (plate IIa) are of Early Iron Age type, indistinguishable from specimens recovered at Kamnama in Zambia (chapter 6, below) and at Malawian sites. The Chifumbaze site is thus of interest as that of the earliest recorded discovery of Early Iron Age pottery in south-central Africa. It was reinvestigated in 1936 and 1937 by J. R. dos Santos (1938a; 1938b: 297 ff; 1940a: 77-9) who has since published numerous illustrations of the paintings. These extend across the rock for some 10 m and are exclusively schematic, in white and various shades of red, with grid motifs predominating.

A second site discovered by Wiese consisted of further schematic rock paintings at Chicolone, 40 km north-west of Chifumbaze. These were investigated and photographed two years later by J. Spring (Staudinger, 1910), who conducted excavations to a depth of 3 to 4 m at the foot of the rock face, recovering "skeletons and stone artefacts". These, like those found by Wiese at Chifumbaze, appear to have been sent to Berlin; but

THE PREHISTORY OF EASTERN ZAMBIA

Dr Rumpf informs me that they are no longer preserved in the Museum für Völkerkunde. This site also has been revisited and described by dos Santos (1940a: 78-83; 1940b; 1941), who names it Chicolone I. To the Chewa it is renowned as the *mwala olemba* (painted rock) *par excellence*.* The painted area measures some 10 m wide by 7 m high. More than two hundred individual schematic motifs in varying shades of red are preserved. According to dos Santos, these include horizontal ladder designs, chequer-board motifs, concentric circles, grids and sets of parallel lines: more unusual motifs, for this area, are a single anthropomorphic figure and over thirty imprints of hands with outspread fingers. Quartz microliths were collected at the foot of the rock but these, too, following an unfortunate accident, were subsequently lost. The *mwala olemba* is today held sacred to *mzimos* (spirits of the dead).

Within 100 m of the *mwala olemba* is a second rock painting site, Chicolone II. Under a small overhang some 13-15 m above ground level are naturalistic paintings representing "a silhouette of the rear half of an eland and the head of a giraffe-like creature, as well as other indecipherable marks" (dos Santos, 1955: 751-2).

Further to the south, at Katzombo, Spring discovered and photographed further schematic paintings. Staudinger (1910: 142) reports that they were overlain (*sic*) by "drawings of human figures and animals (perhaps the work of Bushmen)" but these "were easily washed off"!

Additional naturalistic paintings are noted by de Oliveira (1971b: 62) at Chiuta and Kazula; those at the former site are illustrated and may be seen to display a marked resemblance to those from Zawi Hill in Zambia, described below (p. 183). Both quadrupeds and birds are represented at Chiuta, alongside schematic motifs.

Other rock painting sites have been reported in the Tete District, but they have not been recorded in detail. Their approximate locations are shown on the accompanying map (fig. 5) which, for Moçambique, is based on that published by de Oliveira (1971a: 4). It may be noted in passing that the distribution of schematic paintings in Moçambique is not restricted to the Tete District: they are also known further to the east, as, for example, at Monte Churo near the Melosa river which forms the border between Moçambique and Malawi east of Zomba, and at Monte Campote, near Lake Chirwa.

It is thus apparent that very little is yet known concerning the prehistory of Moçambique's Tete Province beyond the presence there of rock-shelters decorated with both naturalistic and schematic paintings and containing microlithic industries of 'Late Stone Age' type as well as Early Iron Age and later pottery. The only archaeological excavations which have yet been conducted in the province took place almost seventy years ago and any records which may have been kept, together with almost all the finds, have long since been lost.

II. PREVIOUS ARCHAEOLOGICAL RESEARCH IN EASTERN ZAMBIA

Although the present writer's research has been largely restricted to the Eastern Province plateau south of latitude 13° south, the opportunity is here taken to present a brief summary of archaeological work undertaken prior to 1965 in the whole of the Eastern Province, since the greater part of this material has so far remained unpublished.

Prior to 1965 the detailed archaeological sequence of eastern Zambia remained virtually unknown. The presence of rock paintings in the area had been recorded in the early years of the present century, when Miss Alice Werner (1907: 391) noted "prints on a conglomerate rock in the Chipeta country (N. E. Rhodesia), which are connected by the local Bantu with the creation of man and animals" and concluded that "possibly a Bushman origin should be assigned" to them.

No further interest appears to have been taken in the prehistory of the area until 1935, when Mr F. B. Macrae, who had earlier been District Commissioner at Mumbwa in the Central Province, and who has the distinction of having conducted the first archaeological excavation in the then Northern Rhodesia, at Mumbwa Cave, in 1925 (Macrae, 1926), was appointed District Commissioner at Lundazi. During the years immediately preceding the outbreak of the Second World War, he

and Mr D. Gordon Lancaster, Elephant Control Officer, investigated a number of archaeological sites in the Lundazi District. A brief paper (Macrae and Lancaster, 1937) provided summary details of a 'Middle Stone Age' (mode 3) occurrence beside the Viziwa Stream (c. 10° 48′ south, 33°03′ east) in the Luangwa Valley, and of a rock-shelter at Mtunga (c. 11°20′ south, 33°20′ east) on the plateau, where only slight traces of Stone Age occupation were noted. Both these sites are in the north of the Lundazi District. Also recorded was the rock-shelter at Kanyankunde (c. 11°47′ south, 32°54′ east) in the hilly country of the Luangwa escarpment north-west of Lundazi Boma, where a small excavation was conducted by Lancaster in August 1936. Archaeological deposits reached a depth of 90 cm. The uppermost 50 cm consisted of "guano, earth and ashes" and contained pottery as well as stone artefacts of mode 5 type, including twenty-four varied scrapers but only three geometrics out of thirty retouched implements described. It was separated by a rock fall from a lower layer of "reddish cave earth" in which the pottery was coarser and better fired than that in the upper level, and in which forty-three of the sixty-seven stone implements noted were scrapers. A very faint red schematic painting of 'grid' type was also noted on the wall of the rock-shelter.

Further researches in the Eastern Province were subsequently conducted by both Macrae and Lancaster between 1936 and 1940, but the results were not published: the following details have been extracted from their notes and correspondence which are preserved on file at the Livingstone Museum, and from

---

*The present writer, while excavating at Makwe rock-shelter in 1966, was told of the *mwala olemba* at Chicolone by residents in Chief Kathumba's area, some 70 km to the north-west. Unfortunately, the political situation at that time rendered a visit to the latter site impracticable.

Macrae's entries in the Lundazi District Notebook, now kept at the National Archives of Zambia in Lusaka.

ROCK-SHELTERS

Kambulumbulu (11°53′ south, 32°55′ east) is situated within a few kilometres of Kanyankunde (see above) in the eastern Luangwa escarpment. It was investigated by Macrae and Lancaster in 1937 and by the present writer in 1965. The greater part of Kambulumbulu Hill consists of a vast outcrop of rock, at the south-east end of which is a rock-shelter some 15 m long and 4 m deep. Traces of red schematic paintings survive on the flaking gneiss wall and copies of a selection of these have been published (D. W. Phillipson, 1966: 72-7). Excavations conducted by Lancaster revealed 45 cm of deposit which he divided into three strata of equal thickness: light surface dust containing signs of iron-smelting, humic soil containing a presumably mode 5 industry comparable to that from Kanyankunde, and a bottom layer of humic soil containing similar artefacts in greatly reduced quantities. A burial, probably female, had apparently been inserted into the lower levels in comparatively recent times.

Pandawiri Hill (12°30′ south, 32°25′ east). A rock-shelter near Maluza village in the Lundazi District was noted by Lancaster, who recovered from the surface later Iron Age pottery and some 'Late Stone Age' artefacts which are now preserved in the Livingstone Museum.

Nzuni Hill (12°27′ south, 32°46′ east). Six rock-shelters in this hill, east of Mukuku on the Lusangazi river, were located by Lancaster who collected artefacts from their surfaces. These artefacts have not been preserved in any collection known to me.

Chinunga Hill. Macrae excavated a trial trench through 45 cm of deposit at a rock-shelter close to Ngwanta village in the Lundazi District, locating a few 'Late Stone Age' artefacts, bone and charcoal. No further details are available, nor can the site now be pinpointed with any accuracy.

Mambato (13°27′ south, 32°46′ east). In 1937 Macrae located a rock-shelter on a small hill beside the Chipata-Lundazi road 32 km north of the former township and close to Mambato village. Later Iron Age pottery was noted but not collected. There were "traces of a drawing in red ochre" at the site. Mambato village has moved in recent years but search and enquiry around the areas of both its former and present situations (fig. 19, p. 38) by the present writer have not succeeded in re-locating the rock-shelter unless, as seems improbable, it is that described below (p. 170) under the name Chalumbe.

Katolola. These rock-shelters, described in detail below (see p. 173), were investigated by Lancaster, who made a small excavation in site B. The upper 25 cm of deposit consisted of dark earth, below which gravelly soil with a little ash and charcoal reached a maximum depth of 1.10 m, at which point the presence of large fallen slabs of granite prevented further work. Numerous quartz artefacts were recovered, but no pottery. Macrae recovered from a narrow cleft on the same hill a human skull which is now in the Livingstone Museum.

Simbo Hill. The rock paintings at this site, described on p. 181, were discovered in 1936 by Lancaster, who also noted the presence of pottery which, preserved in the Livingstone Museum, is of later Iron Age type.

OPEN SITES

(A substantial number of 'Middle Stone Age' and earlier occurrences beside the Luangwa river and the lower reaches of its tributaries are here omitted. For details, see J. D. Clark, 1939; 1950b: 84-6, 98; 1954; also Macrae and Lancaster's notebooks in the Livingstone Museum.)

Lundazi Boma (12°18′ south, 33°12′ east). Macrae noted the presence of 'Late Stone Age' artefacts on the footpaths around the Boma. An iron arrowhead, illustrated by J. D. Clark (1950a: 83) was recovered at a depth of between 3 and 5 m while digging a well at the Boma.

Ntembwe of Mwase Lundazi (12°24′ south, 33°22′ east). This large defensive perimeter earthwork, or *linga*, situated 2 km east of the village of Senior Chief Mwase Lundazi, was first investigated by Macrae. Oral traditions which he collected indicated that the site was first occupied by the Chewa five generations before 1938, when the Akafula (see p. 10) who previously resided there were driven away. The earthworks were constructed by the Chewa as a defence against the raiding Ngoni. A small excavation conducted by Macrae revealed two levels. The upper one yielded pottery of recent type, iron slag and pieces of wire, together with a single glass bead. The lower level produced a distinct type of pottery and some mode 5 quartz artefacts. The finds are preserved in the Livingstone Museum. The pottery from the lower level, which is exceedingly fragmentary, does not appear to the present writer to be of Early Iron Age type. It was attributed by Macrae to the Akafula.

Diwa Hill (13°04′ south, 32°57′ east). This prominent, steep-sided, rocky outcrop is situated beside the Lundazi-Chipata road, 100 km south of Lundazi. It was investigated by Macrae and Lancaster in about 1938 and by the present writer and Mr H. W. Langworthy in 1965. The summit of the hill is littered with later Iron Age pottery, which oral tradition relates to use of the hill-top as a place of refuge during the Ngoni wars. Lancaster also reported the discovery of a nose-plug of unspecified material and a glass bead.

Kamangamalindi Hill. Thirty-two kilometres south of Diwa Hill, on the border between the Chipata and Lundazi Districts, is Kamangamalindi Hill, on the summit of which Macrae found pottery similar to that from the former site. Collections from both sites are stored at the Livingstone Museum.

Mkwezi Rocks (13°24′ south, 32°58′ east). This site lies near the Malawi border, some 5 km north of Tamanda Mission in the Chipata District. Macrae noted a surface occurrence of "interesting potsherds" which were not collected.

Sanjika (13°43′ south, 32°46′ east). The Sanjika Hills are a prominent range near the Malawi border north of, and parallel to, the road from Chipata to Mchinji. From a rock-shelter high on Bombwe Hill Macrae recovered a human skeleton and later Iron Age pottery. Comparable pottery was found at the site by the present writer and Mr Langworthy in 1965: both collections are preserved in the Livingstone Museum and are described below (p. 31).

Subsequent researches in the Eastern Province were mainly devoted to the rock paintings, in which field several notable discoveries were made by social anthropologists. In 1949 those at Njazi (c.13°53′ south, 31°44′ east) in the Petauke District and at Zawi Hill (see p. 183) were located by Dr J. P. Bruwer and Mr (now Professor) J. A. Barnes respectively.* A brief description of the Njazi paintings was published by Bruwer (1956), but subsequent attempts by both J. H. Chaplin and the present writer to re-locate the site have proved unsuccessful. In 1955, Mr R. A. Hamilton located several painted sites in the Chadiza area, including Sakwe and Kalemba: the former site was further investigated by Chaplin, the others by the present writer (see pp. 179, 173). Tracings of the Zawi, Katolola and Simbo Hill paintings were made in 1955 by Mr B. Williams of the Northern Rhodesia Monuments Commission. Dr J. D. Clark (1958b; 1959b) has published valuable surveys of the Eastern Province rock art, as known at that time.

In 1957 Mr Chaplin joined the staff of the Monuments Commission, and over the next four years he located and investigated many rock paintings, most of which are

_____

*The Zawi site had previously been visited in 1937 by Dr J. M. Winterbottom (*personal communication*).

described in two papers (Chaplin, 1960; 1962) and which are also discussed in chapter 19 of the present work. Paintings investigated by Chaplin in 1958 were Rukuzye Dam and Manda Hill (both described in Chaplin, 1960), as well as the previously known sites of Zawi, Katolola and Simbo Hill. In 1960 he investigated Sezamanja, Sakwe A (previously reported by Hamilton), Mbozi, Mkoma, Chaingo and Masinja, as well as five sites in the Chipangali Resettlement Area reported by Mr P. Greening: all these sites were published (Chaplin, 1962). In the following year (1961b), Chaplin investigated a number of nineteenth century refuge sites, notably those at Milanzi, Kamwara, Simbo and seven sites in Chief Sandwe's area of the Chipata District. Iron-smelting furnaces were also located immediately south of Lundazi township and on Mr H. Rangeley's farm at Petauke.

By 1965 it may thus be stated that the archaeological potential of eastern Zambia had been established. The presence of 'Late Stone Age' and Iron Age sites had been demonstrated but no satisfactory excavations had yet been conducted. Many rock painting sites were known and had been painstakingly recorded: it was clear that several successive styles of these could be recognised, some of which were probably of relatively recent date. This was the state of knowledge when the present project was initiated in 1965.

Chapter 4

Typology and Definitions

As explained in chapter 1, the prehistoric artefacts here discussed are described in terms of broadly defined categories which are applied uniformly to the material from all the sites investigated. Minor typological variations together with metrical data and stylistic observations are discussed separately for each site. In this chapter, working definitions are offered of the various classes used in the analysis of the pottery and chipped stone artefact aggregates, and of the terms used in their mensuration and description.

I. POTTERY

Pottery collections may be classified both according to the vessel shapes represented, and in terms of decorational techniques and motifs. The former method will result in a functionally orientated classification, the relative frequencies of the various vessel shapes being mainly indicative of function. Emphasis on such traits as rim form and decoration, on the other hand, will provide a cultural-stylistic classification. It is this which is attempted here, the main aim of the present analysis being the differentiation of stylistic traditions. The primary division of the pottery collections is therefore made on criteria of decoration.

The terms used in the pottery analyses recorded in this volume are defined as follows:

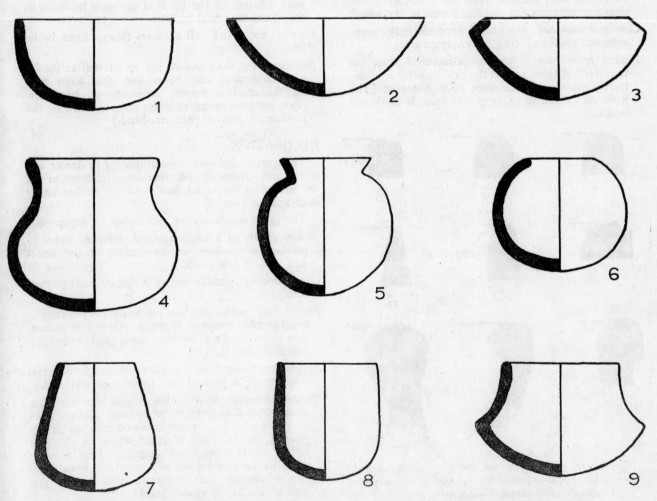

Fig. 6. Pottery vessel forms: 1, 2—open bowls; 3—in-turned bowl; 4—necked vessel; 5—pot with up-turned rim; 6—globular vessel; 7—convergent-mouthed pot; 8—beaker; 9—carinated vessel.

FORM

In the context of pottery descriptions, the term *vessel* relates to any ceramic receptacle. *Pots* are vessels of which the height exceeds the maximum diameter. The maximum diameter of *bowls* exceeds their height. All Iron Age vessels here discussed have rounded bases.

The following vessel shapes are recognised (fig. 6):

Open bowls. These are bowls which have no concavity or carination in their external profile. The maximum diameter is at the rim. (These vessels are generally approximately hemispherical, with the sides at the rim close to vertical.)

In-turned bowls are distinguished from open bowls by the presence of sharply inverted rims. (The rim may be differentiated from the body of the bowl by an angle of almost ninety degrees.)

Necked vessels have rounded shoulders, externally concave necks, and a slight eversion above the neck. Their maximum diameter is at or slightly below the shoulder.

Pots with up-turned rims. These are pots with near globular bodies that are constricted just below the rim. The rim is approximately vertical or slightly everted, and is defined by a sharp angle.

Globular vessels are approximately spherical in overall shape. The rim diameter is appreciably less than the maximum body diameter. The rim is in-turned and does not interrupt the globular profile of the vessel.

Convergent-mouthed pots have approximately semi-spherical bases and straight convergent sides.

Beakers are similar to convergent-mouthed pots, but have vertical sides, so that the rim diameter approximately equals the maximum body diameter. (The maximum diameter rarely greatly exceeds the vessel height.)

Carinated vessels. Any vessel on which the convexity of the wall is keeled or interrupted by an angle. (In practice, this form is rare in eastern Zambia and, the diagnostic carination being generally located at some distance below the rim and decorated zone, carinated vessels are usually represented in the archaeological collections here discussed only by undecorated body sherds.)

The *lip* of a vessel is the upper surface of the edge connecting the interior and exterior surfaces of the vessel wall.

Lip profiles (fig. 7) are described as:

Rounded: a smooth curve links the exterior surface of the vessel wall with the interior surface.

Bevelled: the profile of the lip is facetted with two or more flat faces running around the periphery of the vessel.

Squared: a squared lip has only a single bevel.

Fluted: this is broadly similar to a bevelled lip, but the section of each facet is concave (Soper, 1971: 16).

The *rim* of a pottery vessel is here understood to comprise that part of the vessel wall immediately adjacent to the lip. It may be differentiated from the rest of the wall in terms of thickness or decoration.

The various rim forms (fig. 7) are defined as follows:

Undifferentiated: the portion of the vessel wall immediately adjacent to the lip is of the same thickness as the rest of the vessel wall.

Tapered: the vessel wall becomes thinner towards the lip.

Thickened: the thickness of the vessel wall at the lip is greater than that below the rim. Rims may be thickened *externally*, *internally* or *bilaterally*. (Externally thickened rims are often attained by the production of a distinct rim-band.)

DECORATION

The term *decoration* is here employed to denote any intentional, primarily non-functional elaboration of the surface of the vessel wall involving designs either in intaglio or in relief.

The following decorative techniques are recognised:

Stamping: use of a single toothed stamp or stylus to produce depressions in the surface of the vessel wall while it is still soft.

Comb-stamping: similar use of a linear multi-toothed stamp.

Rocked-comb impressions are produced by pivotting a multi-toothed stamp on alternate ends as it is 'walked' across the surface of the vessel and repeatedly impressed into the clay.

Bangle impressions: here, a spirally wound wire or metal strip bangle is pressed into the surface of the clay.

Grooving/Incision: these terms denote the use of a narrow-ended instrument to produce concave lines in the vessel wall, whether by depression or by gouging, and whether executed when the clay was soft or hard. When used alone, the term *grooving* refers to the gouging out of a relatively broad line: *incision* signifies the production of a narrow line with a 'V'-shaped cross-section.

Wiping is the use of a flexible object, such as a straw, drawn lightly across the soft surface of the clay.

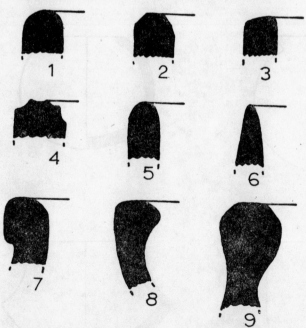

Fig. 7. Lip profiles and rim forms of pottery vessels: 1—rounded lip; 2—bevelled lip; 3—squared lip; 4—fluted lip; 5—undifferentiated rim; 6—tapered rim; 7—externally thickened rim; 8—internally thickened rim; 9—bilaterally thickened rim.

Applied decoration consists of mammillations or ribs raised above the surface of the vessel wall, produced by the affixing of additional pieces of clay.

For the purposes of description in the present work, the decoration of the pottery recovered from archaeological contexts in eastern Zambia has been codified into a series of numbered types. Separate type-listings have been employed for the Early Iron Age pottery and for that of the later Iron Age, since the styles of the two traditions are markedly distinct and very few motifs are common to both. Although pottery from all sites has been described in these terms, variant types and atypical forms are individually described for each site, and their listings are thus not of general applicability. For ease of reference, the listings are repeated on a fold-out sheet at the end of the volume.

EARLY IRON AGE DECORATIVE TYPES

To facilitate comparisons, this typological classification is conformable with that used by the writer in descriptions of Early Iron Age ceramics from other regions of Zambia (D. W. Phillipson, 1968c; 1970; 1972a). Types appearing in the following list in parentheses are not represented in the Early Iron Age sherd collections currently available for study from the Eastern Province of Zambia. They are included here because reference is made to them in chapter 21. Examples of types most frequently occurring in Eastern Zambia are illustrated in fig. 8.

A: decoration based on single stamp impressions
(*Type A1.*) A horizontal band of opposed impressions of a triangular stamp, forming a chevron design in false relief.

Type A2. A horizontal band of single stamp impressions.

B: comb-stamped decoration
Type B1. A horizontal band of diagonal comb-stamping.
(*Type B2.*) Horizontal comb-stamped lines.
(*Type B3.*) A broad band of massed comb-stamping.

C: decoration of grooving/incision
Type C1. One or more parallel horizontal grooves.
Type C2. Type C1 decoration elaborated with downward kinks or pendant loops of grooving.
(*Type C3.*) Vertical parallel grooves.

(*B/C: decoration based on a combination of comb-stamping and grooving.* This occurs on pottery of the Chondwe group of the Zambian Copperbelt.)

D, E, and F: incised decoration
Type D1. A horizontal band of diagonal incision.
Type D2. A horizontal band of criss-cross incision.
(*Type E1.*) A horizontal band of herring-bone incision.
(*Type E2.*) A horizontal band of interlocking triangular blocks of incision, differentiated by the direction of the hatching.
Type F. A horizontal incised chevron line.

G: decoration formed by wiping
Type G: A curvilinear meander of parallel lines, apparently formed by wiping with straws or similar objects.

Undecorated

Atypical. Vessels bearing decoration which could not be classified into any of the above types are listed and described separately at each site.

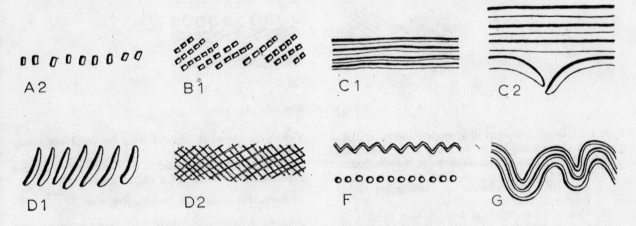

Fig. 8. Decorative types of Early Iron Age pottery.

LATER IRON AGE DECORATIVE TYPES

The later Iron Age pottery of eastern Zambia is attributed to the Luangwa tradition (D. W. Phillipson, 1974). The only analyses of Luangwa tradition assemblages which have so far been published are those of material from Twickenham Road, Lusaka (D. W. Phillipson, 1970) and Chondwe near Ndola (Mills and Filmer, 1972). Unfortunately, it has not proved practicable here to employ a classification compatible with those already published. The following types are recognised (fig. 9):

1: *comb-stamped decoration,* and
2: *incised decoration.* (The break-down of these two classes is the same.)
Type 1/2a. A single horizontal line of comb-stamping/incision.
Type 1/2b. A horizontal row of vertical comb-stamp impressions/incisions.
Type 1/2c(i). One or more horizontal bands of diagonal comb-stamping/incision.
Type 2c(ii). One or more horizontal bands of criss-cross incision.
Type 1/2d. One or more horizontal bands of herring-bone comb-stamping/incision.

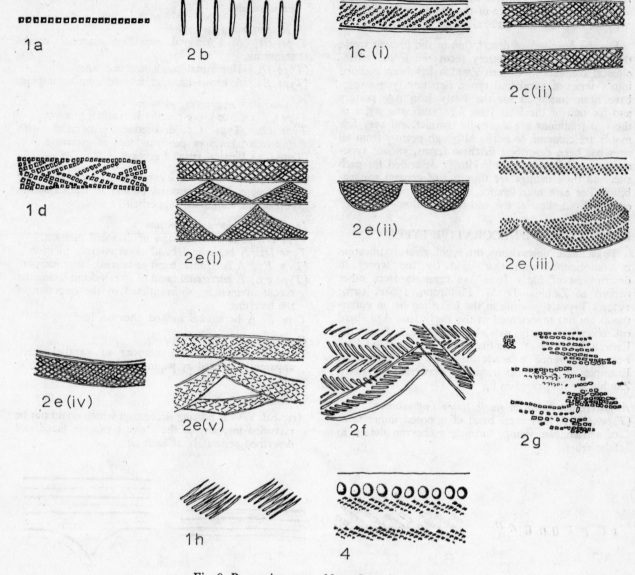

Fig. 9. Decorative types of later Iron Age pottery.

Type 1/2e. Banded designs of triangles, loops, scallops etc., in comb-stamping or incision, often combined with a single band of 1/2c decoration, subdivided as follows:
  (i) One or more bands of upwards-pointing triangular blocks,
  (ii) One or more bands of hemicircular blocks,
  (iii) One or more rows of scallop-shaped blocks,
  (iv) A single festooned band,
  (v) More complex festooned bands.
Type 1/2f. Bands of triangular blocks of herring-bone comb-stamping/incision.

Type 1/2g. Areal designs of irregular comb-stamping/ incision.
Type 1h. A horizontal band of diamond-shaped designs produced by means of a rocked comb.

3: *decoration made with bangle-impressions*

4: *applied decoration* (often used in conjunction with comb-stamping)

Undecorated

Atypical

II. CHIPPED STONE ARTEFACTS

The analysis of chipped stone artefact aggregates has followed a hierarchical classification. Initially, each piece was examined and attributed to one of the following categories:

Cores. These are the nuclei, or parent blocks, from which flakes have been removed.

Shatter-chunks. Angular fragments, not retaining sufficient of a flake release surface to be regarded as broken flakes. (Shatter-chunks are regarded as being mostly the shattered remnants of mis-struck or worked-out cores. At several sites, notably Makwe, the inversely proportional occurrence of cores and shatter-chunks serves to confirm this hypothesis.)

Whole flakes. Flakes are defined as sharp-edged pieces of stone, removed from a core by percussion or pressure, and retaining recognisable traces of conchoidal fracture. Whole flakes retain their striking platforms and are sufficiently complete for their original lengths and breadths (see below) to be measured.

Broken flakes. These are too fragmentary for the above measurements to be taken. (Microburins, being regarded as waste-products (McBurney, 1967:217), are included in this category.)

Retouched implements. Cores, shatter-chunks and whole or broken flakes which show signs of intentional flaking resulting in modification of their shape to produce a usable tool are thus classified. Assessment of these criteria is necessarily subjective but is assisted by the high degree of standardisation of many tool types. It should be noted that, for reasons explained below, specimens whose retouch was judged to be due solely to utilisation were not classified as retouched implements.

It was found that traces of utilisation, as opposed to intentional retouch, could not be distinguished with any degree of confidence from damage caused to the artefacts accidentally. Such damage is frequently observed on specimens recovered from rock-shelters, where the density of artefacts is often such that any movement by the site's prehistoric inhabitants (or its modern excavators) could grind specimens together, producing considerable damage. Experiments have shown (Phillipson and Phillipson, 1970) that artefacts which are to be subjected to analysis of utilisa-

tion damage must be recovered from contexts where such accidental damage may be assumed to have been minimal, and that they must be excavated, sorted and stored with the minimum of handling, especial care being taken to avoid any post-excavation damage. For practical reasons such recovery techniques could not be followed on the excavations here described. Furthermore, at all sites ancient, probably accidental, damage to the artefacts was observed to be frequent. No analysis of utilisation patterns was therefore attempted.

CORES

The cores from all sites show remarkably little standardisation in size, shape or technology. Difficulty was encountered in the establishment of any logical typological subdivision, as the types appear to merge into a multidimensional continuum of variation. The diagram prepared by Gabel (1965:45), on the basis of the cores recovered by him at Gwisho A, illustrates this problem clearly. The typology here employed is similar to that devised by Gabel.

In shape, the cores display such little standardisation that the only practicable subdivision is one based primarily on the number, orientation and minor characteristics of the striking platforms. It is in comparatively few categories that the overall shapes of the cores have been regularly determined by such factors.

Cores are classified in the following types (fig. 10):

Unilateral single-platform cores. Here, flakes were removed only from one edge of a single striking platform. (These cores tend to yield flakes with

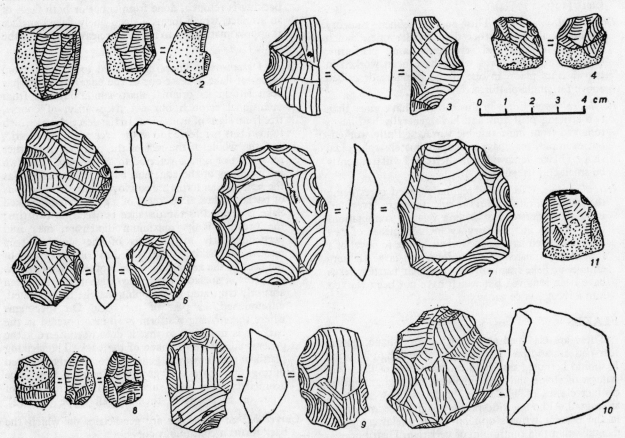

Fig. 10. Types of cores: *1, 2—unilateral single platform; 3, 4—bilateral single platform; 5, 6—radial; 7—tortoise; 8—bipolar; 9—double platform; 10—polyhedral; 11—irregular.*

broadly parallel dorsal scars and simple striking platforms.)

Bilateral single-platform cores. These cores are flaked from both edges of a single striking platform which consequently assumes a sharp, jagged chopper-like form. (Bilateral single-platform cores may produce flakes with either parallel or convergent dorsal scars, the latter predominating, especially on those cores with extended striking platforms. A high proportion of flakes from such cores show pseudo-facetted striking platforms from having been struck at the point where two previous flake-scars intersect on the opposite side of the core.)

Radial cores. These are specimens on which the striking platform, whether unilaterally or bilaterally worked, extends around the whole of the core's periphery. From one or both edges of this platform flakes were struck, leaving scars which converge upon the centre of the core's face, and producing a core of discoid, conical or biconical form. (Flakes struck from such cores show convergent dorsal scars; and many have pseudo-facetted striking platforms.)

Tortoise cores. These may be regarded as a sub-class of the radial cores, characterised by the striking of a single large flake, separated on a plane approximately parallel to that of the core's striking platform, which removes the greater part of the core's face, truncating the scars of all previously removed flakes.

Bipolar cores. Two parallel striking platforms are situated at opposite ends of an elongated core. One or both platforms show crushing. (Parallel-sided flakes were apparently removed from each end by percussion against an anvil, as described and illustrated by J. D. Clark (1959a: 173–4).)

Double-platform cores. This poorly defined category subsumes all cores, other than bipolar ones, which have two distinct and separate striking platforms. (The majority are cores which have been worked in two distinct places in one of the manners described above for single-platform cores.)

Polyhedral cores. Cores in this category have more than two striking platforms and have generally had flakes removed from most suitable surfaces. Fully worked-out examples may have an approximately spheroidal shape. (Flakes removed from such cores will frequently be small and irregular.)

Irregular cores. (Neatly and regularly flaked cores being the exception rather than the rule, the term 'irregular' must be understood as having relative connotations only.) Cores in this category include pieces of raw material which have been worked by the removal of a few flakes, apparently at random, and large shatter-chunks or flake-fragments from which further flakes have been removed but which have not been worked into a recognisable core-type.

FLAKES

These are classified according to size, shape, dorsal scar-pattern, and position and type of striking platform. It should be noted that rigid categorisation of flakes on criteria of shape and size, involving the recognition of distinct classes of 'blades' or 'bladelets', has not been attempted. Although widespread, this practice imparts—in the present writer's opinion—an artificial compartmentalisation to a continuum of variation. Distributions of sizes and shapes of flakes are here indicated by means of scatter-diagrams.

In the descriptions and analyses of flakes, the following terms are employed:

Length. This is the maximum dimension of the flake measured perpendicularly to the chord of its striking platform.

Breadth is the greatest dimension of the flake at right angles to, and in the same plane as, its length.

Thickness is the maximum dimension of the flake measured perpendicularly to its main release surface.

End-struck flakes have a length which equals or exceeds their breadth.

Side-struck flakes have a breadth which is greater than their length.

Striking platforms are classed as *plain*—comprising a single surface only—or *prepared*—having two or more facets being parts of the scars of small flakes removed from the parent core prior to the detachment of the flake, apparently as preparation for this detachment.

Pseudo-factetted platforms, as noted above, bear traces of two or more scars of previously removed flakes which are not interpreted as deliberate platform preparation.

Dorsal scar-patterns may be either *parallel*, from one or opposed directions, or *convergent*.

RETOUCHED IMPLEMENTS

The typological subdivision of the retouched implements follows the hierarchy of classes illustrated diagrammatically in fig. 11 (which is *not*, it should be noted, an evolutionary dendrogram).

Backed tools are almost invariably made on flakes. Backing is retouch, done from either or both faces of an artefact, which forms a steep finely flaked surface at approximately 90° to the main release surface of the flake.

Backed geometrics. These are backed tools made from pieces of flake at least one of the edges of which has been left in its original sharp condition, free from intentional retouch but not necessarily, of course, free from signs of utilisation. In the descriptions which follow, this is referred to as the *edge* of the geometric, and the whole of the rest of the periphery, whether retouched or not, is referred to as the *back*. The two intersections of the edge and back are here known as the *tips*. Similar terms are employed in the descriptions of backed flakes. The *length* of a geometric or backed flake is defined as the distance between its two tips; the breadth is its maximum dimension measured perpendicularly to the axis of the length. Steep retouch, or backing, is employed to trim all or part of the back of the geometric to the required shape. Areas of cortex or surfaces where the original flake has been abruptly truncated by snapping may be incorporated, unretouched, as part of the back. On specimens where the striking platform is so incorporated in the back, it is modified so that it does not interrupt the general curvature or shape of the back. The striking platform was, however, generally completely removed during the process of geometric manufacture. The geometrics have been subdivided into a number of types on the basis of their overall shape (fig. 12).

Curved-backed geometrics are geometrics on which the back forms a continuous curve.

Pointed lunates. On these specimens the back forms a constant curve and the shape is thus approximately

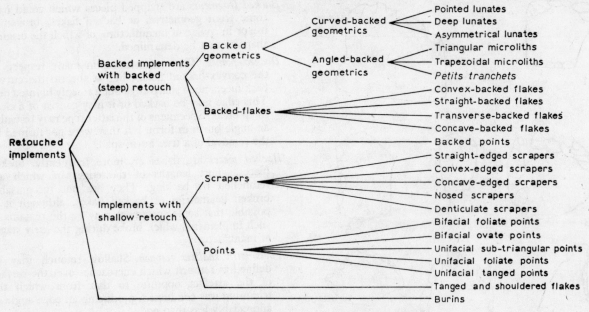

Fig. 11. Classification of retouched implements.

symmetrical about a line perpendicular to the edge at its mid-point. The two intersections of back and edge (tips) form sharp points.

Deep lunates. This type tends to merge imperceptibly into that of the pointed lunates. Deep lunates are symmetrical lunates on which the back and edge meet at both tips at angles of approximately 90 degrees. Their mean length/breadth ratio is consistently smaller than that of the pointed lunates, but there is considerable overlap in the ratios of individual specimens.

Asymmetrical lunates have a continuously curved back which joins the edge at a point at one tip only, the other (generally the bulbar) tip being squared, as on the deep lunates, or rounded.

Angled-backed geometrics are geometrics on which the curvature of the back is interrupted by one or more sharp angles.

Triangular microliths include all specimens in which the back forms a single sharp angle (in practice this usually approximates to a right angle) with the edge of the geometric as hypotenuse.

Trapezoidal microliths. Here, there are two angles on the back. The part of the back between these two angles is generally approximately parallel to the edge, and may be backed or left in its original sharp state.

Petits tranchets. These are short sections of straight-edged flakes, generally substantially broader than they are long. The back consists of two converging straight lines meeting at a rounded point, and is nearly always completely retouched. These specimens are almost invariably symmetrical about a line perpendicular to the edge at its mid-point.

Backed flakes are differentiated from the geometrics by their retention of the striking platform in a basically unmodified form. The striking platform is separated from the back by a pronounced angle. Complete specimens made on flakes from which the striking platform had previously been removed by a fracture at right angles to the edge are also included in this category. (It should be noted that the backed flake category here includes artefacts often referred to as 'backed blades'.) The backed flakes have been subdivided into four types on the basis of their overall shape (fig. 13).

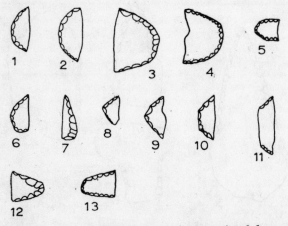

Fig. 12. Types of geometrics: 1, 2—pointed lunates; 3–5—deep lunates; 6,7—asymmetrical lunates; 8, 9—triangular microliths; 10, 11—trapezoidal microliths; 12, 13—petits tranchets.

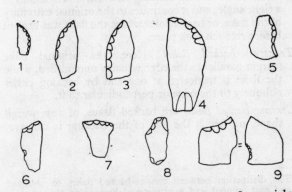

Fig. 13. Types of backed flakes: 1–4—convex; 5—straight; 6, 7—transverse; 8, 9—concave.

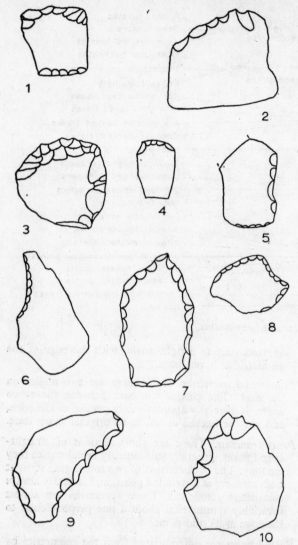

Fig. 14. Types of scrapers: 1, 2—straight; 3, 4—convex;
5, 6—concave; 7, 8—nosed; 9, 10—denticulate.

Convex-backed flakes. The back is a continuous curve
from its junction with the striking platform to its
intersection with the edge. The latter intersection may
form a sharp point or a right angle, and there is a
continuous gradation between these two extremes.*

Straight-backed flakes. The back is retouched to a
straight line approximately parallel to the edge. Its
intersection with the striking platform approximates to
a right angle, and it continues to the original extremity
of the flake, or to the point where the flake was broken
before retouch took place.

Transverse-backed flakes. Here, the original flake
margin parallel to the edge remains unmodified, while
the flake is truncated at one end by backing either
obliquely to the edge or perpendicular to it.

Concave-backed flakes are backed flakes, of any overall
shape, on which the line of the backing is concave.

Backed fragments are snapped pieces which could have
come from geometrics or backed flakes, broken in
use or in course of manufacture, of which the original
shape cannot be determined.

Backed points. These are similar in many respects to
the convex-backed flakes, but at the tip the curved
back meets not a sharp edge but a steeply blunted one.
This edge may be backed or it may consist of a clean
steep break. Specimens of the latter type may resemble
an angle burin in form, but they were not formed by
the removal of a true burin spall.

Backed pieces are flakes or, more frequently, broken
pieces, short lengths of the edges of which are
retouched by backing. They are not recognisably
broken geometrics or backed flakes, although it is
possible that some specimens may be the remains of
such implements which broke during the early stages
of manufacture.

Tools with shallow retouch. Shallow retouch may be
defined as retouch which encroaches over the surface
of the artefact opposite to that from which the
trimming was conducted, producing an edge angle of
appreciably less than 90°.

Scrapers are flakes, cores or shatter-chunks bearing
shallow retouch on one or more of their margins but
where little attempt has apparently been made to
modify the overall shape of the implement. Scrapers
are classified according to the shape of their retouched
edges. The terms used (*straight, convex, concave, nosed*
and *denticulate*) are self-explanatory (fig. 14).

Points, almost invariably made on flakes, are trimmed by
means of shallow retouch to produce a regularly
shaped implement with convergent margins and a
sharp point at one end. Points are here classed as
unifacial or *bifacial* according to the occurrence of
their trimming. Their overall shapes are designated

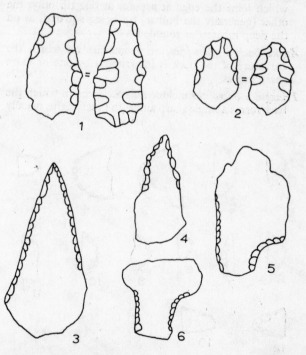

Fig. 15. Types of points, shouldered and tanged flakes:
1—bifacial foliate point; 2—bifacial ovate point;
3, 4—unifacial sub-triangular points; 5—shouldered flake;
6—tanged flake.

---

*The distinction between convex-backed flakes on the one
hand and pointed and asymmetrical lunates on the other is
further considered below (p. 218) in the light of evidence from
studies of edge wear and hafting methods.

foliate, ovate or *sub-triangular*. Some specimens are *tanged* by the production of two opposed notches at the end opposite to their point (fig. 15).

Tanged and shouldered flakes. These bear either two opposed or one (respectively) notches at one, generally the bulbar, end but are not otherwise retouched.

Burins, as here represented, are flakes or flake-fragments from which a spall has been struck from one end roughly parallel to the original flake margin, to produce a narrow transverse edge.

Chapter 5

Later Iron Age Pottery from Village and Refuge Sites in Eastern Zambia

The material described in this chapter* includes all the diagnostic sherds (excluding small fragments and undecorated body sherds) from a number of small surface collections made by J. H. Chaplin, A. Craven, H. W. Langworthy, the present writer and others from refuge and village sites in eastern Zambia. Most of the sites are known either from written records or from oral traditions to have been occupied for the last time during the nineteenth century AD. Other sherds, which are assumed on typological grounds to be broadly contemporary, were collected from the surface deposits in several painted rock-shelters.

No systematic reconnaissance for later Iron Age sites has yet been attempted in this region of Zambia; and most of the material available for study comes from uncontrolled surface collections made at widely scattered sites. Since none of the sherds are from excavated collections it may not be assumed either that they represent the total range of styles present in nineteenth century Eastern Province wares, or that no sherds of earlier or later periods have been included. Because of this absence of adequate chronological control, no detailed analysis has been attempted. The following notes and their accompanying illustrations are offered in the belief that they provide a general overview of the later Iron Age pottery of eastern Zambia, with particular emphasis on the nineteenth century AD. This pottery may all be subsumed within the Luangwa tradition of the present writer's (1974) classification of Zambian later Iron Age ceramics. The Eastern Province collections here described are of particular significance since, although the geographical and temporal parameters of the Luangwa tradition are broadly known (*op. cit.*: 7-10), published surveys of relevant material, whether archaeological or ethnographic, are still almost totally lacking. The affinities and significance of the Luangwa tradition are discussed in a later chapter.

FORM†

Only five basic vessel shapes are represented: beakers, necked vessels, globular vessels and open bowls, with a single convergent-mouthed pot. All have rounded bases.

Reconstructable beakers range from 10 to about 50 cm in height and from 10 to 45 cm in maximum body diameter. The external rim diameter is within 10 per cent of the body diameter. Most of the beakers have straight, undifferentiated rims. Others have tapered, slightly everted rims. On some vessels this is combined with either a slight inwards taper of the vessel walls or a slight constriction below the rim.

The necked vessels generally have an unthickened rim that may be either straight or everted: most do not display a pronounced shoulder below the neck. The majority of the reconstructed necked vessels range in height from 10 to 30 cm. The maximum body diameter is usually approximately equal to the height: it may be as much as 25 per cent more but is very rarely less. Both the minimum external neck diameter and the external rim diameter are nearly always within 20 per cent of the vessel height.

Both the globular vessels and the open bowls have heights between 8 and 20 cm. This is usually equal to or slightly less than the maximum diameter. Their rims, which are unthickened, may be straight, everted or—rarely—inverted.

None of the sherds from any of the sites have pronouncedly thickened or particularly elaborated rim profiles. Undifferentiated or tapered rims were the norm. Most have the lips neatly rounded or squared. Bevelled or fluted lips are not represented. A few sherds from Kongwe, Bombwe and Rukuzye bear comb-stamped decoration on the lip, but otherwise decoration on most vessels begins below the rim and the rims themselves are unadorned.

All the larger reconstructed vessels are beakers or necked pots. Decorative patterns begin immediately below the rims of beakers and open bowls, but at the base of the neck of most necked pots. With these two exceptions there is no apparent correlation between vessel shape and size and either the pattern or the quality of the decoration.

DECORATION

By far the most common decorative technique, being present on 451 (88 per cent) of a total of 513 decorated sherds examined, is that of comb-stamping done with a small comb usually 1 to 2 cm long and having between four and eight square teeth set in a single row. On some sherds the comb impression is slightly curved, as might be expected if the comb were made of a broken piece of calabash. Comb-stamping is frequently used to fill pattern-areas which were first delineated with a shallow groove or faint line, or by a single line of comb-stamping. On a few sherds the comb-stamping is so neatly and regularly executed that it appears at first sight to have been done with a roulette. On some sherds, particularly those where the comb-stamped areas are unbounded, the design may be more irregular and casually executed. Only three sherds have rocked comb impressions and none have dragged comb impressions.

Thirty-three sherds have cross-hatched incised patterns and a further 31 display other decorative

*This chapter is based on analyses and notes prepared by Dr Laurel Phillipson. The analyses are summarised in table 1.
†The terms used in this and the following sections are defined in chapter 4.

techniques including diagonal hatching, applied mammillations and ribs, stylus impressions, and impressions of a twisted metal bangle.

Undecorated body sherds were not examined (nor, in most cases, were they collected), but 141 undecorated rim sherds were included in the tabulated total of 654 sherds. Some specimens show traces of burnishing or graphite burnishing, but this was not tabulated since conditions of preservation differed markedly at the various sites.

The decorative motifs on the sherds may be divided into a limited number of basic patterns, which have been codified above (pp. 23-4). Most of these are closely related to one another and involve a combination of filled horizontal bands, rows of triangles, scallops or festoons located below the rim or at the base of the neck. Decoration is rare on the neck or elsewhere on the body of the vessel.

THE SITES*

Bombwe Hill, Sanjika (13°43′ south, 32°46′ east). Fig. 16:1, 2.

The site, located by F. B. Macrae, has been described above (p.19). Five undecorated beakers have reconstructed heights between 12 and 18 cm. Other rim sherds show decoration respectively of types 1c, 2c(i), and 2c(ii). Two sherds have type 1e(i) decoration; one of these also has a comb-stamped band on the flattened lip. A small, slightly carinated sherd with a finely wrought pattern of diagonal incision and cross-hatching may have been part of the bowl of a large smoking pipe.

Chafisi (13°58′ south, 32°32′ east).

The shelter (see p. 170) yielded only two diagnostic sherds, both rim pieces with type 1c decoration. The forms of the parent vessels cannot be ascertained. On one sherd the decoration is on what appears to be a thickened rim band: this specimen may be Early Iron Age.

Chaingo (13°47′ south, 32°12′ east). Fig. 16:3.

This site, together with its rock paintings, is described below (p. 170). From the surface of the rock-shelter deposits were recovered sherds of two open bowls (one H—14 cm, Rd—12 cm). There are sherds of a necked pot and a beaker with type 1c decoration at the rim. One body sherd has type 1d comb-stamping. There is also a sherd from the neck of a necked vessel (type 4) with applied mammillations and a pattern of unbounded comb-stamping.

Chikwapa's Linga (13°52′ south, 31°33′ east).

Seven kilometres south of Sandwe, on the bank of the Luangwa river, is this fortified village site. Remains of mud walls which encircled the site, and which were said to have been built for the grandmother of the man who was Chief Sandwe in 1961, were still then standing to a height of a metre or so (Chaplin, 1961b). Sherds collected from the area inside the wall include part of an undecorated globular vessel (H—15 cm, Rd—16 cm, Bd—18 cm). Two further rim sherds are undecorated,

ten have type 1c decoration, one type 1e(i) and one type 1e(ii). One body sherd bears type 2c (ii) decoration, while another has shallow parallel grooves. There is also part of the ring base of a moderately large vessel.

Chilenga Hill (14°05′ south, 32°22′ east). Fig. 16:4-6.

Chilenga Hill, the site of two small rock-shelters one of which has a collapsed dry-stone wall across its front, is located 4 km south-east of Nsadzu Mission. A small collection of sherds was recovered from both shelters and from the slopes of the hill. A whole beaker (H—16 cm, Rd—17 cm, Bd—16 cm) is undecorated. Two sherds have type 1c decoration, another type 2c(ii). Part of a necked vessel has type 1e(i) comb-stamping at the base of the neck; another has type 1e(iii). There is one body sherd with type 1e(v) decoration; and five sherds, including one of a beaker (H—12 cm, Bd—c. 20 cm), have type 1g.

Chiwaula's Linga (13°13′ south, 32°01′ east).

Most of the sherds in this collection come from a village adjacent to the fortified site of Chiwaula's *linga*, situated near the Msandile river about 50 km south of Nsefu Game Camp on the Luangwa river (Chaplin, 1961b). There are four undecorated beakers (H—28, 28, 26, 20 cm; Bd—26, 24, 23, 18 cm), six sherds with type 1c decoration, two with type 1e(i), three with type 1e(iv) and one each with types 1e(iii) and 2e(i).

Diwa Hill (13°04′ south, 32°57′ east). Fig. 16:7-9.

This site, first investigated by Macrae and Lancaster in about 1938 (p. 19 above), served as a Chewa refuge during the Ngoni wars. Pottery from the summit and slopes of the hill includes nine beakers (H—12 to 25 cm), two globular vessels and seven necked vessels (H—15 to 22 cm), all of which are undecorated. The decorated sherds include two of type 1c, one of type 2c(ii) and three of type 2c(i). There are also three of type 1e(i) and two of type 1f, one of which is from a fine and very large convergent-mouthed pot (Rd—36 cm). A single sherd has type 4 decoration with applied mammillations and comb-stamping.

Duzduje (14°25′ south, 31°57′ east).

Only 2.5 km from the major excavated site of Makwe, Duzduje is the small hill on the top of which is located the Zambia/Moçambique border beacon no. 19. Six decorated sherds, three with type 1e(i) decoration and three with undiagnostic comb-stamping, were recovered from the top of the hill, together with an undecorated rim sherd.

Fort Young (13°50′ south, 32°37′ east).

Fort Young, now a declared National Monument, was established in 1896 by Lt.-Col. Gardiner Warton for the North Charterland Exploration Company, held during the Ngoni wars of 1897-8, and abandoned in about 1902 (Chaplin, 1961a; see also O'Mahoney, 1963a). It is situated to the north-east of the Chipata-Chadiza road some 25 km from Chipata. A few sherds were collected from an area outside the brick wall of the fort on the south-west side. One has type 1e(iii) comb-stamping; the others bear traces only of undetermined comb-stamped motifs.

Jumbe's Linga (13°16′ south, 32°05′ east).

This is a fortified village-site on the Msandile river (Chaplin, 1961b) which yielded a fairly large collection

---

*The following abbreviations are employed in these descriptions: H=vessel height, Rd=rim diameter, Nd=minimum neck diameter, Bd=body diameter, Md=maximum diameter of vessel. The codifications of decorative types and techniques are defined in chapter 4, pp. 22-4, and summarised on a fold-out sheet at the end of the volume.

of decorated and rim sherds, but no reconstructable vessels. Most of the decorated pieces are comb-stamped: they include nine with type 1c decoration, seven with type 1e(i), nine with 1e(iv) and one each with types 1f and 1g. There is one example of type 2c(ii) decoration.

Katolola (13°45′ south, 32°39′ east).

The rock paintings at Katolola, 14 km south of Chipata, are described on p. 173 below. Pottery was collected from an unadorned shelter on the same *kopje*. There are four almost complete undecorated vessels, with traces of black burnishing on their exterior surfaces, comprising a beaker (H—14 cm, Rd—17 cm, Bd—18 cm), a globular vessel (H—8 cm, Rd—12 cm, Md—14 cm) and two necked vessels (both H—*c*.11 cm, Rd—9 cm, Nd—8 cm, Bd—10 cm). A single large undecorated body sherd comes from a thick-walled vessel, the body diameter of which must have exceeded 50 cm. One globular vessel (H—9 cm) has 1a decoration; another has 1c. A black-burnished necked vessel (H—22 cm, Rd—12 cm, Nd—11 cm, Bd—14 cm) has 1e(i) decoration.

Kawala (c. 13°37′ south, 31°54′ east).

Kawala, also known as Msoro's *linga*, is a fortified village site attributed to the first Chief Msoro. The collection includes sherds of six undecorated beakers, plus nine sherds bearing type 1c decoration, four with type 1e(i) and one each with types 1e(iii) and 1e(iv).

Kongwe Hill (13°08′ south, 32°47′ east). Figs. 16:10-12; 17:1-3.

Kongwe Hill is a domed *kopje* 1 km north-east of Chipangali Tsetse Control Camp. Numerous sherds were collected from a landing part of the way up the hill, and from the summit. They include a beaker (H—*c*. 17 cm, Md—14 cm) with type 1c decoration, rims of two globular vessels with type 2c (i) decoration apparently executed by means of a stylus, and three sherds with type 2c(ii) decoration. Thirteen sherds are of type 1d, eight of type 1e(i) and six of type 1e(iv). Three have type 1f decoration similar to examples from Diwa and Bombwe. One sherd has type 1f comb-stamped hemicircles bordered with triangular stylus impressions.

In addition, a number of atypical sherds were collected at Kongwe. These include the lower part of a perforated vessel which was presumably used for salt-making, and a small, crude globular vessel only 3 cm high with stylus impressed decoration. One sherd has concentric circular impressions probably made with a twisted wire bangle, and another has a row of diamond-shapes roughly executed with a pointed stylus.

Mbarazio Hill (14°19′ south, 32°27′ east). Fig. 17:4-6.

This is the hill on which the Zambia/Moçambique border beacon no. 26 is erected, and is the largest of the Mbizi group of hills. Pottery was found scattered on the western slope of the hill, particularly on a landing about half way up the slope. A nearly complete beaker (H—16 cm, Rd—17 cm, Md—18 cm) and a second very large beaker both bear type 1c comb-stamping. A necked vessel (H—*c*. 25 cm, Rd—21 cm, Nd—17 cm, Md—46 cm) has decoration of type 1e(i), while part of a second necked vessel of similar dimensions has type 2e(i) and is finely finished with black graphite burnishing in the pattern areas contrasting with the natural red colour of the clay elsewhere on the body. Other sherds include a body sherd of type 2g and part of a mammillated bowl (type 4).

Mbozi (14°00′ south, 32°49′ east). Fig. 17:7.

This painted rock-shelter site, located in the south-east of the study area, has been described by Chaplin (1962) and is noted also below (p. 177). In addition to the sherds he collected from the surface of the shelter deposits, Chaplin (*loc. cit.*:11) mentions having left several whole pots standing in position where he found them in the shelter. All four decorated sherds are comb-stamped: one is part of a large necked vessel with type 1f decoration comparable to examples from Diwa.

Mkoma (13°54′ south, 32°12′ east).

The rock-shelter, described in detail below (p. 178) has yielded seventeen sherds. The only reconstructable vessel is an open bowl (H—9 cm, Rd—12 cm) with type 1e(i) comb-stamping. There are rim sherds of two undecorated necked vessels and one beaker with type 1e(iv) decoration. Other sherds include three with type 2c(ii) decoration, two with 1e(i) and two with bands of diamonds produced by a rocked comb technique (type 1h) paralleled only at Rukuzye.

Mtovu Hill (14°24′ south, 31°45′ east).

A shelter half way up the north side of this hill, which is near Nyanje Mission, is said to have been used as a refuge during the Ngoni raids. It must also have been used for iron-working since several tuyeres were found nearby. Most of the pottery has comb-stamped decoration. Seven sherds bear comb-stamping of type 1c, six of type 1e(i) and five of type 1e(iii). There are eleven sherds, including part of an open bowl (H—*c*.15 cm, Rd—*c*. 28 cm) with type 1g decoration.

Nchingalizya (14°20′ south, 32°00′ east).

Several localities on this large, isolated hill were apparently used as refuges at the time of the Ngoni raids. Traditions recorded by Dr H. W. Langworthy (*personal communication*) refer to a chief's area on the summit of the hill and an area for common villagers on a lower landing. The sherds collected from the two localities include the same vessel-forms and decorative types in about the same proportions. They include two reconstructable undecorated necked vessels (H—12 cm, Rd—15 cm, Nd—13 cm, Bd—19 cm; and H—10 cm, Rd—12 cm, Nd—11 cm, Bd—14 cm) and parts of two undecorated beakers (both H—*c*. 20 cm, Rd— 36 cm). Another necked vessel (H—*c*.14 cm, Rd—14 cm, Nd—12 cm, Bd—18 cm) bears type 1c decoration below the rim and at the base of the neck. One beaker is of type 1e(i) and two of type 2e(i): one of the latter is nearly complete (H—15 cm, Rd—16 cm, Bd—16 cm). There are four vessels, including one necked and one globular, with 1e(iv) decoration, one with 2e(iv) and fifteen with 1g. Nine sherds are of type 1c, fourteen of type 13(i).

Rukuzye (13°21′-22′ south, 32°49′-51′ east). Figs. 17:8; 18:1, 2.

A few sherds were collected from Rukuzye sites A, E and F (see p. 179 below). In addition to the rims of six undecorated beakers (one Rd—20 cm) and three undecorated necked vessels, a number of atypical sherds were recovered. One has an unusually fine comb-stamped design bounded by rows of comb-stamping and triangular stylus-impressions. A globular vessel (H—15 cm, Rd—18 cm, Bd—22 cm) is decorated with a single row of diamonds produced by a rocked comb

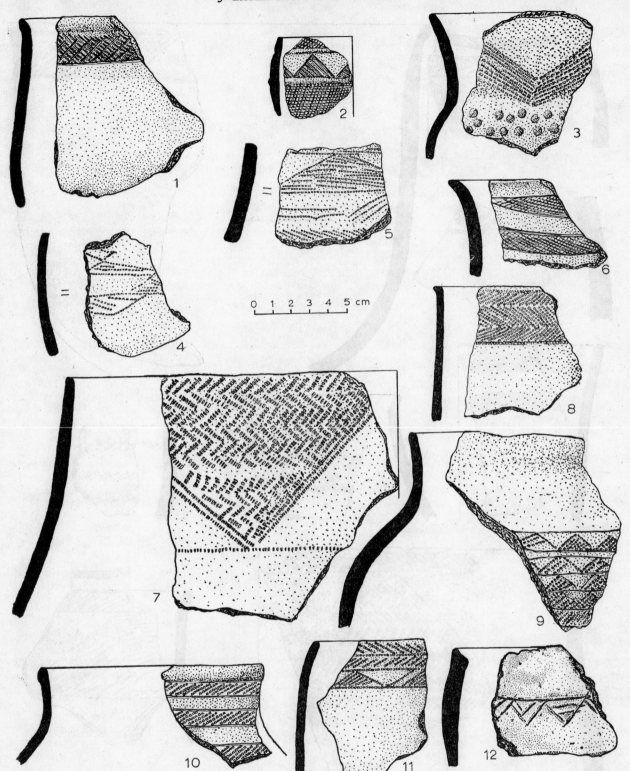

Fig. 16. *Later Iron Age pottery: 1, 2—from Bombwe; 3—from Chaingo; 4-6—from Chilenga; 7-9—from Diwa; 10-12—from Kongwe.*

(type 1 h). There is also one example each of decorative types 1e(i) and 2d.

Sasare Mine (13°55′ south, 31°22′ east). Fig. 18:3.

This, probably the first European-run mine in what is now Zambia, commenced production of gold in about 1900 (Anon., 1953). From the old compound site, which is delineated by mango trees, part of a well-

made globular vessel (H—17 cm, Rd—15 cm, Rd—18 cm) was collected. It bears type 1g decoration comprising two horizontal rows of comb-stamped crosses more careully executed than 1g specimens from other sites.

Sevwa Hill (14°18′ south, 31°46′ east).

The hill is 8.5 km north of Nyanje Mission. Sherds collected from its slopes include a beaker (H—19 cm,

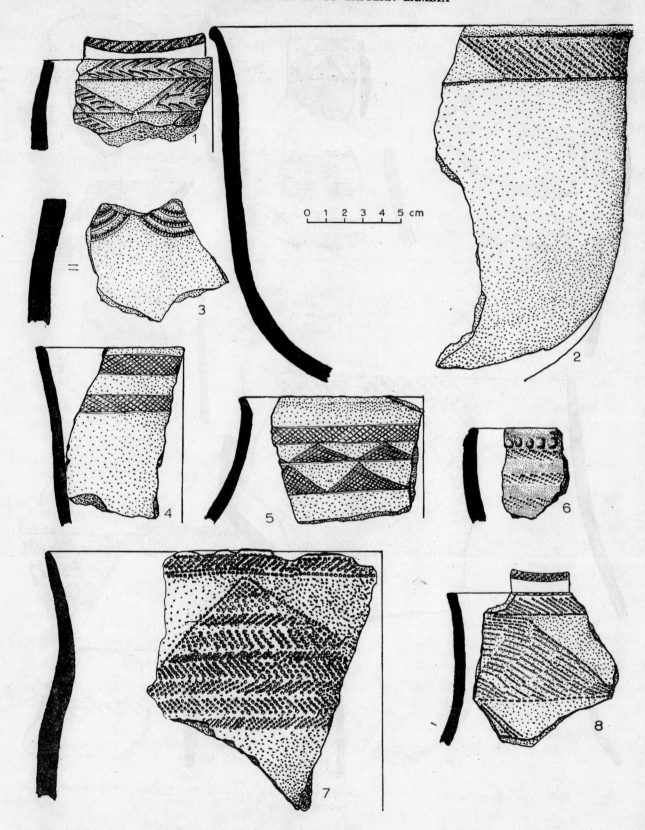

Fig. 17. Later Iron Age pottery: 1–3—from Kongwe; 4–6—from Mbarazio; 7—from Mbozi; 8—from Rukuzye.

Rd—20 cm, Bd—20 cm) and a globular vessel (H—15 cm), both with type 1c decoration. There are also body sherds from four beakers and two other vessels of type 1e(i), and one sherd each of types 1c, 1d and 1e(ii).

Simbo Hill (14°17′ south, 31°12′ east). Fig. 18:4.
The Simbo Hill site, some 16 km west of Petauke, is described on p. 181 below. Sixty-two of the sixty-four diagnostic sherds bear comb-stamped decoration,

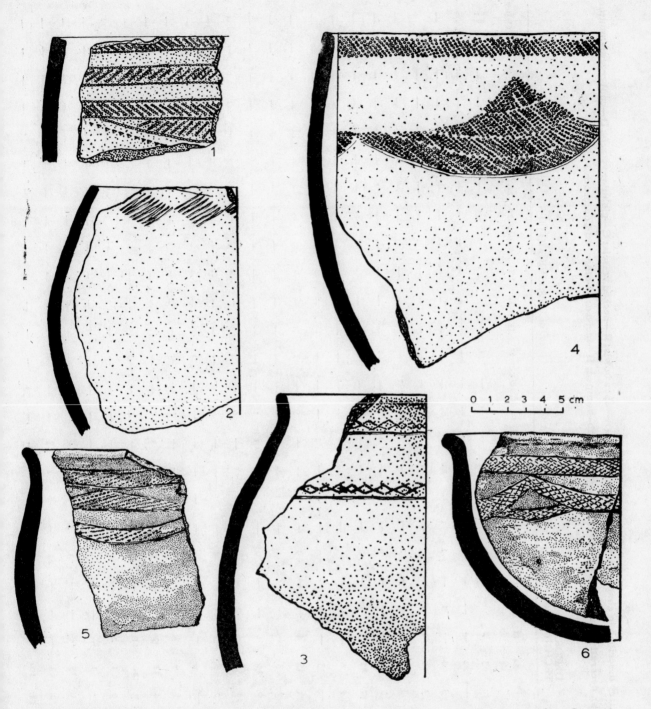

Fig. 18. Later Iron Age pottery: 1, 2—from Rukuzye; 3—from Sasare Mine; 4—from Simbo; 5, 6—from Songwe.

mostly of types 1c and 1e(iii): the other two are undecorated. One beaker (H—20 cm, Rd—29 cm) has very neatly and evenly executed comb-stamping closely resembling rouletting, but most of the sherds in this collection are small pieces from which neither the vessel shape nor the decorative pattern may be reconstructed.

Songwe Hill (14°22′ south, 32°08′ east). Fig. 18:5, 6.

Situated near the confluence of the Kapoche and Katete rivers, this may be the site of the village of the first Chief Songwe to settle in Zambia (Langworthy, *personal communication*); but all the sherds collected from the site appear to be of more recent date. In addition to undecorated rim sherds and sherds with decorative types 1c, 1d and 1e(i), an open bowl (H—18 cm, Rd—34 cm, Md—36 cm) bears type 1e(i) comb-stamping. There are two other well made bowls, one (H—13 cm, Bd—16 cm) with type 2e(v) decoration and one (H—16 cm, Rd—16 cm, Md—17 cm) with type 1e(v).

Table 1. Summary of later Iron Age pottery described in chapter 5, showing vessel shapes (A—open bowls; B—necked vessels; C—globular vessels; D—convergent-mouthed pots; E—beakers), decorative techniques (F—undecorated; G—comb-stamped; H—incised; I—other) and decorative motifs.

	VESSEL SHAPES					DECORATIVE TECHNIQUES				DECORATIVE MOTIFS																				Other sherds	Total sherds
	A	B	C	D	E	F	G	H	I	1a	1c	1d	1e(i)	1e(ii)	1e(iii)	1e(iv)	1e(v)	1f	1g	1h	2c(i)	2c(ii)	2d	2e(i)	2e(iv)	2e(v)	2g	3	4		
Bombwe Hill	—	—	—	—	6	14	5	2	1	—	1	—	2	—	—	—	—	1	—	—	1	1	—	—	—	—	—	—	—	1	22
Chafisi	—	1	—	—	—	—	2	—	1	—	2	—	—	—	—	—	—	—	—	—	—	1	—	—	—	—	—	—	—	—	2
Chaingo	2	2	—	—	2	3	4	—	—	—	2	1	—	—	1	—	—	1	—	—	1	—	—	—	—	—	—	—	1	—	8
Chikwapa's Linga	—	—	1	—	—	3	12	2	1	—	10	—	—	1	1	—	1	1	5	—	—	—	—	—	—	—	—	—	1	1	18
Chilenga Hill	—	2	—	—	2	5	9	2	1	—	2	—	—	1	1	—	1	—	5	—	—	1	—	—	—	—	—	—	—	—	16
Chiwaula's Linga	—	1	—	—	4	7	20	3	—	—	6	—	3	—	1	3	—	—	—	—	—	—	—	1	—	—	—	—	—	—	30
Diwa Hill	—	9	2	1	10	37	11	5	1	—	2	—	3	—	1	—	2	2	—	—	3	3	—	—	—	—	—	—	1	—	48
Duzduje	—	—	—	—	—	1	6	—	—	—	—	—	3	—	—	—	—	—	—	—	—	—	—	—	—	—	—	—	—	—	7
Fort Young	—	1	—	—	—	—	5	—	—	—	—	—	—	—	1	—	—	—	—	—	—	—	—	—	—	—	—	—	—	—	5
Jumbe's Linga	—	—	—	—	—	6	45	4	—	—	9	—	7	—	1	9	—	1	1	—	—	1	—	—	—	—	—	—	—	—	55
Katolola	1	3	2	—	1	7	3	—	1	—	1	—	—	—	—	—	—	—	—	—	1	—	—	—	—	—	—	—	—	—	10
Kawala	2	—	—	—	6	6	16	1	1	1	9	—	4	—	1	1	—	—	—	—	—	—	—	—	—	—	—	—	—	—	23
Kongwe Hill	4	8	2	—	3	11	52	5	7	1	1	13	8	1	1	6	—	4	3	—	2	—	—	—	—	—	1	1	—	3	75
Mbarazio Hill	1	3	—	—	4	5	9	3	1	—	4	8	1	—	1	6	—	1	3	—	—	3	—	—	—	—	1	1	1	—	18
Mbozi	—	1	—	—	—	—	4	—	—	—	1	—	1	—	—	1	—	—	—	—	—	—	—	—	—	—	—	—	1	—	4
Mkoma	2	2	—	—	1	5	9	3	—	—	1	—	3	—	1	1	—	—	2	2	—	3	—	—	—	—	—	—	—	—	17
Mtovu Hill	1	1	—	—	6	4	31	2	—	—	7	—	6	—	5	—	—	—	11	2	—	—	—	—	—	—	—	—	—	—	37
Nchingalizya	3	4	1	—	5	7	119	11	—	—	10	15	15	—	5	4	—	15	15	—	—	—	—	2	—	—	—	—	—	—	137
Rukuzye	1	3	1	—	6	9	1	2	1	—	—	—	—	—	4	—	—	—	1	—	—	—	—	2	—	—	—	—	—	1	13
Sasare Mine	—	—	1	—	—	1	1	—	1	1	—	1	—	—	—	—	1	—	1	1	—	1	1	—	—	—	—	—	—	1	3
Sevwa Hill	—	1	1	—	5	1	15	—	—	—	3	6	—	1	—	—	—	1	1	—	—	—	—	—	—	—	—	—	—	—	16
Simbo Hill	2	1	—	—	3	2	62	—	—	1	21	3	6	1	18	—	—	—	1	—	—	1	—	—	—	—	—	—	—	—	64
Songwe Hill	1	5	—	—	6	14	10	4	—	1	1	2	2	—	—	—	1	—	—	—	—	—	—	1	—	1	—	—	—	—	28

DISCUSSION

Manipulation of the data presented in table 1, including rough matrix sorting based on the presence or absence of the various decorative types at each site, failed to reveal any significant regional or sub-regional clusters. It is possible that there were significant variations in the frequency with which particular pottery styles were represented in different parts of eastern Zambia in later Iron Age (particularly nineteenth century) times, but the collections from most of the sites are too small to reveal this. Furthermore, many of the collections come from refuge sites belonging to a time of considerable population movement and disturbance. It cannot necessarily be expected that any local patterns in the distribution of ceramic wares, such as may have existed in more settled times, would be reflected at such sites. However, the material here discussed gives some indication of the degree of variation present in the Luangwa tradition within a relatively circumscribed area, standardised elements of vessel-shape and decoration being regularly accompanied by less formal, even casual, elements. Much more detailed investigations will be needed to elucidate the local subdivisions of the Luangwa tradition and their respective time–depths. The wider connections and affinities of the eastern Zambian later Iron Age are discussed in chapter 21, below.

Chapter 6

The Early Iron Age Village Site at Kamnama

I. THE SITE

The Kamnama site is located at latitude 13°31′ south, longitude 32°50′ east, 25 km north-east of Chipata, in the area of the Chewa Chief Mkanda. The site is traversed by the barely motorable track from Mgwazo School to Kamnama village and is equidistant, at 1.5 km, from these two settlements. Kamnama village is situated beside Chazangombe Hill, on the Luangwa/Lake Malawi watershed, which is here followed by the

border between Zambia and Malawi. In this area, the watershed is at an altitude of 1210 m above sea level.

The site (plate IIb) lies on the western side of the Mutapo *dambo*, which forms one of the headwaters of the Mlozi river, and at the foot of the eastern slope of Ngonzi Hill. A map of the Kamnama area is reproduced at fig. 19. The Mutapo *dambo* is locally recognised as a

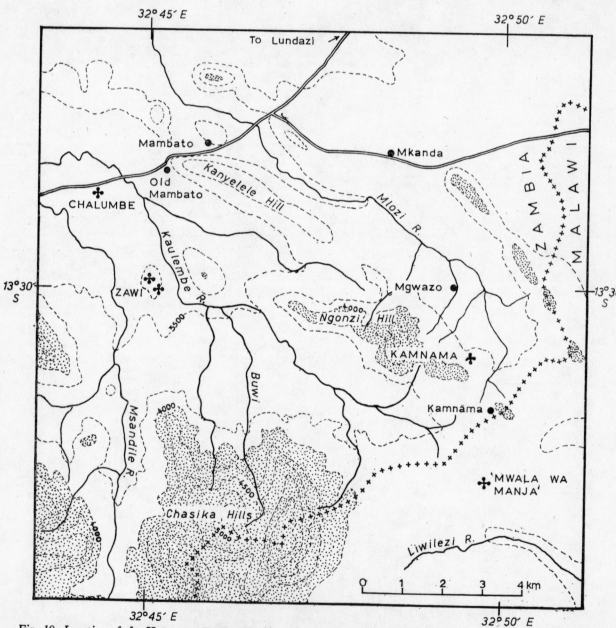

Fig. 19. Location of the Kamnama Early Iron Age site. (Contours are at 250 ft/75 m intervals, and land over 4000 ft/1230 m is stippled.)

38

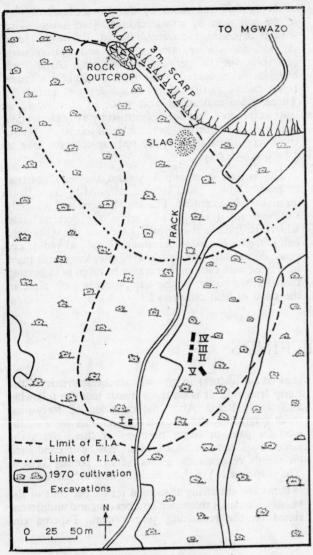

Fig. 20. Plan of the Kamnama site.

June 1970, while on a reconnaissance of Chief Mkanda's area. Trial excavations, as described below, were conducted later the same month. Investigation showed that Early Iron Age pottery occurred as a surface scatter extending over an area of approximately 5 ha of almost flat cultivated land. The area of Early Iron Age occupation (see plan, fig. 20) was visible as a series of patches of soil slightly darker grey than that seen elsewhere: the densities of potsherds within these darker patches was appreciably higher than that prevailing in the intervening areas. Although irregular in distribution, shape and size, these patches rarely exceeded 15 m in maximum diameter. They were interpreted as areas where cultivation had penetrated the thin overburden into the underlying occupation horizon: subsequent excavation confirmed this hypothesis.

The site covers an approximately oval area, 400 m in maximum extent from north to south and 150 m from east to west. At the north end occupation was evidently extended westwards along the top of a 3-m rocky scarp as far as a small outcrop which provides an extensive view to the north-west down the Mlozi valley. The area of the site is poorly drained and is said to be wet and muddy for some months after the rains have ended.

Over the northern half of the Early Iron Age site, and extending beyond the latter's area to the north, west and east, is a scatter of later Iron Age (Luangwa tradition) pottery of very recent appearance. This material is probably to be linked with a Chewa village of about the beginning of the present century. Such a village is remembered by the older inhabitants of Mgwazo and is indicated by the presence of a number of well-established mango trees on this part of the site. Although this later Iron Age pottery is readily distinguishable, both by typology and by physical condition, from that of the Early Iron Age, surface collection and excavation were restricted to the southern half of the site in order to preclude any possibility of admixture. The occurrence of later Iron Age pottery showed no correlation with that of dark soil. No collections of the later Iron Age material were made.

To the west of the Mgwazo to Kamnama track and just above the scarp was located a dense patch of iron slag, some 18 m in diameter, associated with abundant fragments of clay tuyeres and pieces of burnt *daga*, presumably from a furnace wall. This area, which appeared to mark the site of at least one iron-smelting furnace, lay within the distribution of both the later and the Early Iron Age pottery scatters. Elderly inhabitants of a Chewa village on the other side of the Mlozi valley recalled that a furnace at or near this spot had been worked by their fathers to smelt limonite (bog iron) which, although giving a very poor yield, was readily available in the Mutapo *dambo*.

source of clay suitable for potting; and its name is said to be derived from this characteristic.

In this watershed area, human settlement and cultivation are restricted to the valleys and to the margins of the water-retentive *dambos*, where the indigenous bush cover has been almost completely cleared for cultivation. Maize, finger-millet, sorghum and groundnuts are the principal crops. The surrounding stony hills, which reach 1700 m above sea level, are frequented only by hunters. The present sparse population of the area incorporates both Chewa and Ngoni elements.

The presence of potsherds of Early Iron Age type at Kamnama was noted by the present writer early in

II. THE EXCAVATION

Although the Kamnama site had evidently been badly disturbed by prolonged cultivation it was, and still is, the only Early Iron Age village site known from the Eastern Province of Zambia. It was therefore decided to conduct small-scale excavations to ascertain whether the lower portions of the occupation horizon had escaped disturbance. Five trenches were laid out, in the positions

shown in fig. 20. Trenches I and III measured 4 by 2 m: the others were 5 by 2 m. Trench I was placed near the southern extremity of the site, at the edge of the cultivated area, where the surface scatter of pottery was dense. It was found that sherds occurred to a maximum depth of 18 to 20 cm, but that almost the whole of this depth had been disturbed by cultivation. Trenches

II to V were subsequently excavated on the margins of a concentration of sherds located 100 m north-east of trench I. Only in trench V were clearly undisturbed deposits located, in a slight hollow in the subsoil protected from hoeing by a large stone slab.

Sections of trenches I and V are representative and are reproduced in fig. 21. The light grey-brown sandy topsoil, which was only slightly humic, extended to a mean depth of 12 to 15 cm below the bottoms of the cultivation furrows. The limit of this hoe disturbance

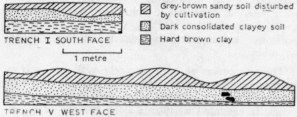

TRENCH I SOUTH FACE

⊟ Grey-brown sandy soil disturbed by cultivation
⊞ Dark consolidated clayey soil
⊞ Hard brown clay

1 metre

TRENCH V WEST FACE

Fig. 21. Sections of the Kamnama excavations.

could be followed more by the texture and density of the soil than by colour change. Several successive seasons of cultivation were indicated. Below this level the soil was darker, more organic and consolidated, probably due to periodic waterlogging. Artefactual material was restricted to the upper 10 cm of this lower layer, except in the south-east quadrant of trench V. There were indications that most of this layer, at least in trench I, had been disturbed by early cultivation but had subsequently become reconsolidated. Below the artefact-bearing level the soil rapidly gave way to a hard brown clay.

The hollow in trench V yielded the only charcoal fragments which could be demonstrated to come from an undisturbed context. The sample recovered was only sufficient for a single radiocarbon age determination which, in 'radiocarbon years' based on the 5568-year half life, gave the following result: N-908: ad 350 ± 110 years. Since only one date is available, this result must be treated with caution, but it may be taken as indicating that the occupation of the site probably took place in the third to fifth centuries ad.

III. THE FINDS

POTTERY (figs. 22-24)

Since very few potsherds were recovered from the excavations at Kamnama, and since it was clear that the southern half of the site had only witnessed a single, brief period of occupation, a complete collection was made of potsherds exposed on the surface of that part of the site which lies to the south of trench II. These sherds, combined with those from the excavations, gave a total of 2802 specimens, of which 2475 were undecorated body sherds. The remaining 327 sherds, retaining traces of decoration and/or part of the rim,

showed no features in any way uncharacteristic of the Early Iron Age. It is on these sherds that the following analysis is based. After the exclusion of forty-nine small fragments, the remaining specimens were examined for pairs or larger numbers of sherds from the same vessel and the final analysis has been conducted on sherds representing a total of 231 pottery vessels. The shapes of 163 of these could be determined (table 2).

Rims are externally thickened on 62 per cent of the vessels, internally thickened on 2 per cent and undifferentiated on the remaining 36 per cent. Tapered rim

Table 2. Kamnama Early Iron Age pottery: vessel shapes and sizes

	Total no.	Rim diameter	
		No. measured	Mean
Open bowls	20 (12%)	9	23.6±8.4 cm
In-turned bowls	17 (10%)	9	27.6±2.5 cm
Necked vessels	109 (67%)	37	24.8±8.5 cm
Pots with up-turned rims	16 (10%)	6	16.6±5.3 cm
Carinated vessel	1 (1%)	—	—
	163		

Table 3. Kamnama Early Iron Age pottery: distribution of lip profiles, rim forms and vessel shapes

Vessel shape	Rim form	Lip Profile			
		Rounded	Squared	Bevelled	Fluted
Open bowls	Undifferentiated	8	2	4	3
	Internally thickened	—	—	3	—
In-turned bowls	Undifferentiated	13	—	—	1
Necked vessels	Undifferentiated	9	10	—	—
	Externally thickened	45	24	3	—
Pots with up-turned rims	Externally thickened	5	2	8	—
		80	38	18	4

Table 4. Kamnama Early Iron Age pottery: distribution of decorative types, rim forms and vessel shapes

Vessel Shape	Rim Form	Decorative type A	B	C	D	F	G	Undecorated	Total
Open bowls	Undifferentiated	1	4	6	2	—	—	4	17
	Internally thickened	—	—	—	3	—	—	—	3
In-turned bowls	Undifferentiated	1	1	—	4	6	1	4	17
Necked vessels	Undifferentiated	3	5	—	9	—	—	5	22
	Externally thickened	1	20	—	41	—	—	17	79
	?	5	—	—	1	—	2	—	8
Pots with up-turned rims	Externally thickened	—	15	—	1	—	—	—	16
Carinated vessel	?	1	—	—	—	—	—	—	1

Total in sample 163
Shape undiagnostic 68
231

forms are not represented. The distribution of rim forms by vessel shape shows considerable standardisation.

The majority (57 per cent) of the lips are simply rounded and a further 27 per cent are slightly squared by a single bevel. Multiple bevels occur on 13 per cent of the lips and fluting on 3 per cent. Table 3 shows the distribution of lip profiles in relation to vessel shapes and rim forms.

The assemblage contains sixty-one vessels of which the rim diameter can be estimated: these data are summarised in table 2. Mean rim diameters of the open bowls, in-turned bowls and necked vessels are all between 23 and 28 cm, but the in-turned bowls are more standarised in size than the other two vessel types. The pots with up-turned rims are generally smaller.

Traces of burnishing were observed on only six vessels. In each instance it is associated with graphite coating. The weathering to which almost all sherds have been subjected makes it appear likely that a much higher proportion of the Kamnama pottery was originally burnished. It is nevertheless significant that five of the six burnished vessels are in-turned bowls: the other is an open bowl.

It is on decoration that the main typological subdivision of the Kamnama pottery is based (tables 4 and 5). Both grooving/incision and the use of various types of stamp were practised. The following decorative types are distinguished:

Type A2(i). This decoration is done with an elongated rectangular stamp, applied to produce a horizontal row of diagonal impressions. It occurs on six vessels, on four of which the stamp has been 'walked' across the surface of the clay from one impression to the next. Five of the vessels decorated in this manner are necked; on three of them the stamping is in the concavity of the neck while on the others it is immediately below the rim, in which position it also occurs on one open bowl.

Type A2(ii). Here a single row of impressions was made with a triangular or sub-rectangular stamp. Of seven vessels in this group, two are necked and the decoration

is on the shoulder. Type A2(ii) decoration also occurs on the shoulder of the only carinated vessel in the Kamnama assemblage. On this specimen, which is badly weathered, there are possible traces of further decoration above the stamping. The shapes of the other four vessels cannot be determined.

A2(ii) variant. A double row of stamp impressions occurs below the rim on two necked vessels, and just below the angle on one in-turned bowl.

Type B1. In its simple form it occurs on a total of seventy-one vessels of which twenty-three are necked, fifteen are pots with up-turned rims, while there are

Table 5. Typological summary of Kamnama Early Iron Age pottery

Type	Number of vessels	
A2(i)	6 (2.6%)	
A2(ii)	7 (3.0%)	
A2(ii) variant	3 (1.3%)	
Total type A		16 (6.9%)
B1	71 (30.7%)	
B1 variants	5 (2.2%)	
Total type B		76 (32.9%)
C1	3 (1.3%)	
C1 variant	2 (0.9%)	
C2	2 (0.9%)	
C2 variant	1 (0.4%)	
Total type C		8 (3.5%)
D1	62 (26.8%)	
D1 variant	4 (1.7%)	
D2	19 (8.3%)	
Total type D		85 (36.8%)
F	4 (1.7%)	
F variants	3 (1.3%)	
Total type F		7 (3.0%)
G	5 (2.2%)	
		5 (2.2%)
Undecorated	34 (14.7%)	
		34 (14.7%)
Total vessels in sample	231	

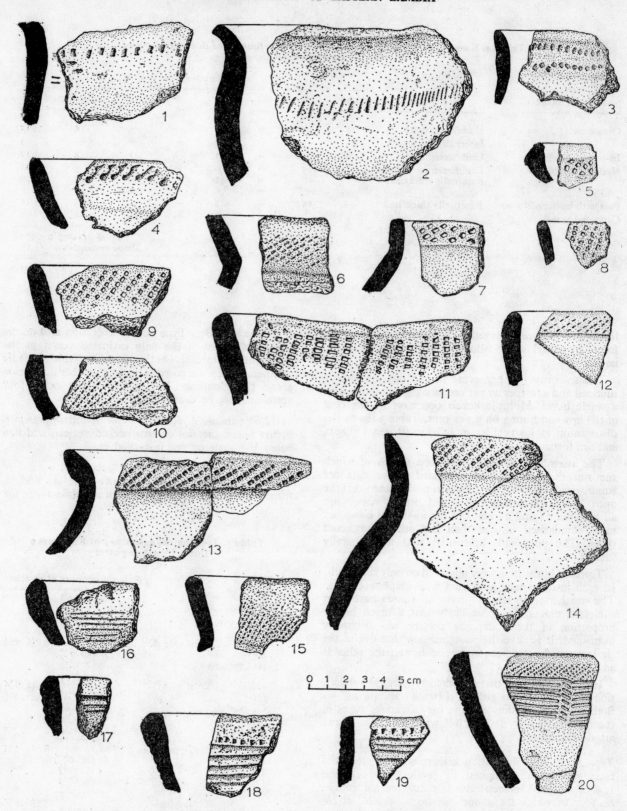

*Fig. 22. Early Iron Age pottery from Kamnama: 1, 2, 4—type A2(i); 3—type A2(ii) variant; 5–15—type B1;
16, 17—type C1; 18, 19—type C1 variants; 20—type C2 variant.*

one open bowl and one in-turned bowl. On all examples except the in-turned bowl, where the decoration is on the top of the rim, the comb-stamping is applied immediately below the rim, often on a thickened rim band. It is remarkable that on the pots with up-turned rims the comb-stamping is invariably much finer than on any other vessels.

B1 variants. (i) Three open bowls bear type B1 decoration above a single horizontal narrow groove. (ii) Two necked vessels have a row of stamp impressions

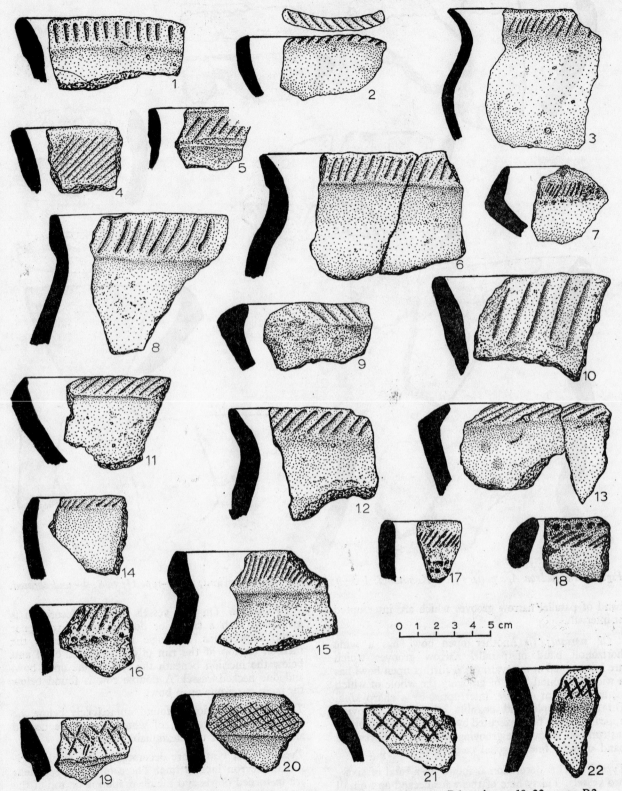

Fig. 23. Early Iron Age pottery from Kamnama: 1–15—type D1; 16–18—type D1 variants; 19–22—type D2.

below the type B1 decoration. On one the stamp used was triangular and on the other square.

Type C1. On two open bowls, this decoration is immediately below their undifferentiated rims. The shape of one other vessel is undeterminable.

C1 variant. Two vessels, at least one of which appears to have been an open bowl, bear type C1 decoration below a horizontal row of impressions of a triangular stamp.

Type C2. Two further open bowls bear a horizontal

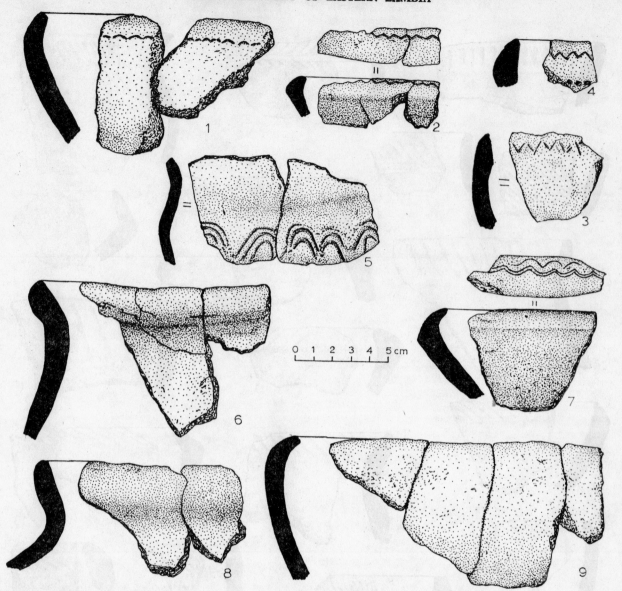

Fig. 24. Early Iron Age pottery from Kamnama: 1–3—type F; 4—type F variant; 5, 7—type G; 6, 8, 9—undecorated.

band of parallel narrow grooves which are interrupted at intervals.

C2 variants. (i) Another open bowl has a wide horizontal band of parallel narrow grooves which are interrupted at intervals. (ii) A further open bowl has a wide horizontal band of grooving the whole of which is, at one point at least, interrupted by a sharp kink. On this example, and possibly others, the grooving appears to have been executed by means of some toothed instrument. Above the grooving is a narrow horizontal band of very fine diagonal comb-stamping.

Type D1. This decoration is found on a total of sixty-two vessels. Thirty-nine of them are necked and on all but two of these the decoration is immediately below the rim: on the exceptions it is on the shoulder. Much finer and more carefully applied incision is present on the rim band of one pot with an up-turned rim. Type D1 decoration also occurs on three open bowls, being immediately below the rim on two examples and on top of the rim on the other, and on top of the rim of three in-turned bowls. It is also found on sixteen vessels of undeterminable shape.

D1 variants. On four vessels type D1 decoration is associated with a single or double row of triangular stamp impressions. A single row occurs above the incision on top of the rim of one in-turned bowl and below the incision beneath the rim of one open bowl and one necked vessel. A double row is found below the incision on one open bowl.

Type D2. Decoration is found immediately below the rim on nineteen vessels, of which eleven are necked and the others of undeterminable shape.

Type F. Four vessels are decorated with a single horizontal chevron incised line. Three of these specimens are in-turned bowls and the decoration is on top of the rim: the shape of the other vessel is undeterminable. On one in-turned bowl the lines comprising the chevron are slightly curved and may have been executed with the finger nail.

F variants. (i) Type F decoration occurs below the angle of two in-turned bowls which have diagonal grooving on top of the rim. (ii) A further in-turned bowl bears type F decoration on top of the rim and a row of single stamp impressions below the angle.

Type G. Such wiped decoration occurs on the shoulders of two necked vessels, on top of the rim of one in-turned bowl and on two body sherds of vessels of undeterminable shape.

Undecorated. A total of thirty-four vessels are undecorated. They comprise twenty-two necked vessels, four open bowls, four in-turned bowls and four vessels of which the shape cannot be determined.

OTHER FINDS

The Kamnama site yielded evidence for small-scale iron working during the Early Iron Age occupation. Small quantities of slag occurred in all trenches, being most frequent in trench I, while single pieces of tuyere came from trenches I and II. A corroded fragment of iron strip from trench I was the only finished metal object recovered from the site.

Small pieces of *daga*, found at all levels in all the trenches, were poorly preserved, presumably due to the periodic waterlogging of the site. They did not retain any traces of their original outer surfaces or of pole impressions.

Little organic material was preserved. Undiagnostic slivers of bone came from trenches I, II and V, and two fragmentary upper molar teeth, probably of antelope but possibly of sheep or goat, were recovered from the lowest undisturbed levels in trench II. A similar situation in trench V yielded a piece of elephant ivory 17 by 5 by 4 cm, its weathered surface retaining no tool marks or other indication of working.

From the surface in the vicinity of trenches I and II, an area from which later Iron Age surface pottery was absent, came a heavily used pounder of quartz and half of a quartzite lower grindstone which had been worn completely through its 11 cm thickness. These two objects cannot be linked with any certainty to the Early Iron Age occupation.

IV. CONCLUSIONS

The Kamnama site may be regarded as that of an extensive Early Iron Age village which was occupied for a comparatively brief period. The single radiocarbon date indicates that the occupation most probably took place between the third and the fifth centuries ad. Fragments of *daga* attest the presence of structures of that material, but no details of their type or mode of construction could be deduced. Iron was worked at or near the site, but there was no evidence for copper, nor were there any traces of more exotic trade goods. With the exception of a single piece of elephant ivory, the few fragments of animal bone which were recovered could not be positively identified. There was no indication of the purpose for which the ivory had been brought to the site.

The pottery, including that collected from the surface in those parts of the site which appear not to have been subject to later Iron Age settlement, forms an apparently homogeneous assemblage, which belongs to the same tradition, although differing in detail, as the Early Iron Age pottery recovered from the Eastern Province rock-shelter excavations discussed below. The broader affinities of the Kamnama material, and of the eastern Zambian Early Iron Age in general, are discussed in chapter 21.

Chapter 7

Excavations at Thandwe Rock-Shelter

I. LOCATION AND ENVIRONMENT

The Thandwe Hills (also known locally as the Kufwakwalizwe or Finye Hills) lie in Chief Nzomane's area of the Chipata District, at latitude 13°49′ south, longitude 32°28′ east. They form part of the ridge of high ground, 1000 to 1100 m above sea level, which locally forms the watershed between the tributaries of the Luangwa and those of the Zambezi.

Detailed geological mapping of the Thandwe area is not yet available. The region is one of Precambrian gneisses heavily weathered to produce sandy plateau soils, now leached and of low inherent fertility. The gently undulating terrain is interrupted by outcrops of gneiss which, as at Kazimuli Hill 8 km south-south-west of Thandwe, reach a height of up to 1300 m above sea level. The Thandwe Hills are a group of such outcrops which rise some 100 m above the plateau, but whose rocky relief is largely obscured by trees. The surrounding country, especially along the *dambo* margins, is intensively cultivated; and the indigenous

Brachystegia-Julbernardia woodland has been almost completely cleared. Streams rising in *dambos* north and south-west of Thandwe form the headwaters of the Makungwa river which flows northwards to join the Lutembwe 8 km downstream of Madzimoyo.

The present population of the area is predominantly of Ngoni stock; and ChiNgoni is still spoken by a few of the oldest inhabitants. These people practise a mixed farming subsistence economy. Cattle, goats and chickens are kept in some numbers; while maize and groundnuts are the principal crops.

Thandwe is easily reached from the Great East Road at Kasukanthanga, 35 km west of Chipata. From this point a road leads south-eastwards past Chief Nzomane's village and joins the old main road 5 km north of Mkuzo. From Mkuzo a track is followed eastwards to Kamukwamba village, whence the Thandwe rock-shelter is clearly visible (see map, fig. 25). The site is now a declared National Monument.

II. THE SITE

The rock-shelter is situated approximately one-third of the way up the eastern side of a defile eroded in the southern flank of the Thandwe Hills. It is formed by a concavity on the underside of a single enormous boulder of gneiss at least 15 m high, forming an overhang 11 m in maximum depth, sloping to a height of 6.5 m (plate IIIa). The weathering which has produced the shelter is still continuing; and the rock is extremely friable. In plan, the rear wall of the shelter is sharply angled at approximately 90 degrees as shown in fig. 26, to produce two main surfaces, both of which bear rock paintings (see chapter 19), facing north-west and south-west respectively.

The greatest extent of the overhang is to the west, immediately opposite the angle of the rear wall. The area of the shelter in front of the south-west-facing wall is filled with a scree of large rocks sloping steeply upwards and reaching almost to the roof at the eastern end of the overhang. A similar scree of smaller boulders rises at the north end of the north-west-facing wall. The area of level floor available for excavation was thus strictly limited, measuring 5.3 by 4.6 m in maximum extent. Starting just inside the overhang a rocky talus slopes down at about 45 degrees to the level floor of the defile 20 m below. A cross-section of the rock-shelter is presented in fig. 27.

III. THE EXCAVATION AND STRATIGRAPHY

The excavation measured 3.70 by 1.80 m, its long axis being perpendicular to the north-west-facing section of the shelter wall (plate IIIb). The trench, positioned over what was thought to be the greatest depth of deposit, was divided into 92-cm (3-foot) grid squares for horizontal control. The location of the trench, and its subdivisions, are shown on the plan, fig. 26.

The archaeological deposits were removed separately from each grid square. Vertical subdivision of the deposit followed the observed natural stratigraphy: none of the visible strata was so thick as to make further arbitrary subdivision necessary or practicable. The excavated material was passed through a sieve of 4 mm mesh. Samples of charcoal for radiocarbon dating were collected *in situ* by the excavators.

The excavation reached a maximum depth of 1.60 m as shown in the section, fig. 28. The following layers numbered consecutively with increasing depth, were encountered:

Layer 1. Surface dust, dark grey and uncompacted with much charcoal and groundnut shells, occasional potsherds, and very few stones.

Layer 2. Loose grey-brown ashy deposit with many rootlets, particularly in the north-east area of the trench. The upper part of the layer contained frequent lenses of very pale brown ash. Cultural material, both potsherds and flaked stone artefacts, together with bone and shell, occurred throughout this and the succeeding five layers.

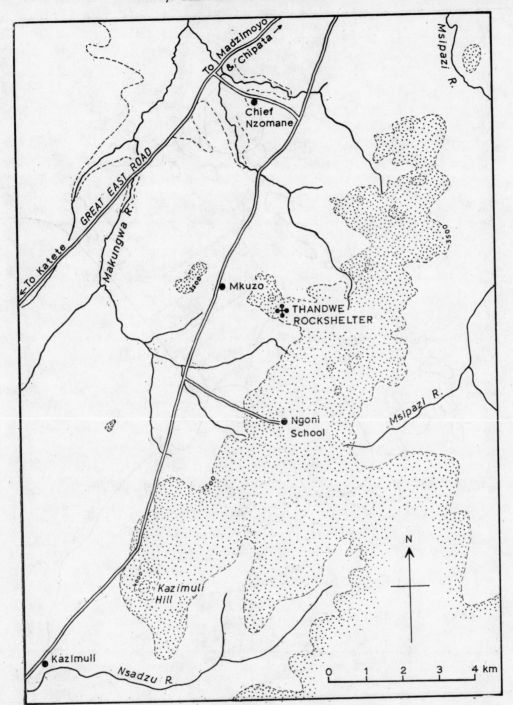

Fig. 25. Location of Thandwe rock-shelter. (Contours are at 250 ft/75 m intervals, and land over 3500 ft/1075 m is stippled.)

In grid square B a small pit dug from near the top of layer 2 reached a maximum depth of 24 cm below the surface and was filled with charcoal overlain by white ash (see fig. 28). A similar but shallower pit in grid square C had a dark grey ash fill overlain by paler ash and was contiguous with a 20-cm deep pit, in grid square F, which contained large quantities of iron slag.

Layer 2a. This layer was restricted to grid squares B and C and small adjacent areas of grid squares E and F. It was paler and more consolidated than the rest of layer 2 and was penetrated by the lower parts of the pits described above. It capped a slight rise in the surface of layer 3, caused by the presence of underlying boulders.

Layer 3. Pale grey ash with very few stones. Pale, dusty and powdery in grid square A against the shelter wall, it become progressively damper and darker towards grid squares D and G. A few rootlets were present in grid squares F and G.

Layer 4. Similar to layer 3 but more homogeneous and with more stones, becoming slightly browner and darker with depth. Local differences in moisture and texture were less apparent than in layer 3.

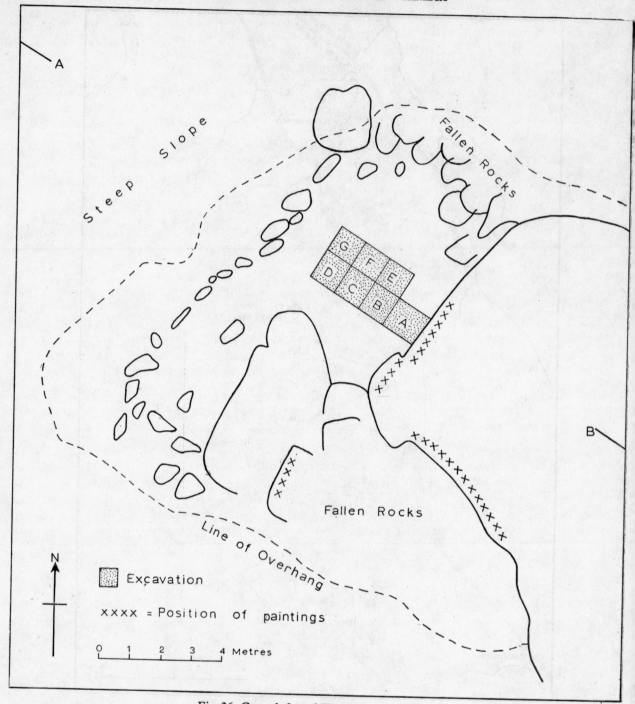

Fig. 26. Ground plan of Thandwe rock-shelter.

Layer 5. Indistinguishable from layer 4 in colour. Over the whole trench this layer was substantially harder and contained a greatly increased quantity of exfoliation and decomposed rock. This feature undoubtedly extended uninterrupted over the whole area of graves 1 and 2 (see below) and ruled out any possibility that these features could be intrusive from above layer 5. Also, a large fallen rock with its bottom in this layer directly overlay stone I (see fig. 29) in the north-east wall of grave 1.

Layer 6. Fine palish-brown ashy soil filling the interstices of rubble from decomposed rock. This layer was also continuous over the grave area. The six potsherds recovered from this layer were the last to

be encountered: the chipped stone industry continued into layers 7 and 8.

Layer 7. The grave-fill of grave 1, similar to layer 6 but a somewhat darker brown and containing less decomposed rock, it was rather looser in texture than layer 6. Between 3 and 5 cm of this stratum lay below the lowest bones of skeleton 1 and presumably represented a brief period of time intervening between the interment of the two skeletons.

Layer 7a. Pedologically, this was indistinguishable from layer 7. It comprised the apparently contemporary deposit between and outside the line of stones I-III which form the north-eastern retaining wall of grave 1.

Layer 8. The fill of grave 2 was similar to layer 7 but more consolidated and containing a higher proportion of decomposed rock, much less artefactual material and no charcoal. This layer filled a shallow scoop dug into layer 9.

Layer 9. Decomposed rock fragments. The minute quantity of chipped stone and of bone fragments, restricted to the top 8 cm of the layer, was probably due to disturbance connected with the digging of grave 2.

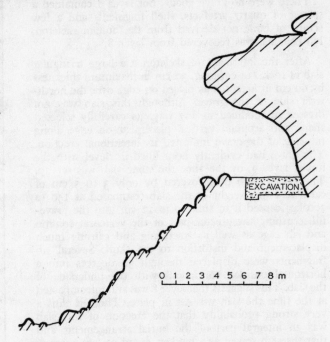

Fig. 27. *Section through Thandwe rock-shelter on line marked A–B on fig. 26.*

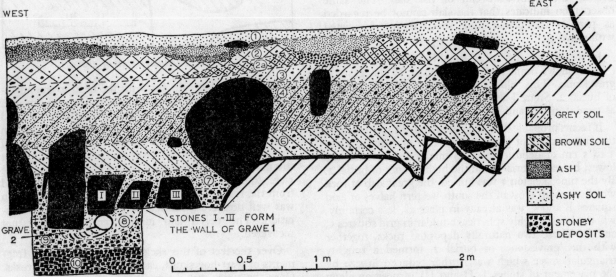

Fig. 28. *Section through the Thandwe deposits on line marked A–B on fig. 26.*

IV. THE GRAVES

Two elaborate human burials disclosed by the Thandwe excavations are best described at this point. An anatomical description of the remains is given in chapter 9.

The earlier human skeleton at Thandwe was buried in a shallow elliptical grave, designated grave 2, 1.0 m (from north-east to south-west) by 60 cm (from north-west to south-east), scooped 20 cm into the decomposed rock rubble of layer 9. The grave was apparently made soon after the initial occupation of the rock-shelter. The grave fill, which was removed as layer 8, was a looser but similar rubble mixed with grey-brown ashy soil, well compacted and densely packed around

the bones. The body, apparently of an adult female, was buried in a very tightly contracted position with the spine flexed and the right knee overlying the skull. The body lay on its left side, the head towards the north-east, facing south-eastwards towards the shelter wall. The corpse appears to have been fully articulated on burial, but subsequently the skeleton was much crushed and compressed. The pelvic area, which was tightly wedged against the south-west side of the grave pit, was distorted and forced upwards from its true position: this was probably done while cramming the body into too small a grave at the time of the original burial.

There were no grave goods, but layer 8 contained a scatter of quartz artefacts, shell fragments and a few scraps of bone not derived from the human skeleton. No charcoal was recovered from layer 8.

After the interment of skeleton 2 a large triangular slab of rock 114 cm long, 37 cm in maximum thickness by 69 cm in height, was placed on edge over the north-west side of the grave. Although this slab was not dressed or modified in any way, its carefully selected shape and accurate vertical placement on edge along the side of the grave indicated its intentional erection. The grave had evidently been filled in, level with the top of layer 9, by the time the stone slab was set up. The bones were thus covered by only 3 to 5 cm of earth and the weight of the slab (estimated at 150 to 200 kg) caused it to sink 10 to 12 cm into the grave-fill, crushing the greater part of the vertebral column and rib cage as well as fracturing and causing much displacement and distortion to the skull. Several rib fragments were displaced through 90 degrees into a horizontal position contiguous with the underside of the slab. This suggests that layer 8 was still uncompacted at the time the slab was set in place. There is thus a very strong probability that the erection of this slab was an integral part of the burial arrangements and that the slab served as a marker, guard or 'gravestone'.

The slab can be shown to have been in place and partly buried by the time of the interment of a second burial (burial 1), since the skull of that burial partly overlay the south-west end of the slab. The same observation indicates that the slab cannot be regarded as part of the demarcating stone setting associated with grave 1.

In the section (fig. 28) a roughly square stone block ('I') is shown immediately south-east of the grave 2 gravestone. This block overlay the skull and knees of burial 2. Stone I was part of the setting of grave 1, as were stones II and III immediately to the south-east.

It seems probable that no long period of time separated the construction of grave 1 from that of grave 2. Only 3 to 5 cm of deposit (layer 7) intervened between the lowest bones of burial 1 and the highest ones of burial 2. By the time skeleton 1 was buried, the great slab of rock which takes up most of the south-western halves of grid squares B and C was already in place as, less certainly, was the large roughly spherical boulder in grid squares C and F. These two naturally deposited rocks, together with the 'gravestone' of burial 2, formed a roughly triangular space which was further reduced in size by the placement of stones I, II and III in position along the boundary between grid squares C and F (see plan, fig. 29), and of three other similar stones roughly parallel to them in grid square D forming an arc just inside the line of the western edge of grave 2. The three latter stones (IV, V, VI in fig. 29) were at a slightly higher former and were probably put in place after the burial level than the was interred. The setting of stones I, II and III, however, clearly predates the disposition of the bones.

It appears that no pit or grave was dug to receive burial 1, but that the body was placed in the roughly rectangular walled-in area, described above, which measured some 85 cm from north-west to south-east and 60 cm from north-east to south-west. Burial 1 thus largely overlay burial 2 but was centred a few centimetres further to the south-west.

Like skeleton 2, skeleton 1 lay in a tightly contracted

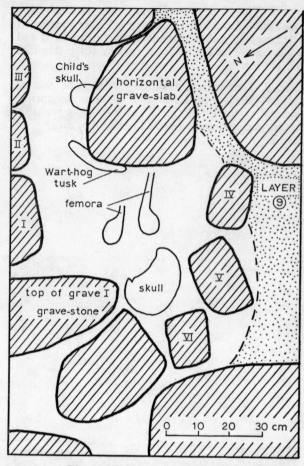

Fig. 29. Thandwe: plan of grave 1.

position on its left side, but with the head to the north-west. The skull partly overlay the gravestone of burial 2. It appears that the skeleton was partly disarticulated or dismembered before burial. One femur was broken and the two halves widely separated. The facial region of the skull, together with the maxilla, was missing, but the mandible was present. The atlas and axis vertebrae were found articulated with the skull but separated from the rest of the vertebral column. The atlas, which was well preserved, showed no sign of forceful decapitation. The pelvis and lumbar vertebrae were not recovered.

Over the feet of this skeleton were placed two fragments of wart-hog skulls, each retaining a pair of tusks. Over the tibiae was set another such fragment with a single massive tusk. Immediately to the east of this tusk lay a mass of crushed bone fragments which proved to be the remains of the skull of a young child. This individual is designated skeleton 1a. Only very fragmentary postcranial remains of this child were recovered. The arrangement is shown in plate IVa.

A rectangular slab of stone, measuring 38 by 25 cm and 9 cm in thickness, had been placed over the lower part of the main skeleton, covering also the wart-hog and child's skulls. This slab was neatly aligned in the rock cleft at the south-east end of the grave area, and was almost perfectly horizontal. It was probably at this stage in the proceedings that the stones IV, V and VI, forming the western wall of the grave, were set in place.

Subsequently, the whole grave area appears to have been covered with a thin layer of decomposed rock mixed with ashy soil incidentally containing mode 5 quartz artefacts. Such artefacts also occurred in small quantities along with shell fragments throughout the grave fill (layer 7). Layer 6 began to be deposited at the level marked by the tops of stones I–VI and the flat top of the horizontal grave slab, while the top of burial 2's gravestone still rose over 30 cm above the ground. This and higher layers appear to have accumulated gradually in the course of intensified occupation of the rock-shelter. Pressure of subsequent activity and the weight of overlying rocks compressed both burials and caused fractures in most of the bones, without greatly displacing the component parts.

V. CHRONOLOGY

Three radiocarbon age determinations were obtained from charcoal samples recovered during the Thandwe excavations. The results of these determinations, calculated in 'radiocarbon years' on the basis of the 5568-year half life, are as follows:

N-905	Grid square G, layer 5	ad 1060±110 years
N-906	Grid squares F and G, layer 6	ad 890±110 years
N-907	Grid squares D and G, lower part of layer 7	ad 330±115 years

These dates form an internally consistent series and indicate that occupation of the site took place mainly during the last two millennia. This finding is in keeping with the evidence noted above that the weathering, which resulted in the formation of the rock-shelter, has been a comparatively rapid process.

It will be noted that date N-907 may be attributed to the apparently brief interval between the interment of the two burials described above.

Chapter 8

The Prehistoric Industries from Thandwe

I. THE CHIPPED STONE INDUSTRY

Terms used in the following analysis and descriptions are defined in chapter 4. For the purposes of analysis the artefacts recovered from layers 2a and 7a have been combined with those from layers 2 and 7 respectively.

Chipped stone artefacts occurred in all layers of the Thandwe excavation. A total of 13,106 specimens was recovered.

Quartz, in both clear crystalline and opaque vein varieties, was the only raw material employed. Crystalline quartz accounted for slightly over 60 per cent of the artefacts in the assemblage. This figure shows relatively little fluctuation between layers (table 6), although there is a slightly lower incidence in the deeper levels. Cortex fragments indicate that most, if not all, of the raw material was obtained in the form of rounded quartz pebbles and small cobbles, such as are occasionally encountered on the lower slopes of the Thandwe Hills and are common beside the Makungwa *dambos*.

The primary categories of the chipped stone industry from each layer are shown in table 6. There is a marked and steady increase in the proportion of retouched implements from 1.6 per cent in layer 7, their lowest occurrence (the chipped stone aggregates from layers 8 and 9 are exiguous), to the remarkably high figure of 4.2 per cent in layer 1. There is an accompanying but less pronounced increase in the proportion of flakes, interrupted only in the two most recent layers. In the higher levels cores are slightly more frequent than they were in earlier times, but they comprise only 1.0 per cent of the assemblage as a whole. This increase, at the expense of the shatter-chunks, may indicate a reduction in the tendency to work out cores until they disintegrated. Since this was accompanied by an increase in the number of flakes produced, a concomitant improvement of flake-production techniques

is also indicated. The over-riding factor, however, was probably the nature of the raw material employed; it will be observed how the fluctuations in the proportion of shatter-chunks present in each level closely follow those of the incidence of vein quartz (fig. 30).

CORES, SHATTER-CHUNKS AND FLAKES

In view of the marked similarity between the chipped stone industry from Thandwe and that from the upper levels of Makwe, where a much larger assemblage was obtained (see chapter 12), the cores, shatter-chunks and flakes from the former site have not been analysed in detail. They are, however, preserved at the Livingstone Museum for future study.

RETOUCHED IMPLEMENTS

The primary categories of the 291 retouched implements from Thandwe are shown in table 6; and selected specimens are illustrated in fig. 31. In view of the small numbers of specimens recovered from some layers, the figures for layers 1 and 2 and for layers 5 to 7 have been combined for the calculation of percentage frequencies. There were no retouched implements in layers 8 and 9. The respective percentage frequencies of these categories show some fluctuations from layer to layer, but the only consistent trends which are apparent are on a very small scale. There are slight reductions through time in the frequencies of scrapers and backed points, and corresponding increases in those of backed flakes and backed pieces. The occurrence of geometrics appears to have been remarkably steady throughout the period of the site's occupation. However, in view of the small numbers of specimens available from each layer, these figures should be treated with reserve: none of the changes is statistically significant.

Geometrics

Geometrics are by far the largest category, representing 66 per cent of the retouched implements. A breakdown into the classes defined in chapter 4 is given in table 7. Of the 193 geometrics recovered, 161 (84 per cent) are curved-backed forms of which the large majority (70 per cent) are pointed lunates, another 13 per cent being asymmetrical lunates; while the remaining 17 per cent are deep lunates. Of the 32 angled-backed geometrics, 65 per cent are triangular and 29 per cent trapeziform: there are only two examples of *petits tranchets*, representing 6 per cent of the angled-backed geometrics. Sample sizes are not adequate to permit a definitive assessment of the degree of differential vertical distribution of geometric types present in the Thandwe sequence: in no case does the difference in proportions of any type in two adjacent levels exceed twice its standard error. There appear to have been no significant changes in the relative frequencies of

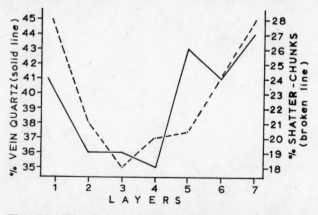

Fig. 30. Thandwe: comparison between the relative frequencies of vein quartz (as a percentage of the total raw material) and shatter-chunks (as a percentage of the total chipped stone artefacts).

Table 6. Summary of Thandwe artefact occurrences

Layer:	1	2	3	4	5	6	7	8	9	Total all layers
CHIPPED STONE ARTEFACTS	144	2007	3785	2891	2411	1303	555	6	4	13106
% in crystalline quartz	59%	64%	64%	65%	57%	55%	56%			61%
CORES	2 (1.3%)	28 (1.4%)	39 (1.0%)	23 (0.8%)	25 (1.0%)	12 (0.9%)	4 (0.7%)	—	—	133 (1.0%)
SHATTER-CHUNKS	40 (27.8%)	419 (20.9%)	680 (18.0%)	573 (19.8%)	495 (20.5%)	310 (23.8%)	156 (28.1%)	—	2	2675 (20.4%)
FLAKES	96 (66.7%)	1507 (75.1%)	2974 (78.6%)	2235 (77.3%)	1842 (76.4%)	959 (73.6%)	386 (69.5%)	6	2	10007 (76.4%)
RETOUCHED IMPLEMENTS	6 (4.2%)	53 (2.6%)	92 (2.4%)	60 (2.1%)	49 (2.0%)	22 (1.7%)	9 (1.6%)	—	—	291 (2.2%)
Geometrics	4	34 (64%)	63 (68%)	39 (65%)	32 (65%)	17 (77%)	3	—	—	192 (66.0%)
Backed flakes	1	13 (25%)	9 (10%)	10 (17%)	4 (8%)	2 (9%)	2	—	—	41 (14.1%)
Backed fragments	1	4 (8%)	12 (13%)	7 (12%)	6 (12%)	1 (5%)	1	—	—	32 (11.0%)
Backed points	—	—	2 (2%)	—	3 (6%)	1 (5%)	—	—	—	6 (2.1%)
Backed pieces	—	2 (3%)	5 (5%)	3 (5%)	1 (2%)	—	2	—	—	13 (4.5%)
Scrapers	—	—	1 (1%)	1 (2%)	3 (6%)	1 (5%)	1	—	—	7 (2.4%)
GROUND STONE AXES	—	1	—	—	1	1	—	—	—	3
KNAPPING HAMMER	—	—	—	—	—	1	—	—	—	1
POUNDING STONES	—	—	1	—	1	—	—	—	—	2
BONE BODKIN	—	—	1	—	—	—	—	—	—	1
CONICAL BONE POINTS	—	—	4	—	—	—	—	—	—	4
SHELL DISC BEADS	1	7	4	6	2	—	—	—	—	20
GLASS BEAD	1	—	—	—	—	—	—	—	—	1
SHELL PENDANTS	—	—	2	—	—	—	—	—	—	13
WORKED IRON	12	4	—	—	—	—	—	—	—	16
IRON SLAG	Qty	—	—	—	—	—	—	—	—	Qty
HAEMATITE	—	—	—	—	—	1	—	—	—	1
TUYERES	—	8	—	4	2	—	—	—	—	14
POTSHERDS Total	55	105	78	42	15	6	—	—	—	301
Undecorated body sherds	48	93	69	36	14	6	—	—	—	266
Early Iron Age	2	3	7	5	1	—	—	—	—	18
Later Iron Age	5	6	1	1	—	—	—	—	—	13
Tradition doubtful	—	3	1	—	—	—	—	—	—	4

% in crystalline quartz and percentages of chipped stone artefacts are noted for cores, shatter-chunks, flakes and retouched implements. Percentages are of total retouched implements for geometrics, backed flakes, backed fragments, backed points, backed pieces and scrapers.

Table 7. Thandwe: sub-division of geometrics

Layer	CURVED-BACKED GEOMETRICS Pointed lunates	Asymmetrical lunates	Deep lunates	Total	ANGLED-BACKED GEOMETRICS Trapezoidal microliths	Triangular microliths	Petits tranchets	Total
1	1 }(66%)	1 }(16%)	— }(16%)	2	1	1	—	2
2	19	4	5	28				
3	31 (59%)	11 (21%)	10 (19%)	52	2	4	—	6
4	28 (77%)	3 (8%)	5 (13%)	36	3 (27%)	8 (72%)	—	11
5	23 }(79%)	1 }(4%)	2 }(17%)	26	1	1	1	3
6	9	1	4	14	1	4	1	6
7	2	—	1	3	—	2	—	3
	113 (70%)	21 (13%)	27 (17%)	161	9 (29%)	20 (64%)	2	31

Table 8. Thandwe: curved-backed geometrics

Layer	No.	% of geometrics	Length (mm) Range	Mean	% eared	% fully backed	Mean % backed	Direction of backing a	b	c	d	e
1	2 }	79%	11–21	15.1±2.6	20%	63%	80%	50%	—	17%	27%	7%
2	28											
3	52	83%	7–27	14.9±3.9	15%	60%	88%	79%	—	4%	13%	4%
4	36	92%	7–23	16.1±3.5	6%	72%	90%	42%	3%	14%	31%	11%
5	26 }	83%	10–25	16.3±3.3	5%	77%	92%	49%	—	14%	37%	—
6	14											
7	3											
	161	84%	7–27	15.6±3.5	11%	68%	88%	57%	1%	11%	26%	5%

Key: a. backed from ventral surface; b. backed from dorsal surface; c. backing totally bi-directional; d. backing partly bi-directional; e. backed from alternate directions.

Table 9. Thandwe: geometrics

	Layer	No.	% of geometrics	Length (mm) Range	Mean	Length/Breadth Range	Mean	% eared
POINTED LUNATES	1	1 }	53%	12–19	15.2±1.9	1.5–3.0	1.9±0.3	15%
	2	19						
	3	31	49%	10–27	15.6±3.9	1.3–2.1	1.7±0.3	13%
	4	28	72%	12–23	17.0±3.0	1.5–3.8	1.8±0.4	7%
	5	23 }	65%	10–25	16.7±3.4	1.4–2.8	1.8±0.3	6%
	6	9						
	7	2						
		113	59%	10–27	16.2±3.3	1.3–3.8	1.8±0.3	10%
DEEP LUNATES	Total	27	14%	7–21	14.3±3.7	1.0–1.5	1.3±0.2	10%
ASYMMETRICAL LUNATES	Total	21	11%	10–23	13.9±2.9	1.3–2.3	1.6±0.3	19%
TRAPEZOIDAL MICROLITHS	Total	9	5%	9–22	15.1±4.1	1.2–2.2	1.5±0.3	10%
TRIANGULAR MICROLITHS	Total	20	10%	9–21	13.6±3.6	1.2–2.4	1.6±0.3	11%
PETITS TRANCHETS	Total	2	1%	7, 11		0.7, 0.6		—

curved and angled-backed geometrics. Within the curved-backed category, however, asymmetrical lunates steadily increase in frequency through time at the expense of the pointed lunates, while the occurrence of deep lunates remains fairly steady. No significant variation may be discerned within the small number of angled-backed geometrics available for study, but it should be noted that the two *petits tranchets* occurred respectively in layers 4 and 5. Of the nine trapezoidal microliths, one was completely backed: on six the back between the two angles retains the original sharp flake edge: on the remaining two the back is blunted by a single break.

Table 8 provides data, layer by layer, on the curved-backed geometrics as a whole. The mean length of all such specimens from Thandwe is slightly less than 16 mm. Almost 70 per cent are fully backed: on rather over half the backing is uni-directional, almost invariably from the ventral surface. Bi-directional backing is complete on only 11 per cent of the curved-backed geometrics. On others it is concentrated at the tips or is done from alternate directions along different sections of the back. This concentration on the tips of the curved-backed geometrics is emphasized by the occurrence of well defined 'ears' on 11 per cent of the specimens, a proportion which increases from only 5 per cent in

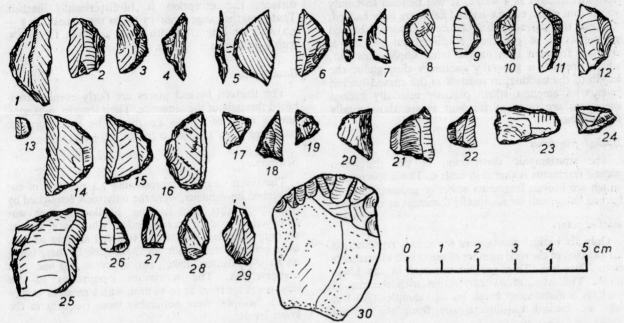

Fig. 31. Thandwehipped stone artefacts: 1–12—pointed lunates; 13–16—deep lunates; 17–20—triangular microliths; 21, 22— trapezoial microliths; 23, 24—petits tranchets; 25–27—convex-backed flakes; 28—transverse-backed flake; 29—backed point; 30—convex scraper.

the lower levels to 20 per cent in the highest layers. No other significant temporal change in the curved-backed geometrics could be detected. Further details of the six classes of geometrics are presented in table 9. Only in the case of pointed lunates are the numbers available sufficient to permit examination of the change from layer to layer; and here again it is only in the incidence of eared specimens that any significant change may be detected.

Backed flakes

Within the backed flakes (table 10), which together total 41 (14 per cent of the retouched implements from all levels), convex-backed flakes are the most frequent type. They show a steady decrease in frequency from 88 per cent of the total backed flake aggregate from layers 5 to 7 combined, to 57 cent in the uppermost two levels. There is a corresponding increase in the occurrence of transverse-backed flakes from 12 to 36 per cent. Straight-backed flakes are represented by only two examples: concave-backed flakes are completely absent. There are insufficient specimens to permit significant tabulations of the typology and metrical characteristics of the individual types of backed flake from individual layers, but table 11 gives the relevant information on the convex and transverse-backed

Table 10. Thandwe: backed flakes

Layer	Convex	Straight	Transverse	Total
1	1 ⎫	— ⎫	— ⎫	1
2	7 ⎬(57%)	1 ⎬(7%)	5 ⎬(36%)	13
3	6	—	3	9
4	7 (70%)	1 (10%)	2 (20%)	10
5	3	—	1	4
6	2	—	—	2
7	2	—	—	2
	28 (68%)	2 (5%)	11 (27%)	41

Table 11. Thandwe: backed flakes from all levels

| | No. | Length (mm) | | Length/Breadth | | % fully backed | Mean % backed | Direction of backing | | |
		Range	Mean	Range	Mean			a	b	c
Convex	28	10–25	15.3±3.4	10–2.3	1.7±0.3	30%	70%	86%	3%	11%
Straight	2	11, 22		1.2, 2.4		—	60%	both	—	—
Transverse	11	10–20	14.1±2.7	0.8–2.0	1.4±0.3	N/A	N/A	73%	27%	

Key: a. backed from ventral surface; b. backing totally bi-directional; c. backing partly bi-directional.

flake assemblages as a whole. It will be seen that only 30 per cent of the convex-backed flakes are fully backed, whereas the corresponding figure for curved-backed geometrics is 68 per cent. Bi-directional backing is also less frequent than on the latter implements but, where present, it generally continues throughout the length of the backing, in contrast to the curved-backed geometrics amongst which partially bifacially backed specimens are twice as frequent as are those totally so retouched.

Backed fragments

The stratigraphic distribution of the thirty-two backed fragments is shown in table 6. These specimens, which are broken fragments either of geometrics or of backed flakes, call for no special comment at this stage.

Backed points

Only six backed points were recovered, representing 2.1 per cent of the total number of retouched implements from Thandwe. They are concentrated in the lower levels. The edge, at its intersection with the curved back, is a clean steep break on all examples. All but one are backed uni-directionally from the ventral

surface; the exception is bi-directionally backed. Their lengths range from 17 to 29 mm (mean 20.8 ± 4.2) and the length/breadth ratios are from 1.1 to 2.3, with a mean of 1.7 ± 0.37.

Backed pieces

The thirteen backed pieces are fairly evenly distributed throughout the sequence. Their lengths, 9-21 mm, have a mean of 13.9 ± 4.0 mm. The length/breadth ratios are from 1.1 to 2.0 (mean 1.6 ± 0.31).

Scrapers

The seven scrapers, representing 2.4 per cent of the retouched implements, were the only tools retouched by techniques other than backing. Shallow retouch was empoyed to produce scraping edges which were convex on four examples, concave on two and straight on one. Four scrapers were made on flakes (one of these being on an old patinated flake), two on cores and one on a shatter-chunk. The maximum dimensions of the scrapers range from 22 to 38 mm, with a mean of 32 mm ± 6.2. Scrapers were noticeably more frequent in the lower levels.

II. GROUND STONE ARTEFACTS

The only type of ground stone artefact represented at Thandwe is the axe. A complete example came from layer 3 and fragments were recovered from layers 2 and 5.

The complete specimen (fig. 32:1) is of dark grey dolerite, measures 87 by 58 mm, and was made on part of a slab, 22 mm thick and of parallelogrammatic cross-section, clearly selected as requiring minimal modification to produce the desired axe. The slab was flaked, partly bifacially, to reduce it to an oval outline with a sharp edge extending around three quarters of the periphery: the broader, more rounded end was left blunt. Grinding was only partial, being restricted to

the cutting edge at the narrow end: even there the flake scars were not completely obliterated. The curved, adze-like cutting edge, bifacially ground for a length of 26 mm to an angle of approximately 40 degrees, shows signs of heavy use.

The two fragments, also of dolerite, are too small to provide information concerning the overall shape of the parent axes. Grinding on both specimens appears to have been more extensive than on the complete example described above. That from layer 2 had evidently been flaked both before and after the grinding operation, while the axe from layer 5 had been shaped by extensive pecking prior to grinding.

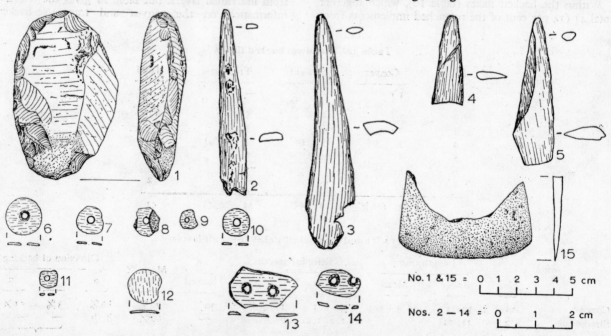

Fig. 32. Artefacts from Thandwe: 1—ground stone axe; 2—bone bodkin; 3-5—conical bone points; 6-11—shell disc beads; 12—shell disc; 13, 14—shell pendants; 15—part of iron axe.

III. HAMMERSTONES

Knapping hammer

A water-rounded spheroidal quartz pebble from layer 6, 55 mm in maximum dimension and weighing 70 gm, bears a small area of fine pitting at one end.

Pounding stones

Two fragments of larger cobbles bearing less localised pitting were recovered from layers 4 and 5. They were made of gneiss and coarse granular quartz respectively.

IV. BONE ARTEFACTS

The five bone points recovered at Thandwe fall into two classes.

?Bodkin: a broken point from layer 5 has a flat, subrectangular cross-section and rounded tip (fig. 32:2). The surviving parts of both sides are fully smoothed, but retain clear scratch marks, probably resulting from its having been shaped by means of a stone cutting-tool.

Conical points: these are made on splinters of long bone which are trimmed and ground to a point at one end only, the remainder of their length being unmodified (fig. 32:3-5).

The four examples come from layers 7, 5 (two specimens) and 3. The lengths of the three complete points are 49, 63 and 66 mm.

V. SHELL ARTEFACTS

These also fall into two classes.

Disc beads

Nineteen specimens were recovered, and were represented in all layers above and including layer 5 (fig. 32:6-11). Beads made of ostrich egg shell were not found. *Achatina* snails were the most frequent source of shell for the manufacture of disc beads (twelve examples): other land snails (four) and water snails (three) were also represented in layers 3 to 5. Bead diameters range from 5 to 10 mm, with a mean value of 6.6 mm: no significant variation is apparent from layer to layer. Both 'hour glass' and straight perforations occur in all layers, the former being the more frequent. All but 16 per cent of the beads have ground edges, producing an almost perfectly circular outline on half of them. The three untrimmed beads come from layer 2 and 3.

Layer 2 yielded a trimmed, unground, disc of *Achatina* shell 9 mm in diameter. It is interpreted as the unperforated rough-out for a disc bead (fig. 32:12).

Pendants

From layer 5 came an oval pendant of water snail shell, 12 by 7 mm, with neatly ground edges (fig. 32:13). Two perforations close to the wider end were drilled from the inside of the curvature, as would probably be essential to avoid breakage.

A broken piece of water snail shell measuring 19 by 11 mm came from layer 3. It has two perforations, close together and drilled only from the inside of the curvature (fig. 32:14). There are no signs of edge trimming or grinding, but the shell could have been intended for grinding down to produce a pendant like that described above from layer 5.

VI. POTTERY

The stratigraphical distribution of the 301 potsherds recovered from Thandwe is shown in table 6 (p. 53). Pottery occurs in the upper six layers but is common only in layers 1 to 4. Two hundred and sixty-six of the sherds are undecorated body fragments: of the remainder, all but four small fragments may be attributed with confidence to either the Early Iron Age or the later Iron Age (Luangwa) ceramic tradition. Descriptions of types are summarised on the fold-out at the end of the volume.

EARLY IRON AGE POTTERY

Decorated and/or rim sherds of Early Iron Age type numbered eighteen (fig. 33:1-9). Specimens were recovered from each of the upper five layers but were most frequent in layers 3 and 4 which, between them, yielded 67 per cent of the Early Iron Age sherds.

Type A2. A body sherd of a necked vessel bears a single horizontal row of impressions of a triangular stamp.

Type B1. Decoration is found on the externally thickened rim bands of two necked vessels, both of which have a single bevel on the lip.

Type C1. One necked vessel, represented by a body sherd only, is decorated in the concavity of the neck by at least seven parallel horizontal grooves, which were clearly carved individually into the dry clay after the pot had been lightly burnished. This sherd shows traces of use of the coil technique of manufacture.

C1 variant. Three small body sherds are decorated with parallel horizontal grooves associated with lines of single triangular stampings. On these specimens the grooving was apparently executed whilst the clay was still wet.

C2 variant. Another body sherd bears a comparable combination of decorative motifs in which the grooving is interrupted by pendant loops.

Type D1. Decoration occurs on the undifferentiated rim of one necked vessel, with a single bevel on the lip.

D1 variant. Similar decoration occurs on the externally thickened rim band of a necked vessel. The lip bears a single bevel on which a lightly incised chevron line is superimposed.

Type D2. This decorative type occurs on top of the undifferentiated rim of an in-turned bowl with single-fluted lip, and on the externally thickened rims of two necked vessels. The lip of one of these is not preserved: the other bears four bevels.

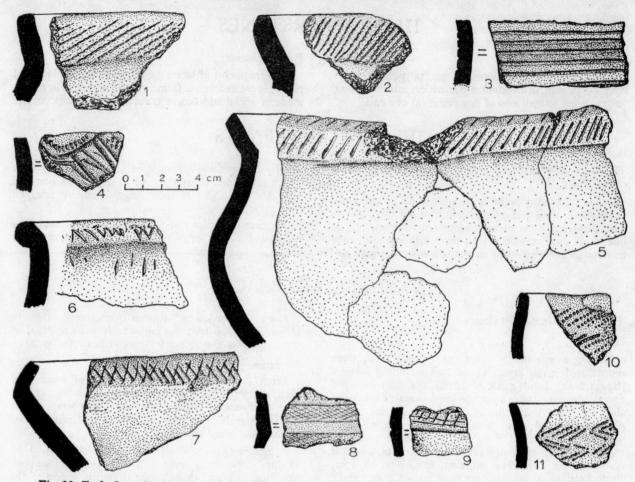

Fig. 33. Early Iron Age (1–9) and later Iron Age (10, 11) pottery from Thandwe: 1, 2—type B1; 3—type C1; 4—type C2 variant; 5, 6—type D1; 7—type D2; 8, 9—type D2 variants; 10—type 1c(i); 11—type 1d.

D2 variant. Two body sherds bear bands of fine D2 decoration delineated by broad shallow grooves. One of these sherds, from layer 5, is burnished.

Undecorated. Undecorated vessels comprise one necked vessel with externally thickened rounded rim, one open bowl with an externally thickened rim and single-bevelled lip, and a third vessel, the shape of which cannot be determined, with an undifferentiated rim and single flute on the lip.

LATER IRON AGE POTTERY

Diagnostically later Iron Age potsherds numbered thirteen, of which all but two came from layers 1 and 2 (fig.33:10, 11). Unless otherwise stated, all these vessels have a tapered rim and rounded lip. The following types are represented:

Type 1c(i). One open bowl.

Type 1d. One beaker.

Traces of comb-stamped decoration also occur on one open bowl with a tapered rim and squared, nicked lip, on one necked vessel and on four body sherds.

Type 2a. One body sherd of a necked vessel.

Undecorated. These comprise one open bowl with undifferentiated rim and rounded lip, one necked vessel, one straight-sided vessel, and one vessel of which the original shape cannot be determined.

VII. GLASS BEAD

A single opaque, white, snapped cane bead, 7 mm in diameter by 6.5 mm in maximum length, was recovered from layer 1. It is the only object recovered from the excavation at Thandwe which is not clearly of local manufacture. It is probably of very recent date, perhaps belonging to the same period of the site's use as do the iron objects, described below, which appear to have been locally forged from imported metal.

VIII. METAL

Haematite

A single unmodified fragment came from layer 3.

Slag

Fragments of iron slag were numerous in layers 1 and 2, but were completely absent from all lower layers. A small pit in grid square C, originating in layer 2 and cut into the upper part of layer 2a, contained several kilograms of slag.

Iron artefacts

These likewise occurred only in the upper two layers.

Layer 1 yielded the snapped-off cutting edge of an axe (fig. 32: 15). The edge survives to its complete original length of 72 mm and the fragment has a maximum thickness of 5 mm. A fragment of a small tang, from layer 2, most probably comes from a razor. The other pieces of iron are all small broken fragments of irregular shape, of which eleven were recovered from layer 1 and three from layer 2. The size and shape of these fragments suggest that they represent scrap broken for reworking. Their limited distribution (six of the fourteen pieces come from grid square A and six from square C) lends support to this hypothesis. The regular thickness and smooth finish of three of the fragments from layer 1 suggest that they may be derived from imported objects.

Tuyeres

A total of fourteen small fragments of baked clay tapering cylindrical tuyeres were recovered at Thandwe. Two came from layer 1, eight from layer 2 and four from layer 4. The last are from an earlier context than any of the other artefacts indicative of metalworking, and may have been introduced into the rock-shelter from elsewhere. All the tuyere fragments are crudely made of a coarse gritty clay. Internal diameters range from 25 to 30 mm and wall thicknesses from 9 to 14 mm. None has slag adhering and none is vitrified: this indicates that they were probably used in connection with forging rather than with smelting, or that they were broken before use.

Chapter 9

Thandwe: Specialist Reports

I. FAUNAL REMAINS
(Identifications by John M. Harris)

Identifications have been restricted to teeth, mandibular and maxillary material, which was represented only in layers 1 to 6 and by the wart-hog (*Phacochoerus* sp.) remains included in grave 2. Table 12, compiled from data kindly supplied by Dr John M. Harris of the National Museums of Kenya, shows the stratigraphical occurrence of specimens attributed to the various species which have been identified.

The data recorded in the table call for little special comment. All the species represented are known to have occurred in the general area of the site in recent times (Ansell, 1960; Wilson, 1975: 347-51). The smaller and medium-sized antelope are notably well represented, especially in layers 4, 5 and 6. Wart-hog and zebra are also of frequent occurrence. Throughout the sequence there is a significant number of small creatures—dassies, mongoose, lizards, hares and rodents—suggesting that the trapping of these, presumably for food, was a regular activity of the site's inhabitants. The bovid species represented probably indicate exploitation of the open plains and *dambos* to the west of the site in preference to the rocky hills to the east. No domestic species was identified.

Table 12. Thandwe faunal remains

Layer:	1	2	3	4	5	6	Total
CERCOPITHECIDAE							
Vervet monkey (*Cercopithecus aethiops*)	1	—	—	—	—	1	2
Baboon (*Papio* sp.)	2	—	1	—	—	—	3
VIVERRIDAE							
Slender mongoose (*Herpestes* cf. *sanguineus*)	—	—	1	—	—	—	1
HYAENIDAE							
Spotted hyena (*Crocuta crocuta*)	1	—	—	—	—	—	1
ORYCTEROPODIDAE							
Ant bear (*Orycteropus* sp.)	—	2	—	—	—	—	2
PROCAVIIDAE							
Hyrax (*Dendrohyrax* sp.)	—	—	1	—	1	—	2
EQUIDAE							
Zebra (*Equus burchelli*)	—	—	2	—	2	—	4
SUIDAE							
Wart-hog (*Phacochoerus* sp.)	—	1	1	2	—	—	4
BOVIDAE							
Eland (*Taurotragus oryx*)	—	1	1	—	—	—	2
Buffalo (*Syncerus caffer*)	—	—	—	—	1	—	1
Wildebeest (*Connochaetes* sp.)	—	—	—	2	1	—	3
Bushbuck (*Tragelaphus scriptus*)	—	—	1	—	—	—	1
Waterbuck (*Kobus ellipsiprymnus*)	—	—	—	—	2	—	2
Reedbuck (*Redunca* sp.)	—	—	—	—	1	—	1
Duiker (*Sylvicapra* sp./*Cephalophus* sp.)	—	—	—	1	—	1	2
Sharpe's Grysbok (*Raphicerus sharpei*)	—	—	—	—	—	1	1
Oribi (*Ourebia ourebia*)	—	—	—	1	—	—	1
Undeterminable	—	3	2	3	1	2	11
LAGOMORPHA							
Undeterminable	—	—	—	—	1	—	1
HYSTRICIDAE							
Porcupine (*Hystrix* sp.)	—	1	2	—	—	—	3
MURIDAE							
Mouse (*Mus* sp.)	—	—	—	—	—	1	1
Undeterminable rodent	1	1	—	3	1	—	6
REPTILIA							
Monitor lizard (*Varanus* sp.)	—	1	1	—	1	1	4
Undeterminable lizard	—	1	—	—	—	—	1

II. HUMAN SKELETAL REMAINS
by Hertha de Villiers

GRAVE I

Grave I (the upper of the two graves at Thandwe) contained the remains of two persons, designated Sk I and Sk Ia.

SK I

The cranial material consists of fragments of the frontal, parietal, temporal and occipital bones, a fragment of the right maxilla containing the root of the canine tooth, and a very worn second premolar.

The extant portion of the mandible comprises most of the corpus mandibulae, that is, to the area below the third molar tooth on the right side and the complete corpus including the angle on the left side. The ramus is, however, missing. In addition, the right angle, coronoid and condyloid processes are preserved. On the left there is a fracture passing through the socket of the central incisor tooth.

Of the mandibular teeth the right lateral incisor, second premolar, root of the first premolar and the left first molar are *in situ*. These show marked attrition with dentine exposure and uneven wear. The sockets for the right central incisor, right second molar and left canine indicate that these teeth may have been lost *post mortem* or shortly before death. The remaining mandibular teeth were lost *ante mortem* as the sockets have been resorbed.

The following postcranial material was present: twenty-five rib fragments; complete atlas and axis vertebrae; ten other vertebral fragments; manubrium; left clavicle; glenoid cavity, coracoid and acromial process of right scapula; glenoid cavity and acromial process of left scapula; right and left humeri; right radius; shaft and head of left radius; fragmentary right and left ulnae; one carpal; two metacarpals; left ischial tuberosity; right and left femora; right and left tibiae; proximal half of right fibula including head; shaft and distal extremity of left fibula; right and left calcanei; right and left tali; one cuneiform; two metatarsals; two phalanges.

The remains are those of a fully adult, probably elderly, individual as judged by the size and thickness of the cranial vault bones, the mandible, postcranial skeleton and teeth.

The absence of the pelvic bones makes it impossible to judge the sex with any degree of accuracy. However, the robust cranial vault bones, the everted angle of the mandible and robust appendicular skeleton suggest that these remains are those of a male. The estimated maximum living stature of this individual is 170.2 cm. This estimation is based on an average obtained from Trotter and Gleser's (1952) formulae for estimating maximum living stature from the measurement of the femur and humerus in American Negro males. However, it is known that different equations are needed for different populations and may even be required for the same populations in successive generations.

Cranium

The cranial vault bones are of moderate thickness and vary between 4.5 mm and 10 mm. Although the cranial vault is not sufficiently complete for accurate measurement, it appears to have been long, of moderate height and breadth.

In *norma verticalis* the parietal contours show a moderate or juvenile degree of bossing. The apparently dolichocranial brain case is thus ovoid. The nuchal surface is convex, with moderately well defined muscular markings. In *norma lateralis* the cranial contour shows a receding forehead of moderate height. The vault apparently reaches its highest point vertically above porion. The temporal squame is incomplete but appears to have been relatively low. The region above asterion is slightly curved. The mastoid process is small (20 mm). The digastric fossa is of moderate depth and not exposed in *norma lateralis*. The mastoid crest is moderately well developed as is the posterior root of the zygoma. The tympanic plate is damaged but appears to have been moderately thickened. The post-glenoid tubercle is of medium size and associated with a glenoid fossa of moderate depth.

Most of the frontal region, facial skeleton and cranial base are missing.

The fragment of the right maxilla contains the antero-inferior portion of what appears to have been an extensive maxillary air sinus. The inferior nasal margin is formed by the fused lateral and spinal crests; the turbinal crest is separate. The anterior nasal spine appears to have been small. The anterior teeth are missing and resorption of the sockets has occurred. The inferior nasal region and hard palate are therefore rather shallow.

Mandible

The corpus mandibulae appears to have been of moderate height (owing to the resorption of the alveolar margin it was not possible to take height measurements). The symphyseal height is 34.5 mm and the thickness is 14.8 mm; the robusticity index is thus 42.8 per cent. The lateral surface of the corpus mandibulae appears to have tapered antero-posteriorly and is marked by a single mental foramen, directed superiorly and posteriorly, which apparently lies below the second premolar. The prominentia lateralis (of Weidenreich, 1936) is slight; anteriorly this prominence divides into a slight upper torus lateralis superior which extends to the mental foramen and a lower faint marginal torus. The torus lateralis superior and marginal torus are separated by a shallow sulcus interoralis. The anterior surface of the symphyseal region presents a moderately well developed mental protuberance. The sub-alveolar depression appears to have been shallow and the upward prolongation of the mental protuberance slight. The overall effect is of a moderately pointed chin. The angle of the mandible is well developed and everted at the masseteric impression. The ramus appears to have been of moderate height and breadth. The mandibular notch is deep with marked bony buttressing between the coronoid and condyloid processes. The coronoid process is large, triangular and stout. It is hooked with an anterior convexity and its apex is directed upwards and backwards. The condyle appears to have been large and oval. On the medial surface of the corpus mandibulae a well marked prominentia alveolaris (of Weidenreich) is apparent. The posterior surface of the symphysis menti is approximately vertical and is marked by two small irregular elevations, the two superior genial tubercles. The inferior surface of the symphyseal region shows two shallow digastric fossae.

Conclusions

The stature (170.2 cm) of the individual represented by the Sk 1 remains, the robustness of the appendicular skeleton, the apparent ortho-ovoidy of the cranial vault, the apparently extensive maxillary air sinus, the morphology of the symphyseal region, angle, coronoid and condyloid processes of the mandible suggest that this individual was of Negroid type. The small mastoid process and apparently low squame of the temporal bone could perhaps suggest a Khoisan influence. However, these features fall within the range of normal variation of the South African Negro male—a small mastoid process was recorded in 27.6 per cent of males and a low temporal squame in 24.1 per cent (de Villiers, 1968).

SK Ia

The cranium is represented by fragments of frontal, including right superior orbital margin; parietal and occipital bones; right half of the maxilla containing the crowns of the unerupted permanent central incisor and first molar teeth.

There is also preserved the greater portion of the corpus mandibulae on the right side with the sockets for the deciduous dentition and the mesial portion of the socket for the unerupted crown of the first permanent molar; the right ramus, coronoid process and part of the angle. On the left side the corpus is missing distal to the socket for the lateral deciduous incisor. The crowns of the two mandibular permanent first molar teeth are also visible.

The following are the extant postcranial remains: two rib fragments; five fragments of vertebrae; distal segment of the sacrum; proximal portion of a radius shaft; proximal two-thirds of shaft, with neck, of left femur; fragmentary right and left iliac blades; one phalanx.

Conclusions

The remains are those of an infant of about 2 to 3 years of age. The crowns of the first permanent molars are large, suggesting a Negroid rather than Khoisanoid infant. The fragmentary state of the cranial remains and the young age of the individual represented make it impossible to state more definitely the population group to which this infant belonged.

GRAVE 2

Grave 2 (the lower of the two graves at Thandwe) yielded the remains of a single individual, designated Sk 2.

SK 2

The cranium is represented by fragmented right and left temporal bones including damaged petromastoid parts; a fragment of frontal bone, including lateral portion of left superior orbital margin; a portion of left maxilla with part of the inferior orbital margin, inferior orbital foramen, maxillary air sinus and zygomatic bone; anterior portions of the right and left maxillae, containing on the right side the canine, premolar and first molar and on the left side a fragmented lateral incisor, complete canine and broken first premolar. The broken root of the second premolar is also present. The sockets of the incisors suggest that these teeth were probably present at the time of death. Also present are four fragments of the parietal bones.

Most of the corpus mandibulae is preserved, that is, the area below the third molars. On the left side the incisors, canine, second and third molars are present, as is the root of the second premolar. On the right side the root of the central incisor and the canine tooth are present. The central incisor teeth are broken and displaced to the right. The remaining mandibular teeth appear to have been lost *ante mortem* as the sockets have been completely resorbed.

The teeth present show marked uneven attrition with pronounced dentine exposure. The second left lower molar appears to be carious.

The following postcranial remains are also preserved: thirty-nine fragments of ribs; very fragmentary right and left scapulae consisting largely of glenoid fossae, coracoid and acromial processes; fragment of right ilium including the greater sciatic notch; fragment of left ilium including the acetabulum; fifty fragments of vertebrae; two carpal bones; five metacarpal bones; eight phalanges; the medial and lateral two-thirds of the right clavicle; the lateral one-third of the left clavicle; both humeri, lacking the left distal extremity; both radii; the proximal one-third of both ulnae; shaft and lateral condyle of the right femur; fragmentary head, neck, shaft and condyles of the left femur; distal one-third of shaft and fragmented condyles of the right tibia; complete left tibia lacking only the anterior part of the condyles and tibial tuberosity; two-thirds of shaft and distal extremity of the right fibula; the trochlear surface of the left talus; fragmented right and left patellae.

The remains are those of a fully adult, probably elderly individual as judged by the cranial vault bones, mandible and teeth. Owing to the incompleteness of the pelvic bones, it is not possible to assess the sex with any degree of accuracy. However, the slender appendicular skeleton, slight posterior root of the zygoma and faint supramastoid crest suggest that these remains are those of a female with an estimated maximum living stature of 157.3 cm. This estimation is based on averages obtained from Trotter and Gleser's (1952) formulae for tibia, humerus, radius and ulna in American Negro females.

Cranium

The left superior orbital margin is notched and somewhat rounded in contour; a slight superciliary eminence gives character to its medial third. The squamous parts of the temporal bones are broken but appear to have been relatively low. The mastoid processes are small (right 24.1 mm and left 22.6 mm), the digastric fossa (right) is shallow and slightly exposed in *norma lateralis*. The mastoid crest is well developed but the supramastoid crest and posterior root of the zygoma show only a slight degree of development. The post-glenoid tubercles appear to have been of medium size and are associated with glenoid fossae of moderate depth. The tympanic parts of both temporal bones have been severely damaged.

The portions of the maxillae indicate that the maxillary air sinuses were well developed. The hard palate appears to have been deep and narrow and the teeth mesodont. The inferior margin of the nasal aperture is formed by the fused spinal and turbinal crests, the lateral crests extend to the intermaxillary suture forming the lower border of a subnasal gutter. The subnasal region appears to have been deep and somewhat corrugated. The anterior nasal spine is missing.

Mandible

The corpus mandibulae appears to have been of moderate height but robust—the thickness at M_2 being 17.1 mm. No measurements of height could be taken as the alveolar margin at M_2 is broken and the inferior margin compressed. The alveolar margin in the region of the symphysis menti is damaged on the labial aspect but an estimated symphyseal height of 30 mm was obtained by reference to the relatively undamaged alveolar margin on the lingual aspect. The symphyseal thickness is 13.6 mm and the symphyseal robusticity index 45.3 per cent. The chord between the mental foramina is 43.8 mm. The lateral surface of the corpus mandibulae apparently tapered anteroposteriorly and is marked by a single mental foramen, directed posteriorly, which appears to have been situated below the second premolar. The prominentia lateralis (of Weidenreich) is moderately well developed and extends downwards to the inferior border. Anteriorly, the prominence extends to the mental foramen. The body of the mandible is thickest in the region of the prominentia lateralis. The anterior surface of the symphyseal region presents a small mental protuberance and two small mental tubercles. A very shallow subalveolar depression can be identified and is divided by an upward median prolongation of the mental protuberance into two shallow fossae mentales on either side of the midline. The overall effect is of a somewhat square

chin. On the medial surface of the corpus mandibulae a well marked prominentia alveolaris is apparent. The posterior surface of the symphyseal region is approximately vertical and is marked by three irregular elevations, the two superior genial tubercles and a single median inferior tubercle. The inferior surface of the symphyseal region shows two shallow digastric fossae separated in the midline by an interdigastric ridge.

Conclusion

The stature (157.3 cm), the morphology of the mastoid process, the digastric fossa, the supramastoid crest and posterior root of the zygoma are in keeping with the apparent female sex of the individual represented by these remains. The deep subnasal region, the apparently deep and narrow hard palate and the apparently well developed maxillary air sinuses suggest a Negroid rather than a Khoisanoid individual. The apparent lowness of the temporal squame could perhaps suggest Khoisan influence.

GENERAL CONCLUSIONS

Unfortunately most of the facial skeleton is missing from each of these three specimens but the remaining parts show Negroid rather than Khoisanoid features—the postcranial remains are robust and the maximum estimated living statures suggest that these individuals were tallish. Both adult mandibles are somewhat robuster than is usual in modern South African Negroes; both are, however, partially edentulous and the broadening and lowering of the corpus may in part be due to the loss of the teeth.

Chapter 10

The Thandwe Sequence

The radiocarbon dates and the typology of the artefacts both indicate that the occupation of Thandwe rock-shelter is of no great antiquity. The earliest evidence of human activity at the site is grave 2 which was scooped into the decomposing bedrock of the shelter floor. The apparently brief interval between this event and the placement of two further burials in grave 1 is dated to between the early third and the mid-fifth centuries ad (N-907). Pottery, absent from the burials, makes its first appearance in the layer (6) which seals the fill of the upper grave. This layer is dated between the late eighth century and the end of the tenth century ad (N-906). The pottery in the overlying layer (5), dated between the mid-tenth and the late twelfth century (N-905), is exclusively of Early Iron Age type. It is replaced in the immediately higher levels by later Iron Age pottery.

The only artefacts demonstrably contemporary with the burials are chipped stone specimens of mode 5 type. They continue with increasing quantity and density until layer 3, by which time later Iron Age pottery had replaced that of the Early Iron Age, and for which a date well into the present millennium is indicated. Substantial numbers of mode 5 artefacts are present in layer 2; and they continue in reduced quantities even into the surface dust, where their presence may be at least partly due to recent disturbance. As will be shown in chapter 19, the present Ngoni inhabitants of the Thandwe area recall human use of the rock-shelter during the period (since about 1870) of their residence in the vicinity. It is likely that the cessation of the manufacture of mode 5 artefacts at Thandwe did not long predate the nineteenth century.

Throughout the period of the site's occupation, there was remarkably little change in the chipped stone industry, in which backed microliths form the most characteristic element. Only two statistically significant trends could be discerned: a steady increase through time in the frequency of retouched implements in the aggregates from successive layers, and an accompanying rise in the numbers of curved-backed geometrics with one or both tips eared. The affinities of the chipped stone industry from Thandwe are discussed below, in chapters 20 and 21.

The two burials unearthed in the lowest levels of the site predate demonstrable contact between the site's stone-tool-making inhabitants and any Iron Age peoples. They may safely be attributed, therefore, to the makers of the mode 5 artefacts. The burial customs illustrated by these discoveries may be regarded as being those of the latter people during the first few centuries AD. Considerable care was taken in the disposal of the dead, even of corpses which—like Sk 1—had evidently suffered some degree of disintegration prior to interment. The incomplete representation of body-parts, coupled with the generally good preservation of those bones which were present, may indicate prolonged exposure of the human remains prior to burial. Such a practice is attested in south-central Africa in more recent times, at least in connection with the burial customs of chiefly dynasties, which may be expected to retain features of those more common in earlier times (Roberts, 1973: 254; Gouldsbury and Sheane, 1911: 20, 185-8).

The interment with Sk 1 of parts of two wart-hog skulls apparently selected for their large size and fine tusks is also worthy of comment. The wart-hog was a significant component of the diet both at Thandwe and at other eastern Zambian sites, as also further afield (see below, p. 108). The burial with which the tusks were interred was that of an adult male, perhaps a hunter: the earlier female burial lacked such an accompaniment. Interestingly, the infant corpse Sk 1a accompanied the body of a male, not a female.

Dr de Villiers' detailed account of the human skeletal material demonstrates the predominantly Negroid affinities of these individuals. In the past it has not infrequently been suggested that the advent of the Early Iron Age to south-central Africa was connected with the spread of Negroid peoples into areas previously occupied by Khoisanoid populations (e.g. Oliver and Fagan, 1975: 94). The evidence from Thandwe, where the apparently Negroid skeletons predate any evidence for contact with Iron Age peoples, suggests that this view may merit reconsideration (see chapter 21, below).

Some time after the interment of the two burials, contact between the stone-tool-making inhabitants of Thandwe rock-shelter and an Early Iron Age population is attested by the presence, in layers 5 and above, of occasional potsherds of characteristic Early Iron Age type. The date at which this contact first took place at Thandwe cannot be ascertained with any exactitude; but date N-906 suggests that it took place around the last quarter of the first millennium ad. This is later, by some four or five centuries, than the Early Iron Age occupation of Kamnama. The typology of the Early Iron Age pottery from Thandwe is in keeping with this hypothesis. It may be concluded that Early Iron Age penetration of the relatively dry and infertile region around Thandwe did not take place until a date significantly later than that of the establishment of Early Iron Age communities in the eastern Zambian region as a whole.

The stratigraphical occurrence of Early Iron Age and later Iron Age sherds in the Thandwe deposits (fig. 34) does not allow a clear chronological distinction to be made between the two traditions. There is, however, no evidence for a typological transition between them. On stratigraphical grounds it is probable that date N-905 marks the approximate period of the first appearance of the later Iron Age material. This is in keeping with the evidence from other sites for the inception of the Luangwa tradition, to which the later Iron Age pottery from Thandwe clearly belongs (D. W. Phillipson, 1974: 7-10).

There is no indication at Thandwe, or at any other site in eastern Zambia, for the practice of any pottery

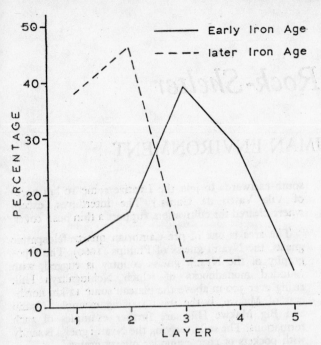

Fig. 34. Stratigraphical distribution of Early Iron Age and later Iron Age pottery at Thandwe, expressed as percentages of the total sherds of each tradition.

tradition other than that of the Early Iron Age or the Luangwa tradition. The few sherds from Thandwe which could not confidently be attributed to one or the other of these traditions could with equal probability have belonged to either. Discussion of the nature of the contact between the makers of the mode 5 industry and those of the Early Iron Age and later Iron Age

pottery is best postponed until chapter 20.

No bones from Thandwe have been identified as those of domestic animals. It appears that the site's inhabitants maintained a hunting-based economy through most if not all of the period of occupation. The wild species represented in the archaeological deposits are all present on the Eastern Province plateau today.

Iron working was practised at the site. The earliest evidence for this is provided by the four tuyere fragments from layer 4—the layer which saw the first appearance of Luangwa tradition pottery. The piece of haematite from layer 3 could, of course, have been intended as colouring matter and may have no metallurgical significance. In the upper two layers, evidence for iron-working is more abundant. It comprises slag, tuyeres and pieces of worked iron, but no complete tools. This material occurred primarily in the two pits associated with layer 2, and in the surface dust. These contexts are shared with the majority of the Luangwa tradition pottery from Thandwe. Use of the site by later Iron Age metallurgists, perhaps sometime during the last three centuries, seems probable. There are no traces of large natural-draught furnaces such as have been used for primary smelting in eastern Zambia during recent times (D. W. Phillipson, 1968b: 102-105). Most probably the activities carried out at Thandwe consisted of the secondary, refining, smelt using the miniature furnace *kantengwa*, and forging. Scrap as well as newly smelted bloom appears to have been used in the latter process.

As will be shown in chapter 19, the most recent use of the site has been by later Iron Age peoples who used the rock shelter in connection with girls' initiation ceremonies. It is to this final phase of the site's occupation that most, if not all, of the rock paintings are to be attributed.

Chapter 11

Excavations at Makwe Rock-Shelter

I. PHYSICAL AND HUMAN ENVIRONMENT

Makwe rock-shelter (14°24.8′ south, 31°56.0′ east) is situated in the extreme south-western corner of the Katete District of Zambia. Access is by way of Kondwelani Primary School, which lies 3.5 km to the north. Beacon no. 19 on the Zambia/Moçambique border lies 2.5 km from Makwe on a bearing of 85 degrees; while the border itself passes 1.0 km to the south of the site. A map of the area is given in fig. 35.

The name Makwe applies to a large granite dome, or monadnock, situated 2.5 km due south of Kondwelani School and 2 km east-south-east of Chikuleni Village, and also to another *kopje* 1.0 km further to the south (plate IVb). To avoid confusion the two hills are here referred to as Big Makwe and Little Makwe respectively.* Makwe rock-shelter is located in the north-east side of the Little Makwe *kopje*.

The area of the site is gently undulating plateau country, sloping almost imperceptibly downwards to the south, at a height above sea level of between 1000 and 1050 metres. It is well watered and relatively fertile, with many open grassy plains, or *dambos*, in which rise the headwater streams of the Mayela River, which flows southwards into Moçambique and then south-eastwards to join the Luatize some 10 km north of Vila Vasco da Gama.† The interfluves, except where cleared for cultivation, support a thin bush cover.

The area is one of pre-Cambrian quartzofeldspathic gneiss, the Nyanji gneiss of Phillips (1960). The topography of the Nyanji gneiss country is rugged, with rounded monadnocks of which Nchingalizya Hill, rising over 300 m above the plateau some 12 km north-east of Makwe, is the most striking example. Nyanji and Big Makwe Hills are further examples of such formations. The soil overlying the Nyanji gneiss is sandy with pockets of coarse angular quartz grains.

The present population of the Makwe area is predominantly Chewa under Chief Kathumba. However, the area is close to that of the Nsenga Chief Nyanji and the population is consequently mixed. The area is appreciably more fertile than that around Thandwe, and it supports a denser population. The economy is almost exclusively agricultural: maize, sorghum, millet, groundnuts, pumpkin, water-melon and burley tobacco are the main crops, while domestic cattle, pigs, goats and chickens are kept.

II. THE SITE

Makwe rock-shelter appears to be widely known to local people; and European members of the colonial Administration are said to have visited the site on more than one occasion and to have photographed the rock-paintings. No report of the site had, however, reached either the Livingstone Museum or the National Monuments Commission until July 1965 when Miss Anna Craven, at that time Keeper of Ethnography at the Livingstone Museum, was told of the site while visiting Chief Kathumba. The present writer was taken to Makwe by the Chief later in the same month.

The rock-shelter is situated on the north-east side of Little Makwe Hill, a rocky *kopje* of quartzofeldspathic rock which rises some 25 m above *dambos* which surround it on all sides except the north and north-west. The upper part of the hill is formed, on the north-east side, by a massive overhang 20 m long, up to 9 m high and extending to a maximum distance of 8.5 m from the back wall. The resultant rock-shelter is further confined by three large boulders, probably originally derived from the underside of the main overhang. These now lie below and in front of the overhang, rising to a maximum height of 3.5 m above the floor of the rock-shelter (see plan, fig. 36 and section, fig. 37). The rock-shelter thus enclosed measures 15.7 m in length (along an axis of 147 degrees magnetic) by 3.1 m in maximum width (5.1 m if areas under a low overhang of the front fallen rocks are included). The floor of the rock-shelter is well protected from wind, from direct sunlight and from all but the most driving rain.

The north end of the rock-shelter is enclosed by a pile of fallen rocks which effectively joins the front fallen boulders to the wall of the main overhang. While it is possible, with considerable difficulty, to gain access to the shelter from this direction, the only really practicable entrance is at the south end. Here a narrow passage, 3.9 m long by 1.1 m wide, is roofed by the uppermost of the front fallen slabs, forming an entrance tunnel only 0.9 m high. Access to the outer end of this tunnel may only be obtained by passing along a sloping ledge, 14 m long and 1.5 to 4 m wide, backed by a vertical rock face and with a precipitous drop in front (plate Va). The fallen boulders in front of the rock-shelter overlook the whole length of this ledge. The rock-shelter is thus easily defensible.

---

*Big Makwe is today sometimes referred to by local people as *Chafisi*, 'the place of hyenas'. The name is appropriate.

†On Portuguese maps, the name Mayela is spelled Moera. Ultimately the waters of the Luatize empty into the Kapoche which itself joins the Zambezi immediately downstream of the Cabora Bassa rapids.

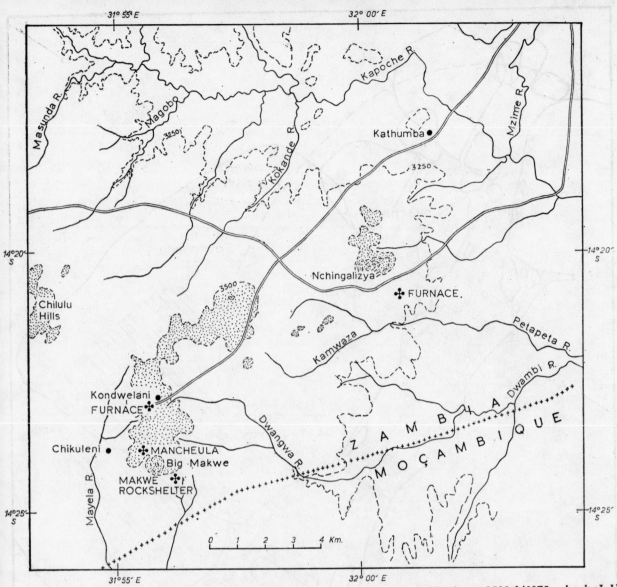

Fig. 35. Location of Makwe rock-shelter. (Contours are at 250 ft/75 m intervals, and land over 3500 ft/1075 m is stippled.)

The upper surfaces of the front fallen boulders form a roughly horizontal area, 14 by 10 m in extent, to which it is just possible to gain access from outside the rock-shelter by means of a precarious scramble round the edge of the slab which forms the roof of the entrance tunnel. The only easy way up, however, is from inside the rock-shelter. The top of these fallen boulders thus provides a useful extension of the living area on the shelter floor, being protected from direct sunlight for most of the morning. A wide view over the country to the east, towards Chadiza, may be obtained (plate Vb). Small smooth-worn pounding or grinding hollows, 10 to 15 cm in diameter and up to 2.5 cm deep, occur along the most sheltered side of this area, that is the part furthest under the overhang,

and confirm its use for presumably domestic purposes by the prehistoric inhabitants of the site.

Prior to the excavations, the floor of the rock-shelter (plate VIa) was largely free from vegetation and was level except at the north end, where the last 3 m of the floor sloped upwards through 0.5 m. Potsherds, maize cobs, fragments of charcoal, pieces of worked wood and bark thongs, together with occasional quartz artefacts, were visible on the surface of the grey ashy deposit.

The rock paintings at Makwe are located on the main wall of the shelter, including parts which can only be reached from the front fallen boulders. Additional examples occur outside the main shelter, adjacent to its entrance. They are described below in chapter 19.

III. THE EXCAVATION

Prior to the commencement of the excavation a grid of 3-ft (92-cm) squares was laid out over the entire floor area of the rock-shelter. Grid lines designated

by letters A to E paralleled the long axis of the shelter on a magnetic bearing of 147°, line A being nearest to the main shelter wall. Lines numbered 6 to 20 ran

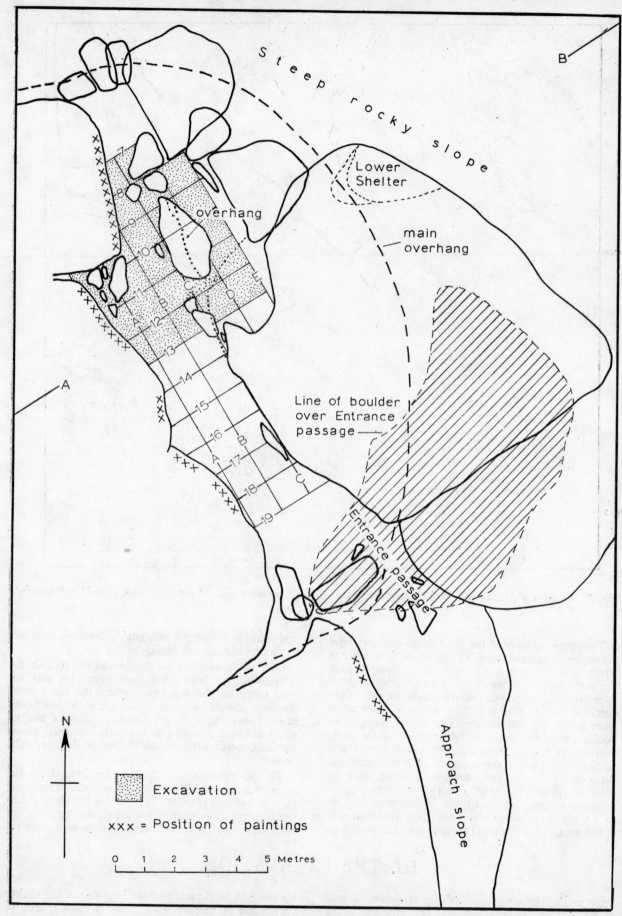

Fig. 36. Ground plan of Makwe rock-shelter.

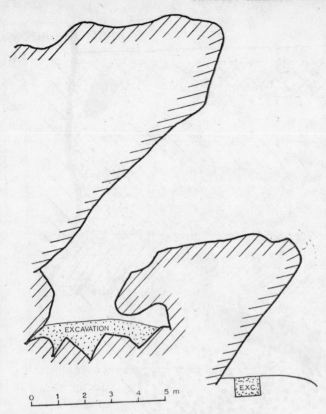

Fig. 37. Section through Makwe rock-shelter on line marked A–B on fig. 36.

perpendicular to the lettered lines, line 6 being at the northern end of the shelter. The resultant grid is shown on the site plan (fig. 36). Each grid square was recorded according to the letter and number of the lines which intersect to form its south-eastern corner: thus square B 8 is delineated by lines A, 7, B and 8.

The surface finds were then collected and recorded. The fine grey surface dust was next removed from the whole of the shelter floor. The depth of this dust, designated layer 1, varied from 1.5 to 5 cm. All obviously recent disturbances, notably a fire-pit which extended to a depth of 13 cm at the intersection of grid lines

C and 12, were also cleared at this stage and the resultant finds were recorded as coming from layer 1.

The excavated material was passed through hand-sieves of 4 mm mesh and all artefactual and faunal remains were retained and bagged. Charcoal samples for radiocarbon dating, however, were, invariably collected *in situ* by the excavators, and not by the sieving team.

Layer 2 was removed from each grid square over the whole area of the rock-shelter north of grid line 19. This layer consisted of humic ashy soil containing rootlets and much organic material. Its thickness increased from 6 cm at the north end of the excavated area to 18 cm at the south. Excavation was then restricted to the northern half of the site, as delineated by grid line 13. The nature of the deposits below layer 2 is discussed below.

In many areas considerable thickness of deposit occurred with no visible subdivision. In such cases the excavation was conducted in arbitrary horizontal spits of 7.5 cm depth, this regimen being interrupted to follow visible stratigraphic changes wherever possible. The grid squares described above provided horizontal control.

An exception to this system was made in the excavation of the 1.85 by 0.45 m area comprising the southern halves of grid squares B 12 and C 12. From the bottom of layer 2 down to bedrock the deposits in this area were excavated in 2.5 cm spits and the resultant material passed through a sieve of 1.0 mm mesh mosquito gauze. The whole of the material retained by this sieve was kept for pedological analysis, subsequently conducted by Laurel Phillipson.

A trial trench was also excavated in the small lower rock-shelter, situated beneath the overhang formed by the eastern side of the main fallen boulder. This trench, 92 cm square, is shown on the section, fig. 37, and is projected onto the plan, fig. 36. It was excavated in 15 cm levels. The deposits showed clear signs of extensive recent disturbance: pottery and both fresh and mineralised bone occurred at all levels, associated with a microlithic stone industry less plentiful than that in the main shelter. The trench was therefore abandoned at a depth of 60 cm.

IV. THE NATURE OF THE DEPOSITS

As excavation progressed, the rocky walls of the shelter were found to close in sharply; and the space available for excavation was further restricted by large fallen boulders in the deposit, particularly towards the north. The maximum depth of deposit, which occurred only in grid square B 12, was 2.08 m. On the east side of the shelter, an overhang of the front fallen boulder was completely filled with deposit. This area was not fully excavated, however, since considerable slumping of the deposits had clearly occurred in the further recesses of the overhang.

The following pedological subdivisions of the deposits were recognised and are shown on the section in fig. 38.

Horizon 6: Loose, pale grey dust on surface.

Horizon 5: Humic, grey-brown, coarse dusty earth, rich in charcoal and with grey ashy lenses.

Horizon 4: Pale grey, loosely packed, ashy soil with a few stones.

Horizon 3: Similar to horizon 4 but darker grey and with fewer stones.

Horizon 2: Brown ashy soil, darker than horizon 3, with little charcoal but many stones. A burned red-brown earth lens occurs in the lower part of this horizon in grid squares B 11 and C 12.

Horizon 1: Darker, rich brown, fine textured earth with no charcoal and very large numbers of stones, including large exfoliated fragments from the shelter wall. Stones become more common with increased depth but give out at the very base of the deposit.

For purposes of description and analysis of finds, horizons 4, 3 and 2 were each arbitrarily subdivided into two components. Horizon 1 was not so subdivided because of the paucity of its contained cultural material.

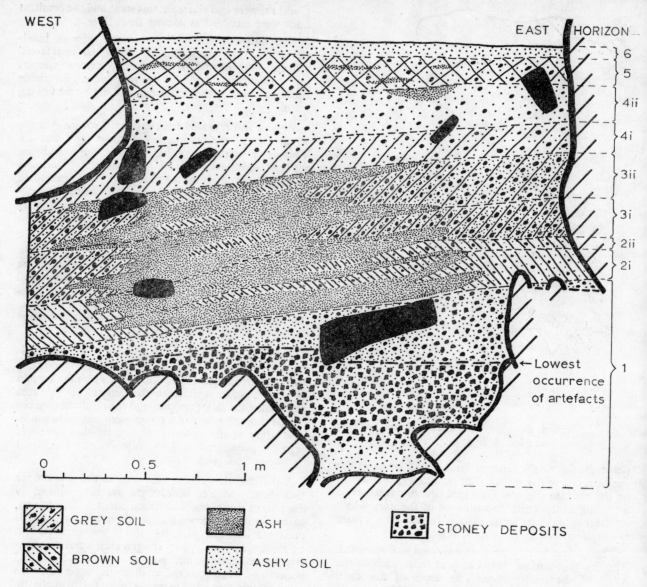

Fig. 38. Section through the Makwe deposits at the mid-point between lines 11 and 12 of the excavation grid.

The designation of these subdivisions follows the system 2i, 2ii, etc., 2i being the lower component. Although each horizon was excavated in levels which at no time exceeded 7.5 cm in thickness, analysis of finds has been conducted according to the horizons and their subdivisions, totalling nine units, here enumerated.

With increased depth, the horizons suffer a reduction in horizontal extent. Horizon 1 occurs only south of a line passing through grid squares A11, B 10, C 11 and D 12; while a line through squares A 10, B 9, C 8 and D 11 similarly delineates horizon 2i. A cross-section of the Makwe deposits, taken at the mid-point between datum lines 11 and 12 is shown in fiig. 38.

Centered in the C squares, but also sometimes extending into B and D was a complex of pale grey ashy lenses which persisted throughout the vertical extent of horizons 3 and 2 (plate VIb). Horizontally, this complex extended from the limit of excavation at datum line 13, northwards into the southern half of square C 11. Throughout their thickness these lenses interdigitated with the adjacent deposits, showing that the ash complex built up slowly, contemporaneously

with the rest of the deposits which comprise horizons 3 and 2. The formation appears to be indicative of repeated use of this same area of the shelter for the lighting of fires.

PEDOLOGICAL ANALYSIS OF THE SAMPLE-COLUMN

Soil samples from the southern halves of grid-squares B 12 and C 12, noted above, were weighed and sieved through a 4 mm mesh. The proportion by weight of each sample which was thus retained is shown graphically in fig. 39. Components in the 1 to 4 mm size-range represent a steady proportion of between 60 and 70 per cent of each sample from horizons 5, 4ii, 4i and 3ii. In horizon 3i there is a marked drop to 40 to 45 per cent. This continues through horizons 2ii, 2i and into the upper part of horizon 1, below which the proportion rises again to almost 70 per cent.

The residue, that is all material retained by the 4 mm mesh, was next sorted manually; and weights of exfoliation from the shelter wall, burnt soil, charcoal, artefacts, bones and shell were recorded. These figures

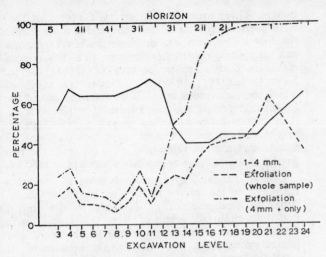

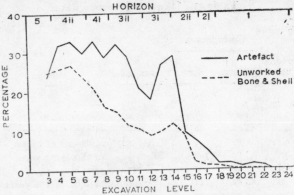

Fig. 41. Pedological analysis of the Makwe deposits: artefacts, bone and shell as percentages, by weight, of each sample.

Fig. 39. Pedological analysis of the Makwe deposits: components over 4 mm as percentage, by weight, of each sample; exfoliation as percentage, by weight, of each sample.

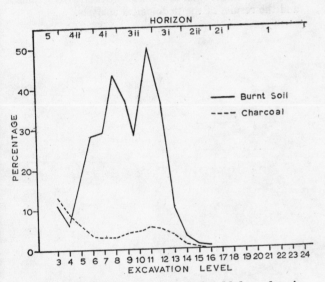

Fig. 40. Pedological analysis of the Makwe deposits: burnt soil and charcoal as percentages, by weight, of each sample.

are shown graphically in figs. 39-41 as percentages of the weight of all material exceeding 4 mm in grain-size.

Exfoliation represents 25 to 30 per cent of the larger components in horizon 5 but drops steadily to only 10 per cent in horizon 4i. Interrupted only by a slight drop at the bottom of horizon 3ii, it then increases sharply and steadily, reaching 95 per cent in horizon 2i and almost 99 per cent in the lower levels of horizon 1.

When quantities of exfoliation are calculated as proportions of the total samples over 1 mm in grain-size a comparable picture emerges for the upper levels, rising to a maximum of 65 per cent in the middle of horizon 1, below which the value drops sharply to 35 per cent. Charcoal represents 13 per cent of the larger material in horizon 5 but drops steadily through horizon 4ii and remains between 6 and 3 per cent in horizons 4i and 3ii, falling to negligible values in horizon 2. Lumps of burned soil show a contrasting distribution, rising from only 6 per cent in horizon 4ii to 50 per cent in 3ii, then sharply falling and virtually disappearing in horizon 2.

The cultural richness of the upper part of the Makwe deposits is shown by the frequency graph for artefactual material (fig. 41). This rises from 24 per cent in horizon 5 to values between 29 and 33 per cent which are maintained throughout horizons 4ii, 4i and the upper part of horizon 3ii, in the lower part of which there is a sharp drop to 18 per cent. In horizon 3i artefacts again rise to 29 per cent, falling again steadily throughout horizon 2 to only 2 per cent, and gradually petering out altogether in horizon 1. This distribution is largely paralleled by that for bone and shell combined, which gradually drop from 25 per cent in horizon 5 to 9 per cent at the top of horizon 3i. A slight increase in the lower part of that horizon, to 12 per cent, is much less marked than the corresponding increase in the proportion of artefacts. In horizon 2ii bone and shell values drop to only 2 per cent and fall still further in horizon 2i. Only minute quantities of bone and shell come from horizon 1. Most of the bone from horizon 2ii was moderately mineralised: all that from horizons 2i and 1 was heavily mineralised. This phenomenon accompanies a marked reduction in the quantity of bone preserved. The significance of these pedological trends is discussed in chapters 14 and 20, below.

V. CHRONOLOGY

A total of thirteen radiocarbon age determinations is available from the Makwe excavations. All dates were run on charcoal samples and all horizons are represented, with the exception of horizon 6 (the manifestly recent surface dust) and horizon 1 (which contained no charcoal). The results of these determinations, calculated in 'radiocarbon years' based on the 5568-year half-life, are listed in table 13.

The sample submitted for dating from horizon 5 was reported by the laboratory to be "too young to date" (SR-212). With one exception, the remaining twelve dates fall neatly into two stratigraphical-chronological

Table 13. Makwe radiocarbon dates

Hori-zon	Co-ordinates		Lab. no.	Age
	Square	Level		
5	C 9	3	SR-212	"too young to date"
4ii	C 12	6	SR-207	ad 750 ± 80 years
4ii	B 12	6	GX-1551	ad 220 ± 110 years
4i	C 11	7–8	SR-206	ad 980 ± 70 years
(4i	B 12	8	GX-1552*	3480 bc ± 140 years)
3ii	C 12	11	N-903	2430 bc ± 130 years
3ii	B 12	11	GX-1553	2695 bc ± 110 years
3ii	C 13	12	N-904	2970 bc ± 130 years
3i	B 12	12	SR-205	2630 bc ± 90 years
3i	B 12	13	GX-1554	2535 bc ± 110 years
3i	B 11	10	SR-208	3035 bc ± 100 years
2ii	B 11	12	SR-204	3060 bc ± 90 years
2i	B 13	14	GX-1555	2865 bc ± 120 years

*Incompletely pretreated for removal of contaminants, due to small size of sample.

groups. Three samples (SR-207; GX-1551; SR-206) from horizons 4ii and 4i have all yielded dates within the first millennium ad, although the results are not stratigraphically consistent. Horizons 3ii to 2i produced eight charcoal samples (N-903; GX-1553; N-904; SR-205; GX-1554; SR-108; SR-204; GX-1555), of which the determined ages fall between the end of the fourth millennium and the late third millennium bc. This group shows a slightly greater degree of stratigraphical consistency: the six dates from horizons 3ii and 3i have a mean value of *c.* 2730 bc, while the two from horizons 2ii and 2i produce a mean of *c.* 2960 bc.

One sample (GX-1552), from horizon 4i, yielded a date close to the middle of the fourth millennium bc. Although stratigraphically belonging to the upper, first millennium ad, group of dates, this reading is in fact older than all the dates of the lower group. The laboratory reported that this sample, because of its small size, was incompletely pretreated for the removal of contaminants; and it is to this cause that its aberrant age determination is probably to be attributed.

The implications of this chronology are discussed in chapter 14 in the light of the Makwe industrial sequence and the results of the pedological analysis.

Chapter 12

The Prehistoric Industries from Makwe

This chapter considers only the artefacts recovered from the main rock-shelter; those from the test excavation conducted in the lower shelter, noted above (p. 69), have not been analysed in detail on account of the disturbed stratigraphy at the latter site. For definitions of the terms used in this chapter the reader is referred to chapter 4. For convenience of reference, the numbered classes of pottery decoration are summarised on a foldout sheet at the end of the volume. (facing p. 215).

I. THE CHIPPED STONE INDUSTRY

During the Makwe excavations a total of 173,058 chipped stone artefacts were recovered from stratified contexts within the main rock-shelter. All but a minute proportion of these artefacts are of quartz. Both vein and crystalline varieties were used, the latter being always predominant but becoming less so as time passed (table 14). A few artefacts of dark grey chert from horizon 4i were the only specimens in materials other than quartz.

Cortex fragments indicate that the majority of the quartz came from stream-rolled pebbles of up to 10 cm in diameter. Such pebbles, mostly bearing a yellow, orange or reddish stain similar to that observed on cortex pieces from the excavation, may readily be picked up on the fringes of the *dambos* within 2 km of the site. It is thus reasonable to suppose that the inhabitants of the rock-shelter used these pebble deposits as the main source of their raw material. The origin of the grey chert was not located.

Table 14 also shows the primary categories of the chipped stone artefacts from each horizon. Two major trends may be discerned. First, there is a gradual decrease in the frequency of shatter-chunks from over 33 per cent of the assemblages in horizons 1 and 2i, to between 14 and 20 per cent in the upper horizons. There is a corresponding increase in the frequency of cores from 0.7 per cent to between 1.5 and 1.7 per cent. These trends may be attributed either to an increasing mastery of flake-striking technique (involving a more careful choice of raw material), or to a decreasing economy in the use of raw material, both of which would tend to reduce the number of mis-strikes which caused the cores to shatter, or to a combination of both factors. A further correlation, as at Thandwe, is between the frequency of shatter-chunks and the proportion of vein quartz used for artefact manufacture.

The second trend is a steady increase in the proportion of retouched implements from only 0.3 and 0.4 per cent of the assemblages from horizons 1 and 2i, to 1.7 per cent from horizon 3ii onwards.

Flakes constitute between 65 and 80 per cent of the assemblage from each horizon, showing a gradual but irregular increase through time, largely correlated with the decreasing frequency of shatter-chunks. Between 87 and 90 per cent of the flakes from each horizon are broken.

In preparing this description of the chipped stone industry from Makwe, all the retouched implements have been studied and analysed in detail; but because of the large numbers of specimens involved further work on the other categories has been restricted to samples.

CORES

The following analysis is based on the 524 cores (26 per cent of the total from the site) which were recovered from grid squares B 12, B 13, C 12 and C 13. Since only four cores were recovered from horizon 6, and none of these came from the sample area, this horizon has been omitted from discussion.

Table 15 shows the proportions in which the various core types are represented in the assemblages from each horizon, and also summarises the data relating to maximum dimensions of the cores in each category, horizon by horizon.

The following core types are recognised. Characteristic examples are illustrated in figs. 42 and 43.

Unilateral single-platform. On the majority of specimens, the platform is parallel to the shorter axis of the core, flakes having been removed parallel to the long axis. These examples were frequently made on split quartz pebbles, the flaked surface being remarkably flat and trimmed back until a thin, slab-like, worked-out core was produced. On a few cores, also subsumed into this category, a part or all of a circular striking platform was employed and the resultant worked-out core was consequently either cylindrical or conical. Unilateral single-platform cores comprise approximately 15 per cent of the cores from horizons 1 and 2i and gradually become more frequent, reaching values of 29 per cent in horizons 4ii and 5. Their mean maximum dimension of 25 to 30 mm shows little variation.

Bilateral single-platform. On some examples working is limited to one end of a pebble: the resultant core, especially if discarded before it was worked out, has the appearance of a small pebble-chopper. Also subsumed in this category are cores on which the bifacially worked platform extends around a greater part of the periphery of the core which, on many examples, thus becomes roughly discoid in shape. These specimens merge into the class of radial cores, on which the striking platform extends around the whole of the core's periphery. Bilateral single-platform cores account for less than 10 per cent of the cores from horizons 1 and 2i, but show values of up to 33 per cent in the higher

Table 14. Summary of Makwe artefact occurrences

Horizon:	6 (top)	5	4ii	4i	3ii	3i	2ii	2i	1	Total all horizons
CHIPPED STONE ARTEFACTS	330	17475	31321	27535	28418	23174	20306	18856	5943	173058
% crystalline quartz	80%	78%	80%	83%	90%	90%	89%	92%	78%	86%
% vein quartz	20%	22%	20%	17%	10%	10%	11%	8%	22%	14%
% chert	—	—	—	0.5%	—	—	—	—	—	0.08%

Percentages are of total chipped stone artefacts

	6 (top)	5	4ii	4i	3ii	3i	2ii	2i	1	Total all horizons
CORES	4 (1.2%)	267 (1.5%)	554 (1.7%)	304 (1.1%)	337 (1.1%)	234 (1.0%)	148 (0.7%)	133 (0.7%)	46 (0.8%)	2027 (1.2%)
SHATTER-CHUNKS	54 (16.4%)	3758 (21.5%)	4975 (15.9%)	4460 (16.2%)	4065 (14.3%)	5691 (24.6%)	6154 (33.3%)	6233 (33.6%)	1977 (33.3%)	37368 (21.6%)
WHOLE FLAKES	26 (7.9%)	1726 (9.9%)	2919 (9.3%)	2627 (9.5%)	3052 (10.7%)	1941 (8.4%)	1475 (7.3%)	1189 (6.4%)	377 (6.3%)	15333 (8.9%)
BROKEN FLAKES	242 (73.3%)	11420 (65.3%)	22333 (71.3%)	19659 (71.4%)	20472 (72.0%)	15112 (65.2%)	12411 (61.1%)	10921 (58.9%)	3525 (59.3%)	116095 (67.1%)
RETOUCHED IMPLEMENTS	4 (1.2%)	304 (1.7%)	540 (1.7%)	484 (1.8%)	491 (1.7%)	196 (0.9%)	118 (0.6%)	80 (0.4%)	18 (0.3%)	2235 (1.3%)

Percentages are of total retouched implements

	6 (top)	5	4ii	4i	3ii	3i	2ii	2i	1	Total all horizons
Geometrics	2	194 (63.8%)	341 (63.3%)	278 (57.1%)	283 (57.5%)	102 (52.8%)	54 (46.2%)	14 (17.5%)	6 (17.5%)	1274 (57.0%)
Backed flakes	1	70 (23.0%)	121 (22.3%)	114 (23.6%)	143 (29.1%)	61 (30.7%)	41 (34.5%)	37 (46.3%)	9 (50.0%)	597 (26.6%)
Backed fragments	1	27 (8.9%)	47 (8.9%)	62 (12.7%)	42 (8.5%)	17 (8.5%)	9 (7.6%)	14 (17.5%)	1 (5.6%)	220 (9.9%)
Backed points	—	1 (0.3%)	11 (2.0%)	8 (1.6%)	1 (0.2%)	2 (1.0%)	—	—	—	23 (1.0%)
Backed pieces	—	4 (1.3%)	11 (1.9%)	14 (2.9%)	10 (2.0%)	3 (1.5%)	3 (2.5%)	5 (6.3%)	1 (5.6%)	51 (2.2%)
Scrapers	—	7 (2.3%)	9 (1.7%)	7 (1.4%)	12 (2.4%)	11 (5.5%)	10 (8.4%)	10 (12.5%)	1 (5.6%)	67 (3.0%)
Others	—	1 (0.3%)	—	1 (0.2%)	—	—	1 (0.8%)	—	—	3 (0.1%)

	6 (top)	5	4ii	4i	3ii	3i	2ii	2i	1	Total all horizons
GROUND STONE ARTEFACTS	—	2	1	4	3	4	—	1	1	16
HAMMERSTONES AND ANVILS	—	8	1	6	4	4	7	1	2	33
RUBBING STONES	—	—	1	—	1	11	1	—	—	14
GRINDSTONES	—	6	—	—	1	1	—	—	—	8
BONE ARTEFACTS (EXCL. BEADS)	4	4	4	3	2	5	3	2	—	27
BONE BEADS	—	3	—	—	—	6	—	1	—	10
SHELL AND TOOTH BEADS AND DISCS	1	26	22	—	—	1	—	9	6	65
GLASS BEADS	1	—	—	—	—	—	1	1	1	4
SHELL PENDANTS	—	1	4	2	—	—	—	—	—	7
POTTERY AND OTHER BAKED CLAY	407	1954	697	116	18	10	—	—	—	3202
METAL ARTEFACTS	8	8	3	—	—	—	—	—	—	19
CLOTH, ROPE AND WOOD ARTEFACTS	4	5	—	—	—	—	—	—	—	9

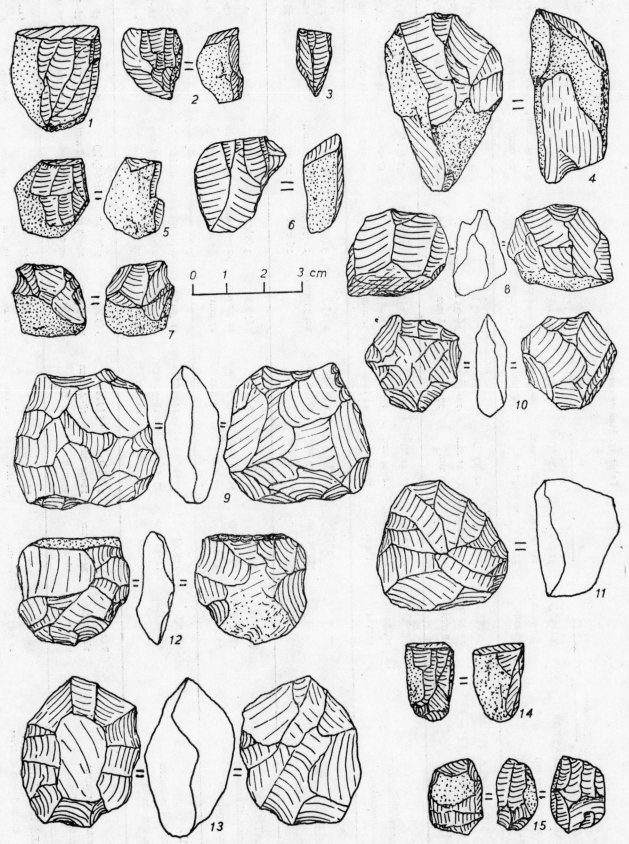

0 1 2 3 cm

Fig. 42. Cores from Makwe: 1–6—unilateral single platform; 7, 8—bilateral single platform; 9–13—radial; 14, 15—bipolar.

Table 15. Makwe cores

	Horizon: 5	4ii	4i	3ii	3i	2ii	2i	1	Total all horizons
UNILATERAL SINGLE-PLATFORM	8 (29%)	31 (29%)	20 (27%)	18 (19%)	14 (25%)	12 (21%)	9 (13%)	6 (18%)	118
Range in max. dimensions	18–40 mm	15–36 mm	18–47 mm	18–39 mm	16–44 mm	18–37 mm	18–38 mm	21–36 mm	15–47 mm
Mean max. dimension	28 mm	27 mm	30 mm	28 mm	27 mm	25 mm	28 mm	27 mm	29 mm
BILATERAL SINGLE-PLATFORM	5 (18%)	31 (29%)	22 (29%)	32 (33%)	7 (13%)	12 (21%)	4 (6%)	3 (9%)	116
Range in max. dimensions	23–37 mm	18–45 mm	17–41 mm	15–47 mm	19–35 mm	22–52	24–45 mm	24–37 mm	15–52 mm
Mean max. dimension	28 mm	30 mm	30 mm	27 mm	28 mm	30 mm	32 mm	31 mm	29 mm
RADIAL	2 (7%)	18 (17%)	16 (21%)	17 (18%)	13 (23%)	11 (19%)	28 (41%)	13 (28%)	118
Range in max. dimensions	26, 34 mm	25–40 mm	21–44 mm	17–44 mm	23–46 mm	17–60 mm	17–45 mm	25–50 mm	17–60 mm
Mean max. dimensions	30 mm	31 mm	33 mm	32 mm	31 mm	34 mm	29 mm	35 mm	32 mm
BIPOLAR	—	2 (2%)	2 (3%)	2 (2%)	2 (4%)	5 (9%)	8 (12%)	—	21
Range in max. dimensions		20, 24 mm	22, 23 mm	28, 35 mm	20, 33 mm	18–34 mm	22–38 mm		18–38 mm
Mean max. dimension						26 mm	27 mm		26 mm
DOUBLE-PLATFORM	3 (11%)	8 (7%)	3 (4%)	7 (7%)	4 (7%)	3 (5%)	6 (9%)	2 (6%)	36
Range in max. dimensions	25–28 mm	28–38 mm	34–43 mm	23–37 mm	21–32 mm	27–50 mm	20–35 mm	17, 27 mm	17–50 mm
Mean max. dimension	27 mm	30 mm	39 mm	28 mm	27 mm	37 mm	27 mm		29 mm
POLYHEDRAL	2 (7%)	9 (8%)	9 (12%)	15 (16%)	11 (20%)	9 (16%)	8 (12%)	4 (12%)	67
Range in max. dimensions	28, 41 mm	18–37 mm	23–54 mm	18–50 mm	19–40 mm	21–42 mm	22–35 mm	21–44 mm	18–54 mm
Mean max. dimension		26 mm	34 mm	29 mm	27 mm	29 mm	29 mm	30 mm	29 mm
IRREGULAR	8 (29%)	8 (7%)	5 (6%)	5 (5%)	5 (9%)	5 (9%)	6 (9%)	6 (18%)	48
Range in max. dimensions	18–41 mm	24–45 mm	26–40 mm	18–41 mm	25–63 mm	29–63 mm	24–48 mm	36–95 mm	18–95 mm
Mean max. dimension	28 mm	36 mm	33 mm	32 mm	37 mm	42 mm	29 mm	57 mm	36 mm
TOTAL CORES IN SAMPLE	28	107	77	96	56	57	69	34	524
Mean max. dimension of all cores	28 mm	29 mm	31 mm	29 mm	29 mm	31 mm	29 mm	36 mm	36 mm

horizons. Mean maximum dimensions are between 27 and 32 mm throughout the sequence.

Radial. With the exception of a very few examples made on flat quartz slabs, all of these are bifacially worked. Cross-sections show a continuous range from flat to biconical, the latter predominating. The cores are nearly always approximately symmetrical about the plane of the striking platform. No clear cases were noted of platform preparation on the cores. The frequency of radial cores shows a marked reduction through the Makwe sequence: they comprise approximately 40 per cent of the cores from the two lowest horizons, but average only 20 per cent thereafter, showing a final drop to only 7 per cent of the cores from horizon 5. Mean maximum dimensions are from 29 to 35 mm.

Bipolar. None of the specimens examined showed undisputable signs of damage due to subsequent utilization: they are not therefore to be classed as *outils écaillés*. Bipolar cores are absent from horizons 1 and 5. They form 12 per cent of the cores in horizon 2i and steadily decrease to a value of only 2 per cent in horizon 4ii. Their maximum dimensions range from 20 to 38 mm, with a mean of 26 mm.

Double-platform. Such cores never form a major component of the assemblage and account for less than 11 per cent of the cores from each horizon. Double-platform cores naturally tend to be somewhat larger than the single-platform specimens: their mean maximum dimensions show considerable variation and range from 27 to 39 mm.

Polyhedral. Polyhedral cores comprise 12 per cent of those from horizons 1 and 2i, rise slightly to between 16 and 20 per cent in the middle horizons, and fall again to below 8 per cent in horizons 4ii and 5. Mean maximum dimensions are from 26 to 34 mm.

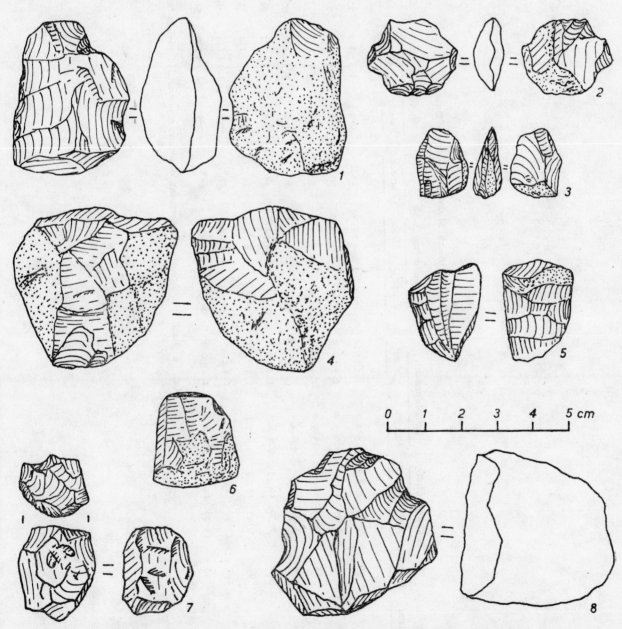

Fig. 43. Cores from Makwe: 1–5—double platform; 6—irregular; 7, 8—polyhedral.

Table 16. Makwe: typology of flakes

Horizon	Flakes in sample	Length (mm) Range	Length (mm) Mean	Length/breadth Range	Length/breadth Mean	Thickness (mm) Range	Thickness (mm) Mean	Side-struck	No. dorsal scars Range	No. dorsal scars Mean	Dorsal scar-pattern a	b	c	d	Platform e	f	Utilized
5	56	9–55	18±8	0.5–2.3	1.4±0.4	1–12	4.2±2.2	25%	0–4	2.3±1.0	75%	—	14%	11%	—	10%	46%
4ii	107	7–45	18±7	0.6–3.0	1.3±0.4	1–11	4.3±2.1	30%	0–6	2.5±1.2	72%	—	21%	7%	—	5%	33%
4i	88	7–40	18±6	0.5–3.6	1.4±0.5	1–10	3.8±2.0	20%	0–5	2.3±0.9	70%	—	25%	5%	—	9%	30%
3ii	95	8–52	17±7	0.6–2.3	1.3±0.4	1–17	3.7±2.5	30%	0–6	2.5±1.0	67%	—	30%	3%	2%	8%	22%
3i	89	7–30	16±5	0.6–2.5	1.4±0.5	1–10	3.2±1.7	25%	0–5	2.3±1.1	68%	—	20%	12%	—	11%	26%
2ii	99	9–45	21±7	0.6–3.0	1.4±0.5	2–15	4.6±2.4	18%	0–8	2.8±1.1	53%	7%	35%	5%	2%	12%	22%
2i	101	10–39	19±7	0.7–4.2	1.4±0.5	1–17	4.8±3.0	27%	0–9	2.9±1.3	51%	8%	37%	4%	1%	14%	41%
1	44	13–46	24±7	0.5–2.9	1.4±0.6	2–15	6.2±3.1	25%	0–5	2.7±1.0	54%	—	39%	7%	2%	14%	48%

Key. a. parallel; b. bipolar; c. convergent; d. cortex; e. prepared; f. pseudo-facetted.

Irregular. In horizon 1 this category accounts for 18 per cent of the cores, including some very large examples (mean maximum dimension: 57 mm), mainly of only slightly modified raw material. Through the rest of the sequence irregular cores form less than 10 per cent, except in horizon 5 where they rise sharply to 29 per cent. Mean maximum dimensions in these horizons are from 28 to 42 mm. The varying frequency of the irregular cores appears to correlate with that of the poor-quality vein quartz.

Although the Makwe cores form a series in which a number of distinct categories have been recognised, the divisions between these categories are poorly defined. Several developmental trends are distinguished, the most notable being the gradual reduction with time in the frequency of radial cores and the corresponding increase in single-platform specimens, both unifacial and bifacial. The mean maximum dimensions of all cores remains virtually constant between 28 and 31 mm in all horizons; the slightly higher figure for horizon 1 being due to the presence of a small number of large irregular cores.

SHATTER-CHUNKS

The implications of the stratigraphical variations in the frequency of shatter-chunks have been discussed above. No typological subdivision of this artefact class appears practicable, and no metrical analysis has been attempted.

FLAKES

Analysis was conducted on all the unbroken flakes recovered from the southern half of grid square B 12, and those from horizon 5 of the southern half of grid square C 12, making a total sample of 679 specimens, being 4.4 per cent of the whole flakes recovered from the site as a whole. Details of the analysis are given in table 16.

Examination of the patterns of dorsal flake scars reveals a steady increase through time in the proportion of parallel scars at the expense of those showing a convergent pattern. Parallel scars are found on between 51 and 54 per cent of the flakes in horizons 1 to 2ii, and increase to 75 per cent in horizon 5. The trend in the frequency of flakes with convergent scar-patterns closely parallels that of the radial cores. The very slight decrease in the mean number of dorsal scars visible on each flake is presumably linked to the decrease in radially struck flakes, which tend to show more scars than do those with a parallel scar pattern. Flakes which were demonstrably struck from bipolar cores were recorded only in horizons 2i and 2ii although, as noted above, the cores themselves indicate the continued though infrequent use of the bipolar technique through horizons 3 and 4.

Flake lengths show a reduction in mean value from 24 mm in horizon 1 to between 16 and 18 mm in horizons 3i to 5. Mean thicknesses display a comparable decrease. Side-struck flakes account for between 18 and 30 per cent of the flakes from each horizon, but no clear trend is apparent in their frequency. True prepared striking platforms are rare. In no horizon do they occur on more than 2 per cent of the flakes examined; and they are completely absent from horizons 4i to 5. 'Pseudo-facetted' striking platforms are found on 14 per cent of flakes in horizons 1 and 2i, but become steadily less frequent thereafter.

Traces of utilisation are, as noted in chapter 4, difficult to recognise. Edge damage which may probably be attributed to use is, however, found on approximately 40 per cent of the flakes in horizons 1 and 2i. Their frequency drops to 20-25 per cent in horizons 2ii, 3i and 3ii, before rising steadily again to about 45 per cent in horizon 5. No detailed analysis of the loci or types of utilization has been attempted.

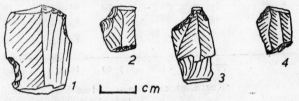

Fig. 44. Makwe microburins.

The frequency of broken flakes in each horizon is shown in table 14. The only specimens which merit special comment are four probable microburins, all of which are illustrated (fig. 44). Two examples come from horizon 3ii and two from horizon 4ii: their lengths range from 12 to 24 mm. Three more doubtful specimens come respectively from horizons 3ii, 4ii and 5. It is possible that all seven were produced accidentally: even if this were not the case, use of the microburin technique was extremely rare and was limited to the later part of the sequence.

RETOUCHED IMPLEMENTS

All the 2,235 retouched implements, representing 1.29 per cent of the chipped stone assemblage, were admitted to analysis.* Representative examples from each horizon are illustrated in figs. 46-51. All but 68 of the retouched implements bear backed retouch. A breakdown of the assemblage from each horizon is given in table 14, where some significant changes are apparent. There is a steady and substantial increase through the sequence in the proportion of geometrics at the expense of the backed flakes. Geometrics rise from less than 18 per cent of the retouched implements in horizon 2i† to almost 64 per cent in horizon 5, while backed flakes show a corresponding decrease from 50 to 23 per cent through the same horizons. Miscellaneous backed pieces account for over 6 per cent of the retouched implements from horizons 1 and 2i but drop sharply thereafter, always remaining less than 3 per cent. Backed points appear in horizon 3i but never become numerous. Scrapers, the only shallow-flaked type of retouched implement recognised in the Makwe assemblage, are not uncommon in the lower levels, comprising over 12 per cent of the retouched implements from horizon 2i: later their frequency steadily declines to less than 2 per cent of the assemblages from horizons 4 and 5. Details of the categories of retouched implements recognised are given below, together with an account of the variation through time which has been discerned within each category.

---

*Sixty specimens retained traces of the mastic used for affixing them to hafts. They have been included in the analysis here presented, but are discussed in detail in the *Appendix* (pp. 215-8).
†The high value of 33 per cent geometrics for horizon 1, based on a total of only eighteen retouched implements, cannot be regarded as definitely indicating that the trend is reversed at the base of the deposit.

Table 17. Makwe: curved-backed geometrics

Horizon	No.	% of all geometrics	Length (mm) Range	Length (mm) Mean	% eared	% fully backed	Mean % backed	Direction of backing a	b	c	d	e
6	2											
5	156	80%	9–29	17.1±3.4	21%	52%	84%	53%	1%	15%	31%	—
4ii	226	66%	8–28	16.8±3.4	20%	79%	95%	54%	—	14%	29%	3%
4i	157	56%	8–26	16.6±3.8	21%	72%	93%	54%	—	14%	27%	5%
3ii	127	45%	10–25	16.9±3.6	18%	68%	90%	65%	—	9%	23%	4%
3i	71	70%	9–29	15.6±3.6	19%	55%	84%	73%	—	8%	15%	4%
2ii	44	80%	7–25	14.2±3.6	5%	55%	86%	70%	—	14%	16%	—
2i	9 }											
1	5 }	70%	9–22	14.1±3.5	14%	50%	86%	71%	—	14%	7%	7%
	797	63%	7–29	16.5±3.5	19%	66%	90%	58%	0.25%	13%	26%	3%

Key: a. backed from ventral surface; b. backed from dorsal surface; c. backing totally bi-directional; d. backing partly bi-directional; e. backed from alternate directions.

Table 18. Makwe: sub-classes of curved-backed geometrics

	Horizon	No.	% of curved-backed geometrics	Length (mm) Range	Length (mm) Mean	Length/Breadth Range	Length/Breadth Mean	% eared
POINTED LUNATES	6	1			15		1.7	—
	5	107	69%	9–29	17.2±3.7	1.3–3.2	1.93±0.3	18%
	4ii	162	72%	11–28	16.9±3.2	1.3–2.6	1.87±0.3	19%
	4i	93	59%	10–26	16.4±3.2	1.3–2.5	1.85±0.2	15%
	3ii	82	65%	10–25	16.8±3.1	1.4–4.0	1.86±0.4	15%
	3i	48	65%	9–29	15.9±3.6	1.4–3.2	1.86±0.3	20%
	2ii	28	64%	10–25	15.7±3.5	1.4–2.1	1.76±0.2	14%
	2i	7 }						
	1	1 }	57%	10–25	14.7±3.5	1.2–3.0	1.76±0.6	13%
		529	66%	9–29	16.7±3.3	1.2–4.0	1.86±0.3	18%
DEEP LUNATES	6	—						
	5	30	19%	10–29	16.2±4.0	0.8–1.6	1.3±0.2	40%
	4ii	42	19%	8–26	16.5±3.8	0.9–1.7	1.3±0.2	36%
	4i	52	33%	8–26	17.7±4.3	0.9–1.6	1.3±0.2	29%
	3ii	31	24%	11–25	18.2±3.4	0.9–1.5	1.3±0.1	29%
	3i	11	15%	11–29	18.1±5.1	0.9–1.5	1.3±0.2	36%
	2ii	8	18%	7–16	11.1±2.6	1.0–1.5	1.2±0.2	—
	2i	2 }						
	1	3 }	36%	9–17	14.0±3.1	0.9–1.7	1.1±0.3	20%
		179	22%	7–29	16.9±4.3	0.8–1.7	1.3±0.2	31%
ASYMMETRICAL LUNATES	6	1			10		1.1	
	5	19	12%	13–19	15.3±1.6	1.2–2.1	1.6±0.2	5%
	4ii	22	10%	10–26	16.4±3.7	1.0–2.0	1.5±0.3	5%
	4i	12	8%	8–18	13.2±3.1	0.8–1.8	1.4±0.3	8%
	3ii	14	11%	10–22	14.5±3.2	1.1–2.1	1.6±0.3	21%
	3i	12	20%	9–17	13.0±2.2	1.3–1.9	1.6±0.2	—
	2ii	8	18%	10–15	12.0±1.8	1.1–2.1	1.5±0.3	12%
	2i	— }						
	1	1 }	7%		10		1.4	—
		89	12%	8–26	14.4±3.1	0.8–2.1	1.5±0.3	9%

Geometrics

These form the largest category of retouched implements, being represented by 1,274 specimens. Details of the 797 curved-backed geometrics are given in table 17. Their mean length, 16.5 mm, shows a slight increase from 14.2 mm in horizons 1 to 2ii to between 16.6 and 17.1 mm in horizons 4i to 5. Data on variations in proportions and shape are presented below for the three sub-categories recognised (see also table 18).

Further variation may be discerned in the quantity and direction of the backing. The proportion of the curved-backed geometrics which bear retouch along the whole back increases steadily from 50 per cent in horizons 1 and 2i to almost 80 per cent in horizon 4ii, followed by a sudden drop in the highest level. This same trend is also indicated, though less markedly, by calculations of the mean of the proportion of backing on each curved-backed geometric in the horizon. Throughout the occupation of the site there is a steady decrease in the proportion of curved-backed geometrics which are backed uni-directionally from over 70 per cent in horizons 1 and 2 to little over 50 per cent in horizon 5. With the exception of two specimens from horizon 5, all the uni-directionally backed specimens are retouched from the ventral surface. In most horizons approximately 14 per cent of the curved-backed geometrics show bi-directional retouch along the entire length of their backing, but their proportion drops to only 8 per cent in horizon 3. A steadily increasing proportion, rising from 7 to 31 per cent through the duration of the site's occupation, bear partly uni-directional and partly bi-directional backing, while a small number from most levels are retouched from the ventral and dorsal surfaces alternately.

The three sub-classes of the curved-backed geometrics are as follows:

Pointed lunates. This is the largest category of geometrics, being represented by 529 specimens, or 66 per cent of all curved-backed geometrics. On 18 per cent of the pointed lunates one tip is emphasised by the making of an eared projection. Among the pointed lunates little significant change can be demonstrated during the Makwe succession, as may be seen in table 18. As a proportion of the total number of curved-backed geometrics, pointed lunates become slightly more frequent in the upper levels, rising from around 60 per cent in horizons 1 and 2 to approximately 70 per cent in horizons 4ii and 5. This trend is accompanied by a barely significant increase in the mean length of the pointed lunates. Variations in the mean length/breadth ratio of these artefacts from each horizon do not appear to be significant, nor do those in the proportions of eared specimens.

Deep lunates. This type is represented by 179 examples, 22 per cent of the total number of curved-backed geometrics. The deep lunates have a mean length/breadth ratio of 1.3, as opposed to 1.9 for the pointed lunates. The type includes 88 per cent of the curved-backed geometrics with length/breadth ratios of less than 1.25. Ears are present on 31 per cent of the deep lunates and are thus almost twice as frequent as on the pointed lunates. There is little temporal variation within the deep lunate category. Their mean length, only 12.2 mm in horizons 1 and 2, rises to 18 mm in horizon 3, showing a slight reduction thereafter. The mean length/breadth ratio remains virtually constant. The proportion of eared specimens, which are virtually absent in horizons 1 and 2, rises to between 30 and 40 per cent from horizon 3i upwards.

Asymmetrical lunates. There are 89 specimens in this category, comprising 12 per cent of the total number of curved-backed geometrics in the assemblage. Only 8.7 per cent are eared. The mean length/breadth ratio of the asymmetrical lunates is 1.54. They form a some-what larger proportion of the curved-backed geometrics in the higher horizons, where they are also, on average, some 2 mm longer than the earliest examples. There is no significant variation in the mean length/breadth ratios, nor in the frequency of eared examples.

The angled-backed geometrics total 477: details and quantifications are presented in table 19. Because of the variety of the three sub-classes, further details of each are presented separately:

Triangular microliths. In shape, the 179 implements in this category generally approximate to a right-angled isosceles triangle, with the edge as hypotenuse on approximately 60 per cent and with the longer sector of the back as hypotenuse on the remainder. Only 68 per cent are fully backed: on 11 per cent a diagonal break on the original flake or blade has been incorporated in the back without further retouch. On the remainder, a small part of the back, nearly always in the region of the mid-back angle, remains sharp. The mean proportion of the back which bears retouch, 90 per cent, is identical with the corresponding figure for the curved-backed geometrics. On 62 per cent the backing is exclusively uni-directional, invariably from the ventral surface. On most others the backing is only partially bi-directional, this generally being restricted to the tips. Triangular microliths bearing completely bi-directional backing and those backed from alternating directions are both rare.

Details of the triangular microliths from each horizon are given in table 19. As they are comparatively infrequent in horizons 1, 2i and 2ii, adequately quantified data for these horizons are lacking. The mean length of the specimens shows a steady increase from 11.1 mm in horizon 3i to 16.6 mm in horizon 5. There is no significant variation in the length/breadth ratios. Eared specimens, which never represent more than 14 per cent of the examples from the lower horizons, rise sharply in horizons 4ii and 5, reaching 28 per cent in the latter level. At the same time there is a slight increase in the proportion of specimens whose backs incorporate an unretouched fracture: the incidence of backing shows a corresponding reduction. Bi-directional backing likewise increases slightly in the upper horizons.

Trapezoidal microliths. The angled-backed geometrics include 118 trapezoidal specimens, only 22 per cent of which are retouched along all three sectors of the back. On a further 16 per cent, the section of the back which parallels the long edge comprises a clean snapped break or cortex area roughly perpendicular to the main flake surface. The remaining 62 per cent are retouched only at the ends and retain two sharp parallel edges. The shapes of the trapezoidal microliths show considerable variation: length/breadth ratios range from 0.7 to 3.3, with a mean of 1.4. As table 19 and fig. 45 show,

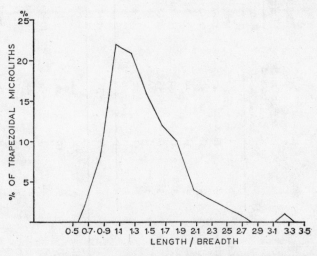

Fig. 45. *Makwe: length/breadth ratios of 118 trapezoidal microliths from all horizons.*

Table 19. Makwe: sub-classes of angled-backed geometrics

Horizon:	No.	% of angled-backed geometrics	Length (mm) Range	Length (mm) Mean	Length/Breadth Range	Length/Breadth Mean	% eared	% fully backed	Unretouched portion of back — Sharp	Unretouched portion of back — Blunt	Mean % backing	Direction of backing — a	b	c	d	e
TRIANGULAR MICROLITHS																
6	—		—	—	—	—	—	—	—	—	—	—	—	—	—	—
5	18	47%	12–26	16.6±3.1	1.1–1.8	1.5±0.2	28%	61%	22%	17%	88%	67%	—	—	—	—
4ii	58	50%	9–21	14.3±2.7	0.9–2.4	1.4±0.6	22%	62%	20%	18%	89%	43%	—	6%	28%	14%
4i	31	26%	9–22	13.8±2.9	0.8–2.1	1.4±0.3	10%	81%	16%	3%	95%	61%	—	9%	33%	10%
3ii	47	30%	8–19	11.4±3.2	0.8–2.3	1.4±0.3	14%	68%	25%	7%	93%	75%	—	3%	26%	5%
3i	18	58%	8–14	11.1±1.5	1.1–1.9	1.4±0.2	11%	72%	17%	11%	92%	83%	—	6%	20%	—
2ii / 2i / 1	5 / 1 / 1	41%	9–18	12.6±3.1	1.1–1.6	1.2±0.2	13%	87%	13%	—	97%	87%	—	—	13%	—
(total)	179	47%	8–24	13.3±3.1	0.8–2.4	1.3±0.3	15%	68%	20%	11%	90%	62%	—	5%	25%	7%
TRAPEZOIDAL MICROLITHS																
6	—		—	—	—	—	—	—	—	—	—	—	—	—	—	—
5	16	42%	7–22	15.0±3.7	0.8–2.2	1.4±0.4	20%	6%	75%	19%	70%	67%	—	7%	20%	7%
4ii	33	29%	10–27	15.9±4.5	0.9–3.3	1.6±0.4	3%	29%	53%	18%	73%	74%	3%	—	20%	3%
4i	25	21%	9–24	15.7±4.2	0.8–2.7	1.4±0.4	12%	12%	76%	12%	72%	65%	4%	—	23%	8%
3ii	28	18%	7–25	14.9±4.3	0.9–1.9	1.2±0.3	—	25%	61%	14%	78%	96%	—	—	4%	—
3i	9	29%	8–25	14.5±5.4	0.9–1.5	1.2±0.2	—	33%	67%	—	81%	89%	—	—	11%	—
2ii / 2i	3 / 4	13% / 18%	11–18	14.9±1.8	1.2–2.3	1.4±0.4	—	30%	25%	44%	73%	86%	—	—	14%	—
(total)	118	25%	7–27	15.3±4.2	0.8–3.3	1.4±0.4	8%	22%	62%	16%	75%	79%	2%	1%	16%	3%
PETITS TRANCHETS																
6	—		—	—	—	—	—	—	—	—	—	—	—	—	—	—
5	4	11%	9–13	11.0±2.0	0.8	0.8±0	—	75%	—	25%	95%	50%	—	—	50%	—
4ii	24	21%	7–15	8.9±2.5	0.5–1.2	0.7±0.2	—	61%	13%	26%	88%	61%	4%	4%	27%	4%
4i	65	54%	6–15	9.7±2.1	0.5–1.1	0.8±0.1	2%	63%	23%	13%	90%	61%	—	5%	31%	2%
3ii	81	52%	5–17	9.8±2.3	0.5–1.1	0.8±0.1	2%	60%	27%	12%	93%	67%	—	6%	22%	5%
3i / 2ii	4 / 2	13% / 18%	7–12	9.2±2.1	0.6–0.8	0.7±0.1	—	67%	17%	17%	95%	33%	—	17%	50%	—
2i	—		—	—	—	—	—	—	—	—	—	—	—	—	—	—
1	—		—	—	—	—	—	—	—	—	—	—	—	—	—	—
(total)	180	38%	5–17	9.6±2.3	0.5–1.2	0.8±0.1	1%	62%	23%	15%	91%	63%	1%	6%	27%	3%

Key. a. backed from ventral surface; b. backed from dorsal surface; c. backing totally bi-directional; d. backing partly bi-directional; e. backed from alternate directions.

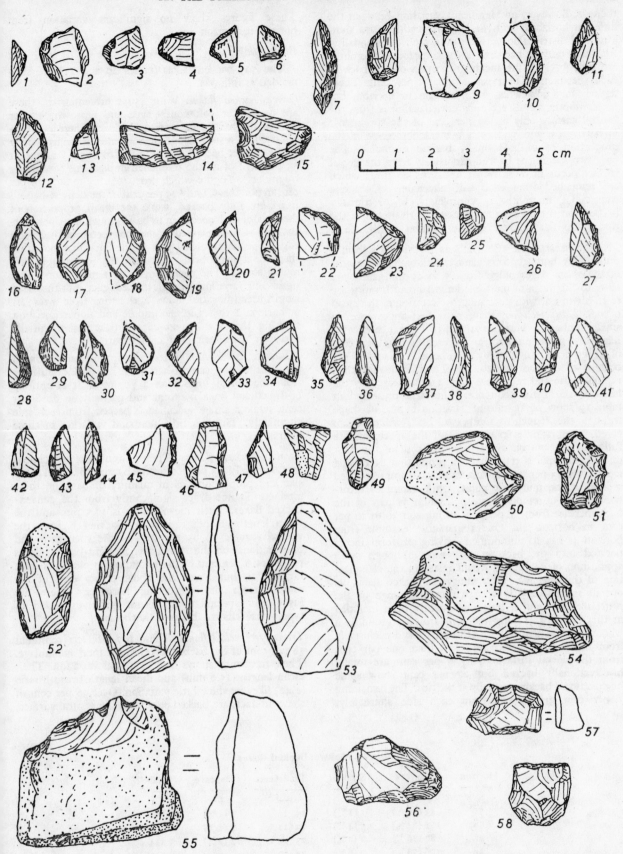

Fig. 46. Retouched implements from horizons 1 (1–15) and 2i (16–58) at Makwe: 1—pointed lunate; 2–4—deep lunates; 5—asymmetrical lunate; 6—triangular microlith; 7–12—convex-backed flakes; 13—backed fragment; 14, 15—scrapers; 16–21—pointed lunates; 22–26—deep lunates; 27–31—asymmetrical lunates; 32—triangular microlith; 33, 34—trapezoidal microliths; 35–44—convex-backed flakes; 45, 46—straight-backed flakes; 47, 48—transverse-backed flakes; 49—concave-backed flake; 50–58—scrapers.

there is, however, no significant variation between the different horizons; and the length/breadth ratios show a normal distribution with no indication of bimodality. Although only 22 per cent of the trapezoidal microliths are fully backed, the mean proportion of the back of each specimen to bear retouch is 75 per cent. These figures vary somewhat from horizon to horizon, but no significant trends are apparent. Backing is from the ventral surface only on 79 per cent of the specimens: in horizons 4 and 5 there is a marked increase in the proportion of bi-directionally backed examples. The only two specimens backed exclusively from the dorsal surface occur in these upper levels, as do three which are retouched from each side alternately. Only one trapezoidal microlith is completely bi-directionally backed: on the others such backing is restricted to the tips or to the thickest central portion of the back.

Petits tranchets. The 180 artefacts in this class form a remarkably homogeneous group. Although the lengths of the sharp edges range from 5 to 17 mm, most are close to the mean of 9.6 mm: length/breadth ratios are from 0.5 to 1.2, with pronounced clustering at the mean of 0.8. *Petits tranchets* make their first appearance, in small numbers, in horizons 2ii and 3i. They then become markedly more numerous, representing 19 per cent of all retouched implements from horizon 3ii and 16 per cent of those from horizon 4i. Their frequency then rapidly falls; and they have almost disappeared by the latest stage in the sequence. The data presented in table 19 show no significant variation in size or shape through the sequence. Only two *petits tranchets* are eared. Slightly over 60 per cent of the specimens are fully backed, but on average 90 per cent of the back of each example is retouched. A proportion decreasing from 27 to 13 per cent have a short, sharp unretouched section at the mid-back point, while examples incorporating an unretouched steep fracture as part of the back increase from 12 per cent in horizon 3ii to 26 per cent in horizon 4ii. One remarkable example from horizon 4i has its unmodified striking platform incorporated into the back in this way: although strict application of definitions would result in the classification of this specimen as a transverse-backed flake, its overall morphology is well within the range of the *petits tranchets* and it has consequently been included in this category. Taking the *petit tranchet* group as a whole, we find that 63 per cent are backed exclusively from the ventral surface and less than one per cent from the dorsal surface. Only 6 per cent are totally bi-directionally backed but 27 per cent show some bi-directional backing, usually at the tips. The remaining 3 per cent are backed from each side alternately.

These figures show no significant variation from horizon to horizon.

Backed flakes

The 597 backed flakes (tables 20 and 21) are sub-divided as follows:

Convex-backed flakes. With 459 representatives, these are by far the commonest type and represent 77 per cent of the backed flakes from Makwe. There is a pronounced decrease through the sequence in the frequency of the convex-backed flakes: in horizon 1 they represent 53 per cent of all the retouched implements (excluding fragments), a figure which drops steadily to only 19 per cent in horizon 5. Only 29 per cent of the convex-backed flakes are fully backed, while the mean proportion of the back of each specimen to bear retouch is 75 per cent. Backing is concentrated at the intersection of back and edge. The unretouched part of the back may be either sharp or a steep break or cortex. Eared examples are totally absent. The mean length, 17.1 mm, shows little significant variation through the sequence, but the mean length/breadth ratio shows a decrease from over 2.1 in horizon 1 to 1.7 in the middle and upper horizons, showing that the convex-backed flakes were initially narrower than their later counterparts.

Backing is exclusively from the ventral surface on 86 per cent of the convex-backed flakes and exclusively from the dorsal surface on 2 per cent. It is entirely bi-directional on 4 per cent and partially so on 8 per cent, while a single specimen is backed from each side alternately. There is little temporal variation in these figures.

Straight-backed flakes. These twenty-six specimens represent only 4.3 per cent of the backed flakes. In mean size and proportions, as in quantity of backing, these artefacts do not differ significantly from the convex-backed flakes. Their mean length is 17.5 mm and the mean length/breadth ratio 1.81. Backing is from the ventral surface on 85 per cent of the specimens and bi-directional on the remainder. Straight-backed flakes represent 8 per cent of the retouched implements from horizon 2i, but never rise above 2 per cent of the sample from the succeeding horizons. There are insufficient specimens to permit an investigation of typological change between horizons.

Transverse-backed flakes. These 107 artefacts represent 18 per cent of the backed flakes in the total assemblage. Their frequency shows little temporal variation. Their mean length (15.6 mm) and mean length/breadth ratio (1.42) likewise show little variation. Over 96 per cent of these artefacts are backed only from the ventral surface,

Table 20. Makwe: backed flakes

Horizon	Convex	Straight	Transverse	Concave	Total
6	1	—	—	—	1
5	53 (76%)	1 (1%)	15 (21%)	1 (1%)	70
4ii	101 (84%)	5 (4%)	13 (11%)	2 (2%)	121
4i	87 (76%)	2 (2%)	23 (20%)	2 (2%)	114
3ii	106 (74%)	9 (6%)	28 (20%)	—	143
3i	43 (70%)	3 (5%)	15 (25%)	—	61
2ii	31 (86%)	1 (2%)	9 (22%)	—	41
2i	28 (76%)	5 (13%)	4 (11%)	—	37
1	9 (100%)	—	—	—	9
	459 (77%)	26 (4%)	107 (18%)	5 (1%)	597

Table 21. Makwe: sub-classes of backed flakes

		Length (mm)		Length/Breadth		% fully backed	Mean % backed	Direction of backing				
Horizon	No.	Range	Mean	Range	Mean			a	b	c	d	e
CONVEX												
6	1	16	—	1.8	—	—	—	1	—	—	—	—
5	53	11–25	17.0±3.1	1.1–3.0	1.71±0.4	15%	70%	79%	—	2%	17%	2%
4iii	101	11–27	17.2±3.8	1.1–3.0	1.83±0.4	42%	79%	88%	1%	4%	7%	2%
4i	87	11–34	17.9±4.4	1.1–2.8	1.81±0.4	28%	74%	82%	5%	5%	8%	—
3iii	106	10–24	16.7±3.2	1.1–2.6	1.73±0.3	33%	77%	88%	1%	6%	5%	—
3ii	43	9–26	15.4±3.7	1.0–2.8	1.70±0.4	19%	70%	88%	5%	2%	5%	—
3i	31	10–33	17.5±5.7	1.2–3.0	1.91±0.5	26%	72%	90%	—	—	10%	—
2i	28	10–24	17.0±3.0	1.3–3.0	2.01±0.4	22%	71%	93%	—	—	7%	—
1	9	14–24	18.1±3.3	1.2–3.4	2.12±0.7	33%	77%	89%	—	—	11%	—
Total	459	9–34	17.1±4.4	1.0–3.0	1.80±0.3	29%	75%	86%	2%	4%	8%	0.2%
STRAIGHT												
Total	26	12–31	17.5±5.6	1.3–2.5	1.8±0.4	N/A	N/A	85%	—	4%	8%	4%
TRANSVERSE												
6	—	—	—	—	—	N/A	N/A	—	—	—	—	—
5	15	10–27	15.3±4.3	0.8–2.7	1.4±0.6	N/A	N/A	100%	—	—	—	—
4iii	13	10–37	16.9±6.9	1.0–2.4	1.7±0.4	N/A	N/A	77%	—	23%	—	—
4i	23	10–35	17.0±5.2	0.9–2.3	1.5±0.3	N/A	N/A	100%	—	—	—	—
3iii	28	8–24	14.8±4.5	0.7–2.6	1.3±0.4	N/A	N/A	100%	—	—	—	—
3i	15	10–22	16.3±3.8	0.8–1.8	1.4±0.2	N/A	N/A	100%	—	—	—	—
2ii / 2i	9 / 4	9–20	15.4±3.8	1.0–2.1	1.4±0.4	N/A	N/A	93%	7%	—	—	—
1	—											
Total	107	8–37	15.9±5.1	0.7–2.7	1.4±0.4	N/A	N/A	96%	1%	3%	—	—
CONCAVE												
Total	5	10–19	18.0	1.0–1.5	1.4	N/A	N/A	100%	—	—	—	—

Key. a. backed from ventral surface; b. backed from dorsal surface; c. backing totally bi-directional; d. backing partly bi-directional; e. backed from alternate directions.

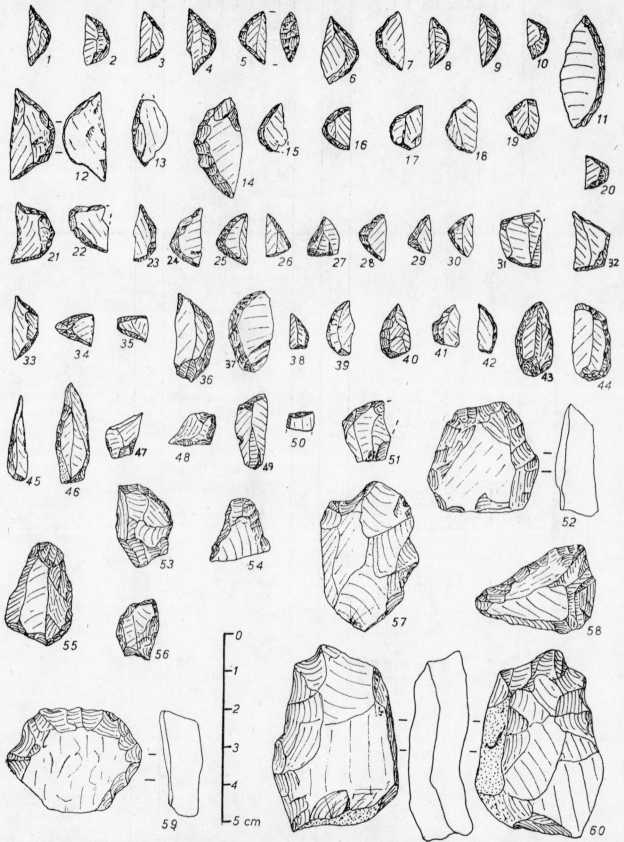

Fig. 47. *Retouched implements from horizon 2ii at Makwe: 1–15—pointed lunates; 16–21—deep lunates; 22–25—asymmetrical lunates; 26–30—triangular microliths; 31–33—trapezoidal microliths; 34, 35—petits tranchets; 36–46—convex-backed flakes; 47, 48—straight-backed flakes; 49–51—transverse-backed flakes; 52–60—scrapers.*

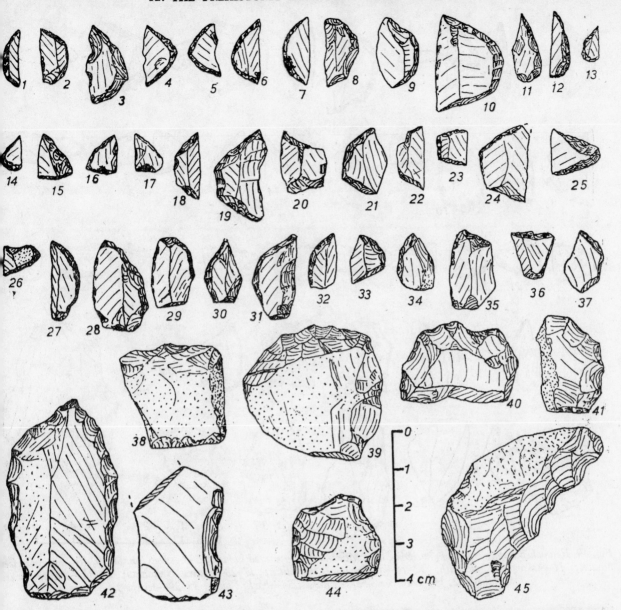

Fig. 48. Retouched implements from horizon 3i at Makwe; 1–8—pointed lunates; 9, 10—deep lunates; 11–14—asymmetrical lunates; 15–17—triangular microliths; 18–24—trapezoidal microliths; 25, 26—petits tranchets; 27–33—convex-backed flakes; 34—straight-backed flake: 35–37—transverse-backed flakes; 38–45—scrapers.

the only exceptions being a single specimen from horizon 2i which is backed from the dorsal surface and three examples from horizon 4ii which are backed bi-directionally.

Concave-backed flakes. This type, with only five examples, represents only 1.0 per cent of the Makwe backed flakes. They occur only in horizon 4i (two specimens), 4ii (two) and 5 (one). The small sample available indicates that artefacts in this class are characteristically short and relatively broad, with a mean length of 18 mm and a mean length/breadth ratio of 1.4.

Backed fragments

There are in the Makwe assemblage 220 snapped fragments of microliths. Their stratigraphical occurrence is shown in table 14.

Backed points

These total twenty-three (or 1.0 per cent of the total of retouched implements). On seven specimens the edge is backed: on sixteen it is a clean steep break. The only two retouched implements in the entire assemblage which are made of chert are both backed points from horizon 4i. Backed points are absent below horizons 3i and never represent more than 2 per cent of the retouched implements from any of the higher levels. All are backed from the ventral surface only, with the exception of two specimens from horizon 4i which are bi-directionally backed. The lengths of the backed points range from 12 to 25 mm (mean 18.5 ± 0.3), and the length/breadth ratios from 1.2 to 2.7 (mean 1.8±0.3). The sample is not sufficiently large to indicate typological change between horizons.

Backed pieces

These number fifty-one, and are most frequent in horizons 1 and 2i where they represent approximately 6 per cent of the total number of retouched implements. In subsequent horizons they never rise above 3 per cent of the implement assemblage. The lengths of

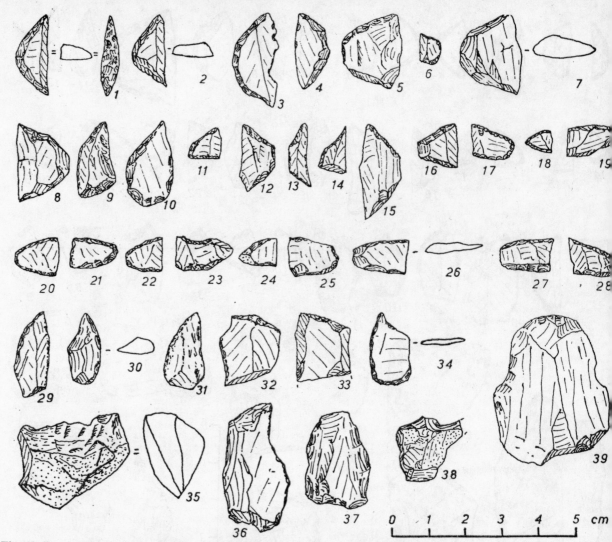

Fig. 49. Retouched implements from horizon 3ii at Makwe: 1–4—pointed lunates; 5–8—deep lunates; 9, 10—asymmetrical lunates; 11—triangular microlith; 12–16—trapezoidal microliths; 17–28—petits tranchets; 29–31—convex-backed flakes; 32, 33—transverse-backed flakes; 34—backed piece; 35–39—scrapers.

these specimens vary from 9 to 27 mm (mean 15.2± 3.5), while their length/breadth ratios are from 1.0 to 2.1 (mean 1.4±0.3).

Scrapers

This is the only category of retouched implement (with the exception of the single adze) which was formed by shallow flaking rather than by backing. In many instances it was not possible to distinguish with any certainty between intentional retouch and that which was caused by utilisation. While an attempt

was made to omit the latter from this section of the analysis, the author has probably erred in the direction of over-inclusiveness. Although the scrapers were few (sixty-seven or 3.0 per cent of all retouched implements), several types were represented. Three (4 per cent) of the scrapers are made on non-artefactual material —two on natural slabs and one on a split pebble. Eleven (18 per cent) are on shatter-chunks. The remaining 79 per cent are on flakes, of which one fourth were broken before retouch. The shapes of the scraping edges and the maximum dimensions of the scrapers are summarised in table 22.

Table 22. Makwe: scrapers from all levels

Shape of scraping edge	No.	Maximum dimension (mm)	
		Range	Mean
Convex	39 (58%)	15–53	30.6±8.8
Concave	16 (24%)	18–59	34.2±13.4
Straight	10 (15%)	21–33	30.3±4.1
Nosed	1 (1%)	25	
Denticulate	1 (1%)	28	
All scrapers	67	15–59	31.3±8.8

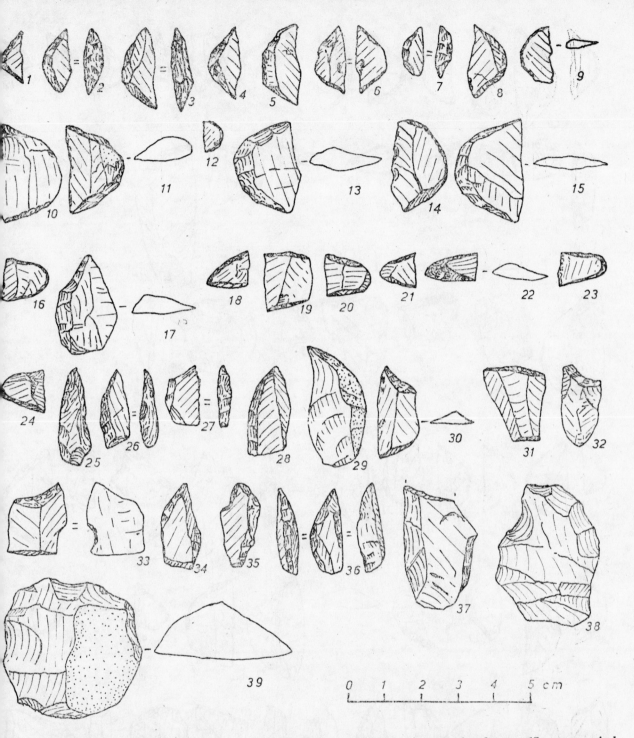

Fig. 50. Retouched implements from horizon 4i at Makwe: 1–8—pointed lunates; 9–16—deep lunates; 17—asymmetrical lunate; 18—triangular microlith; 19—trapezoidal microlith; 20–24—petits tranchets; 25–29—convex-backed flakes; 30, 31—transverse-backed flakes; 32, 33—concave-backed flakes; 34–36—backed points; 37–39—scrapers.

Scrapers represent 12 per cent of the retouched implements from horizons 1 and 2i, falling to 6 per cent in horizon 3i. In the later horizons they never rise above 3 per cent of the implement total. No significant trend in size or shape of scraping edge can be discerned through the sequence.

Adze

A single specimen from horizon 5 was made by careful bifacial flaking of a large shatter-chunk. The resultant evenly curved edge, 26 mm in length, shows signs of crushed and scaled damage presumably resulting from utilization.

Tanged flake

A single flake, 23 by 11 mm and 4 mm in maximum thickness, from horizon 4i, is worked with two opposing notches to form a neat tang at the bulbar end.

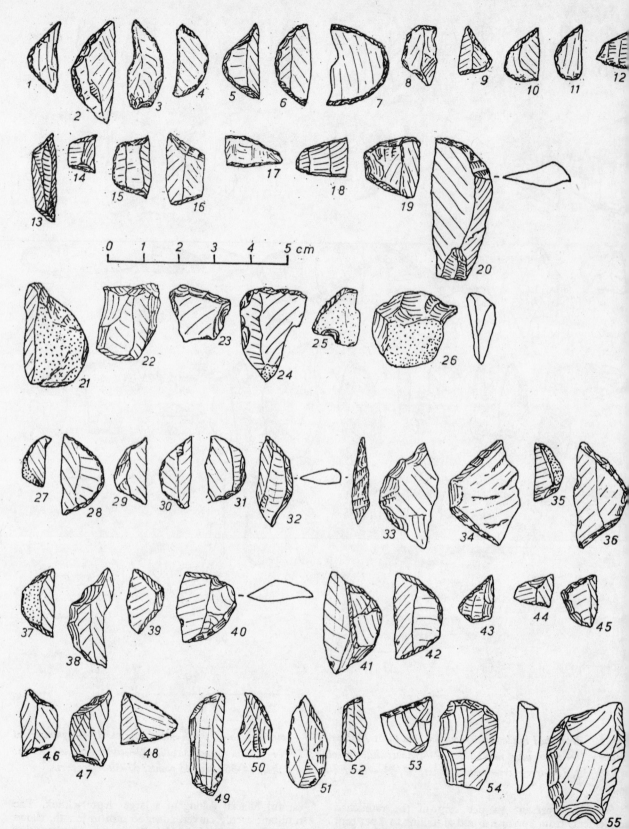

Fig. 51. *Retouched implements from horizons 4ii (1–26) and 5 (27–55) at Makwe: 1–6—pointed lunates; 7, 8—deep lunates; 9–11—asymmetrical lunates; 12—triangular microlith; 13–16—trapezoidal microliths; 17–19—petits tranchets; 20, 21—convex-backed flakes; 22—straight-backed flake; 23, 24—transverse-backed flakes; 25—backed piece; 26—scraper; 27–39—pointed lunates; 40–42—deep lunates; 43—asymmetrical lunate; 44, 45—triangular microliths; 46, 47—trapezoidal microliths; 48—petit tranchet; 49–51—convex-backed flakes; 52, 53—transverse-backed flakes; 54, 55—scrapers.*

II. GROUND STONE ARTEFACTS

All sixteen ground stone artefacts from Makwe are of a fine-grained basic igneous rock. Those which are sufficiently complete for identification comprise six axes and one pestle. Examples or fragments occur at all horizons of the site except 2ii and 6, but they are commonest in horizons 3i, 3ii and 4i. They may probably be assumed to have been in use, in small numbers, throughout the occupation of the site.

Axes

Horizon 3i yielded the broken cutting edges of two axes. One (fig. 52:2) tapers from a width of over 41 mm to a sharp curved cutting edge, only 16 mm wide, at which the faces meet at an angle of approximately 60 degrees. This axe, when complete, was probably oval with a biconvex cross-section. The second specimen, a much smaller fragment, appears to come from an almost identical axe (fig. 52:5). Two ground stone fragments from the same horizon are possibly from the butt ends of similar axes.

From horizon 3ii comes an almost complete ground stone axe. Made on a weathered slab of rock measuring 65 by 36 mm and 20 mm thick, the axe retains the rectangular cross-section of the original slab; it is not ground on the sides or on the main faces away from the cutting edge (fig. 52:3). The underside is completely flat while the upper surface has been ground down to intersect it at an angle of approximately 30 degrees. The slightly curved cutting edge was originally 34 mm wide. Multidirectional striations caused by grinding are clearly visible and, in addition, the cutting edge shows signs of heavy use. With its more acute edge angle this would have been a much more serviceable wood-working axe than those from horizon 3i.

Two broken cutting edges from the oval type of axe represented in horizon 3i were found lying next to each other in grid square C 12 of horizon 4i (fig. 52:4, 6).

One example shows very clearly that it had been pecked to the desired shape. Grinding was restricted to the region of its cutting edge, which is only partly preserved, has an angle of approximately 45 degrees, and shows battering indicative of heavy use. The edge formed by the intersection of the two ground surfaces continues from the cutting edge half way to the butt, the angle subtended by the two surfaces gradually increasing to about 80 degrees. The second example retains the whole of its slightly utilised cutting edge, which has an angle of approximately 40 degrees. Here also the ground edges continue towards the butt, subtending an increased angle. Grinding on this axe is also incomplete. The surviving fragment has a thickness of 25 mm and a maximum width of 45 mm, tapering sharply to a curved cutting edge only 27 mm wide.

Horizon 5 yielded the only complete ground stone axe found at Makwe (fig. 52:1). It appears to have been made on a flat oval pebble which required only comparatively slight modification to attain the desired shape. Both flaking and pecking were employed to produce an axe 86 mm long, 63 mm wide and 27 mm in maximum thickness. Grinding was only used in the manufacture of the cutting edge, which has a width of 48 mm, an angle of approximately 45 degrees and shows extensive damage due to heavy use. The well-defined intersection of the two surfaces extends from the cutting edge around the entire periphery of the axe, which has a biconvex cross-section. The butt shows heavy damage, most probably due to hammering with a large stone, or possibly through use of the axe-butt as a hammer. (If these artefacts were regularly used in conjunction with, or as, a stone hammer, the term 'axe' is, of course, a technical misnomer.)

Pestle

This object, from horizon 4i, is interpreted by comparison with more complete specimens from Kalem-

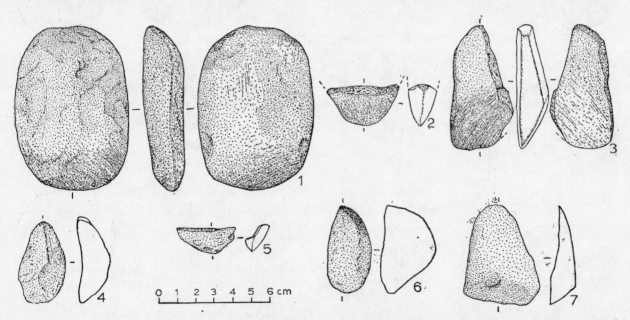

Fig. 52. Ground stone artefacts from Makwe: 1—complete axe (horizon 5); 2–6—axe fragments from horizons 3i (2, 5), 3ii (3) and 4i (4, 6); 7—pestle fragment (horizon 4i).

ba (p. 153 below). It is a flake from what appears to have been an oval or cylindrical cobble, originally approximately 80 mm in diameter and at least 50 mm in length, which had been ground flat and smooth, obliquely, at one end. There are indications that this flat surface was prepared by pecking, before grinding

(fig. 52:7).

The remaining seven ground stone artefacts from Makwe are all tiny fragments, one each from horizons 1, 2i, 4i, 4ii, 5, and two each from horizons 3i and 3ii. They call for no special comment.

III. HAMMERSTONES, ANVILS, RUBBING AND GRINDING STONES

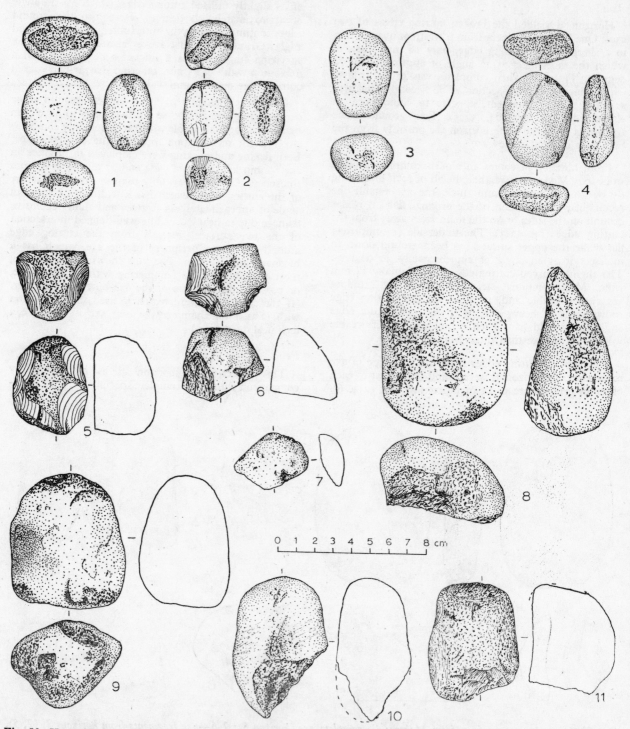

Fig. 53. Knapping hammers (1–6) and pounding stones (7–11) from Makwe: 7—from horizon 1; 10—from horizon 2ii; 4—from horizon 3i; 2—from horizon 3ii; 8, 9—from horizon 4i; 1, 3, 5, 6, 11—from horizon 5.

The stratigraphical distribution of these artefacts is shown in table 23. Several specimens which show signs of more than one type of use have been included in all the relevant categories.

Stones showing signs of hammering or bashing occurred in small numbers throughout the deposits. They may be divided into two classes on the basis of the type of damage they have sustained. Secondary features confirm this dichotomy.

Knapping hammers

This group comprises a total of eighteen specimens, (*e.g.* fig. 53:1-6), made up of ten rounded discoid river-pebbles of quartz and one of gneiss, six almost spherical quartz cores and one well-rolled quartzite core. The unbroken specimens range in maximum dimension from 33 to 55 mm, with a mean of 44 mm. Their weights range from 30 to 120 gm with a mean of 65 gm. All bear a restricted area of fine pitting (plate VII) at one or both ends, invariably on the long axis of the pebble or core. Where disc-shaped pebbles were used, the pitting may extend from the ends for some distance round the edge, even extending in some cases over half of the total circumference. Heavily weathered pebbles and those of coarse granular quartz were evidently avoided. It seems probable that the artefacts in this class were used as hammerstones in the manufacture of the chipped stone industry. No significant correlation

Table 23. Makwe: hammerstones, anvils, rubbing and grinding stones

Horizon	Knapping hammers	Pounding stones	Anvils	Rubbing stones	Grindstones Upper	Lower
6	—	—	—	—	1	—
5	6	2	—	—	5	1
4ii	1	—	—	—	—	1
4i	2	4	—	—	—	—
3ii	1	3	—	11	—	—
3i	3	1	—	1	—	—
2ii	3	2	2	1	—	—
2i	—	1	—	1	—	—
1	2	—	1	—	—	—
	18	13	3	14	6	2

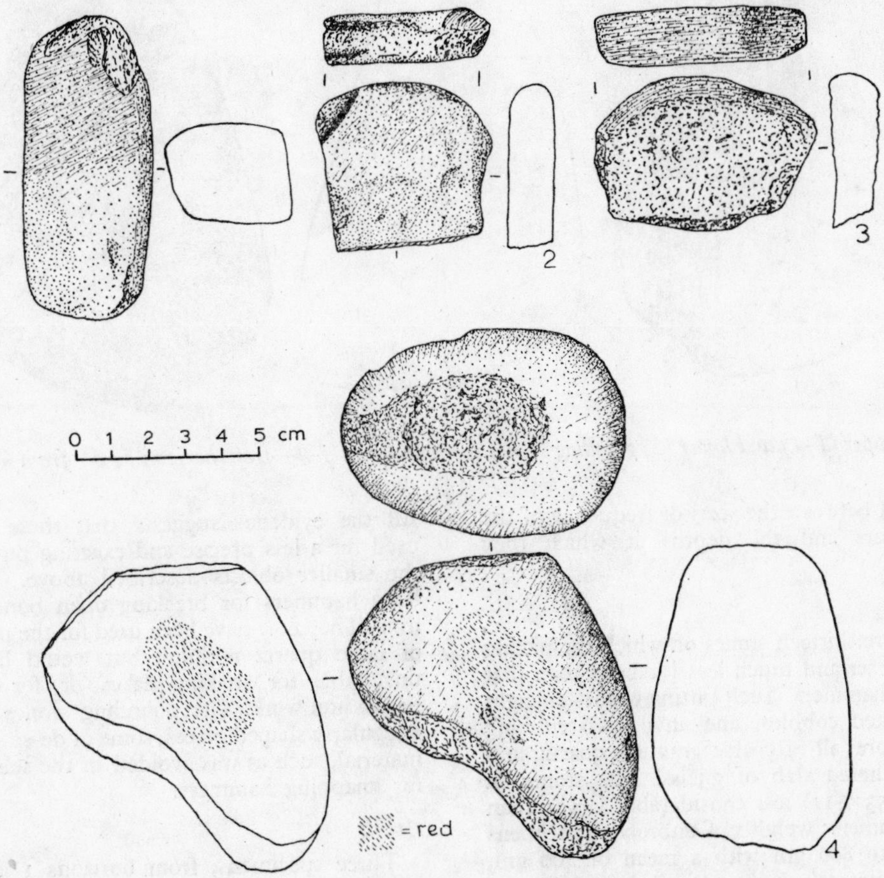

Fig. 54. Rubbing stones from Makwe, all from horizon 3ii. No. 4, which has also been used as a pounding stone, retains traces of red pigment on the rubbed surface.

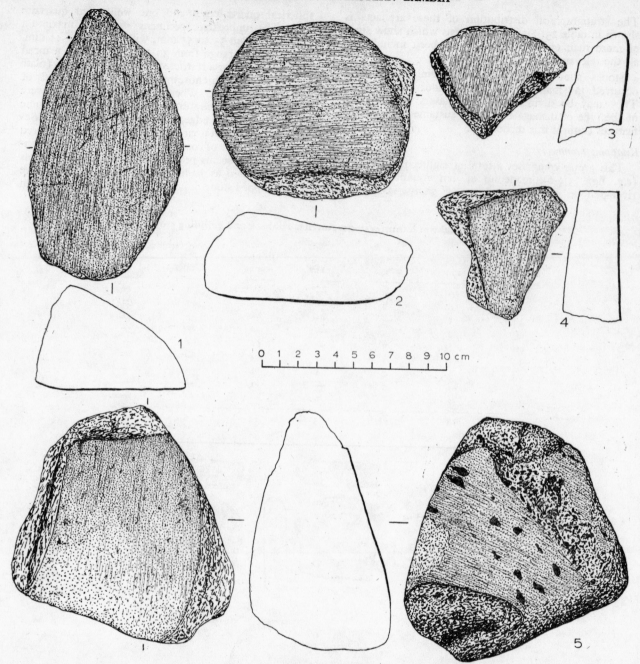

Fig. 55. *Upper (1–4) and lower (5) grinding stones from Makwe: 1–4—from horizon 5; 5—from horizon 4ii.*

may be discerned between the sizes or frequency of the knapping hammers and the depths at which they occurred.

Pounding stones

In this group are thirteen stones on which the pitting (plate VII) is coarser and much less localised than that on the knapping hammers. Such pitting occurs on eight otherwise unworked cobbles, one anvil, two rubbing stones and one core, all of coarse granular quartz, and one heavily weathered slab of gneiss. The stones in this group (fig. 53:7-11) are considerably larger than the knapping hammers: weights of unbroken specimens range from 210 to 800 gm with a mean of 400 gm, while maximum dimensions range from 69 to 140 mm with a mean of 86 mm. The sizes of the two groups of hammerstones are thus seen to be mutually exclusive.

All the evidence suggests that these pounders were used for a less precise and exacting purpose than were the smaller objects described above. They may have been hammers for breaking open bones and cracking nuts. They may have been used for the primary breaking of large quartz nodules, but would have been quite unsuitable for striking flakes or for more exacting percussion work. The pounding stones include several irregularly shaped pieces, some of de-silicified weathered material, such as was avoided in the selection of stones for knapping hammers.

Anvils

Three specimens, from horizons 1 and 2ii, show a restricted area of fine pitting in a slightly concave surface on their short axis. All are cobbles of coarse granular quartz. The single unbroken example weighs

94

470 gm and has a maximum dimension of 90 mm. These specimens are identical to the "dimpled anvils" described by J. D. Clark (1950c: 89) from 'Nachikufan' sites. It has been suggested that the characteristic scars are produced by their use as anvils for the striking of microlithic blades by the bipolar technique.

The rubbing and grinding stones also may be divided into two groups on typological and stratigraphical grounds.

Rubbing stones

The fourteen specimens in this group all come from horizons 2i to 3ii. Eleven are from horizon 3ii. They show little standardisation in size: weights range from 50 to 410 gm and maximum dimensions from 52 to 92 mm. Five examples are on exfoliated slabs of gneiss and two are on cobbles of coarse granular quartz which were subsequently used as pounders. Seven rubbing stones are on weathered pieces of dark grey quartzite: these were all found together in a small alcove of the main rock-shelter wall in horizon 3ii of grid square A 11. All but one of these bear small convex areas of smooth rubbing on the side or end but generally not, or only minimally, on the main flat surfaces (fig. 54:1-3). The exception is a rounded cobble of quartz from horizon 3ii which is rubbed smooth over the greater part of its flattest side (fig. 54:4). Remains of red pig-ment are clearly visible in the centre of the rubbed area.

Grindstones

These eight specimens are restricted to horizons 4ii, 5 and 6. They are made of flat exfoliated pieces of rock, 40 to 75 mm thick, such as are at present weathering from the upper part of Little Makwe Hill above the rock-shelter. They are ground smooth over the whole of one or both sides (fig. 55). Two fragments are from concave lower grindstones (*mphelo*), while the others are upper convex rubbers (*mwana mphelo*) of the type commonly found on Zambian Iron Age sites. One concave fragment has been re-used as a *mwana mphelo*. The complete rubbers range in weight from 650 to 1500 gm.

The rubbing stones and grindstones must clearly have served distinct functions. Their stratigraphical distributions show no overlap. The first group comprises mainly casual artefacts of a type probably used once and discarded. Their purpose is unknown—they possibly served such functions as grinding pigment, dressing hides or breaking down fibrous foodstuffs. The second group are grinders of a common Iron Age type known to have been used for grinding cereal grains. They first become frequent in horizon 5, which is also marked by the first appearance in the Makwe sequence of cultivated maize, as noted in chapter 13.

IV. BONE ARTEFACTS

Bone artefacts occurred at all levels in the Makwe deposits. Examples are illustrated in plate VII.

Bone points

These form the only group sufficiently large to allow detailed analysis. The twenty stratified examples may be divided into two main categories (table 24).

Bodkins. Represented by fourteen fragments and three complete examples, these occur in all horizons except no. 6, but are commoner in the lower horizons. The complete bodkins are 52, 72 and 74 mm in length and are bluntly pointed at both ends. The maximum diameters of all specimens range only from 3 to 6 mm. With one exception (a long splinter of bone with a triangular cross-section, ground to a point at both ends), all are very carefully worked and are ground all over. The cross-sections show a steady progression from round in the lowest horizons, through oval to subrectangular cross-sections in horizons 4i, 4ii, and 5. Representative specimens are illustrated in fig. 56:1-11.

Conical points. Three other bone points, two from horizon 4i and one from horizon 5, offer a marked contrast with the finely finished bodkins (fig. 56:12, 13). They are made from rough splinters of bone which have been trimmed and ground to a point at one end only. They are consequently much thicker than the bodkins and could have been used for heavier work. They appear only in the upper part of the sequence. The only complete specimen is 54 mm long.

Bone ring beads

These, the oldest beads recovered from Makwe, are represented by a single example each in horizons 1

Table 24. Makwe: types of bone points

Horizon	Bodkins					Conical points
	a	b	c	d	Total	
6	—	—	—	—	—	1
5	—	—	1	—	1	—
4ii	—	—	2	—	2	2
4i	—	—	1	—	1	—
3ii	—	1	—	—	1	—
3i	1	2	1	1	5	—
2ii	—	1	—	—	1	—
2i	—	4	—	—	4	—
1	1	1	—	—	2	—
	2	9	5	1	17	3

Key. a. circular cross-section; b. oval cross-section; c. subrectangular cross-section; d. triangular cross-section.

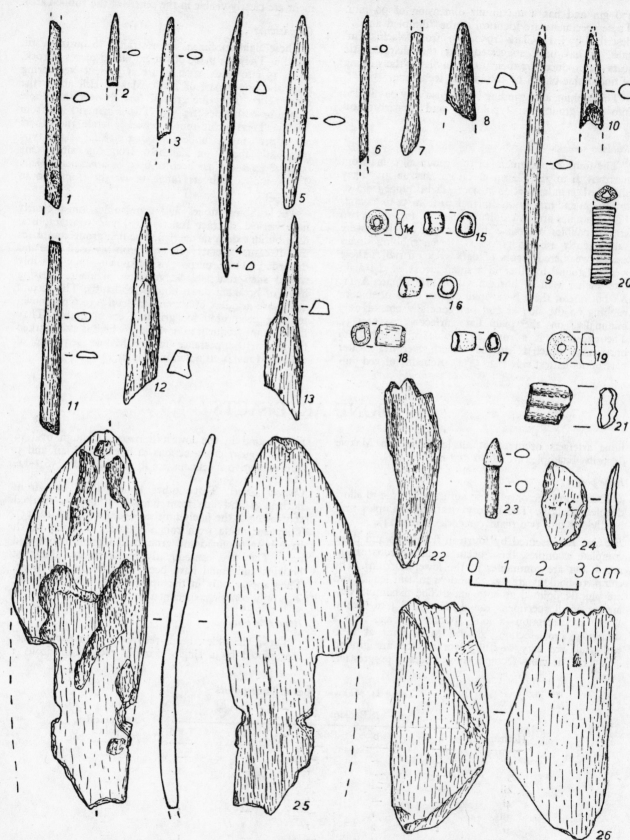

Fig. 56. Bone artefacts from Makwe: 1–11—bodkins from horizons 1 (1), 2i(2), 2ii(3), 3i(4–7), 4i(8), 4ii(9, 10) and 5(11); 12, 13—conical points from horizon 4i; 14—ring bead from horizon 1; 15–18—tube beads from horizon 3i (15–17) and the lower shelter (18); 19—tooth bead from horizon 5; 20—carved tube from horizon 3ii; 21—grooved bone from horizon 4ii; 22—notched bone from horizon 2ii; 23—peg from horizon 5; 24—crescent from horizon 5; 25—scoop from horizon 2ii; 26—possible pottery stamp from horizon 4ii.

and 2i. Both are 6.5 mm in diameter and have a central hour-glass perforation 2.5 mm in minimum diameter (fig. 56:14). The thicknesses are 2.0 mm (horizon 1) and 1.5 mm (horizon 2i). Both are very carefully finished and have been so smoothed, either during production or by wear, that the method of manufacture cannot be determined. The regular circular outline and the thickness of the walls indicate, however, that these beads are not sections of bird long-bones like the tube beads discussed below.

Bone tube beads

Eight stratified examples, from horizons 2ii (2 beads) and 3i (6 beads), are sections of bird long-bones, 5.0 to 6.5 mm in external diameter and 4.5 to 7.0 mm long. Specimens are illustrated in fig. 56:15-18. Their central perforations retain the outline of the original marrow cavity. All these examples are worn, and some are also slightly weathered; but a completely fresh example from the lower shelter clearly shows that the method of manufacture was to encircle the bone with narrow grooves so as to mark off sections of the required length. It was then snapped along the lines of the grooves. This technique has been recorded from sites in the Matopo Hills and a grooved, but unsnapped, length of four beads from Amadzimba has been illustrated by Cooke and Robinson (1954).

At Makwe, although horizons 2ii and 3i are each represented in eighteen excavation squares, in all of which bone was well preserved, all the eight stratified bone tube beads occur in three adjacent squares: A 12 (one example), B 12 (five) and B 11 (two).

?Tooth bead

Horizon 5 yielded a single disc bead, 8.0 mm in diameter and 4.0 mm in thickness, with a parallel-sided perforation (fig. 56:19). It was probably carved from a large tooth.

Bone scoop

Horizon 2ii yielded the broken end of a large flat bone scoop, probably made from the pelvis or scapula of a large bovid. The specimen is 37 mm wide and survives to a length of 99 mm with a maximum thickness of only 3.5 mm. The edges of the scoop have been carefully ground down to a gradually tapering rounded point (fig. 56:25). The slightly convex surface is the original exterior of the bone and retains parallel longitudinal striations, presumably caused by scraping with a stone tool. The other surface cuts through the inner cavities of the bone. There are slight signs of abrasion at the pointed end of the scoop.

Notched bone

A 50-mm section of metapodial of a small antelope from horizon 2ii has had two 'V'-shaped notches cut into the end producing three pointed teeth (fig. 56:22). Although the teeth are very much larger and more widely spaced than those on the possible pottery stamp (from level 4ii, see below), the two artefacts are quite similar. However, this specimen's occurrence in horizon 2ii precludes its being connected with pottery manufacture.

Carved bone tube

Probably part of a bird's long-bone, the tube (from horizon 3ii) is 6 mm in diameter and 21 mm long. It bears fine parallel grooves around its circumference, seven at one end and eight at the other, leaving an undecorated central zone 4 mm in width (fig. 56:20). An almost identical specimen comes from Kalemba (p. 155).

Grooved bone

A small fragment of bone from horizon 4ii has two parallel grooves, 3 mm wide by 1 mm deep, cut into its flat surface parallel to the long axis of the bone. The fragment (fig. 56:21), which at present measures 14 by 11 mm, has been broken since the grooves were cut.

Bone pottery stamp (?)

A 63-mm long fragment of large long-bone, from horizon 4ii, has been worked along one straight end into six small teeth 2 to 3 mm apart (fig. 56:26). It resembles tools made by Chewa and Nsenga women today from pieces of gourd and used to produce the comb-stamped decoration on pottery.

Bone crescent

This specimen, from horizon 5, is a flake of bone carefully flaked into a crescent-shaped artefact 24 by 12 mm. The straight edge bears little retouch but is very blunt (fig. 56:24). The crescent bears no signs of grinding or of use and I am unable to offer any suggestion as to its purpose.

Bone peg

Horizon 5 yielded a small neatly carved bone peg, 23 mm long, with a circular cross-section. For 15 mm the peg has a diameter of 4 mm, it then widens abruptly to 6 mm and tapers to a sharp point. The object (fig. 56:23) could have been worn as an ear or nose plug, but this is pure surmise.

V. SHELL ARTEFACTS

Shell disc beads (see plate VIIIa)

With fifty stratified examples, this is by far the commonest type of bead at Makwe. Shell disc beads first appear in horizon 3ii and are present in constantly increasing numbers in horizons 4i, 4ii and 5. They do not occur in horizon 6. On the available evidence, based as it is on small samples, it seems likely that there was little if any chronological overlap between the vogue for bone tube beads and that for shell disc beads. The appearance of the latter almost certainly preceded the arrival of Early Iron Age peoples in the Kapoche area. The beads (fig. 57:1-9) are indistinguishable from those found on many central African 'Late Stone Age' sites and also on Iron Age sites, except the most recent.

Details of the shell disc beads are presented in table 25, from which it can be seen that water snail shell and ostrich eggshell*, as materials for bead manufacture, decreased in importance as time progressed, while

---

*The ostrich does not now occur in eastern Zambia, but its former presence there is perhaps attested by a rock-painting at Zawi Hill, described in chapter 19. The evidence from Makwe suggests that its local extinction did not take place until later Iron Age times.

Table 25. Makwe: shell disc beads

Horizon:	5	4ii	4i	3i
MATERIAL				
Achatina shell	17	13	5	1
Other land snail	4	1	—	—
Water snail	—	1	2	1
Ostrich eggshell	1	2	1	1
PERFORATION				
'Hour glass'	10	11	6	3
Straight	12	6	2	1
DIAMETER				
Range (mm)	6–11	5–11	5–11	6–13
Mean (mm)	7.8	7.5	6.8	8.8
FINISH				
Smoothed at edge	21	12	4	2
Well rounded	18	10	5	1
Total beads	22	17	8	3

beads made of the shell of the *Achatina* snail (unworked fragments of which occurred in enormous numbers throughout the deposits) become increasingly frequent in the later horizons. Beads made from the very thin shell of a small, flat, spiral land snail, of which it has not proved possible to ascertain the species, first appear in horizon 4ii and are more common in horizon 5.

'Hour glass' perforations are found on all the shell disc beads from horizon 3ii, but these then steadily decrease in frequency as cylindrical perforations, perhaps made with a metal drill, become more common. The inception of the latter technique approximately coincides with that of such Iron Age artefacts as pottery.

There appears to be no significant difference in the size of the shell disc beads from the various levels, nor in the diameter of the perforation. There is, however, a steady improvement through time in the regularity of shape of these beads.

Large pierced shell discs

Three pierced discs of *Achatina* shell, from horizon 4ii (two examples) and horizon 5 (one example), range in diameter from 24 to 42 mm, and are thus clearly distinguishable from the shell disc beads. All are of somewhat irregular circular outline, with the edges ground smooth, and display considerable curvature, although the most carefully made example has been ground flat on the highest point of its convexity (fig. 57:10, 11). The single, roughly central, perforations are punched through from one side only and are crude in comparison with those on the disc beads.

Unpierced shell discs

Five unpierced shell discs (fig. 57:12, 13) may be rough-outs for beads or for larger discs such as those described above:

Horizon	Material	Diameter	Finish of edges
3i	Tortoise carapace	20 mm	trimmed
4i	*Achatina* shell	16 mm	ground
4ii	*Achatina* shell	10 mm	trimmed
4ii	*Achatina* shell	c.35 mm	ground (broken)
5	*Achatina* shell	c.22 mm	trimmed (broken)

A single 32 by 15 mm fragment of *Achatina* shell, from horizon 3i, has been ground down on two sides into a sub-triangular shape (fig. 57:14). It may be an unfinished rough-out for a pendant.

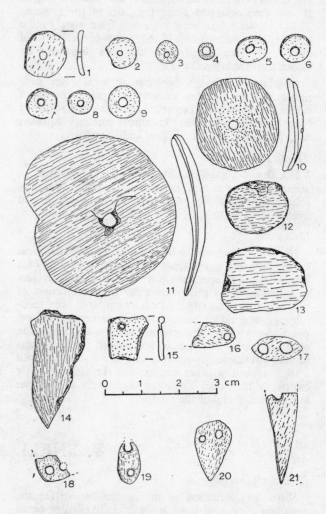

Fig. 57. *Shell artefacts from Makwe: 1–9—disc beads from horizons 4i (1, 2), 4ii (3, 4) and 5 (5–9); 10, 11—pierced discs from horizon 4ii; 12, 13—unpierced discs from horizon 4ii; 14—ground fragment from horizon 3i; 15—pierced fragment from horizon 2ii; 16–21—pendants from horizons 4i (16, 17) and 4ii (18–20) and from the lower shelter (21).*

Untrimmed pierced fragments

The site yielded six fragments of bone and shell which had been pierced, but which bore no other signs of modification.

Horizon	Material	Maximum dimension	Type of perforation
2ii	Ostrich eggshell (fig. 57:15)	14 mm	'hour glass'
3ii	*Achatina* shell	c.10 mm	'hour glass'
3ii	*Achatina* shell	c.10 mm	'hour glass'
3ii	snail shell	14 mm	punched
4ii	tortoise carapace	21 mm	'hour glass'
5	bone	32 mm	punched

Half of these specimens come from horizon 3ii, which also marks the introduction of shell disc beads. In view of their small size these fragments may be bead rough-outs.

The pierced fragment of ostrich eggshell from horizon 2ii is the oldest shell artefact from Makwe. It is the only pierced shell or bone artefact which falls outside the limited stratigraphical range of the shell disc beads.

Shell 'pendants'

The seven stratified examples of this type were restricted to horizons 4i, 4ii and 5. In view of their variety they merit individual description.

(a) Horizon 4i. A broken elongated piece of shell of water snail has neatly ground edges, parallel sides and a rounded end, near which is a neat 'hour glass' perforation. The specimen (fig. 57:16) is 7 mm wide and survives to a length of 12 mm.

(b) Horizon 4i. An extremely delicate oval of water snail shell measures 13 by 7 mm. The outer surface has become detached (or was intentionally removed) to leave a thin sheet of mother-of-pearl. Two large holes occupy most of the surface area (fig. 57:17).

(c) Horizon 4ii. A similar double-perforated oval of thick *Achatina* shell measures 11 by 6 mm. The perforations are smaller than those on specimen (b) and the artefact (fig. 57:19) is less carefully finished.

(d) Horizon 4ii. A carefully ground sub-triangular section of *Achatina* shell, 15 by 10 mm, has two perforations close together at the narrowest, slightly rounded, end (fig. 57:20).

(e) Horizon 4ii. A fragment of a similar object is made from the shell of water snail (fig. 57:18).

(f) Horizon 4ii. A large broken piece of *Achatina* shell, 43 by 32 mm, with two crudely punched holes, is probably an unfinished object.

(g) Horizon 5. A triangular piece of the outer margin of a water snail shell, 16 by 12 mm, shows slight traces of grinding and a single perforation near one corner.

(h) The lower shelter yielded a broken fragment of an elongated triangular object of water snail shell with carefully ground edges and a single perforation at the broad end. The specimen (fig. 57:21) is 8 mm in greatest surviving width and is preserved to a length of 23 mm.

It will be noted that the stratigraphical range of these 'pendants' coincides with that of the shell disc beads. The proportion of these artefacts made from shell or water snail (50 per cent) is substantially higher than the proportion of beads made from this material. Water snails would have to be brought some distance, perhaps from the Kapoche river and, being shinier and more attractive than the *Achatina* shells, they would presumably be reserved for making the more delicate and valued objects.

VI. POTTERY AND OTHER BAKED CLAY ARTEFACTS

More than three thousand potsherds were recovered from stratified contexts within the main rock-shelter. Of these, 83 per cent are undecorated body sherds whose presence is recorded in table 26, but which have been excluded from more detailed analysis. The following description is based on the 542 sherds which retain traces of decoration and/or rim areas.

Two pottery traditions are represented in the Makwe assemblage. An Early Iron Age tradition, bearing a close resemblance to the Kamnama material, is represented by forty-two sherds. The later Iron Age (Luangwa) tradition, related to that of the modern Chewa and Nsenga people, is represented by 488 sherds. Typologically, these traditions are so distinct that even small decorated sherds and rim profiles may be attributed with confidence to their correct tradition. All but twelve of the analysed sherds could be so attributed: these twelve could have belonged to either tradition. There is no evidence for the presence of any pottery tradition other than the two noted above.

The stratigraphical distribution of sherds of the two pottery traditions is shown in table 26. The peak

Table 26. Makwe: pottery summary

Horizon	Total potsherds	Undecorated body sherds	Early Iron Age	Later Iron Age	Tradition doubtful
6	407	349	—	58	—
5	1950	1612	8	321	9
4ii	697	572	24	100	1
4i	116	97	8	9	2
3ii	18	17	1	—	—
3i	10	9	1	—	—
2ii	—	—	—	—	—
2i	—	—	—	—	—
1	—	—	—	—	—
	3198	2656	42	488	12

of the Early Iron Age occurrence is in horizon 4ii, while that of the later Iron Age distribution is in horizon 5. Potsherds are completely absent from horizons 1, 2i and 2ii, are present in very small numbers in horizons 3i and 3ii, and occur in appreciable quantities only in horizon 4i and above. The potsherds in horizons 3i and 3ii all occur in areas of limited horizontal extent: the ten sherds in horizon 3i come only from two adjacent grid squares A 12 and B 13, while of the eighteen sherds from horizon 3ii, all but one come from the area of squares C 12, C 13, D 12 and D 13. It seems probable, therefore, that the presence of these few, probably Early Iron Age, potsherds in such low horizons is due to some minor disturbance or localised irregularity of the stratigraphy which was not observed during the excavation.

EARLY IRON AGE POTTERY

No typological trends or changes with depth are apparent in the small assemblage of Early Iron Age pottery. In the description which follows, the Early Iron Age pottery from Makwe is regarded as belonging to a single occurrence. The probability must, however, be borne in mind that the sherds were made and accumulated over several centuries and that more than one phase of Early Iron Age potting may therefore be represented.

The Early Iron Age pottery assemblage contains eighteen necked vessels, six pots with up-turned rims, five open bowls, and four in-turned bowls, while the remains of a further ten vessels are too fragmentary to enable the original shape to be ascertained. Rims, where preserved, are undifferentiated on six vessels, and thickened externally on sixteen, bilaterally on one and internally on one. Lip-profiles are rounded on fifteen specimens, bevelled on five, squared on four and fluted on three. The fabric is fine-textured, with crushed quartz or sherd temper, and well fired.

Type A2. (One vessel.) One open bowl with an undifferentiated squared rim bears a horizontal band of three parallel lines of upwards-pointing impressions of a triangular stamp (fig. 58:1). The impressions are closely packed and neatly applied; the whole band is delineated by lightly incised lines, apparently executed before the stamping.

Type B1. (Five vessels.) These sherds are decorated with a horizontal band of diagonal comb-stamping on an externally thickened rim band. Coarse comb-stamping (fig. 58:3, 4) is found on two necked vessels: on both the lips are rounded and the concavities of the necks are apparently undecorated. Fine comb-stamping (fig. 58:2) occurs on three pots with up-turned rims, on two of which the lip is bevelled.

B1 variant. One pot with an up-turned rim and lightly bevelled lip bears fine B1 decoration on the externally thickened rim band (fig. 58:6). Between the comb-stamping and the lip bevels is a line of single impressions of a triangular stamp. A round-lipped necked vessel (fig. 58:5) has a row of square stamp-impressions below the externally thickened B1-decorated rim band.

Type C1. (Eleven vessels.) Here, the decoration takes the form of a horizontal band of several broad parallel grooves, which appear to have been executed individually (fig. 58:7-14). Although the dimensions of all the grooves on individual sherds remain reasonably constant,

their widths vary from sherd to sherd between 2 and 6 mm, while depths range from 0.5 to 1.0 mm. On four body sherds, C1 decoration occurs in a broad band low in the concavity of the neck, starting at or just below the point of maximum constriction,* while three other sherds are too small for their position on the parent vessel to be determined. There are five grooves on each of the two sherds on which the whole width of the band is preserved, but more than six evidently occurred on other vessels. An open bowl with an undifferentiated rim is decorated with three parallel horizontal grooves immediately below its squared lip. The remaining three vessels of type C1 are in-turned bowls with two, three or four broad flutes on the lip, and horizontal grooving below. One of these sherds has a projecting boss immediately below the fluted zone.

Three quarters of the sherds bearing C1 decoration are body sherds (eight from necked vessels and six from vessels of undeterminable shape). While none of the rim sherds of types B1 and D can positively be attributed to the same vessels as the type C1 body sherds, no other types of rim sherd, decorated or undecorated, from necked vessels are present in the Makwe Early Iron Age assemblage. It thus seems likely that many of the necked vessels with B1 and D rim decorations also bore broad grooved decoration low in the concavity of the neck or on the shoulder. Decorative type C1 thus presumably does not characterise a distinct class of pottery vessel but a style of decoration which was probably generally associated on the same vessel with types B1 and D.

C1 variant. On two vessels C1 decoration is associated with criss-cross incision. One body sherd from a necked vessel (fig. 58:15) bears a horizontal band of criss-cross incision below a band of parallel horizontal grooving. A rim sherd of an in-turned bowl with squared lip is decorated immediately below the rim with two horizontal grooves, with criss-cross incision superimposed on the interstice (fig. 58:16).

Type C2. (Six vessels.) Horizontal broad grooving occurs on a further six body sherds, of which three are from concave areas of necked vessels and three from vessels of undetermined form. This group is distinguished by the presence of interruptions or curves in the grooving (fig. 58:17-20). On three vessels the whole band takes a downward, 'U'-shaped curve, while on another only the bottom groove curves downwards in a sharp 'V'. Two vessels bear whorls of parallel grooving, but there is no evidence whether these were linked to or associated with bands of horizontal grooving.

Type D1. (One vessel.) This decorative type is characterised by a horizontal band of diagonal incision. In its simple form it occurs, carelessly applied, only on the undifferentiated rim of one necked vessel with a lightly squared lip. This vessel (fig. 58:21) also shows traces of at least two horizontal broad grooves in the concavity of the neck.

D1 variant. Three necked vessels with externally thickened rims and rounded lips bear finely executed

---

*One such sherd of this type bears two impressions of the edge of a bangle of twisted metal strip. Bangles of this kind, made invariably of copper, have been recovered from several Zambian Early Iron Age sites. The impressions are very light and are probably due to a bangle worn by the potter coming into unintentional contact with the pot while the clay was still wet.

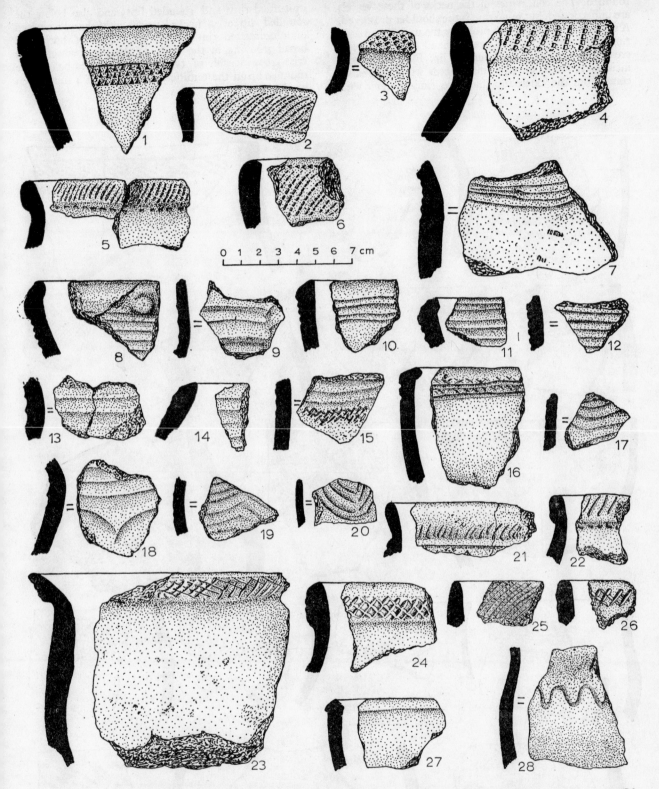

Fig. 58. *Early Iron Age pottery from Makwe: 1—type A2; 2–4—type B1; 5, 6—type B1 variants; 7–14—type C1; 15, 16—type C1 variants; 17–20—type C2; 21—type D1; 22—type D1 variant; 23–26—type D2; 27—undecorated; 28—type G.*

diagonal incision on the rim band. On two examples (*e.g.* fig. 58:22) there is a row of single triangular stamp impressions immediately below the rim band. On the third specimen a similar stamped motif occurs on the rim band above the incision.

Type D2. (Ten vessels.) Here, incision is used to produce a horizontal band of criss-cross lines (fig. 58: 23-6). Deep, widely-spaced incision occurs on the externally thickened rim bands of five necked vessels, one of which has a bevelled lip, the remainder being rounded. The concavities of the necks of these vessels are undecorated, but in no case is the shoulder preserved. A small sherd of what was probably the undifferentiated rim of an open bowl also bears a band of coarse criss-cross incision below the rounded lip. Fine criss-cross incision is found on two small sherds which probably come from the externally thickened rims of pots with

up-turned rims and rounded lips; and also below the rounded lip of a necked vessel with sharply everted undifferentiated rim. There are signs of horizontal broad grooving in the neck of the latter vessel. Fine criss-cross incision of type D2 also occurs below the rounded lip on the undifferentiated rim of a small open bowl.

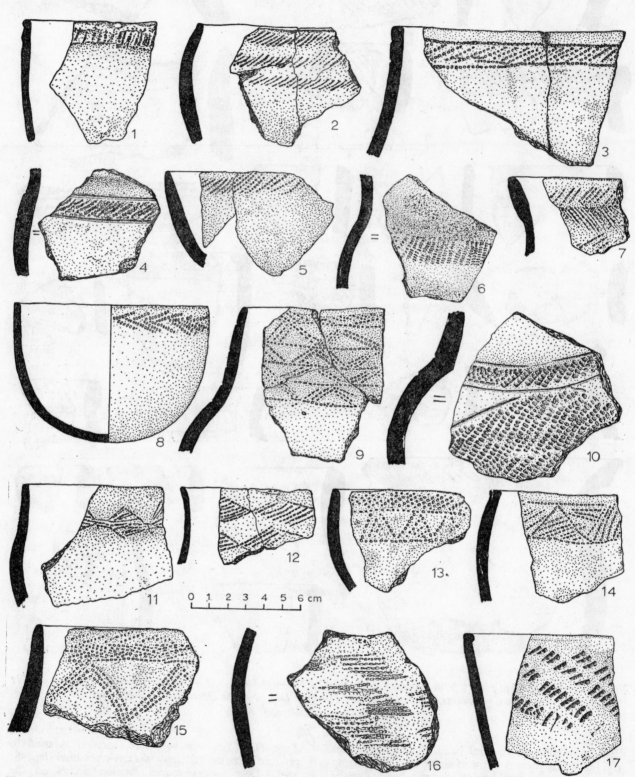

Fig. 59. Later Iron Age pottery from Makwe: 1–6—type 1c(i); 7, 8—type 1d; 9–13—type 1e(i); 14, 15—type 1e(i) variants; 16, 17—type 1g.

Type G. (One vessel.) A horizontal wavy line, evidently executed with a round-ended instrument while the clay was still very wet, occurs on the shoulder of a necked vessel (fig. 58:28), of which the rim is not preserved. A similar wiped line occurs in the concavity of the neck of the same vessel but was not continuous around the whole circumference.

Undecorated. (One vessel.) There is a single sherd of an undecorated open bowl (fig. 58:27) with a slightly bilaterally thickened rim and a bevelled lip.

LATER IRON AGE POTTERY

The Luangwa tradition pottery from Makwe is characteristically of coarser, softer fabric, less well fired and much more fragmented than that of the Early Iron Age: 69 per cent of sherds in the former group, but only 40 per cent of those in the latter, could be fitted into a square 4 by 4 cm. Since the decorative motifs of the Luangwa tradition, tending to be areal rather than banded, require a larger preserved area to be definitively recognised than do those of the Early Iron Age, and since the available sample size was reasonably large (488 sherds), all the fragments fitting into a 4 cm square were excluded from analysis. The description which follows is thus based on a sample of 153 sherds representing 135 vessels.

The shapes of 104 vessels could be determined:

Open bowls	..	..	22 per cent
Globular pots	..	..	12 per cent
Necked vessels	..	..	59 per cent
Beakers	..	..	12 per cent

Rims are almost invariably tapered. On 191 specimens (including some small sherds excluded from the main analysis), only two slightly thickened rims were noted. Lips are rounded on 59 per cent of the sample and squared on 41 per cent. Decorative techniques show little variety: 67 per cent of the vessels represented were decorated with comb-stamping, 28 per cent were undecorated. Only 4 per cent were incised; and a single sherd bore impressions of a metal bangle.

Type 1c(i). One or more horizontal bands of diagonal comb-stamping occur on two open bowls, two beakers and eight necked vessels (fig. 59:1-6). On some of these specimens the comb-stamped band is delineated by incised lines or shallow grooves.

Type 1d. An undelineated herring-bone comb-stamped band occurs on one open bowl (single band) and one necked vessel (multiple bands), as shown in fig. 59:7, 8.

Type 1e(i). Decoration with an areal design of triangular blocks of comb-stamping, sometimes associated with a horizontal band of diagonal comb-stamping, is found

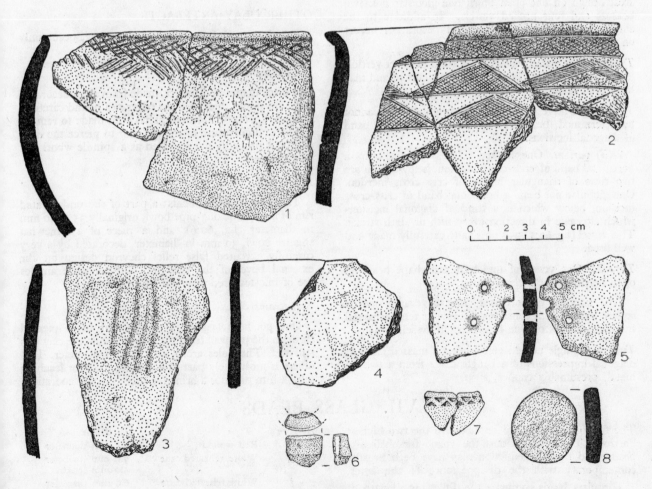

Fig. 60. Later Iron Age pottery (1–4) and other baked clay artefacts (5–8) from Makwe: 1, 2—type 2c(ii) variants; 3, 4—undecorated; 5—sherd of salt-strainer; 6, 7—bowls of smoking pipes.

**Table 27. Makwe: vessel shapes and decorative techniques
of the later Iron Age pottery**

Horizon:	6	5	4ii	4i
VESSEL SHAPE				
Open bowls	6 (33%)	16 (24%)	1 (7%)	—
Globular pots	1 (5%)	4 (6%)	3 (21%)	—
Beakers	5 (28%)	6 (9%)	1 (7%)	—
Necked vessels	6 (33%)	42 (62%)	9 (64%)	4
DECORATION				
Comb-stamped	12 (44%)	76 (74%)	16 (80%)	—
Incised	4 (15%)	1 (1%)	1 (5%)	—
Bangle-impressed	—	1 (1%)	—	—
Undecorated	11 (41%)	25 (24%)	3 (15%)	4

on five open bowls, two globular pots, one beaker and twenty-two necked vessels (fig. 59:9-13).

1e(i) variants. A band of interlocking triangular blocks of comb-stamping occurs immediately below a horizontal band of diagonal comb-stamping. Such decoration (fig. 59:14) is found only on two open bowls and one globular pot. One open bowl and two necked vessels bear comparable decoration with a bold comb-stamped chevron line below the horizontal band (fig. 59:15).

Type 1g. Widely spaced and carelessly applied multiple undelineated horizontal bands of diagonal comb-stamping (*e.g.* fig. 59:16, 17) form a broad band or areal design on one open bowl, one globular pot, two beakers and four necked vessels. In addition to the above, fragmentary comb-stamped decoration occurs on thirty vessels.

Type 2b. One necked vessel has a band of short vertical incisions on the rim. These are slightly curved and may have been done with the finger nail.

Type 2c(i). One vessel, of which the original shape cannot be determined, bears an undelineated horizontal band of diagonal incisions.

2c(ii) variant. One necked vessel (fig. 60:2) bears a horizontal band of criss-cross incision, below which are two rows of triangular blocks of criss-cross incision. One globular pot bears a horizontal band of criss-cross incision, below which is a band of diagonal incisions which alternate in direction every fifth or sixth stroke. This vessel (fig. 60:1) was unusually carefully made and well fired.

Type 2d. One vessel of undetermined shape bears an open herring-bone incised design.

2e(i) variant. A horizontal row of evenly spaced square blocks, each consisting of nine or ten horizontal incisions, occurs on one large necked vessel.

Type 3. A single necked vessel bears a massed band of diagonal impressions of a bangle made from a twisted metal, presumably copper, strip.

Undecorated. Undecorated vessels (fig. 60:3, 4) comprise eleven open bowls, two globular pots, seven beakers and twenty necked vessels.

An attempt was made to evaluate the extent of chronological change which took place within the later Iron Age pottery (table 27). The relative frequency of the four main vessel shapes shows considerable variation, with open bowls and beakers becoming progressively commoner through time, at the expense of the globular pots and necked vessels. Among the decorative types comb-stamping becomes less frequent, while the occurrence of incised and undecorated vessels shows a corresponding increase.

OTHER CLAY ARTEFACTS

Baked clay artefacts, other than pottery, occur only in horizon 5.

Ground sherd disc

A disc, 37 mm in diameter, made from an undecorated potsherd 9 mm thick, has the edges neatly and carefully ground (fig. 60:8). No attempt has been made to remove the natural curvature of the pot, nor to pierce the disc, so it was probably not intended as a spindle whorl but as a stopper.

Pipe bowls

There are two fragments: a part of the undecorated rim of a clay smoking-pipe bowl, originally 35 to 40 mm in diameter (fig. 60:6), and a piece of a somewhat smaller bowl, 30 mm in diameter, decorated by a very carefully executed false relief chevron design on the external bevel of the rim (fig. 60:7). Both examples are of fine-textured clay and well fired.

Salt strainer

One potsherd (fig. 60:5) shows four holes pierced through the pot wall from the outside while the clay was still wet. The holes are 3 to 4 mm in diameter. This object is most likely part of a strainer used for leaching salty ash to produce a brine for subsequent evaporation.

VII. GLASS BEADS

The four glass beads are restricted to the two highest horizons. They thus outlast the vogue for shell disc beads; and their introduction may have been broadly contemporary with the disappearance of the latter.

The glass beads comprise the following (length is measured parallel to the perforation and diameter at right-angles to it):

Horizon	Type	Dimensions
5	Red wound	3.5 mm diameter
5	White reheated cane	7.0 mm diameter 5.0 mm length
5	White reheated cane	6.0 mm diameter 5.5 mm length
6	Red barrel	10.0 mm diameter 11.0 mm length

VIII. METAL

ORE

Small fragments of haematite occurred throughout the deposits except in horizon 6. None shows signs of artificial fracture or other modification such as crushing or grinding for the production of pigment. They were possibly collected and brought to the site as curiosities because of their unusual weight and lustre. It is noteworthy that these fragments of ore become noticeably rarer in horizon 5 and disappear completely in horizon 6, coinciding with the time when metal artefacts were becoming common and the useless metallic objects would consequently be losing their novelty.

SLAG

A single fragment of iron slag was found in horizon 5. This, and the complete absence of tuyere fragments, suggest that while iron was presumably not smelted and worked at the Makwe rock-shelter, it probably was smelted in the immediate area. This was confirmed by the discovery of two iron-smelting furnaces at Kondwelani School, 3.5 km north of Makwe (fig. 35, p. 67), where there is also an opencast quarry for iron ore which was worked until early in this century (D. W. Phillipson, 1968b). The same geological formation could have been the source of the ore fragments described in the previous paragraph.

METAL ARTEFACTS

Metal artefacts occurred only in horizons 4ii, 5 and 6. Iron, as noted above, was worked in the vicinity of the site: copper does not occur locally and must have been traded from some distance.

Horizon 4ii

This horizon yielded two broken fragments of iron rods: one 6.0 by 4.5 mm rectangular cross-section and 62 mm long; the other 5.5 by 5.0 mm and 43 mm long. They may be the tangs of arrowheads. A third piece of iron from horizon 4ii is so corroded as to be completely uninformative.

Horizon 5

Lead ball: this is roughly spherical, 14 mm in average diameter (fig. 61:10). It may be of European or Arab origin and is conceivably a bullet.

Copper razor: the cutting edge is broken away and only the tang and adjoining section of the blade remain (fig. 61:9). At the break are signs of repeated hammering with a sharp object; and the razor appears to have been intentionally broken by bending in a single direction. Carefully made, the elongated tapering tang is a regular 2.0 mm in thickness and survives to a length of 51 mm.

Iron hooks: the two examples are heavily corroded and apparently broken. They are made of rod 5.5 mm in diameter bent to enclose an aperture 10 mm across. Their function is unknown.

Iron triangular arrowhead: this (fig. 61:3) is almost complete and has a total length of 103 mm. The flat tip forms an approximately equilateral triangle of side 18 mm; and the tang is rectangular, 5 by 4 mm in cross-section.

Iron hoe-blade: a fragment, only 42 by 27 mm, retains part of a very worn working edge.

Iron rod: a 33 mm broken length comes from a rectangular cross-sectioned rod identical to that which forms the tang of the arrowhead described above.

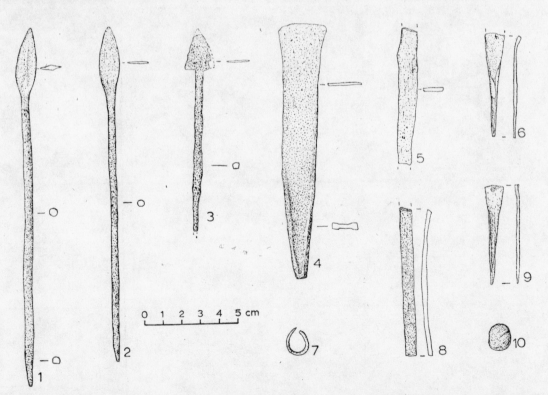

Fig. 61. Metal artefacts from Makwe: 1–3—arrowheads from horizons 5 (3) and 6 (1, 2); 4—axe from horizon 6; 5—copper strip from horizon 6; 6, 9—broken copper razors from horizons 5 (9) and 6 (6); 7—copper ring from horizon 6; 8—iron strip from horizon 5; 10—lead ball from horizon 5.

Iron strip: 7 by 2 mm in cross-section, this survives to a length of 78 mm (fig. 61:8). It is very slightly curved throughout its length, and may be a key from a thumb-piano.

Horizon 6

Copper razor: this is identical in all respects to the razor from horizon 5, described above, and has been hammered and broken in the same way in the same place (fig. 61:6).

Copper ring: this is a length of 1.0 mm thick copper wire bent into a complete circle 12.5 mm in diameter (fig. 61:7).

Copper strip: a 71 mm length of strip measures 10 by 1.5 mm in cross-section (fig. 61:5). Its purpose is unknown.

Iron leaf-shaped arrowheads: the two examples (fig. 61:1, 2) are complete and almost identical, 188 and 177 mm in length. The tips are the shape of laurel leaves 32 mm by 10 mm in maximum width, with a faint central rib. The long straight tangs are circular in cross-section, 4.5 mm in diameter.

Iron axe-blade: this appears to have been made from a 134 mm length of machine-made rectangular iron strip 19 by 3.5 mm in cross-section (fig. 61:4). The tang has been narrowed by hammering on the side of the strip, producing a pronounced flange; and hammering has also been used to achieve a splayed cutting edge 26 mm in width.

Iron buckle and bicycle nut: both are clearly of machine manufacture and twentieth-century date.

IX. CLOTH, ROPE AND WOODEN ARTEFACTS

Cloth and Rope

Horizon 6 yielded a knotted section of sisal rope and a tiny fragment of woven cloth which, although poorly preserved, appears to be of machine manufacture. These finds are probably to be connected with the use of the rock-shelter for the preparation of *Nyau* masks, as is discussed further in chapter 19.

Wooden yoke

A length of wood, found in horizon 6, has two 'V'-shaped notches cut into one edge and is clearly part of a yoke for draft oxen, of a type still made and used in the immediate area of the site in 1966.

Charcoal crayons

Six charred sticks, five from horizon 5 and one from horizon 6, 23 to 55 mm long, have fairly pointed ends on which they are rubbed and abraded. They appear to have been used as crayons and they may have been employed for the drawings of *Nyau* characters which are present on the walls of the rock-shelter (see chapter 19) or for colouring work in the construction of masks.

Makwe: Specialist Reports

I. FLORAL REMAINS

(*Identifications by* Dewan Mohinder Nath Nair *and the* Royal Botanical Gardens, Kew)

Four heavily mineralised fragments of twig (plate VIIIb) were recovered from horizon 1 in grid squares C 12 and C 13 and from horizon 2i in grid square C 12. The Director of the Royal Botanical Gardens reports that a detailed identification of these is not possible.

With the exception of the above specimens, floral remains were preserved only in horizons 3ii, 4ii, 5 and 6. The following species were identified.

WILD SPECIES

Parinari curatellifolia Planch ex Benth. A single fragment of the shell of this nut was the only floral specimen recovered from horizon 3ii. Twenty-five further fragments of nut shell and one complete nut came from horizon 5, and one nut shell from horizon 6. Most of the specimens are charred. This species is still widely eaten in Zambia, the fleshy mesocarp as well as the nut being edible. In English the species is sometimes referred to as the cork tree or monola plum tree; but it is more generally known by its Zambian names, *e.g. mupundu* (ChiBemba), *mbula* (ChiNyanja) or *murula* (ChiTonga and SiLozi).

Citrullus colocynthis Schrad. This is represented by two seeds from horizon 4ii. Known in English as bitter apple, the vine is native to Africa and Asia and is a source of a powerful purgative—the colocynth.

Lagenaria siceraria (Molina) Standley. (Syn. *Lagenaria vulgaris* sw.). A fragment of the woody outer pericarp was found in horizon 5. Known in English as the gourd calabash, bottle gourd or calabash cucumber, this cucurbit is widely used in Africa as a container for liquids.

Strychnos cocculoides Baker. A fragment of the hard fruit coat comes from an unstratified context in the lower shelter. This, the wild orange or kaffir orange, is edible but unpalatable.

CULTIVATED SPECIES

Zea mays L. Pieces of maize cob, mostly slightly charred, come from horizons 5 (eight examples) and 6 (seven examples). The measurable examples from horizon 5 are 11, 11, 13, 13, 15, 16 and 23 mm in maximum diameter. Those from horizon 6 (which in fact all come from the surface and are probably very recent) all measure 24 or 25 mm. It seems likely that two varieties are represented, remains of the older and smaller variety being found only in horizon 5, associated with one example of the larger and more recent variety which is the only type found in horizon 6.

Cucurbita maxima Duchesne. A seed of this species, the pumpkin or hubbard squash, comes from horizon 6. The species is grown in the Makwe area today.

II. VERTEBRATE MACROFAUNA

by Brian M. Fagan

About eighty thousand bone fragments were found in the various levels at Makwe. Identifiable postcranial pieces numbered under two thousand and a total of 951 teeth, mandibular, and maxillary fragments were finally submitted to us for analysis in Santa Barbara.* Only 317 pieces in the California collection could be positively identified.

IDENTIFICATIONS

The following animals are present in the collection. Details of horizon association appear in table 28.

DOMESTIC ANIMALS	
Cattle (*Bos taurus*)	Teeth and mandibles
Goat (*Capra hircus*)	Teeth, mandibles, maxillae
? Dog (*Canis familiaris*)	Maxilla
WILD ANIMALS	
BOVIDAE	
Duiker (*Sylvicapra grimmia*)	Mandibles, maxillae, teeth
Klipspringer (*Oreotragus oreotragus*)	Mandibles, teeth
Kudu (*Tragelaphus strepsiceros*)	Mandible, teeth
Wildebeest (*Connochaetes taurinus*)	Teeth
Impala (*Aepyceros melampus*)	Teeth
Buffalo (*Syncerus caffer*)	Teeth
Reedbuck (*Redunca arundinum*)	Teeth
?Eland (*Taurotragus oryx*)	Teeth
?Haartebeest (*Alcelaphus lichtensteini*)	Teeth
EQUIDAE	
Zebra (*Equus burchelli*)	Mandible, teeth

---

*Mr Michael Bisson, Miss Leah Ristau, and my wife kindly assisted with the analysis of the Makwe bones. (B.M.F.)

Table 28. Makwe: stratigraphical distribution of vertebrate macrofauna.*
The table enumerates identified specimens, not individuals

Horizon:	6	5	4ii	4i	3ii	3i	2	1	Total
DOMESTIC									
Cattle	1	35	10	2	—	—	—	—	48
Goat	—	2	2	—	—	—	—	—	4
Dog	—	—	1?	—	—	—	—	—	1?
WILD									
Duiker	2	2	2	6	1	6	5	1	25
Klipspringer	—	—	1	1	5	2	—	—	9
Kudu	2	3	—	2	—	1	—	—	8
Wildebeest	—	—	2	3	—	—	2	—	7
Impala	—	2	—	—	—	1	3	1	7
Buffalo	—	—	—	—	—	3	2	2	7
Reedbuck	—	—	2	1	—	—	—	—	3
Eland	—	—	—	—	—	—	1?	—	1?
Haartebeest	—	—	—	—	—	—	1?	—	1?
Zebra	—	7	1	4	10	2	1	1	26
Wart-hog	4	25	17	5	3	8	25	1	88
Bush-pig	2	8	2	4	1	3	—	—	20
Lion	—	—	—	—	—	1	—	—	1
Vervet monkey	—	—	—	1	—	—	—	—	1
Porcupine	1	11	6	3	7	1	2	—	31
Monitor lizard	—	10	4	4	8	1	—	—	27
Bird (?francolin)	—	—	—	—	—	—	1	—	1
	12	105	50	36	35	29	43	6	316

*The mammalian macrofauna was submitted to Dr Fagan at an early stage in the analysis of the Makwe material, before it had been decided to separate the assemblages from horizon 2i and 2ii. Dr Fagan's report therefore treats these horizons as a single stratigraphical unit. (D.W.P.)

SUIDAE
Wart-hog (*Phacochoerus aetheopicus*) — Mandibles, maxillae, teeth
Bush-pig (*Potamochoerus porcus*) — Mandibles, maxillae, teeth

FELIDAE
Lion (*Panthera leo*) — Tooth

CERCOPITHECINAE
Vervet monkey (*Cercoithecus* sp.) — Mandible

HYSTRICIDAE
Porcupine (*Hystrix* sp.) — Teeth, mandibles, maxillae

Only one bird fragment, that of a limb bone of a francolin (?) came from horizon 2; monitor lizard fragments were found in horizons 3i to 5.

This faunal list calls for little special comment; the wild fauna is typical of a savannah woodland environment, with a combination of both browsing and grazing animals being taken by the inhabitants. With two exceptions, the species represented are frequently encountered in the Makwe area today: wildebeest and impala are not recorded from the southern Eastern Province plateau, although both occur in the Luangwa valley and on the plateau further north (Ansell, 1960: 67, 70).

Domestic animals first occur in horizon 4i, where a fragmentary adult ox mandible occurs in grid square D 13 and a single, lower second molar in grid square D 12.† Cattle are relatively abundant in horizons 4ii and 5, while the first goat remains occur in horizon 4ii. An adult goat mandibular fragment and a lower third molar are present in grid squares A 12 and B 10 respectively. A single maxilla fragment from horizon 4ii in grid square D 11 may be that of a domestic dog, or conceivably a jackal. Unfortunately, the domestic animal bones are too fragmentary for detailed metrical analysis.

The wild animal fragments are dominated by the bones of wart-hog, zebra, duiker, and bush-pig; while a wide range of medium sized antelope were also taken upon occasion. Buffalo occurs only in horizons 1, 2 and 3i. Samples are too small for any significant trends in hunting practices to be discernible. Wart-hog seems, however, to have been a prominent source of food through the occupation. A similar emphasis on zebra and wart-hog was found at the third millennium bc site of Gwisho B, in southern Zambia, where the latter was the second most commonly hunted animal (Fagan and van Noten, 1971: 53-71). Broom (1942: 197-8) also listed wart-hog as the principal component of the 'Wilton' fauna at Mumbwa Cave, to the north of Gwisho. The !Kung of the Dobe area, Botswana, regularly hunt wart-hog, and regard it as a primary meat source today (Lee, 1966: 116). Bush-pigs at Makwe are less common than wart-hogs, as is the case at Gwisho (Fagan and van Noten, 1971). Medium-sized antelope were dominant among the bovidae at Gwisho, in contrast to Iron Age sites in southern Zambia where smaller buck were the favourite prey (Fagan, 1967: 70-78; Fagan and Phillipson, 1965: 265-265). The same pattern may occur in the successive horizons at Makwe, but the evidence is inadequate for positive conclusions.

---

†Numerous authorities have emphasized the difficulties in distinguishing isolated buffalo and cattle teeth from each other. This distinction is hard to make at Makwe where samples are small, and measurements unreliable. The mandible in gridsquare D 13, horizon 4i is, however, certainly that of a domestic ox. (B.M.F.)

Table 29. Makwe: ages at death of mammalian macrofauna

		Old	Adult	Adolescent	Immature	Totals
Cattle	Maxillae	—	2	1	—	3
	Mandibles	1	3	1	—	5
Goat	Mandibles	—	1	1	—	2
Wart-hog	Maxillae	—	2	1	1	4
	Mandibles	—	3	—	2	5
Bush-pig	Maxillae	—	2	—	2	4
	Mandibles	—	2	1	—	3
Duiker	Maxillae	—	3	—	—	3
	Mandibles	—	—	3	1	4
Zebra	Mandible	—	1	—	—	1
Klipspringer	Maxillae	—	2	—	—	2
	Mandible	—	1	—	—	1
Wildebeest	Mandibles	—	2	—	—	2
Impala	Mandible	—	1	—	—	1
Reedbuck	Maxilla	1	—	—	—	1
Buffalo	Maxilla	—	1	—	—	1
Total	(Domestic)	1	6	3	—	10
	(Wild)	1	20	5	6	32

BUTCHERY AND KILLING

No body-part analysis was undertaken, and conclusions on butchery techniques are consequently impossible. The few more-or-less complete jaws and maxillae from Makwe were categorized as old, adult, adolescent, or immature according to the criteria established by the author some years ago (Fagan, 1967: 76). The results of this analysis are given in table 29. Only one of the thirty-two wild animals included was an old individual; most were either young adults, or nearing adulthood, as if they had been killed in their prime. The Suidae are remarkable for the number of immature specimens relative to adults. These figures might be due to the presence of wart-hog or bush pig litters near the rock-shelter, as pigs are normally hunted or trapped near their burrows. Selective hunting appears to have favoured young adult individuals. The domestic animal figures are insufficient for detailed analysis.

DISCUSSION

The Makwe animal bone collection shows few remarkable features. The pre-Iron Age levels, with their preponderance of wart-hog, zebra, and duiker, show hunting preferences which are duplicated at Gwisho B, and possibly Mumbwa. Domestic animals first appear in the Iron Age horizons and, if date GX-1551 is dependable, may have been present at Makwe by as early as the third century ad—a not impossible date in view of the early date for domesticated small stock from Mabveni in Rhodesia (Robinson, 1961; Fagan, 1966: 503), and the domestic animal bones from the basal layer of Kalundu Mound (Fagan, 1967: 65-70, 218). The Makwe fauna suggests that domestic animals probably arrived in parts of eastern Zambia early in the Iron Age.

III. CUT AND SMASHED BONE

(D.W.P.)

A careful examination of all the bone fragments from Makwe produced only twenty-eight which showed tool marks apparently resulting from butchery. Several specimens show deep, straight, clean cuts which appear to be the work of metal tools; but on nearly half of the pieces studied either stone or metal implements could have been responsible. With the exception of single examples from horizons 2 and 3i, all the specimens come from levels containing pottery and consequently date from periods during which there is reason to believe metal tools may have been available. The marks on the two oldest examples are slight and could easily have been done with stone tools.

The exceedingly shattered nature of the vast majority of the bone from Makwe and the scarcity of tool marks shows that bones were generally shattered, presumably for the extraction of marrow, by simple percussion.

IV. MICROFAUNA

(*Identifications by* D. H. S. Davis)

The microfauna is represented by 989 specimens, representing 3.2 per cent of the total bone assemblage in horizon 5, 1.8 per cent in horizon 4ii, and less than 1.0 per cent in all lower horizons.

The skull and mandible remains have been examined by Dr D. H. S. Davis, formerly of the South African Medical Research Unit, who has drawn up table 30. This shows the occurrence of the various species in each horizon, and is based upon the approximate number of individuals represented, rather than on actual numbers of specimens.

Table 30. Makwe: stratigraphical distribution of identified microfauna

	Approximate minimum number per horizon							Totals
	5	4ii	4i	3ii	3i	2	1	
INSECTIVORA								
Macroscelididae								
Elephantulus (Nasilio) brachyrhynchus (Short-nosed Elephant Shrew)	—	1	1	—	1	—	—	3
Soricidae (shrews)								
Suncus varillus	—	—	—	—	—	—	—	
Crocidura hirta	—	—	—	1	—	—	—	1
C. cf. *luna*	5	7	2	—	—	—	—	14
C. cf. *bicolor*	4	—	1	—	—	—	—	5
CHIROPTERA								
Molossidae								
Tadarida (?) (Free tailed Bat)	1	—	—	—	—	—	—	1
PRIMATES								
Galagidae								
Galago senegalensis (Bushbaby)	—	2	2	—	—	—	—	4
CARNIVORA								
Viverridae								
Herpestes sanguineus (Slender mongoose)	1	—	—	—	—	—	—	1
HYRACOIDEA								
Procaviidae								
Heterohyrax brucei (Yellow-spotted Dassie)	—	—	1	—	—	—	—	1
RODENTIA								
Bathyergidae								
Cryptomys cf. *lugardi* (Mole Rat)	5	6	2	3	3	4	7	30
Thryonomyidae								
Thryonomys swinderianus (Cane Rat)	3	—	—	—	—	2	—	5
Sciuridae								
Paraxerus cepapi (Bush Squirrel)	—	—	1	2	—	—	—	3
Muscardinidae								
Graphiurus murinus (Dormouse)	1	3	—	—	—	—	—	4
Muridae-Murinae								
Thamnomys (Grammomys) dolichurus (Thicket Rat)	1	1	—	—	—	—	—	2
Aethomys kaiseri walambae (Kaiser's Bush Rat)	3	2	—	1	—	—	—	6
A. chrysophilus (African Bush Rat)	1	5	1	—	—	—	—	7
Thallomys paedulcus (Tree Rat)	1	2	1	—	—	—	—	4
Dasymys incomtus (Swamp Rat)	7	8	2	1	—	—	—	18
Pelomys fallax (Creek Rat)	1	2	1	1	—	—	—	5
Lemniscomys griselda (Single-striped Mouse)	1	1	—	—	—	—	—	2
Praomys (Mastomys) natalensis (Multimammate Mouse)	11	17	5	2	—	—	—	35
Saccostomus campestris (Pouched Mouse)	2	—	—	—	—	—	—	2
Cricetidae-Dendromurinae								
Dendromus cf. *mystacalis* (Lesser Climbing Mouse)	1	2	1	—	—	—	—	4
Cricetidae-Gerbillinae								
Tatera valida (Savanna Gerbil)	5	4	3	3	—	—	—	15
T. leucogaster (Bushveld Gerbil)	1	2	—	—	—	3	—	6
	55	66	24	14	4	9	7	179

Dr Davis comments on the data presented in table 30 (*in litt.*, 21st August 1972) as follows:

"Mole rats (*Cryptomys*) were the only species to be found in all horizons, but they could perhaps have dug down from outside the shelter at any time. The Murinae are represented by the assemblage of species one would expect to find in grassy open woodland with old termite hills and dampish patches of coarse vegetation: there is nothing remarkable about the species-composition or frequency of this occurrence. The multimammate mouse (*Praomys natalensis*) is most common and this is to be expected as it is semi-commensal and might invade a shelter more frequently than other species. Otherwise the bones of rats, mice and gerbils are what one would expect to be derived from owl pellets or from hunting. The elephant shrew (*Elephantulus brachyrhynchus*) lives in rocky places, but the ordinary shrews occur in grass. One thing does strike me and that is that there were only five pieces (in horizons 2 and 5) of the teeth of cane rat (*Thryonomys*) which is today a prized item of diet."*

The list contains three species not recorded by Ansell (1960:3, 6, 108) from south-eastern Zambia. *Suncus varillus* is not recorded from Zambia: *S. Lixus* does occur, but has not been reported from the eastern regions. *Crocidura luna* is not known in the Eastern Province south of the Nyika Plateau of northern Lundazi District. *Tatera valida* is "believed absent" by Ansell (*op. cit.*: 108) from the Luangwa Valley and Eastern Province plateau.

---

*Thryonomys occurs frequently around Makwe at the present time. (D.W.P.)

V. FISH

(*Identifications by* G. Bell-Cross)

Fish-bones were rarely preserved in the Makwe deposits, never exceeding 0.11 per cent of the bone fragments from any horizon, and being absent from horizons 6, 2i and 1.

All fish bones from Makwe may be attributed to a species of *Clarias*, probably *C. gariepinus* (catfish or barbel).

Fifty-nine specimens were identified, comprising twelve vertebrae, eleven pectoral spines, two pelvic spines and thirty-four neurocranium fragments. All but one appear to come from fish in the 500 to 1000 gm size-range. The exception is a 4-kg individual represented in horizon 5.

VI. MOLLUSCS

(D.W.P.)

Shell fragments, mostly comminuted, were extremely numerous throughout the deposits, except in horizon 1 where only occasional tiny pieces were recovered. It has unfortunately not proved possible to obtain a specialist report on this material. My own examination indicates that the great majority of specimens are of the giant land snail *Achatina*, with a few other land snails and freshwater molluscs also represented in small numbers.

VII. HUMAN REMAINS

(D.W.P.)

These comprise one incisor tooth from horizon 2ii, two molars and one fragment of radius from horizon 4i, and one molar from horizon 4ii. No specialist report is available. Unlike the other Eastern Province rock-shelter sites investigated, Makwe, rock-shelter appears not to have been used for the burial of the dead. The resence of the radius fragment is, however, difficult to explain.

VIII. PRINCIPAL COMPONENTS ANALYSIS OF THE MAKWE CHIPPED STONE INDUSTRY

by Ian Hodder

The methodology of principal components analysis in an archaeological context has been described and evaluated by Doran and Hodson (1975: 190-7). This method of analysis identifies a series of axes (eigenvectors or principal components) which each account for a stated proportion of the total variance in the data. The first axis accounts for most variance. Each axis represents some combination of the variables, and the part played by each variable on each axis can be assessed. Because we can determine which axes account for most of the variance in the data, we learn something about the variables themselves. Also, since we can convert each original observation (*i.e.* from each horizon) to what is called a *score*, and project it onto the principal axes, we can produce a scatter diagram which shows the relationship between the data pertaining to each horizon in terms of the two or three principal axes.

Twelve variables were considered in this analysis of data relating to the Makwe chipped stone industry, with regard to each of the eight horizons:

  (i) Shatter chunks as a percentage of all chipped stone artefacts
 (ii) Radial cores as a percentage of total cores
(iii) Retouched implements as a percentage of all chipped stone artefacts
 (iv) Geometrics as a percentage of all retouched implements
  (v) Backed points as a percentage of all retouched implements
 (vi) *Petits tranchets* as a percentage of all retouched implements
(vii) Mean flake length
(viii) Eared geometrics as a percentage of all geometrics
 (ix) Mean length of pointed lunates
  (x) Mean length/breadth ratio of pointed lunates
 (xi) Mean length of triangular microliths
(xii) Mean length/breadth ratio of convex-backed flakes.

Analyses were carried out for three reorganisations of the data:

Trial 1. The data as listed above (twelve variables)
Trial 2. The data omitting variable xi because of the very small samples available for horizons 1 to 2ii (eleven variables)
Trial 3. The data omitting variables ix, x and xi, for which relatively small samples are available (nine variables).

For trial 1 the first three axes account for 86 per cent of the total variance in the data (axis 1: 62.7 per

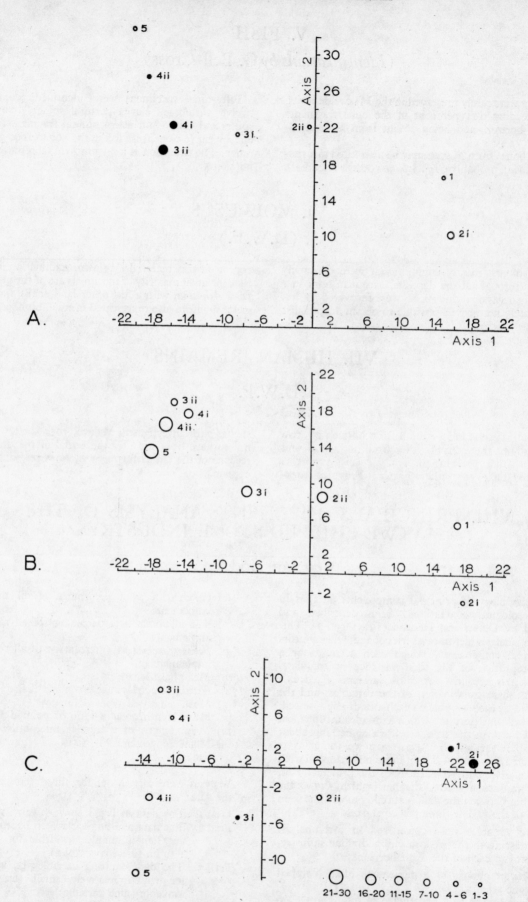

Fig. 62. *Principal components analyses of the Makwe chipped stone industry (see p. 111).*

cent; axis 2: 12.8 per cent; axis 3: 11.1 per cent). The first axis thus accounts for by far the greatest variance. Table 31 shows the 'loadings' for the twelve variables on the first three axes or eigenvectors. The magnitude of these 'loadings' (plus or minus) indicates the relative importance of each variable on each axis. This shows, for example, that in terms of axis 1 (which accounts for most of the variance) the main differences between the horizons are the decreases in variables i, ii and xii, and the increases in variables iii, iv, viii and ix. The second axis (which accounts for much less of the total variance) represents mainly variables x and xi; while the third axis has highest loadings for variables vi and x.

The scatter diagram in fig. 62a shows the relationship between the horizons in terms of the first two principal axes. The sizes of the circles (filled circles for positive scores, open circles for negative scores) represent each horizon's score on the third axis.

In trial 2, the first three axes account for respectively 67.4, 12.5 and 8.3 per cent of the total variance in the data—a total of 88.1 per cent. The 'loadings' (table 32) again show that axis 1 represents all the variables fairly evenly, with slight emphasis on decreases through time in variables i and xii, and on increases in variables iii, iv, viii and ix. The highest 'loading' on axis 2 is for variable x and on axis 3 for variable vi. The score of each horizon on the first three principal axes is plotted in fig. 62b.

In trial 3, axis 1 accounts for 70.3 per cent of the total variance, axis 2 for 10.9 per cent and axis 3 for 8.5 per cent. Thus, the first three axes represent 89.8 per cent of the total variance. The most important elements in axis 1 are the decreases through time in variables i, ii and xii, and the increases in variables iii, iv, and viii (table 33). The highest 'loading' on axis 2 is for variable vi; and the highest on axis 3 is for variable v. The first three axes of trial 2 are summarised in fig. 62c.

Discussion of the results of these three trials is best conducted with reference to the scatter diagrams (fig. 62). In each trial, the first axis (representing overall change in all variables, but in particular the increases in variables iii, iv, viii and—to a certain extent—ix, and the decreases in variables i, xii and—to a lesser extent—ii) accounts for by far the largest variance: it reflects chronological variation. This latter point is clear because the horizons occur in approximate chronological sequence from horizon 1 to horizon 5 with reference to the first axis; that is, the analyses have roughly ordered the horizons from right to left on all three of the scatter diagrams. But, in the overall gradual change through time, horizons 1 and 2i are always separate from the others. Horizons 3ii, 4i, 4ii, and 5 form another cluster; while horizons 2ii and 3i are intermediate. This would suggest that the periods of greatest change, or the longest gaps in sequence, were between horizons 2i and 2ii, between horizons 2ii and 3i, and between horizons 3i and 3ii. The biggest changes between these horizons are in variables i, iii, iv, viii, xii and—to a lesser extent—in variables ii and ix.

Trial 3 (fig. 62c) in particular suggests that it is horizons 3ii and 4i which show most deviation from the sequence on the second principal axis. Horizons 1, 2i, 2ii, 3i, 4ii and 5 are ordered fairly well along this

second axis, with horizons 3ii and 4i showing significant deviation from this sequence. This suggests that horizons 3ii and 4i are slightly anomalous (given the overall pattern of change through time) in reference to the second axis. This axis in trials 1 and 2 mainly reflects change in variables x and xi; in trial 3 variable vi has a dominant effect. It is noteworthy that these three variables all relate to geometrics.

A break between horizons 3i and 3ii is even more marked if we consider the third axis in trial 1. Horizons 1 to 3i all have negative scores on this axis, represented by open circles in fig. 62a. Horizons 3ii and 4i both have fairly large positive scores, represented by filled circles. Axis 3 in trial 1 largely represents variation in variables vi and, to a lesser extent, x. This evidence supports the picture of a marked break between horizons 3i and 3ii, and of the slightly anomalous position of horizons 3ii and 4i.

Table 31. Trial 1: loadings of the twelve variables on the first three components

Variable	Eigenvectors		
	1	2	3
i	.33	.01	-.33
ii	.30	-.23	.10
iii	-.34	.12	.19
iv	-.32	.23	.16
v	-.22	.09	.20
vi	-.20	-.28	.56
vii	.29	.36	.17
viii	-.32	.11	-.21
ix	-.34	-.09	-.20
x	.19	.43	.48
xi	-.13	.64	-.28
xii	.33	.14	.11

Table 32. Trial 2: loadings of the eleven variables on the first three components

Variable	Eigenvectors		
	1	2	3
i	.33	-.28	-.20
ii	.30	-.04	.42
iii	-.34	.23	.05
iv	-.32	.27	-.31
v	-.22	.23	.00
vi	-.21	.32	.69
vii	.30	.34	-.21
viii	-.32	-.11	-.25
ix	-.34	-.22	-.01
x	.19	.64	-.25
xii	.33	.16	.09

Table 33. Trial 3: loadings of the nine variables on the first three components

Variable	Eigenvectors		
	1	2	3
i	.37	-.31	-.01
ii	.33	.27	.42
iii	-.37	.16	-.03
iv	-.36	-.07	-.18
v	-.25	.11	.78
vi	-.24	.74	-.21
vii	.31	.17	-.18
viii	-.34	-.35	.21
xii	.35	.25	.19

Chapter 14

The Makwe Sequence

That the accumulation of horizons 4i, 4ii, 5 and 6 at Makwe took place during the last two thousand years is shown both by the radiocarbon dates for these horizons, and by the frequent presence in them of Iron Age pottery. They are thus broadly contemporary with the occupation of Thandwe.

Horizons 2i, 2ii and 3i belong to a period between the end of the fourth millennium bc and the middle of the third. The eight radiocarbon age determinations from these horizons, allowing one standard deviation, suggest a maximum duration of this occupation in the period from 3150 to 2300 bc.

No radiocarbon dates are available for horizon 1. The deposits here are more consolidated and their artefact content very much sparser than in the higher levels. Artefacts are, indeed, virtually absent from the lowest 50 cm of the deposit. It seems probable that horizon 1 accumulated slowly over a substantial period, prior to the late fourth millennium bc, during which the Makwe rock-shelter was only infrequently visited by man. The floor of the shelter at this time would have been a relatively narrow crack much obstructed by boulders, and thus less suitable for occupation than the open uninterrupted floor of later times.

The radiocarbon dates thus suggest that there may have been a hiatus in the occupation of the Makwe rock-shelter, covering approximately the last two millennia bc, at around the point in the depositional process represented by horizon 3ii. This possibility is discussed further later in this chapter, in conjunction with the evidence of artefact typology and that of the pedology of the deposits.

The artefact assemblages recovered from the various horizons at Makwe show considerable typological constancy (fig. 63). The chipped stone industry is dominated throughout by the use of non-radial cores for the production of end-struck flakes, among which fine parallel-sided 'blades' or 'bladelets' are exceptional. Retouched implements are, with the exception of a few informal scrapers, almost exclusively backed flakes and backed geometrics. As will be shown below, there is typologically more change among the bone and shell artefacts, notably among the beads, than there is among the chipped stone artefacts. Pottery and metal objects occur only in the upper horizons.

The main trends discerned in the development of the Makwe chipped stone industry are as follows:

General composition

(i) The frequency of shatter-chunks shows a steady reduction through the sequence (fig. 64), coinciding with a slight increase in the frequency of cores. (This may be linked with changes in raw material.)

(ii) Radial cores (fig. 64) and flakes with convergent dorsal scar patterns become progressively less frequent through the period of the site's occupation.

(iii) Retouched implements increase from only 0.4 per cent of the total chipped stone assemblage in horizon 1 to 1.8 per cent in horizon 5.

(iv) Through the sequence there is a steady increase in the frequency of geometrics from 24 per cent of the retouched implements (excluding fragments) in the lowest levels, to 71 per cent in the most recent horizons (fig. 64). There is a corresponding decrease in the frequency of backed flakes from 63 per cent to 26 per cent, and in that of scrapers from 14 to 2 per cent.

(v) Backed points, which never exceed 2 per cent of the retouched implements in any horizon, occur only in horizon 3i and above.

(vi) *Petits tranchets* are virtually restricted to horizons 3ii, 4i and 4ii (fig. 64).

Metrical and stylistic trends:

(vii) There is a steady trend towards reduced flake size (fig. 65).

(viii) Less than 5 per cent of the geometrics in the lowest horizons are eared, increasingly steadily to 22 per cent at the top of the sequence (fig. 64). Among the curved-backed geometrics a sharp distinction occurs between horizons 2ii and 3i. Below this break between 5 and 7 per cent are eared, above it the proportion in each horizon varies between 18 and 21 per cent. Among the angled-backed geometrics, none are eared in horizons 1, 2i or 2ii; in horizons 3i to 4ii the proportion is between 3 and 9 per cent; the figure increases to 26 per cent in horizon 5.

(ix) There is a steady increase in the mean length of the pointed lunates from 14.7 mm in horizons 1 and 2i to 17.2 mm in horizon 5 (fig. 65). Deep and

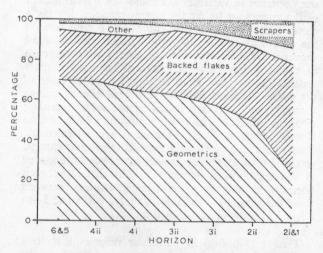

Fig. 63. Primary classes of retouched implements through the Makwe sequence.

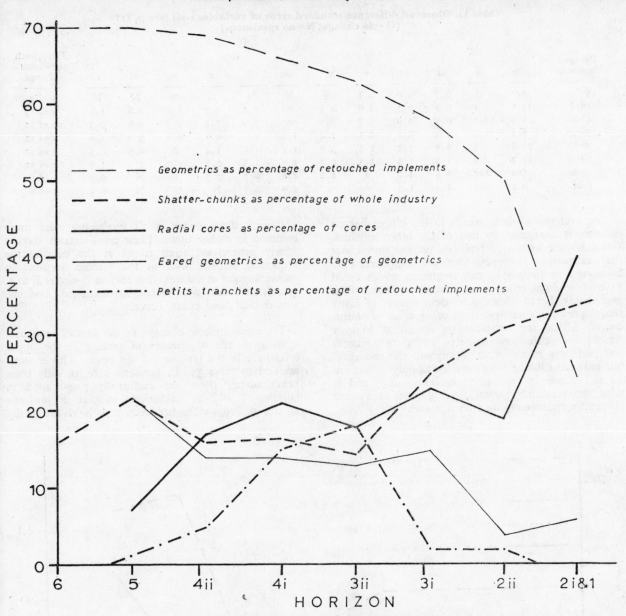

Fig. 64. Principal trends in the Makwe chipped stone artefact aggregates.

asymmetrical lunates show a similar but less regular increase.

(x) The mean length/breadth ratios of the pointed lunates increase from 1.76 in the lower horizons to 1.93 in the upper ones (fig. 65).

(xi) The triangular microliths show a steady increase in mean length from 11-12 mm in the lower levels to over 16 mm at the top of the succession (fig. 65).

(xii) The convex-backed flakes are significantly narrower in the lower horizons (fig. 65), thus opposing the trend among the pointed lunates.

Each of the above trends has been subjected to a rudimentary test for statistical significance by calculating the standard error of the difference between the means (or proportions) observed in adjacent horizons, and comparing this with the observed difference. Where the observed difference is more than twice its standard error it may be assumed that the means or proportions are significantly different (Chambers, 1958: 39-41, 46-9). In many cases, significant change between adjacent horizons could not be demonstrated (table 34); but when differences between more widely separated horizons were examined, statistical significance could be demonstrated in each case. It will be seen that the greatest degree of significant variation between adjacent horizons is between horizons 2i and 2ii, where five of the eleven trends investigated register significant differences.

The data summarised above have also been subjected to a principal components analysis by Dr Ian Hodder, whose report has been presented above (p. 111). Dr Hodder concludes that the chipped stone aggregates from successive horizons represent a continuous developmental sequence in which the greatest changes took place between horizons 2i and 2ii and between horizons 3i and 3ii. Horizons 3ii to 5 yielded aggregates which cluster closely together, as did horizons 1 and 2i. The material from horizons 2ii and 3i is intermediate between that of these two clusters. The geometrics from horizons 3ii and 4i appear to differ somewhat from those of the rest of the sequence.

Table 34. Observed difference/standard error of variables i-xii (see p. 111)
(O=no change; N=no specimens)

Between horizons	i	ii	iii	iv	v	vi	vii	viii	ix	x	xi	xii	Traits with significant change
5-6	2.2	N	0.7	0.6	0.1	N	N	N	N	N	N	N	1 of 4
4ii-5	15.6	0.1	0.2	0.1	2.0	2.5	0	1.1	0.7	1.6	2.8	1.8	4 of 12
4i-4ii	1.3	0.7	0.5	2.0	0.5	6.7	0	1.0	1.2	1.3	0.8	0.3	2 of 12
3ii-4i	6.3	0.5	0.4	0.1	2.3	1.4	1.0	0.5	0.8	0.6	3.4	1.6	3 of 12
3i-3ii	29.8	0.8	8.5	1.1	1.4	5.3	1.1	1.1	1.4	0	0.5	0.5	3 of 12
2ii-3i	13.3	0.5	3.3	1.1	1.5	0.2	5.7	1.8	0.2	1.7	1.2	1.9	3 of 12
2i-2ii	7.0	2.7	2.3	4.2	0	1.2	2.0	0.2	0.7	0	N	0.9	5 of 11
1-2i	0.4	0.3	1.4	1.5	0	0	4.0	0.7	N	N	N	0.5	1 of 9

The evidence of these trends in the chipped stone industry is confirmed by that of the other artefacts. Ground stone axes were probably present throughout the occupation. However, they are represented in horizons 1 to 2ii only by tiny fragments which could have come from other ground stone artefacts, albeit improbably. Bored stones, a frequent feature of many contemporary assemblages from other areas of south-central Africa, are conspicuously absent at Makwe. Among the other stone artefacts, knapping hammers and pounding stones occur throughout the sequence, but informal rubbing stones are found only in horizon 3ii and below. In the highest horizons, 4ii, 5 and 6, their place is taken by formal grinding stones such as are frequently encountered on Iron Age sites.

Bone bodkins occur at all levels, but were more common in earlier times. Their cross-sections show a steady progression from round at the base of the sequence, through oval in the middle horizons to subrectangular at the top. It is only in horizons 4i to 5, associated with the rectangular-sectioned bodkins, that conical bone points occur.

The most striking changes in the Makwe sequence, apart from the appearance of pottery in the upper levels, are in the typology of the beads. This is summarised in table 35. In horizons 1 to 3i, only bone beads occur; these are exclusively ring-shaped in horizons 1 and 2i, exclusively tubular in horizons 2ii and 3i. From all higher levels bone beads are totally

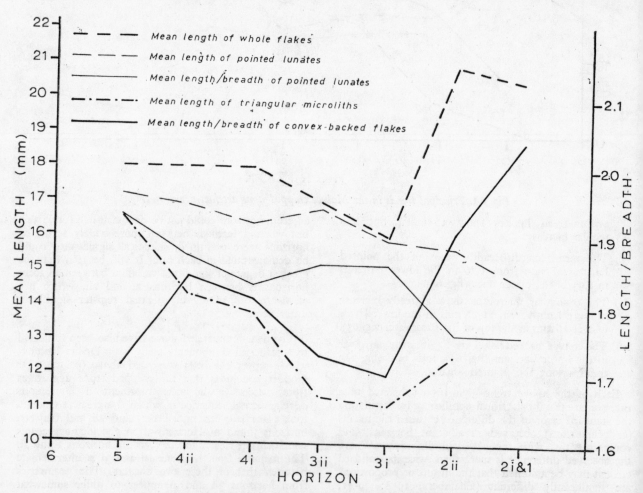

Fig. 65. Further trends in the Makwe chipped stone artefact aggregates.

Table 35. Makwe: bead types

Horizon	Bone ring	Bone tube	Shell disc	?tooth disc	Glass
6	—	—	—		1
5	—	—	22	1	3
4ii	—	—	17	—	—
4i	—	—	8	—	—
3ii	—	—	3	—	—
3i	—	6	—	—	—
2ii	—	2	—	—	—
2i	1	—	—	—	—
1	1	—	—	—	—
	2	8	50	1	4

absent. In horizons 3ii to 5 shell disc beads are encountered; and in all but the highest of these horizons they are the only bead type present. Glass beads are restricted to horizons 5 and 6.

Other shell artefacts tend to share the distribution of the shell disc beads, with the exception of a single fragment of ostrich eggshell, pierced but untrimmed, from horizon 2ii. The shell pendants all come from horizons 4i to 5, and are thus contemporary with the shell disc beads.

Pottery first becomes frequent in horizon 4i. The few sherds recovered from horizons 3i and 3ii occurred in areas of limited horizontal extent and were probably introduced from higher levels. Certainly there can be no question that the pottery is contemporary with the third millennium bc dates obtained from samples taken in these horizons. As at Thandwe, two ceramic traditions —Early Iron Age and Luangwa tradition—are represented. The few sherds which could not surely be attributed to one of these traditions could have derived from either. As is shown in fig. 66, the peak of the Early Iron Age sherd distribution is in horizon 4ii, while that of the later Iron Age Luangwa tradition material is in horizon 5. As at Thandwe, therefore, the chronological separation of the two traditions can be demonstrated, although the nature of their interface is not clear.

Three radiocarbon dates from horizons 4i and 4ii suggest that their deposition covered the greater part of

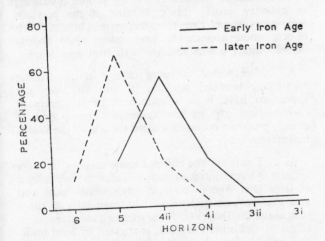

Fig. 66. Stratigraphical distribution of Early and later Iron Age pottery at Makwe, expressed as percentages of the total sherds of each tradition.

the first millennium ad. Date GX-1551 suggests that Early Iron Age material was probably present from the first half of that millennium, which is significantly earlier than the corresponding event at Thandwe. This is in keeping with the typological evidence, for— as will be shown in chapter 20—the Early Iron Age pottery from Makwe has greater affinities with that from Kamnama than does the material from Thandwe. Evidence from elsewhere in Zambia suggests that the inception of the Luangwa tradition took place around the eleventh century ad. The evidence from Makwe is in keeping with this, but allows no precise dating of the event. Metal objects and grindstones occur at Makwe only in the pottery-bearing levels, as do bones of domestic animals.

It is abundantly clear that the chipped stone industry continued without major modification, until long after the advent of the later Iron Age pottery. The appearance of the Early Iron Age material was accompanied in horizon 4i by a number of other innovations, notably the appearance of shell pendants and conical bone points; but there is no reason to believe that these share a common origin with the pottery, since they are not types which are generally recovered from Early Iron Age village sites. It is more reasonable to suppose that the makers of the mode 5 stone industry continued to practise a viable and developing culture alongside that of Early Iron Age immigrants with whom they established contact and from whom they obtained characteristic Early Iron Age pottery. This view is confirmed by the uninterrupted continuation, in the chipped stone industry of horizons 4i to 5, of developmental trends which had been established in considerably earlier periods. The interrelationship between Iron Age peoples and the makers of the chipped stone industries is discussed at length in chapter 20.

The faunal assemblage of horizon 3ii and below contained exclusively wild species which, with a few exceptions already noted, occur in the general vicinity of the site at the present time. Wart-hog and zebra were important elements in the diet. Buffalo and perhaps eland (the latter only tentatively identified) were the largest species represented; significantly they occur only in the lower horizons 1 to 3i. Domestic animals are restricted to the upper part of the sequence, cattle appearing for the first time in horizon 4i and goat in horizon 4ii. Their presence thus does not pre-date the earliest occurrences of Iron Age pottery. Wild species continue to be represented in these levels alongside the domestic ones, which remain in a clear minority throughout. Fish remains, although rare, are present at all levels except the lowest, where their absence may be due to poorer conditions of preservation. They indicate that the range of territory exploited by the site's inhabitants extended at least as far as the Kapoche river 15 km distant: this is confirmed by the occurrence of water snail shells, used for making beads and pendants, in horizons 3i to 5.

Remains of food plants were preserved only in the upper levels, their lowest occurrence being in horizon 3ii. The limited number of species represented, like their restricted stratigraphical distribution, is probably due more to accidents of preservation than to cultural preferences or varied availability. The *mbula* nuts and kaffir oranges were presumably collected for use as food, the colocynth for medicinal purposes, and the gourd for use as a container. Only in horizons 5 and 6 are domestic crops represented, and these are restricted to maize and pumpkins. In the same horizons there occur grindstones comparable with those frequently found on Iron Age sites and known from recent ethnographic observations to have been used for grinding cereals.

It is only in horizons 5 and 6, representing the period of the later Iron Age, that we find evidence for trade-contact or resource exploitation outside the immediate area of the site. Both the cultivated crops there attested are of New World origin; the glass beads likewise attest contacts, albeit indirect, with the coastal trade. Copper artefacts are also present and presumably represent trade either with the trans-Luangwan regions of Zambia and Shaba or with the Rhodesian plateau to the south of the Zambezi.

It is now appropriate to return to the problem of the hiatus in the accumulation of deposits to which reference was made above. The radiocarbon dates suggest that the Makwe rock-shelter contains no deposits which accumulated during the greater part of the last two millennia bc. The gap in the radiocarbon dates falls at the interface between horizons 3ii and 4i. The basic continuity in the industrial succession has already been emphasised; and it is remarkable that such a long gap in the sequence as is indicated by the radiocarbon dates should not show up as a significant discontinuity in the analysis of the artefacts from successive levels. Such a discontinuity is, however, indicated between horizons 3i and 3ii.

Twelve major trends in the development of the Makwe chipped stone industry have been enumerated on p. 111 above. The difference between the percentage frequencies of retouched implements in the chipped stone assemblages in horizons 3i and 3ii is particularly striking. On this criterion horizon 3ii clearly belongs with the upper part of the sequence. The change from bone to shell beads also occurs between horizons 3i and 3ii, as does the very marked increase in the frequency of *petits tranchets*. Against these observations must be set the facts that, pedologically, horizon 3ii belongs with the ash lens complex of horizons 2i to 3i, and that horizon 3ii has yielded three charcoal samples which have been dated by radiocarbon to the third millennium bc, horizon 4i being placed by a single determination (supported by the evidence of its contained pottery) in the first millennium ad.

Nowhere in this part of the sequence is there any indication of a sterile layer, or of any discontinuity in the accumulation of the deposits. Natural erosion of any deposits, sterile or otherwise, which may have

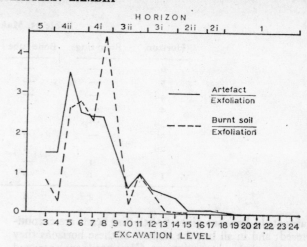

Fig. 67. *Artefact/exfoliation and burnt soil/exfoliation ratios at Makwe.*

accumulated during this time can, for topological reasons, be regarded as improbable. There is likewise no indication of the removal of such deposits by any human agency. It seems likely, therefore, that the interruption of occupation suggested by the radiocarbon dates was accompanied by a virtual cessation of the accumulation of deposits. The only pedological changes which can be interpreted as reflecting a temporary cessation of occupation are the dips in the proportions of artefacts and of burned soil which are indicated in figs. 40 and 41 (p. 71). The steady trends towards increased incidence of both commodities show an appreciable interruption in layers 10 and 11, which form the middle and lower parts of horizon 3ii. This is more clearly shown in fig. 67, in which are plotted the respective occurrences of artefacts and burned soil, by weight, relative to that of exfoliation for each 7.5-cm layer in the deposits. A temporary decrease in the incidence of materials derived from human activity, relative to those attributable to natural phenomena, is clearly indicated.

It must be concluded that a major gap in the Makwe succession is marked by horizon 3ii at the top of the ash lens complex rather than by one of the actual interfaces between horizons. The indications are that re-occupation of the shelter was by people producing an industry closely similar to that of the previous inhabitants some two thousand years before. This re-occupation appears to have taken place shortly before contact was established with Iron Age peoples.

An earlier period of major change in the artefact aggregates, between horizons 2i and 2ii, does not appear to have been accompanied by a significant chronological gap in the sequence. This period of change probably occurred around the end of the fourth millennium bc.

As at Thandwe, the chipped stone mode 5 industry appears to have continued until well after the appearance of later Iron Age pottery, in other words until well into the present millennium. In more recent times still, use of the shelter by *Nyau* societies, for preparation of masks and other purposes, is attested by local tradition and confirmed by the charcoal drawings on the site's walls. The detailed evidence for this, together with an account of the Makwe rock paintings, is presented in chapter 19.

Chapter 15

Excavations at Kalemba Rock-Shelter

I. LOCATION AND ENVIRONMENT

The Kalemba rock-shelter lies at latitude 14°07′ south, longitude 32°30′ east, on the south-eastern side of the Chipwete valley, 3 km to the north-east of Mbangombe village (fig. 68). The Chipwete source is in the range of hills which rise a few kilometres to the east of the administrative centre of Chadiza and which continue southwards into Moçambique and eastwards to the Mwangazi and beyond. The headwaters of the Chipwete are located in high plains, lying some 1180 metres above sea level, on which Mbangombe village is sited. These plains are surrounded by hills which reach a maximum altitude of 1350 m. Further to the south on the same plain rises the Mkandabwako, which flows westwards to join the Nsadzu river some 15 km south-west of Chadiza. The Chipwete, however, flows initially in a north-easterly direction and drops rapidly through a narrow valley, with steep, densely wooded sides, for some 7 km before emerging into a more open valley, through which it flows eastwards to its confluence with the Mwangazi some 20 km from Mbangombe. It is in the first, steep, section of the valley that the Kalemba rock-shelter is located, rather over two-thirds of the way up the precipitous (*c.* 60°) slope, at a height of some 90 m above the river (plates IXa and IXb).

Mbangombe village is best reached from Chadiza *via* Zingalume and Sakwe, which is 1 km to the east of the latter place. From Sakwe a rough track follows the approximate line of the Mkandabwako valley to Mbangombe: this last section of the route is only passable by motor vehicles during very dry weather unless bridges are built.

The stony hill country around Kalemba is covered for the most part with dense bush. Land suitable for cultivation is restricted to the high, but well watered, plain around Mbangombe, and to the Mkandabwako valley further to the west. Maize, pumpkins, bananas, plaintains and tobacco are widely grown, the last-named being an important cash-crop. Cattle, goats, pigs and chickens are herded; some cattle are used as draught animals. To the north, the upper Chipwete valley where lies Kalemba is uninhabited and largely unfrequented, being traversed only by a rarely used footpath leading to Chimsitu, a village some 13 km downstream on the eastwards-flowing lower Chipwete. The lower valley formerly bore scattered settlement, but is now largely depopulated. Herds of buffalo and of the larger antelope are there frequently encountered. The human population of the area is almost exclusively Chewa, under Chief Mwangala.

Geologically, the area is one of much eroded Basement rocks with deep colluvial deposits. Domed granitic hills are characteristic, and rock-shelters are of frequent occurrence. Kalemba is one of the largest such shelters yet located in Zambia, but the area further to the east is inadequately explored, and further comparable sites may there await discovery.

II. THE SITE

The rock-shelter is widely known to local people and has given its name, Kalemba (the painted place), to the whole range of hills bordering the south-east side of the upper Chipwete valley. So far as I have been able to ascertain, it was not brought to the notice of outsiders until the visit, in 1955, of Mr R. A. Hamilton, by whom it was reported to the then Rhodes-Livingstone Museum. A photograph by Hamilton of some of the Kalemba rock paintings was published in 1959 (J. D. Clark, 1959*b*: 201); but no further investigation was made until the visit of the present writer in 1970.

The rock-shelter is formed by a massive outcrop of granite gneiss over 30 m in height, jutting from the hillside (plate IX). On the north-west side, facing the Chipwete valley, a finely domed overhang with a maximum height of 4.5 m extends 7.0 m to protect an open area 9.0 by 11.0 m in extent (plate X, figs. 69, 70). The flat, uninterrupted floor is further enclosed on the north-east by a steep rocky promontory of the main hillside. To the north-west and south-west are further rock outcrops, the tops of which may only be reached from within the rock-shelter. These provide extensions to the living space of the shelter floor, and serve as vantage points overlooking much of the upper Chipwete valley. Adjacent to the south-west end of the main shelter is a second, smaller overhang, facing south-west. Its 6 by 12 m floor is less well protected. The easiest access to both rock-shelters from below is at the southern corner: from the hills, or from following the contour of the shelter, entrance at the north end of the main shelter is also practicable. Paintings extend for a distance of 12 m along the rear wall of the main shelter, and there is a smaller panel beneath the south-western overhang also. Both series are described and discussed in a later chapter.

III. THE EXCAVATION

A grid of 3-foot (92-cm) squares was laid out over the floor of the main shelter. Numbered lines run parallel to the painted wall of the shelter in a north-east to south-west direction. Line 10 closely follows the line of the wall, while line 21 intersects the front of the rock outcrop which demarcates the floor on the north-west.

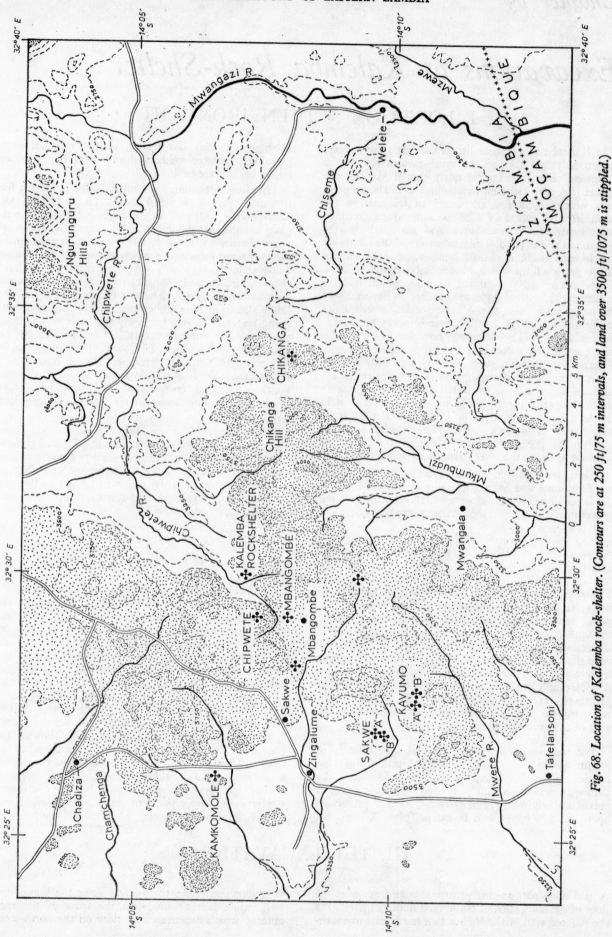

Fig. 68. Location of Kalemba rock-shelter. (Contours are at 250 ft/75 m intervals, and land over 3500 ft/1075 m is stippled.)

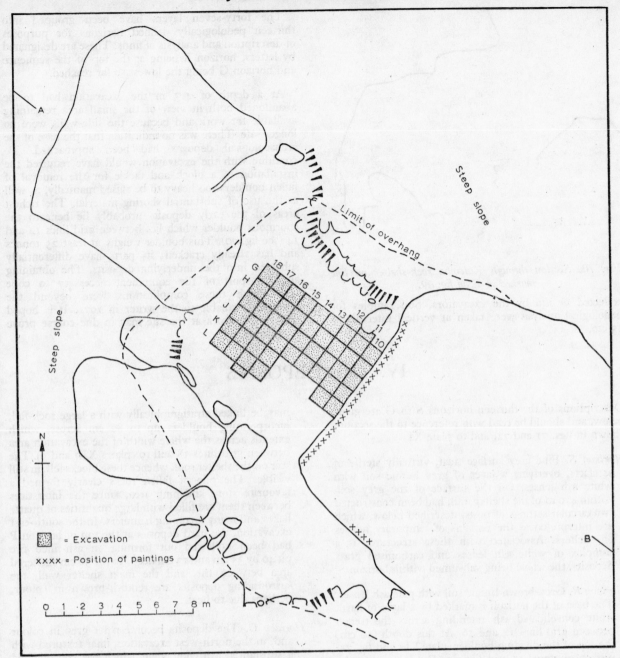

Fig. 69. Ground plan of Kalemba rock-shelter.

Lettered lines run perpendicularly to the numbered ones, designated from D at the extreme north-east of the floor to P at the south-west. Each square was recorded by the designations of the grid lines which intersect to form its eastern corner. Thus square G 10 is demarcated by grid lines G, 10, H and 11.

Excavation was originally restricted to the ten grid squares H and I, 10 to 15, but with increasing depth substantial lateral extension became necessary so that the side-walls could be stepped to avoid collapse. A massive fallen boulder, with its top 50 cm below the surface, was found to occupy most of the trench between grid lines 12 and 14. It lay roughly parallel to the main shelter wall and effectively divided the excavation area into two parts. Further extension of the excavation to the north-west was therefore required to enable the

lower levels to be reached. The total area of the excavation, as shown in fig. 69, eventually covered 40.2 sq.m. As the sections indicate, however, the lowest levels, at a depth of 4.30 m, were reached only in a single area less than 1 sq.m in extent.

The excavation was conducted according to the observed natural stratigraphy, arbitrary horizontal subdivisions being made of layers exceeding 8 cm in thickness. The deposits were thus removed in forty-seven layers, horizontal control being provided by the 92-cm grid noted above. All excavated material, with the exception of some removed in the course of extending the trench or stepping the side-walls, was passed through sieves of 4-mm mesh; and all artefactual and faunal remains thus recovered were retained. In the upper layers charcoal samples for radiocarbon dating were

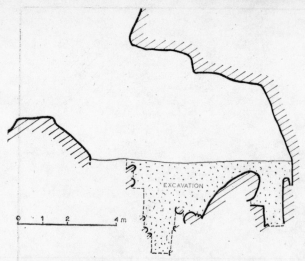

Fig. 70. Section through Kalemba rock-shelter on line marked A-B on fig. 69.

collected *in situ* by the excavators. Soil samples for pedological analysis were taken at vertical intervals of 15 cm.

The forty-seven layers have been grouped into thirteen pedologically defined horizons for purposes of description and analysis of finds. These are designated by letters, horizon S being at the top of the sequence and horizon G being the lowest so far reached.

At a depth of 4.3 m the excavation had to be abandoned both in view of the small area remaining available for work and because the side-walls were no longer safe. There was no indication that the base of the archaeological deposits had been approached. To continue with the excavation would have required the installation of a block and tackle for the removal of fallen boulders too heavy to be raised manually, as well as the use of substantial shoring material. The richest areas of the early deposits probably lie beneath the enormous boulder which lies between grid lines 12 and 14 (see fig. 70). This boulder weighs at least 25 tonnes and has already cracked; its parts have differentially subsided into the underlying deposits. The obtaining and transport of the equipment necessary to cope safely with these complications were beyond the resources available to the writer in 1971. It is hoped that further work at the site may in due course prove practicable.

IV. THE DEPOSITS

Descriptions of the thirteen horizons S to G are given below, and should be read with reference to the sections shown in figs. 71 and 72, and to plate XI.

Horizon S. Fine grey surface dust, virtually sterile of artefacts, overlying a layer of grey humic soil with white ash lenses. On the surface of the grey soil, within 4.0 m of the shelter wall, had been constructed two circular settings of posts, described below, which are interpreted as the remains of temporary houses or shelters. Associated with these structures is a complex of white ash lenses and carbonised grass deposits, the whole being subsumed within horizon S.

Horizon R. Grey-brown humic soil with pale ash lenses. The base of the horizon is marked by a layer of hard, white consolidated ash extending across the trench between grid lines 14 and 16. At this depth (50 cm) the top of the dividing boulder (plate XIa and fig. 71) was encountered at grid line 12. From here on, the excavation was perforce conducted in two separate areas, north-west and south-east.

Horizon Q. Similar to horizon R but becoming browner with increased depth, this horizon contains progressively more pieces of exfoliated rock in the lower levels. The base of the horizon is marked in the north-west excavation by an extensive lens of exfoliated fragments associated with a large fallen stone weighing some 30 kg. As in other horizons down to horizon K, decomposed rock fragments are concentrated on the sloping surface of the dividing boulder. The deposits of horizon Q in the south-east excavation are essentially similar.

Horizon P. Greyer in colour than those of the overlying horizon, the deposits are more consolidated and contain yet more exfoliation. In the north-west excavation an extensive lens at the base of the horizon consisted of almost pure exfoliation. This occurrence

may be linked stratigraphically with a large rock-fall, incorporating boulders up to 80 cm across, which extends across the whole width of the excavation area between grid lines 18 and 19 (plates XIb and c). The scar on the shelter roof, whence these blocks fell, in still visible. The pile of fallen rocks clearly formed a favourite stone-knapping area, since the interstices between them are filled with large quantities of quartz flakes and many knapping hammers. In the south-east excavation, the hard deposits at the top of horizon P had been hollowed out forming an ash-filled fire pit 40 by 35 cm and 13 cm deep. In the 50 cm sheltered area between this and the main shelter wall, the surrounding deposits are reddish-brown in colour, perhaps due to heat.

Horizon O. The deposits become paler grey in colour and, in the north-west excavation, finer textured with a substantial ash component which has consolidated into nodules. In the lower part of the horizon the quantity of exfoliation decreases. In the south-east excavation the deposits are humic rather than ashy, and the reduction in exfoliation is less marked. This is interpreted as due to a slower rate of accumulation caused by less intensive occupation. Parts of this horizon, in the limited area investigated between the dividing boulders and the shelter wall, had been removed through the excavation of a grave, described below, dug from this level into horizon L.

Horizon N. In the north-west excavation the consolidated ash nodules increase in size and frequency. There is a further reduction in the quantity of exfoliation. In the south-east excavation there are no deposits which can be attributed to this horizon.

Horizon M. The grey ashy deposits continue in the north-west excavation. Exfoliation, almost absent at the top of the horizon, increases again with depth.

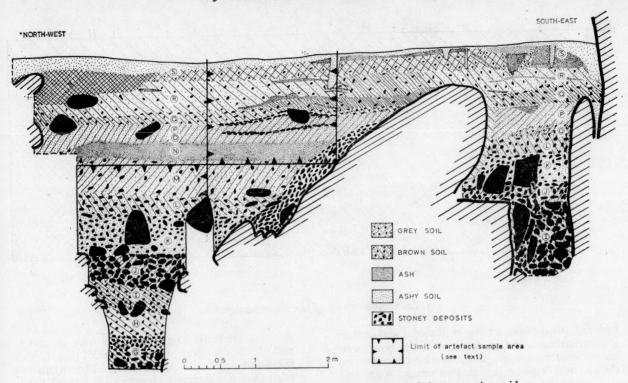

GREY SOIL
BROWN SOIL
ASH
ASHY SOIL
STONEY DEPOSITS

Limit of artefact sample area
(see text)

0   0.5   1   2 m

Fig. 71. Section through the Kalemba deposits on line H of the excavation grid.

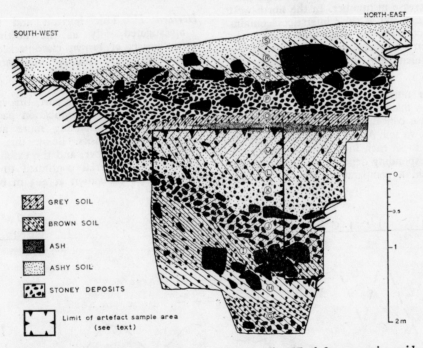

GREY SOIL
BROWN SOIL
ASH
ASHY SOIL
STONEY DEPOSITS

Limit of artefact sample area
(see text)

0
0.5
1
2 m

Fig. 72. Section through the Kalemba deposits on line 17 of the excavation grid.

This horizon has no counterpart in the south-east excavation.

Horizon L. In the north-west excavation, the deposits are browner and less ashy; exfoliation continues to increase with depth. On the inner side of the dividing boulder, horizon L (which is here overlain directly by horizon O) is marked by a thick red sandy layer with heavy exfoliation, becoming coarser and more gravelly with increased depth. The floor-space here at this time was at the bottom of a 1.0 m deep cleft,

only 1.1 m wide, between the main shelter wall and the dividing boulder.

Horizon K. On both sides of the dividing boulder, this horizon is marked by fallen rocks up to 60 cm across; by a large quantity of exfoliation in the fine-textured brown soil; and by increased artefact density. It is probable that the dividing boulder itself fell from the shelter roof at this time, but since (for obvious reasons) its under surface has not been examined, this suggestion must remain tentative. Beneath the

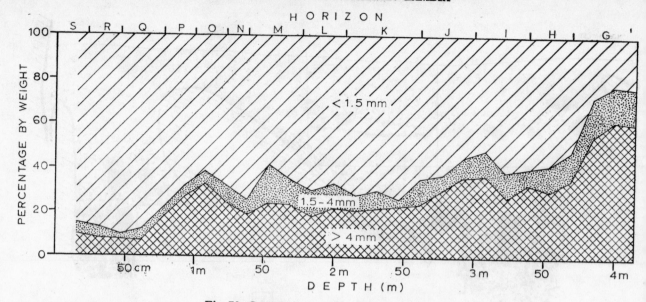

Fig. 73. Granulometry of the Kalemba deposits.

rock-fall, the deposits are greyer in colour and contain less exfoliation. Artefact densities in the north-west excavation remain high. In the south-east excavation the deposits show signs of weathering, suggesting slow accumulation, and contain relatively few artefacts.

Horizon J. In both of the areas investigated, large slabs of fallen rock increase in number. In the north-west excavation, the grey soil in their interstices contains abundant artefacts. In the south-east excavation, which now penetrates a narrow crevice only 55 cm in width, the fallen slabs are closely packed and artefacts are few.

Horizon I. In the north-west excavation, exfoliated fragments show a marked decrease, and the deposit consists of a dense concentration of artefacts closely packed in fine brown soil. At the base of the horizon is a layer of fallen rocks each measuring up to 25 cm across. The corresponding deposits in the south-east excavation contain a comparable rock-fall but are

sterile of artefacts. The fallen rocks were so densely packed in the deep narrow crevice that further excavation proved impracticable. The south-east excavation was therefore abandoned at a depth below the surface of 3.2 m, no artefacts having been encountered below 2.75 m.

Horizon H. This horizon and horizon G were investigated only in the north-west excavation. It consists of brown close-packed earth with few artefacts and steadily increasing quantities of exfoliation.

Horizon G. In its upper part, this horizon consists of small fragments of exfoliation packed in rich red-brown earth containing more artefacts than the horizon H deposits. Below this, artefacts further increase in number, and the exfoliated fragments in size. This material continued to the base of the north-west excavation at 4.3 m below the surface.

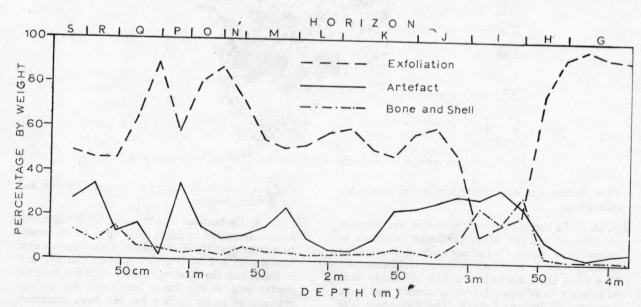

Fig. 74. Pedological analysis of the Kalemba deposits.

PEDOLOGICAL ANALYSIS

Samples of the deposits, taken at vertical intervals of 15 cm, have been examined by Laurel Phillipson. The mean weight of the samples was 2.2 kg. They were all taken on grid line H, at its intersection with grid line 16 from the surface to a depth of 1.80 m, at the mid-point between grid lines 16 and 17 from 1.95 to 2.70 m, and at grid line 17 for the remainder of the sequence.

The granulometry of the samples is summarised in fig. 73. This shows a fairly steady increase with depth in the components in the 1.5 to 4.0 mm and over-4.0 mm size-ranges at the expense of those smaller than 1.5 mm. In fig. 74 are shown the respective percentage frequencies, by weight in the over 4.0 mm components, of exfoliation, artefact and bone and shell.*
Exfoliation shows a steady increase through horizons S to Q, followed by fluctuating high levels in horizons P to N. In horizons M to K it returns to moderate levels, drops to its lowest values in horizon I before reaching a further peak in horizon G at the bottom of the sequence. Artefact frequencies fluctuate between 1 and 40 per cent, with peaks in horizons S, P, M and I, in which last bone and shell also reach their greatest quantities. Further discussion of the implications of the stratigraphy and pedology are postponed to chapter 18 where they are considered in the light of the industrial sequence and of the chronology.

V. FEATURES

GRAVES

Four separate human burials were located during the Kalemba excavation: three are associated with horizon O and one with horizon Q. The skeletal remains are described by Dr Hertha de Villiers in chapter 17.

In horizon O of the south-east excavation, in grid square I 11 and extending partly into H 11, a pit 60 cm by 1.2 m had been dug along the east face of the dividing boulder for 30 cm into the underlying horizon L. At the bottom of this pit a row of stones was placed parallel to the face of the dividing boulder and 50 cm distant from it. The line of stones clearly separated the coarse red sandy deposit of horizon L from the grave-fill, which was of grey soil containing little exfoliation and closely similar to the deposits of the lower part of horizon O. Near the centre of grid square I 11, close to the south-western end of the grave, a neat pile of stones occurred at the same level (plate XIIa). On the removal of the upper-most of these stones, the crushed remains of an adult human skull and cervical vertebrae were exposed (plate XIIb). Centered 25 cm to the south-east were found the very badly crushed remains of an infant skull, together with a few postcranial bones of the same individual. Careful examination of the rest of the grave-fill, and screening of the deposits, failed to reveal any further remains. It was discovered, however, that the northern half of the dividing boulder had, at some time subsequent to the interment, shifted some 10 to 12 cm to the north-west, settling slightly downwards in the process. This movement is indicated by the lateral displacement of the two halves of the boulder, visible in plate XIIa, and by the crevice alongside the eastern face of the boulder exposed in the northern section of the south-eastern excavation (plate XIIIa). This move-ment of the dividing boulder had disturbed the grave contents, and further remains of the adult skull, but no postcranial material, were found displaced downwards in the resultant crack as much as 25 cm below the level of their fellows. Although a quantity of chipped stone artefacts was found in the grave-fill, none could be regarded as grave-goods.

Also in horizon O, in grid square J 15, the fragmented incomplete skull of a child was found, placed beneath a stone slab. There were no indications that any pit had been dug to receive these remains. The skull had evidently been broken before burial and the pieces were separated. There were no postcranial remains and no grave-goods.

Some 8 cm above the burial last described, at the junction between grid squares J 15 and K 15, a small pile of stones overlay a shallow depression containing postcranial human bones which were much charred and fragmented.

In horizon Q, at the intersection of grid line K with the main shelter wall, a small pit only 20 cm in diameter was found. This had been scooped out of the underlying deposits and used for the interment of much fragmented human remains. The pit was lined with three pieces of a human pelvis and one skull fragment. In the area thus demarcated were placed, one at each end, the two halves of a mandible. Between these was a pile of vertebra and rib fragments, a few bits of shattered long-bone and two pieces of the temporal. A few unidentified animal bones were also included. The human remains from this interment all appear to have belonged to the same, adult, individual.

On the dividing line between grid squares H 16 and I 16, in horizon S, was found a complete later Iron Age open bowl buried inverted in a shallow pit dug, little larger than the vessel itself, from a level 12 cm below the modern surface of the deposits. The base of the bowl, now uppermost, was level with the top of the pit. Any contents which the bowl may have had when buried had been destroyed by termites which had constructed a nest inside the vessel. Chewa workmen interpreted this feature as the burial of a still-born infant, interred according to their own tradition.†
For stratigraphical reasons, this feature appears to be contemporary with the pole and bamboo-framed shelters described below.

POLE AND BAMBOO-FRAMED SHELTERS

Beneath the surface dust, in the excavated area within 4.0 m of the shelter wall, were found the charred remains of wooden posts and bamboo (*Oxytenanthera abyssinica*) stakes, roughly pointed by means of a metal tool, and driven—rather than set in post-holes—into the underlying deposits (plates XIVa, XIVb). A plan of these features is shown in fig. 75. Three separate but apparently inter-related structures may be distinguished. An approximately semicircular post-setting, 1.6 by 1.2 m, adjacent to the shelter wall is best interpreted as the remains of a lean-to structure, utilising the main rock face as its rear wall. A central gap in the setting, facing

---

*The figures given in fig. 74 are in several cases only approximate, in view of the heavy encrustation surrounding the components from the middle and lower horizons.

†For a comparable custom among the Bemba, see Gouldsbury and Sheane, 1911: 177–8.

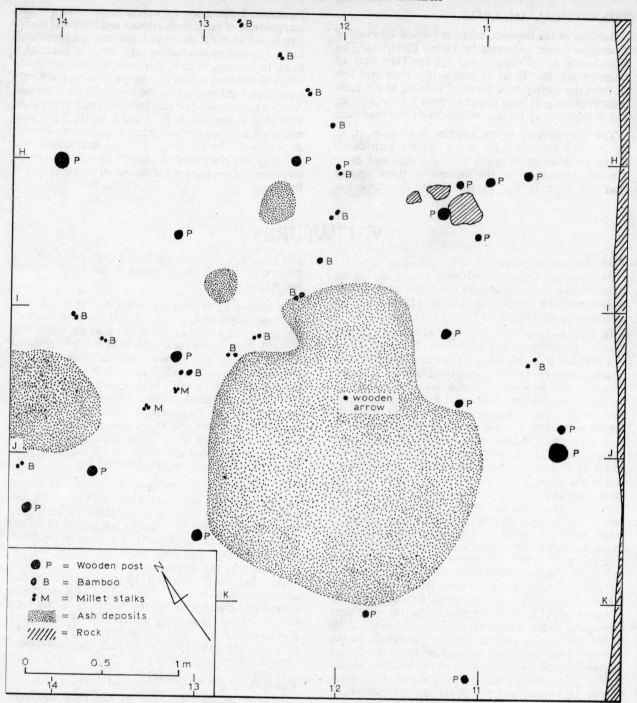

Fig. 75. Kalemba: plan of structures and other features in the upper part of horizon S.

north-west, may represent an entrance. In front of this, only 75 cm away, is a curved line of split bamboos which appear to form part of a roughly circular setting some 3.0 to 3.5 m in diameter, the north-western half of which has not been preserved. The split bamboos occur, generally in pairs, at an average distance of 25 to 30 cm apart. Adjacent to one pair, marking the southern end of the line, is a substantial post 8 cm in diameter; and nearby, continuing the line of the bamboos, are two bundles of millet stalks driven into the ground. It is reasonable to interpret this second structure as a lightly constructed circular hut with a door or entrance barrier of millet stalks. Traces of charred grass located inside the structure may be the remains of the original roof or of bedding material. Two further pairs of split

bamboos and one post, set inside the line of the wall, may represent some internal partition or structure.

To the south-east, a line of wooden posts 0.7 to 1.2 m apart may represent a fence protecting both structures from the direction of the rock-shelter entrance. Within the fence and between the two structures a deposit of ashy soil had accumulated. Embedded almost vertically into this was found the wooden arrow-point described on p. 160 below.

At the division of grid squares L 16 and M 16, at a depth of 10 cm below the modern surface, the top of a large necked pot was exposed, covered by a small stone slab. Excavation revealed an intact, undecorated necked vessel of later Iron Age type, almost completely filling the pit in which it had been buried (plate XIIIb). The vessel, whose exterior retained soot encrustations, was filled to slightly over half its depth with beans (probably *Canavalia virosa*) above which, in an inverted position, was placed an undecorated later Iron Age beaker. It is reasonable to regard this feature as an abandoned food-store of the inhabitants of the pole and bamboo-framed shelters described above. A 45 to 55 cm diameter, 45 cm deep, pit in grid square K 17, dug from the same level as that containing the pot of beans, contained later Iron Age sherds and was probably associated with the same period of occupation.

Local tradition recalls the use of the Kalemba rock-shelter as a refuge during the time of Ngoni raiding in the nineteenth century. It is to this period that the structures and other recent features here described are best attributed. This hypothesis receives some degree of confirmation from the radiocarbon age determination (N-1389) of ad 1835 ± 70 years obtained from beans from the later Iron Age pot noted above.

VI. CHRONOLOGY

Thirteen radiocarbon age determinations have been obtained from samples excavated at Kalemba. Details are enumerated in table 36. Those from levels between the top of horizon O and the surface of the deposits were run on charcoal samples: those from lower levels, where charcoal was not preserved, were run on bone apatite.* All samples comprised fragments recovered throughout the thickness of the relevant layer: the charcoal samples were mainly of pieces 5 to 10 mm in maximum dimension, the bone ones of unidentifiable fragments up to 5 cm in length. The results given in the table are uncorrected and are expressed in 'radiocarbon years' based on the 5568-year half-life of radiocarbon. They are given to one standard deviation, except for the minimum dates GX-2767 and GX-2609 which have 95 per cent confidence (2 sigma). The reasonably close agreement between the charcoal-based date from horizon O and that obtained from bone apatite recovered

Table 36. Kalemba radiocarbon dates

Grid square	Layer	Horizon	Material	Lab. no.	Age
L/M 16	2 (pit)	S	Beans from pot	N-1389	ad 1835 ± 70 years
I 14	6	top of Q	Charcoal	N-1387	2530 bc ± 90 years
I 15	8	bottom of Q	Charcoal	N-1386	3090 bc ± 110 years
H 15	10	lower P	Charcoal	N-1385	5080 bc ± 105 years
H/I 15	11, 12	upper O	Charcoal	N-1388	4860 bc ± 105 years
H 15	12	middle O	Bone apatite	GX-2770	5965 bc ± 300 years
H 15	15	middle N	Bone apatite	GX-2769	13380 bc ± 1100 years
H 16/17	19	middle M	Bone apatite	GX-2768	24350 bc + 1500 years — 1200 years
H 16/17	24	middle L	Bone apatite	GX-2767	>29000 bc
H 17	27	top of K	Bone apatite	GX-2766	12850 bc ± 1000 years
H 16/17	30	lower K	Bone apatite	GX-2611	22470 bc + 2000 years — 1000 years
H/I 17	40	top of H	Bone apatite	GX-2610	22650 bc + 2000 years — 1000 years
H 16	46, 47	bottom of G	Bone apatite	GX-2609	>35000 bc

from the adjacent underlying layer suggests that one may accept with some confidence the series of dates obtained from the latter material.

On the whole, the sequence of dates is consistent with the stratigraphy. The minor inversion of N-1385 and N-1388 is not significant since these dates are, to all intents and purposes, contemporary. The only major inconsistency is between horizons M and K, where at least two dates are clearly in error. Since GX-2769 and GX-2766 are contemporary, the most economic view is to regard GX-2768 and GX-2767 as too early, and to postulate a major hiatus in the accumulation of deposits at the level marked by horizon K. Other gaps in the sequence are indicated around horizons M and H. Further consideration will be given to these possibilities in chapter 18, in the light of the evidence provided by the industrial succession.

*The bone samples were pre-treated as follows: the bone was generally cleaned of foreign material and crushed to approximately 10 mesh. The sample was then reacted with cold dilute acetic acid to remove carbonates. As soon as carbonate carbon dioxide evolution ceased, the sample was filtered, washed thoroughly, and dried. The sample was then hydrolysed with hydrochloric acid which released a second generation of carbon dioxide from the apatite fraction of the bone. This bone apatite carbon dioxide was used for the analysis.

Chapter 16

The Prehistoric Industries from Kalemba

In this chapter, sections I, III and VII—presenting respectively the descriptions of the chipped stone artefacts, the hammerstones and rubbing stones etc., and the pottery—are based on samples of the total material recovered. The details of the sampling procedure which was adopted in each case is stated at the beginning of the relevant section. In all other sections the total assemblage is considered.

I. THE CHIPPED STONE INDUSTRY

The total number of chipped stone artefacts recovered from the Kalemba excavation was, at a conservative estimate, probably in the region of three quarters of a million. In view of the impracticability of analysing in detail the whole of this material, the following account has been based on the artefacts recovered from grid squares H 14, H 15, I 14 and I 15 for horizons S to N inclusive and those from grid squares H 16, H 17, I 16 and I 17 for the underlying horizons M to G. These parts of the site, which are clearly marked on the sections presented in the previous chapter, provide unobstructed stratigraphic columns free of major disturbance or rock-falls. They have yielded a total of 275,042 chipped stone artefacts, from approximately 10.5 cubic metres of deposit.

Quartz is the dominant raw material. It is abundantly available in the valleys of the Chipwete and its tributaries in the immediate vicinity of the rock-shelter. It occurs in the form of water-worn cobbles and pebbles in the river bed, as well as in occasional outcrops on the valley sides. The other materials used vary indistinguishably from a brown, highly silicified sandstone, or quartzite, to a dark grey chert. Many of these materials occur as cobbles in the bed of the Chipwete, particularly in the three-kilometre stretch of its course which lies immediately downstream of the site. No exact parallels for the finest grey chert were observed here, however; and it is possible that this was brought from further afield or, alternatively, that its desirability for tool-making purposes led to exhaustion of its supply in areas within easy reach of the rock-shelter. The former suggestion may be considered as the more probable in view of the evidence, cited below (p. 162), that the hunting range covered by the site's inhabitants was more extensive during the earlier phases of the occupation than it was subsequently. This would explain the marked decrease in the fine chert's occurrence in the upper horizons of the excavation.

Table 37 shows the relative frequency of vein and crystalline quartz and of the quartzite/chert materials among the retouched implements. It should be noted that the materials with finer flaking characteristics were more frequently represented among the tools than they were in the industry as a whole. To illustrate this point, the occurrence of quartzite/chert artefacts as a percentage of the total aggregate from each horizon is also shown in parentheses. It will be noted that the proportion of quartzite/chert is extremely low in the upper horizons, shows a tendency to increase very slightly with depth, and reaches significant proportions only in the two lowest horizons, H and G, reached in the excavations. In the most recent horizons implements of crystalline quartz outnumber those of vein quartz by a factor of approximately three to one; but with increased depth these proportions are gradually reversed. This tendency may be linked, at least in part, with the increased

Table 37. Summary of Kalemba chipped stone artefact occurrences in sample area (see above)

Horizon:		S	R	Q	P	O	N
CHIPPED STONE ARTEFACTS		7366	6027	7248	15808	23503	24999
% crystalline quartz		27%	17%	32%	26%	37%	71%
% vein quartz		73%	83%	68%	74%	60%	24%
% chert/sandstone		— (0.1%)	— (0.2%)	— (0.1%)	— (0.2%)	4% (0.5%)	5% (0.5%)
Percentages are of total chipped stone artefacts	CORES	65 (0.9%)	50 (0.8%)	63 (0.9%)	79 (0.5%)	126 (0.5%)	118 (0.5%)
	SHATTER-CHUNKS	1853 (25.2%)	1476 (24.5%)	2131 (29.4%)	5645 (35.7%)	9253 (39.4%)	7718 (30.9%)
	WHOLE FLAKES	618 (8.4%)	470 (7.8%)	507 (7.1%)	863 (5.5%)	1233 (5.2%)	1471 (5.9%)
	BROKEN FLAKES	4718 (64.1%)	3922 (65.1%)	4470 (61.6%)	9171 (58.0%)	12839 (54.6%)	15650 (62.6%)
	RETOUCHED IMPLEMENTS	112 (1.5%)	109 (1.8%)	77 (1.1%)	50 (0.3%)	52 (0.2%)	42 (0.2%)
Percentages are of total retouched implements	Geometrics	73 (65.2%)	66 (60.5%)	33 (42.9%)	18 (36.0%)	16 (30.8%)	2 (4.8%)
	Backed flakes	19 (17.0%)	26 (23.9%)	21 (27.3%)	16 (32.0%)	18 (34.6%)	16 (38.1%)
	Backed fragments	9 (8.0%)	8 (7.3%)	6 (7.8%)	3 (6.0%)	1 (1.9%)	
	Backed points	—	2 (1.8%)	1 (1.3%)	1 (2.0%)	1 (1.9%)	2 (4.8%)
	Backed pieces	8 (7.1%)	6 (5.5%)	9 (11.7%)	—	1 (1.9%)	1 (2.4%)
	Scrapers	3 (2.7%)	1 (0.9%)		—	2 (3.8%)	1 (2.4%)
	Points	—	—	7 (9.1%)	11 (22.0%)	13 (25.0%)	20 (47.6%)
	Other	—	—	—	1 (2.0%)	1 (1.9%)	1 (2.4%)

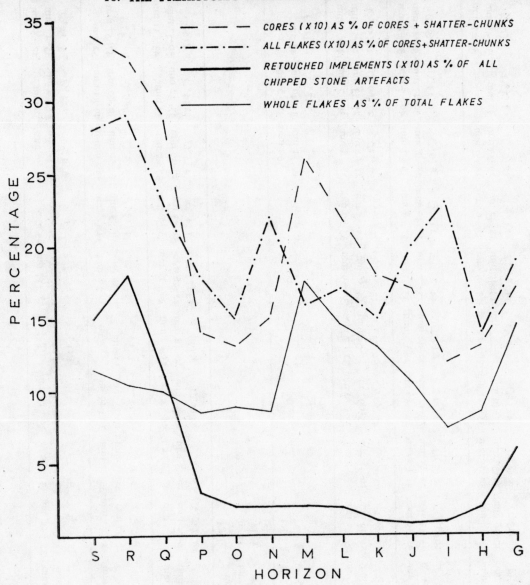

Fig. 76. Kalemba: selected ratios in the chipped stone industries.

Table 37, continued.

	M	L	K	J	I	H	G	Total all horizons
	17466	16495	46631	46283	47290	8155	7771	275042
	79%	76%	86%	89%	84%	76%	79%	
	21%	24%	11%	11%	4%	12%	9%	
	— (0.4%)	— (0.3%)	4% (0.3%)	— (0.5%)	12% (0.7%)	12% (1.2%)	13% (2.7%)	
	178 (1.0%)	135 (0.8%)	325 (0.7%)	253 (0.5%)	173 (0.4%)	45 (0.6%)	47 (0.6%)	1657
	6618 (37.9%)	5875 (35.6%)	18195 (39.0%)	14953 (32.3%)	13959 (29.5%)	3330 (40.8%)	2654 (34.2%)	93660
	1857 (10.6%)	1502 (9.1%)	3651 (7.8%)	3227 (7.0%)	2464 (5.2%)	412 (5.1%)	734 (9.4%)	19009
	8779 (50.3%)	8949 (54.3%)	24404 (52.3%)	27805 (60.1%)	30643 (64.8%)	4351 (53.4%)	4289 (55.2%)	159990
	34 (0.2%)	34 (0.2%)	56 (0.1%)	45 (0.1%)	51 (0.1%)	17 (0.2%)	47 (0.6%)	726
	2 (5.9%)	—	—	2 (4.4%)	2 (3.9%)	—	—	210
	8 (23.5%)	4 (11.8%)	5 (8.9%)			—	—	137
	—	—	—					27
	—	—	1 (1.8%)	1 (2.2%)	3 (5.9%)			31
	22 (64.7%)	29 (85.3%)	46 (82.1%)	37 (82.2%)	40 (78.4%)	14 (82.4%)	42 (89.4%)	285
	1 (2.9%)	1 (2.9%)	4 (7.1%)	5 (11.1%)	6 (11.7%)	2 (11.8%)	5 (10.6%)	26
	1 (2.9%)					1 (5.9%)		3

Table 38. Kalemba cores

Horizon:	S	R	Q	P	O	N	M	L	K	J	I	H	G
UNILATERAL SINGLE-PLATFORM	9 (14%)	7 (14%)	11 (17%)	14 (18%)	16 (13%)	9 (8%)	4 (5%)	4 (6%)	11 (6%)	12 (7%)	12 (9%)	1 (2%)	6 (13%)
Range in max. dimension	13–57 mm	20–30 mm	22–38 mm	18–41 mm	17–36 mm	20–37 mm	23–49 mm	20–55 mm	13–46 mm	17–42 mm	29–53 mm	43 mm	30–49 mm
Mean max. dimension	31±13 mm	27±3 mm	30±6 mm	30±6 mm	27±6 mm	30±5 mm	35±11 mm	36±13 mm	25±9 mm	33±6 mm	38±7 mm	43 mm	37±7 mm
BILATERAL SINGLE-PLATFORM	10 (15%)	7 (14%)	9 (14%)	9 (12%)	10 (8%)	8 (7%)	8 (11%)	6 (9%)	14 (7%)	4 (2%)	8 (6%)	6 (13%)	4 (9%)
Range in max. dimension	23–36 mm	20–34 mm	21–35 mm	16–46 mm	23–43 mm	23–48 mm	27–127 mm	22–42 mm	27–77 mm	27–46 mm	28–48 mm	30–47 mm	35–41 mm
Mean max. dimension	29±4 mm	27±4 mm	27±4 mm	28±8 mm	31±6 mm	31±8 mm	49±30 mm	28±7 mm	33±14 mm	37±8 mm	39±7 mm	40±5 mm	37±2 mm
RADIAL	16 (25%)	16 (32%)	15 (24%)	28 (35%)	51 (40%)	65 (55%)	47 (62%)	51 (73%)	130 (67%)	128 (72%)	96 (72%)	27 (60%)	26 (55%)
Range in max. dimension	19–36 mm	19–39 mm	17–45 mm	16–71 mm	14–46 mm	16–48 mm	15–69 mm	17–54 mm	14–56 mm	21–55 mm	21–62 mm	25–53 mm	26–53 mm
Mean max. dimension	28±5 mm	29±6 mm	28±7 mm	31±11 mm	29±7 mm	31±8 mm	33±10 mm	32±7 mm	30±9 mm	35±7 mm	38±8 mm	39±7 mm	40±7 mm
TORTOISE	—	—	—	—	—	—	—	1 (1%)	—	1 (1%)	2 (2%)	3 (7%)	1 (2%)
Range in max. dimension								47 mm		45 mm	49, 51 mm	34–40 mm	45 mm
Mean max. dimension											50 mm	37±2 mm	
BIPOLAR	3 (5%)	1 (2%)	2 (3%)	2 (3%)	1 (1%)	—	—	—	—	—	—	—	—
Range in max. dimension	14–36 mm	19 mm	25, 39 mm	19, 23 mm	30 mm								
Mean max. dimension	29±10 mm	19 mm	32 mm	21 mm	30 mm								
DOUBLE-PLATFORM	9 (14%)	12 (24%)	10 (16%)	5 (6%)	18 (14%)	15 (13%)	4 (5%)	6 (9%)	13 (7%)	7 (4%)	4 (3%)	2 (4%)	3 (6%)
Range in max. dimension	20–38 mm	24–41 mm	22–55 mm	26–33 mm	16–60 mm	20–43 mm	23–42 mm	20–48 mm	21–96 mm	31–53 mm	27–46 mm	37, 42 mm	30–57 mm
Mean max. dimension	28±5 mm	29±6 mm	31±10 mm	30±3 mm	30±9 mm	28±6 mm	34±8 mm	35±9 mm	36±18 mm	36±8 mm	37±7 mm	39 mm	43±11 mm
POLYHEDRAL	9 (14%)	4 (8%)	11 (17%)	10 (13%)	11 (9%)	12 (10%)	9 (12%)	1 (1%)	24 (12%)	24 (13%)	6 (5%)	4 (9%)	2 (4%)
Range in max. dimension	26–47 mm	24–35 mm	22–37 mm	22–35 mm	22–97 mm	24–45 mm	17–45 mm	33 mm	20–56 mm	19–53 mm	30–56 mm	30–80 mm	47, 57 mm
Mean max. dimension	35±7 mm	31±4 mm	28±4 mm	29±4 mm	34±21 mm	33±7 mm	34±10 mm	33 mm	33±8 mm	34±8 mm	38±9 mm	49±19 mm	52 mm
IRREGULAR	9 (14%)	3 (6%)	5 (8%)	11 (14%)	9 (15%)	9 (8%)	4 (5%)	1 (1%)	3 (2%)	2 (1%)	5 (4%)	2 (4%)	5 (11%)
Range in max. dimension	24–46 mm	23–41 mm	20–35 mm	19–41 mm	18–74 mm	22–46 mm	23–60 mm	24 mm	16–40 mm	23, 27 mm	35–52 mm	37, 40 mm	35–47 mm
Mean max. dimension	31±6 mm	34±8 mm	26±5 mm	28±7 mm	35±12 mm	33±7 mm	39±13 mm	24 mm	28±10 mm	25 mm	42±6 mm	38 mm	42±5 mm
TOTAL CORES IN SAMPLE	65	50	63	79	126	118	76	70	195	178	133	45	47
Mean max. dimension of all cores	30±6 mm	29±6 mm	28±7 mm	29±8 mm	30±10 mm	31±7 mm	35±13 mm	32±8 mm	31±10 mm	34±7 mm	38±8 mm	40±9 mm	40±8 mm

occurrence in the lower levels of large implements, notably scrapers, which are characteristically made on larger pieces than are generally available in crystalline quartz, and for which the more friable, coarser-grained materials may have been found more suitable.

In table 37 are presented the major chipped stone artefact categories for each horizon. The steady trends in the relative frequency of the retouched implements should be noted: representing 0.6 per cent of the aggregate from horizon G, they fall sharply in frequency to only 0.1 per cent in horizons I, J and K, climbing slowly but steadily thereafter to 0.3 per cent in horizon P, before jumping to much higher frequencies of between 1 and 2 per cent in the most recent horizons. The relative frequencies of the other categories are too inter-dependant for the figures shown in table 37 to display immediately significant trends, but they enable various ratios to be calculated which provide a clearer picture of the composition of the aggregates (fig. 76). The parallelism between the curve showing the relative incidence of whole and broken flakes and that calculated in respect of cores and shatter-chunks is particularly noteworthy: comparable trends are apparent in the ratio of whole and broken flakes to cores plus shatter-chunks, and also in the relative frequency of retouched implements.

CORES

The following analysis is based on a total of 1245 cores, comprising all those yielded in the sample areas by horizons G, H and N to S, with random samples of those from the more prolific horizons I to M.

The maximum dimensions of the cores show a steady decrease with time: the mean values, to one standard deviation, are shown in fig. 77.

The following core-types are represented in the assemblage (see also table 38, fig. 78 and fig. 79):

Unilateral single-platform. These are mostly irregular and minimally worked. Flat, fully worked out examples—such as were noted at Makwe—are exceptional, and their occurrence is restricted to the upper five horizons.

Conical or cylindrical types are not here represented. Unilateral single-platform cores comprise 13 per cent of the cores in horizon G and less than 10 per cent in horizons H to N; their frequency rises again to between 14 and 18 per cent in the four most recent horizons. Their mean maximum dimension shows an irregular decline through the sequence from 37 to 27 mm.

Bilateral single-platform. The frequency of this type remains at between 7 and 15 per cent through the greater part of the succession. They show a reduction in mean maximum dimension from about 38 mm in the lower horizons to about 28 mm at the top of the sequence. The bilateral single-platform cores show greater standardisation than the unilateral examples, those from the lower horizons in particular being worked around much of their periphery in a manner comparable with that employed in the production of the radial cores. In the upper horizons, their counterparts are frequently elongated, and worked at one end to produce a chopper-like edge.

Radial. In every horizon this core-type is the most frequent. Representing between 50 and 60 per cent of cores in horizons G and H, their frequency increases to between 67 and 73 per cent in horizons I to L, falling steadily thereafter to figures below 30 per cent in the upper levels. Their mean maximum dimensions show a parallel decline from 40 mm to 28 mm. Remarkably small specimens are characteristic of the upper horizons: this is the only core-type which regularly includes specimens less than 20 mm in maximum dimension. Almost all the radial cores are bifacially worked, biconical types being predominant, biconvex types uncommon, and flat examples extremely rare. Asymmetrical specimens are more frequent than at Makwe, particularly in the lower levels.

Tortoise. This sub-type is represented by a total of only eight examples, their distribution being restricted to horizons G to L. Their maximum dimensions range from 34 to 51 mm. They are radial cores which have been carefully prepared for the removal of a single flake in a plane parallel to that of the peripheral striking platform. One example has been thus worked on both sides; the others are radially flaked on the reverse face. These are the only cores at Kalemba to show clear signs of platform preparation.

Bipolar. The occurrence of bipolar cores is restricted to the upper five horizons, where they never represent more than 5 per cent of the total number of cores. The mean maximum dimension of the nine bipolar cores is 27 mm. None show signs of significant damage attributable to utilisation after striking.

Double-platform. These are found in all levels but are uncommon below horizon M. Their mean maximum dimensions show a steady decline from 43 mm in horizon G to 28 mm in horizon S.

Polyhedral. These show frequency and size distributions similar to those of the double-platform cores, but tend to be slightly larger in most horizons. They are irregular and unsystematically worked.

Irregular. In no horizon do irregular cores represent more than 15 per cent of the total. They are particularly uncommon in horizons J to L. Mean maximum dimensions vary from 25 to 42 mm, with a tendency towards higher values in the lower horizons. The majority of cores in this category appear to be broken

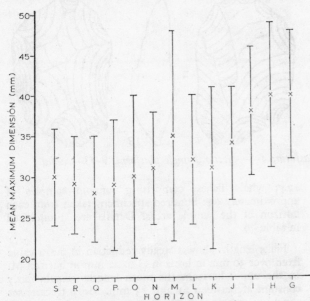

Fig. 77. Mean maximum dimensions (to one standard deviation) of Kalemba cores.

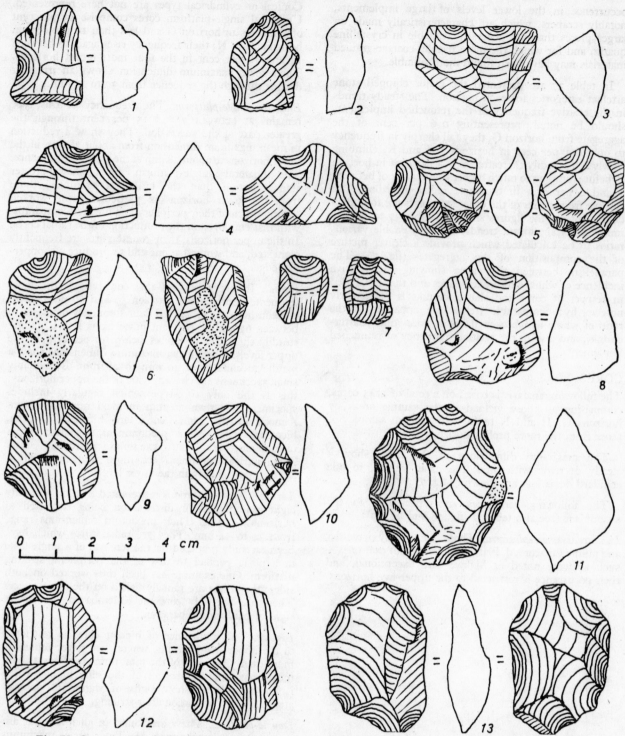

Fig. 78. Cores from Kalemba: 1–3—unilateral single platform; 4–8—bilateral single platform; 9–13—radial.

worked out cores of other types (*i.e.* shatter-chunks) which have been subjected to minimal further working.

SHATTER-CHUNKS

The stratigraphical occurrence of the shatter-chunks is shown in table 37, and its implications have been discussed briefly above. No typological or metrical analysis of these artefacts has been attempted.

FLAKES

The following description is based on the analysis of

1243 whole flakes, comprising random samples of approximately one hundred specimens taken from each horizon of the sample areas. Details are summarised in table 39.

Flake lengths show a steady reduction in mean value from over 30 mm in horizon G to 22 mm in horizon M. In the upper horizons the mean lengths remain fairly constant at between 21 and 23 mm. Mean thicknesses show a corresponding, but not precisely parallel, decrease from 8.2 mm in horizon G to between 4.6 and 4.8 mm in horizons Q to S. Mean length/breadth

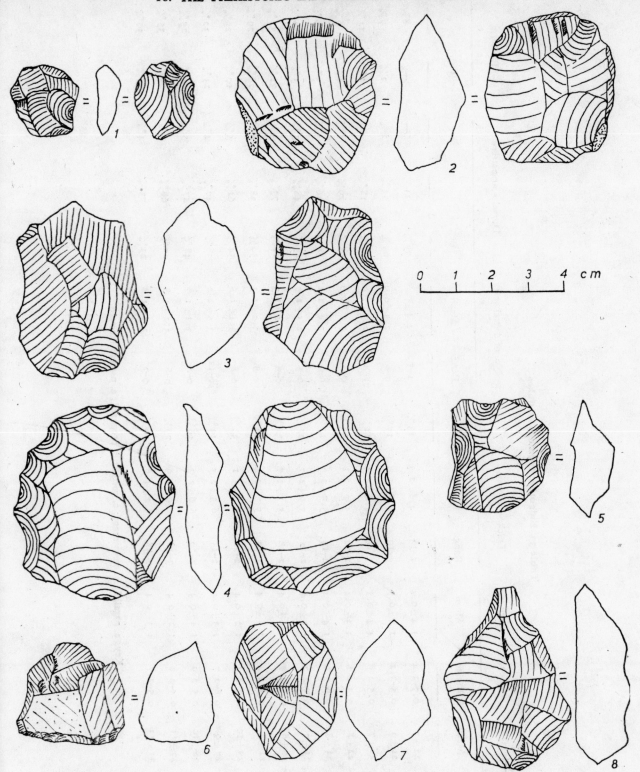

Fig. 79. Cores from Kalemba: 1–3—radial; 4—tortoise; 5—double platform; 6, 7—polyhedral; 8—irregular.

ratios vary erratically within the relatively narrow limits of 1.45 and 1.19 as shown in table 39. A clearer picture of variation in flake sizes and proportions is provided by the length/breadth scatter-diagrams (fig. 80), and by calculation of the mean weight of the flakes from each horizon (fig. 81).

The mean number of dorsal flake-scars present on each flake shows a consistent pattern, with values of between 3.0 and 3.5 in horizons G to M, and between 2.2 and 2.5 in the subsequent horizons. In general terms this decrease may be correlated with the reducing frequency of flakes with convergent dorsal scar-patterns; and the erratic fluctuations in the latter figures for horizons J to N are to a certain extent reflected in those for the mean number of dorsal scars, as is shown in fig. 82.

An interesting trend is seen in the percentage frequency of flakes bearing prepared striking platforms.

Table 39. Kalemba: typology of flakes

Horizon	Flakes in sample	Length (mm) Range	Length (mm) Mean	Length/Breadth Range	Length/Breadth Mean	Thickness (mm) Range	Thickness (mm) Mean	Side-struck	No. of dorsal scars Range	No. of dorsal scars Mean	Dorsal scar pattern a	b	c	Platform d	e
S	97	10-44	22±7	0.7-2.4	1.4±0.4	2-13	4.8±2.3	13%	1-5	2.4±0.8	79%	21%	—	—	8%
R	96	9-45	21±6	0.5-3.2	1.4±0.5	2-10	4.6±1.9	17%	0-6	2.3±0.9	65%	33%	2%	2%	8%
Q	84	9-47	22±7	0.5-2.6	1.4±0.5	1-15	4.8±2.4	11%	1-8	2.3±1.0	82%	18%	—	1%	11%
P	98	10-42	22±8	0.4-2.8	1.3±0.4	2-22	5.7±3.1	26%	0-4	2.2±1.0	65%	29%	6%	1%	6%
O	77	10-55	23±8	0.6-3.0	1.4±0.4	2-14	5.7±2.6	17%	0-6	2.4±1.1	59%	36%	5%	3%	29%
N	92	9-41	23±7	0.5-2.3	1.3±0.4	2-15	5.9±2.7	21%	0-5	2.5±1.0	49%	48%	3%	3%	20%
M	100	8-46	20±6	0.5-2.7	1.2±0.4	2-18	5.1±2.7	31%	0-6	3.0±1.3	20%	77%	3%	31%	32%
L	100	10-45	21±8	0.5-2.4	1.3±0.4	1-12	5.3±2.4	23%	0-8	3.2±1.3	59%	38%	3%	28%	29%
K	100	7-55	25±10	0.3-2.4	1.2±0.4	2-22	6.4±3.1	32%	0-8	3.1±1.8	34%	61%	5%	10%	29%
J	100	13-64	27±9	0.6-2.7	1.3±0.4	2-15	6.3±2.5	13%	0-12	3.5±2.2	56%	40%	4%	23%	30%
I	100	10-52	28±10	0.5-2.9	1.4±0.4	2-20	6.6±2.7	16%	0-8	3.1±1.7	48%	47%	5%	14%	25%
H	99	8-57	27±11	0.5-2.2	1.2±0.4	3-18	7.0±2.9	29%	0-8	3.1±1.8	27%	66%	7%	5%	35%
G	100	12-83	31±13	0.5-2.7	1.3±0.4	2-38	8.2±4.6	20%	0-9	3.2±1.8	23%	73%	4%	4%	30%

Key: **a.** parallel; **b.** convergent; **c.** cortex; **d.** prepared; **e.** pseudo-facetted.

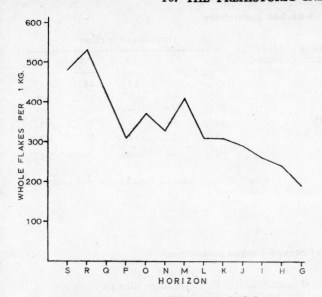

Fig. 81. Kalemba: weights of whole flakes.

From only 4 and 5 per cent in the two lowest horizons, this rises fairly steadily to over 30 per cent in horizon M, but thereafter never exceeds 3 per cent. Pseudo-facetted platforms are found on between 25 and 35 per cent of the flakes from horizons G to M, decreasing to less than 10 per cent in the upper levels.

RETOUCHED IMPLEMENTS

A total of 726 retouched implements was recovered from the sample areas and has been analysed in detail. The primary categories of these for each horizon are summarised in table 37. The trends in the stratigraphic occurrence of each type are, in most cases, readily apparent and do not need to be elaborated at this stage. Backed specimens first appear in the sequence in horizon I and increase steadily in frequency, representing over 97 per cent of the implements from the two most recent horizons. Six geometrics retain traces of mastic;

and these are described and discussed in the appendix (pp. 215-8) along with the similar specimens from Makwe. The remaining implements are predominantly scrapers, with a minority of bifacial and unifacial flake points in the lower levels. A selection of the retouched implements from each horizon is illustrated in figs. 83-6, 89-94.

Curved-backed geometrics

Details of the 141 curved-backed geometrics are presented in table 40. Implements of this type first appear in small numbers in horizon M: in horizons O to R they represent approximately 30 per cent of the retouched implements,* rising to 60 per cent in the most recent horizon, horizon S. There is a slight but steady reduction in mean length from over 21 mm in the earliest specimens to rather less than 17 mm in the most recent. There is a remarkable pattern in the trend towards increased incidence of bi-directional backing, which rises from 25 to 60 per cent in horizons M to P and again from 19 to 60 per cent in horizons Q to S. The same configuration, although slightly less pronounced, is apparent among the bi-directionally backed geometrics as a whole. There are less marked increases continuing through the sequence in the proportion of the back of each curved-backed geometric which bears retouch. A more detailed picture is provided by examination of the three sub-types (table 41) into which the curved-backed geometrics have been divided.

Pointed lunates. These appear through time to represent a progressively larger proportion of the curved-backed geometric category. The specimens from horizons M to P are too few for the variation in frequency in individual horizons to be treated as significant, but pointed lunates represent 59 per cent of the total curved-backed geometrics from these four horizons taken

---

*The drop in frequency in horizons Q and R is a reflection of the large numbers of angled-backed geometrics present in those horizons.

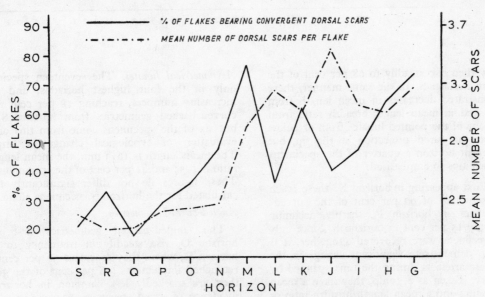

Fig. 82. Kalemba whole flakes: incidence of convergent dorsal scars compared with mean number of dorsal scars per flake.

Table 40. Kalemba: curved-backed geometrics

Horizon	No.	% of all geometrics	Length (mm) Range	Length (mm) Mean	% eared	% fully backed	Mean % backing	Direction of backing a	b	c	d	e
S	62	85%	11–27	16.8±3.4	31%	69%	91%	40%	—	13%	44%	3%
R	29	44%	12–25	17.4±2.8	7%	59%	89%	59%	—	7%	35%	—
Q	16	48%	10–25	17.3±3.5	12%	62%	90%	81%	—	7%	19%	—
P	15	83%	11–32	18.0±3.4	27%	60%	88%	40%	—	—	19%	—
O	15	94%	14–24	18.5±2.3	27%	40%	83%	40%	—	7%	40%	13%
N	2	100% }	17–26	21.5±3.0	—	100%	100%	53%	7%	13%	27%	—
M	2	100% }						75%	—	—	—	25%

Key: a. backed from ventral surface; b. backed from dorsal surface; c. backing totally bi-directional; d. backing partly bi-directional; e. backed from alternate directions.

Table 41. Kalemba: sub-classes of curved-backed geometrics

	Horizon	No.	% of curved-backed geometrics	Length (mm) Range	Length (mm) Mean	Length/Breadth Range	Length/Breadth Mean	% eared
POINTED LUNATES	S	42	68%	11–27	17.0±3.6	1.2–2.4	1.6±0.2	26%
	R	19	66%	14–25	18.1±2.7	1.4–2.4	1.8±0.3	5%
	Q	10	63%	15–25	18.4±3.5	1.2–2.6	1.7±0.4	10%
	P	5	33%	18–32	22.8±5.5	1.3–2.0	1.6±0.2	—
	O	12	80%	16–24	19.4±2.6	1.5–2.7	2.0±0.3	—
	N	1 }	75%	19–26	23.0±2.9	1.8–2.1	2.0±0.1	—
	M	2 }						
		91	65%	11–32	18.2±3.4	1.2–2.7	1.7±0.3	14%
DEEP LUNATES	S	9	15%	12–23	16.3±3.7	1.0–1.8	1.4±0.2	33%
	R	6	21%	12–22	16.3±3.4	1.0–1.5	1.2±0.2	17%
	Q	5	31%	10–19	15.0±3.5	1.0–1.4	1.2±0.1	—
	P	9	60%	11–18	15.2±2.6	0.9–1.5	1.2±0.2	33%
	O	3	20%	14–16	15.0±1.0	1.2–1.6	1.4±0.1	67%
	N	1 }	25%	17		1.1		—
	M	— }						
		33	23%	10–23	15.7±3.0	0.9–1.8	1.3±0.2	27%
ASYMMETRICAL LUNATES	S	11	18%	12–20	16.2±2.6	1.3–1.7	1.5±0.1	45%
	R	4	14%	12–17	15.8±2.3	1.3–1.7	1.5±0.1	—
	Q	1 }	7%	17, 19	18.0	1.3, 2.1	1.7	—
	P	1 }						
		17	12%	12–20	16.3±2.3	1.3–2.1	1.5±0.1	41%

together. They then rise steadily to 68 per cent of the specimens from horizon S. In the same manner, there may be demonstrated decreases in mean length from 21 to 17 mm and in mean length/breadth ratio from 1.9 to 1.6. None of the pointed lunates from or below horizon P bears an eared projection at the tip, but in the most recent horizon a quarter of the specimens have one of their tips so emphasised.

Deep lunates. First appearing in horizon N, these reach a maximum frequency of 60 per cent of the curved-backed geometrics in horizon P, sharply declining thereafter to only 15 per cent in horizon S. Since only thirty-three specimens were recovered altogether, it is not possible to demonstrate significant change in the typology of these artefacts during the time spanned by their occurrence. Taken as a group, they have a mean length of 15.7 mm and a mean length/breadth ratio of 1.3, while 27 per cent are eared. (The corresponding figures for the pointed lunates as a whole are 18.2 mm, 1.7 and 14 per cent.)

Asymmetrical lunates. The seventeen specimens occur only in the four highest horizons, and in steadily increasing numbers, reaching 18 per cent of the total curved-backed geometrics from horizon S. Since all but six of the specimens come from this one horizon, evaluation of typological change is impracticable. The mean length is 16.3 mm, the mean length/breadth ratio is 1.5; and 41 per cent of the specimens are eared. These figures do not differ significantly from those calculated for the horizon S specimens alone.

Angled-backed geometrics

The angled-backed geometrics first appear in horizon O, rise steadily in frequency to a peak in horizon R, where they represent 37 per cent of all the retouched implements (56 per cent of the geometrics); they are markedly less common in horizon S. The incidence of eared specimens (38 per cent) is higher than among the curved-backed geometrics. The four geometric microliths from horizons O and P are all trapezoidal; in horizon Q they are joined by both

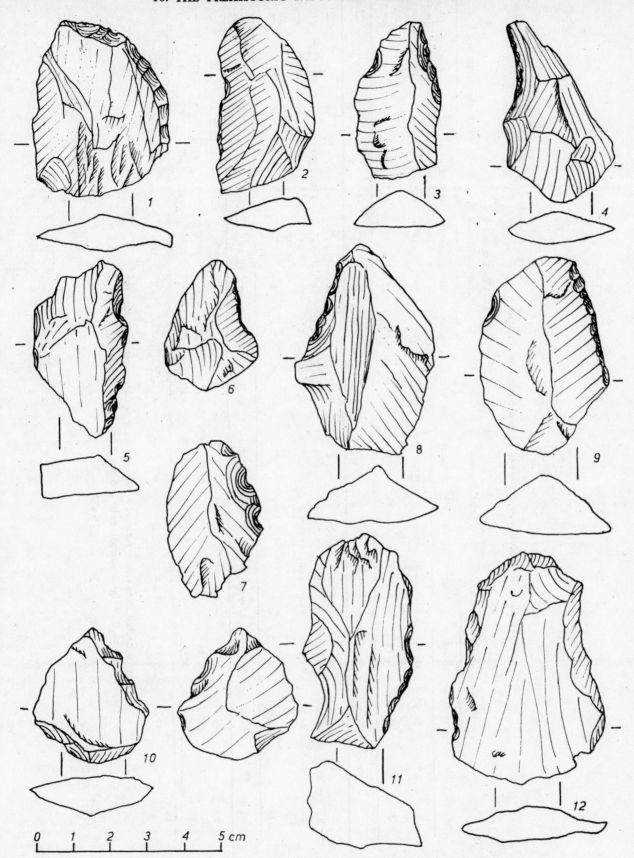

Fig. 83. Retouched implements from horizon G at Kalemba: 1–12—scrapers.

Table 42. Kalemba: sub-classes of angled-backed geometrics

Horizon	No.	% of angled-backed geometrics	Length (mm) Range	Length (mm) Mean	Length/Breadth Range	Length/Breadth Mean	% eared	% fully backed	Unretouched portion of back Sharp	Unretouched portion of back Blunt	Mean % backing	Direction of backing a	b	c	d
TRIANGULAR MICROLITHS															
S	6	54%	11-17	14.7±2.1	0.9-1.5	1.2±0.2	17%	67%	16%	16%	95%	67%	—	33%	—
R	5	13%	13-17	14.6±1.7	1.0-1.8	1.3±0.3	80%	80%	20%	—	98%	60%	20%	20%	—
Q	3	18%	9-13	10.6±1.7	0.9-1.2	1.1±0.1	100%	67%	33%	—	97%	100%	—	—	—
	14	20%	9-17	13.8±1.9	0.9-1.8	1.2±0.2	57%	71%	21%	7%	96%	71%	7%	21%	—
TRAPEZOIDAL MICROLITHS															
S	5	45%	14-18	15.8±1.5	1.3-1.9	1.5±0.2	80%	40%	40%	20%	66%	100%	—	—	—
R	11	30%	11-23	15.3±3.8	0.7-2.3	1.4±0.4	36%	18%	64%	18%	71%	64%	—	27%	9%
Q	7	41%	11-21	15.6±3.5	1.1-1.8	1.4±0.2	43%	29%	29%	43%	73%	71%	—	29%	—
P	3	100%	16-24	18.5±3.2	1.2-2.2	1.8±0.4	50%	—	75%	25%	52%	50%	—	50%	—
O	1	100%	—	—	—	—	—	—	—	—	—	—	—	—	—
	27	39%	11-24	15.9±3.2	0.7-2.3	1.5±0.3	48%	22%	26%	22%	68%	70%	—	26%	4%
PETITS TRANCHETS															
S	—	—	—	—	—	—	—	—	—	—	—	—	—	—	—
R	21	57%	6-15	10.5±2.2	0.4-1.0	0.7±0.2	24%	48%	19%	33%	87%	43%	—	57%	—
Q	7	41%	5-15	11.0±3.3	0.3-0.9	0.8±0.2	29%	71%	—	29%	93%	57%	—	43%	—
	28	41%	5-15	10.6±2.5	0.3-1.0	0.7±0.2	25%	54%	14%	32%	88%	46%	—	54%	—

Key: a. backed from ventral surface; b. backing totally bi-directional; c. backing partly bi-directional; d. backed from alternate directions.

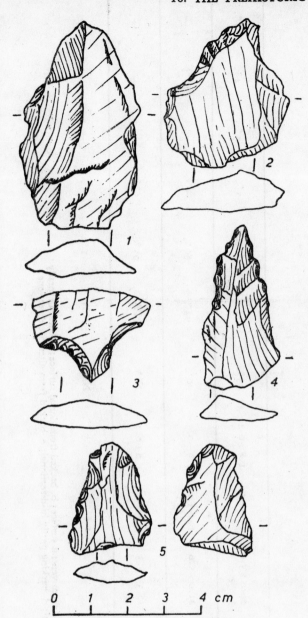

Fig. 84. *Retouched implements from horizon G at Kalemba:1–5—points.*

triangular and *petit tranchet* forms. The latter type occurs only in horizons P and Q, where it represents respectively 41 and 57 per cent of the angled-backed geometrics, frequencies of the other types showing a corresponding depression (table 42). It is only in the uppermost horizon that triangular microliths are dominant.

Trapezoidal microliths. Taken as a group, these have a mean length of 15.9 mm and a mean length/breadth ratio of 1.5. The apparent tendency for both figures to reduce slightly in the higher levels is probably not significant. On 22 per cent of the twenty-seven specimens backed retouch extends over the entire back; on the others the central portion of the back (*i.e.* that approximately parallel to the edge) is left sharp (on 52 per cent) or forms a naturally blunt break (26 per cent). On 70 per cent of the trapezoidal microliths the backing is uni-directional, exclusively from the ventral surface; the others are only partly retouched by bi-directional backing, specimens completely so retouched not being represented in the Kalemba collection. Almost half the microliths of this type are eared; but here, as with the other characteristics, the sample is not sufficiently large for the demonstration of significant typological change through the sequence.

Petits tranchets. As noted above, these occur only in horizons Q and R, which yielded seven and twenty-one specimens respectively. No significant morphological distinctions could be made between the assemblages from the two horizons. The *petits tranchets* have a mean length of 10.6 mm and a mean length/breadth ratio of 0.7. Backing on 54 per cent is partly bi-directional, and uni-directional from the ventral surface on the remainder. The mean percentage of the back of each specimen to bear retouch approaches 90 per cent. One quarter of the *petits tranchets* are flared or eared.

Triangular microliths. Fourteen specimens were recovered, all from the upper three horizons. They all form approximately isosceles triangles with the edge, which has a mean length of 13.8 mm, as hypotenuse. The mean length/breadth ratio is 1.2. On three quarters of the specimens the backing is exclusively from the ventral surface; and there is only one example on which the backing is completely bi-directional. Eight triangular microliths are flared or eared.

Backed flakes

These total 137, first appear in horizon I and reach a peak frequency in horizons N, O and P, where they

Table 43. Kalemba: backed flakes

Horizon	Convex	Straight	Transverse	Concave	Total
S	12 (63%)	1 (5%)	5 (24%)	1 (5%)	19
R	21 (81%)	2 (8%)	3 (12%)	—	26
Q	16 (76%)	1 (5%)	4 (19%)	—	21
P	14 (87%)	2 (12%)	—	—	16
O	15 (83%)	2 (11%)	1 (6%)	—	18
N	12 (75%)	1 (6%)	3 (18%)	—	16
M	6 } (75%)	1 } (8%)	1 } (17%)	—	8
L	3	—	1	—	4
K	5 } (89%)	—	— } (11%)	—	5
J	1	—	1	—	2
I	2	—	—	—	2
	107 (78%)	10 (7%)	19 (14%)	1 (1%)	137

Table 44. Kalemba: sub-classes of backed flakes

Horizon	No.	Length (mm) Range	Length (mm) Mean	Length/Breadth Range	Length/Breadth Mean	% fully backed	Mean % backed	Direction of backing a	b	c	d	e
CONVEX												
S	12	13–27	19.6±4.4	1.3–2.1	1.7±0.2	17%	61%	100%	—	—	—	—
R	21	13–24	18.0±3.0	1.4–2.7	1.8±0.3	52%	85%	86%	9%	5%	—	—
Q	16	13–24	16.4±3.1	1.1–2.0	1.6±0.2	44%	81%	82%	—	6%	12%	—
P	14	13–31	21.0±5.2	1.4–2.7	1.9±0.4	50%	83%	79%	—	14%	7%	—
O	15	13–31	19.3±5.1	1.2–4.0	1.9±0.7	40%	75%	80%	—	7%	7%	7%
N	12	12–49	22.4±8.9	1.5–2.6	1.8±0.3	17%	67%	100%	—	—	—	—
M	6 }											
L	} 3	15–40	24.7±7.7	1.4–2.4	1.9±0.3	—	54%	100%	—	—	—	—
K	5 }											
J	1 } 2	20–38	26.4±5.0	1.1–3.2	2.0±0.6	—	64%	100%	—	—	—	—
I												
Total	107	12–49	20.0±5.0	1.1–4.0	1.8±0.4	33%	74%	88%	3%	5%	4%	1%
STRAIGHT												
Total	10	15–33	21.0±5.6	1.4–3.0	1.9±0.5	70%	94%	80%	—	10%	10%	—
TRANSVERSE												
Total	19	11–33	20.3±6.3	0.9–2.5	1.6±0.4	N/A	N/A	95%	5%	—	—	—
CONCAVE												
Total	1	14		1.6		N/A	N/A	1	—	—	—	—

Key: a. backed from ventral surface; b. backed from dorsal surface; c. backing totally bi-directional; d. backing partly bi-directional; e. backed from alternate directions.

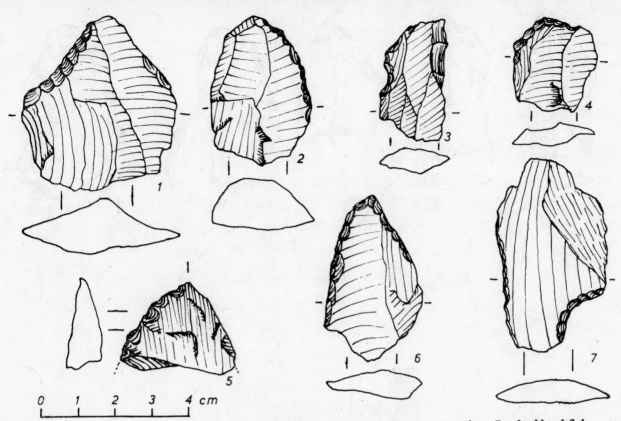

0 1 2 3 4 cm

Fig. 85. Retouched implements from horizon H at Kalemba: 1–4—scrapers; 5, 6—points; 7—shouldered flake.

represent between 34 and 38 per cent of the retouched implements, declining again in frequency thereafter. At all levels, convex-backed flakes predominate; straight and transverse forms appear respectively in horizons M and J and continue to be found in small numbers through the succeeding horizons (table 43). The single example of a concave-backed flake comes from horizon S. No backed flakes bear ears such as are frequently observed on the geometrics. In view of the number of specimens represented, metrical data on the backed flakes are best presented under the heads of these sub-types.

Convex-backed flakes. Details of the convex-backed flakes are presented in table 44. There is a significant decrease in mean length from over 25 mm in the lowest horizons (I to M) to 16 mm in horizon Q, rising slightly again in the two most recent horizons. The mean length/breadth ratio shows a slight but rather more steady decrease from 1.9 to between 1.6 and 1.7 through the sequence. Only one third of the convex-backed flakes are retouched along their entire length; and the mean proportion of the back to be retouched is 74 per cent. These figures both rise somewhat in horizons O to R, which is the only part of the sequence where bi-directional backing occurs on convex-backed flakes; even here, however, it does not occur on more than one fifth of the specimens from any one horizon.

Straight-backed flakes. There are only ten examples, so typological change cannot be demonstrated. They have a mean length of 21.0 mm and a mean length/breadth ratio of 1.9. All but two are backed only from the ventral surface.

Transverse-backed flakes. The seventeen specimens have a mean length of 20.3 mm and a mean length/breadth ratio of 1.6. An apparent tendency for both these measurements to be somewhat less with regard to the specimens from the three most recent horizons cannot be shown to be significant. The backed edge is oblique to the long axis of the artefact on all but one example; on this specimen, from horizon Q, it is approximately perpendicular to the long axis. All are uni-directionally backed and, again with one exception (from horizon Q), from the ventral surface.

Concave-backed flake. The single example comes from horizon S, has a length of 14 mm, and is backed from the ventral surface.

Backed fragments

There are twenty-seven broken fragments which could have come either from geometrics or from flakes. They occur in horizons O to S inclusive, as is shown in table 37.

Backed points

The seven implements in this category are restricted to the upper part of the sequence, where they occur in horizons N to R. Their mean length is 22.6 ± 4.4 mm and the mean length/breadth ratio 2.0 ± 0.3. On two specimens, from horizons Q and R, the edge is backed adjacent to the tip; on all other specimens it is a clean break roughly perpendicular to the main flake surface. All backing on the backed points is from the ventral surface only. Abrasion and scaling of the point on the majority of specimens indicates heavy use: indeed it is not certain whether or not the two specimens from horizons O and P are intentionally backed or whether the damage to the back was caused exclusively by use.

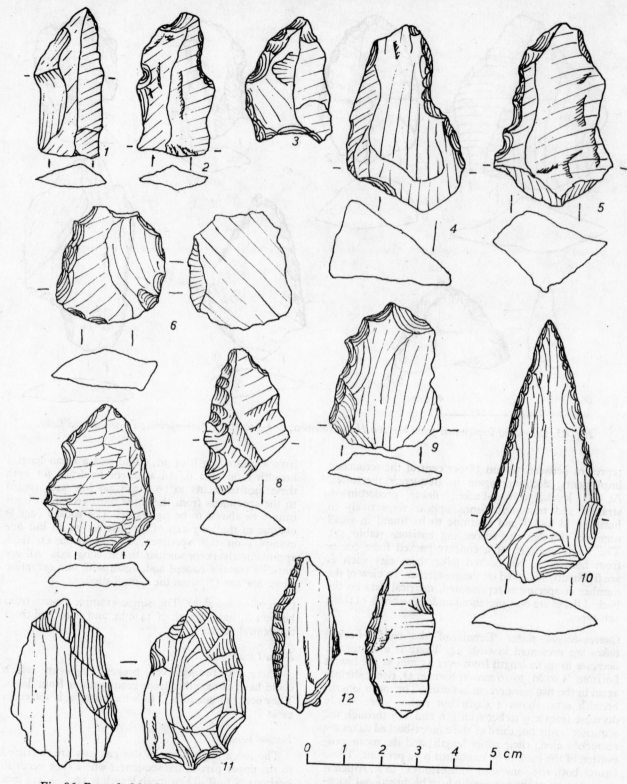

Fig. 86. Retouched implements from horizon I at Kalemba: 1–9—scrapers; 10, 11—points; 12—backed flake.

Backed pieces

Together with the backed flakes these are the earliest backed implements to appear in the Kalemba sequence. Their first occurrence is in horizon I: thereafter they are present at most levels. The thirty-one specimens have a mean maximum dimension of 16.6 ± 3.2 mm,

with the figure for examples from the two most recent horizons being approximately 10 per cent higher than that for the earlier specimens. No change is demonstrable in the mean length/breadth ratio which, for the whole collection, is 1.4 ± 0.4. All the backed pieces are uni-directionally backed from the ventral surface.

Scrapers

The 285 scrapers comprise the largest category of retouched implements from Kalemba. They account for about 90 per cent of the retouched implements from the lowest excavated horizon, G, and steadily decrease in frequency thereafter to a level of less than 1 per cent in horizon R. There is a slight but probably significant increase in the highest horizon. Typologically, the scrapers show considerable but continuous variation in which no clustering into discrete types is apparent. It has therefore been considered more appropriate not to separate them into mutually exclusive sub-types, but to record for each specimen a number of well-defined traits and measurements which can then be used to illustrate the scrapers' range of typological variation and the degree to which this changes in different parts of the sequence. Data recorded for each scraper consist of the material and nature (*i.e.* whole flake, shatter-chunk, etc.) of the piece on which it was made; its length and breadth (defined as the lengths of the sides of the smallest rectangle into which the scraper could be fitted) and thickness; the profile of the retouched scraping edge (whether concave, straight, convex or denticulate); the axis of the implement on which this scraping edge was produced; the angle of retouch; and the length of the retouched edge. The information thus recovered is summarised in table 45.

The scrapers in horizon G have a mean length in excess of 40 mm; this steadily decreases to 32 mm in horizon M, rises slightly and then decreases again to a figure of only 30 mm for the scrapers from the three highest horizons. The length of the retouched scraping edge shows considerable variation, but the mean percentage of this relative to the length of the individual implement shows significant change through the Kalemba sequence (fig. 87). In horizons G and J the value is approximately 75 per cent but there is a marked drop in the intervening levels. From J to M the mean decreases steadily, reaching a level of 60 per cent in the latter horizon. Thereafter it climbs to almost 100 per cent in horizons Q to S. The angle of retouch also varies considerably, ranging on individual specimens from 30 to 80 degrees. The mean value for all scrapers is 55 degrees, while the corresponding figure for the

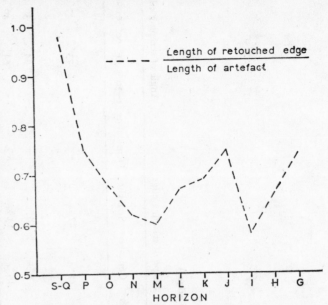

Fig. 87. *Mean relative length of retouched edge on scrapers from Kalemba.*

assemblages from individual horizons varies between 50 and 60 degrees, with no general trend being apparent. The relative frequency of the various shapes of cutting edge does, however, show significant change. Concave and denticulate scrapers represent respectively some 25 and 15 per cent of those from horizons G to L; thereafter they both become steadily less common, neither being represented at all in the small assemblage from the three most recent horizons. There is a corresponding increase in the occurrence of convex scrapers from approximately 35 to 40 per cent in horizons G to L, thereafter increasing steadily to over 75 per cent. Straight scrapers remain reasonably constant in frequency at between 20 and 25 per cent of the total from each horizon.

The selection of artefacts to form the base for scraper manufacture also raises points of interest. The graph (fig. 88) shows many irregularities due to the small

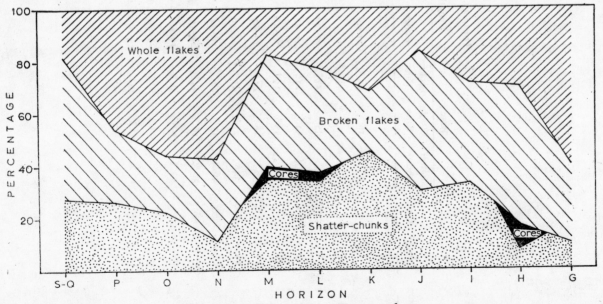

Fig. 88. *Kalemba: bases for scraper-manufacture.*

Table 45. Kalemba: scrapers. (LSE = length of retouched scraper edge.)

Horizon	No.	Base				Length (mm)		Length/Breadth		Mean LSE (mm)	Shape of scraping edge				Angle of scraping edge		
		Core	Shatter-chunk	Whole flake	Broken flake	Range	Mean	Range	Mean		Convex	Concave	Straight	Denticulate	0–30°	31°–60°	61°–90°
S	3 }																
R	1 }	—	27%	18%	55%	21–46	30.1±6.9	1.1–1.7	1.2±0.2	29.4	73%	—	27%	—	—	73%	27%
Q	7 }																
P	11	—	27%	45%	27%	27–42	33.7±5.2	1.1–2.6	1.4±0.4	25.3	73%	9%	18%	—	—	64%	36%
O	13	—	23%	54%	23%	21–46	36.2±8.0	1.2–1.8	1.5±0.2	24.6	62%	15%	15%	8%	—	54%	46%
N	20	—	10%	55%	35%	26–52	36.4±7.1	1.1–2.1	1.4±0.3	22.8	60%	20%	15%	5%	—	75%	25%
M	22	5%	36%	18%	41%	17–63	32.0±9.4	1.0–3.3	1.4±0.5	19.0	32%	23%	27%	18%	—	82%	18%
L	29	3%	34%	21%	41%	22–56	34.0±8.1	1.1–1.8	1.3±0.2	22.3	31%	38%	31%	—	3%	72%	24%
K	46	—	46%	33%	22%	18–54	33.8±8.6	1.0–2.3	1.4±0.3	23.6	35%	28%	26%	11%	2%	65%	33%
J	37	—	30%	16%	54%	25–55	36.1±7.5	1.0–2.3	1.4±0.3	27.2	41%	30%	16%	14%	2%	51%	49%
I	40	—	33%	30%	38%	17–62	37.0±8.9	1.0–2.9	1.5±0.4	20.9	40%	28%	23%	10%	—	85%	15%
H	14	7%	7%	29%	57%	25–56	39.1±8.6	1.0–1.7	1.3±0.2	25.1	50%	7%	29%	14%	—	100%	—
G	42	—	10%	62%	29%	25–61	40.4±8.9	1.0–2.4	1.4±0.3	29.4	40%	26%	19%	14%	5%	69%	26%

sizes of the samples from several horizons. The general picture, however, appears to be as follows. In the lowest horizon some 60 per cent of the scrapers are made on whole flakes, a further 30 per cent on broken flakes, and only 10 per cent on shatter-chunks. In successive horizons there is an increase in the incidence of scrapers made on the latter two artefact classes and a corresponding decrease in those made on whole flakes until, in horizons J to M inclusive, only 25 per cent are made on whole flakes, 35 per cent on broken flakes and 40 per cent on shatter-chunks. Between horizons M and N there is a sudden change brought about primarily by a return to a strong preference for whole flakes as a base for scraper manufacture. In horizon N and all subsequent horizons some 50 per cent of the scrapers are made on whole flakes, while broken flakes and shatter-chunks each form the base of 25 per cent of the scrapers. Scrapers made on cores are of intermittent occurrence and are rare in all horizons.

Points

These are differentiated from the backed points of horizons N to R by the presence of shallow flaked retouch instead of backing and by their distinctive sub-triangular, foliate or ovate shape. They represent between 10 and 12 per cent of the retouched implements

in each of horizons G to J, thereafter becoming much less frequent, only single specimens occurring in each of horizons L to O and none in the higher horizons. There is thus very little overlap, restricted to horizon N and O, in the stratigraphic distribution of the points and the backed points.

The twenty-six points range in length from 28 to 70 mm, with a mean of 42 ± 8 mm; their length/breadth ratios extend from 1.0 to 2.1 (mean 1.5 ± 0.3). They may be divided primarily into unifacial and bifacial types, which do not differ from each other in size or general proportions, and further subdivided according to their shape. Bifacial points occur only in horizons J and L. The distribution of the six types of points recognised is summarised in table 46.

Bifacial foliate points. There are two of these, one each from horizons J and L. The earlier specimen is of chert and is somewhat rolled: it may have been found elsewhere and brought to the site when already in this condition. Its tip is much worn and was perhaps slightly broken before being subjected to rolling. Coarse shallow flaking covers the whole of both surfaces leaving irregular edges although the overall shape, including the 13 mm-thick lenticular cross-section, is regular. One edge is partly broken away. This point is 46 mm in length and

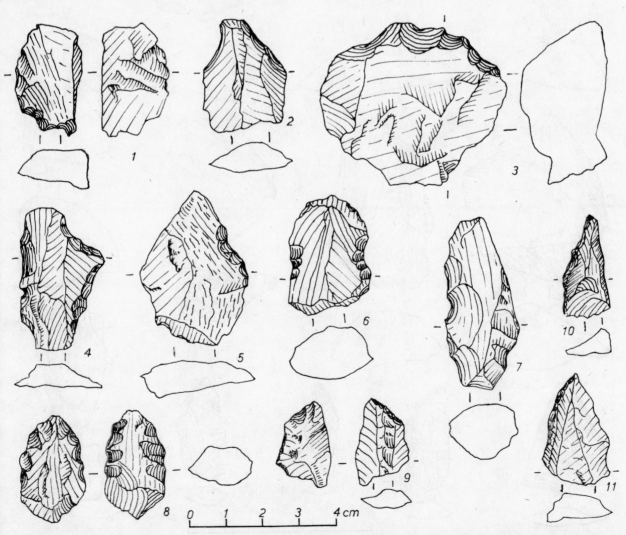

Fig. 89. Retouched implements from horizon J at Kalemba: 1–6—scrapers; 7, 8—points; 9–11—backed flakes.

Table 46. Kalemba: points

| Horizon | Bifacial | | Unifacial | | | |
	Foliate	Ovate	Sub-triangular	Foliate	Tanged	Other
O	—	—	—	—	—	—
N	—	—	1	—	—	—
M	—	—	1	—	—	—
L	—	—	1	—	—	—
K	1	—	4	—	—	—
J	—	—	3	—	—	—
I	1	1	6	—	—	—
H	—	—	2	—	—	—
G	—	—	2	1	1	1

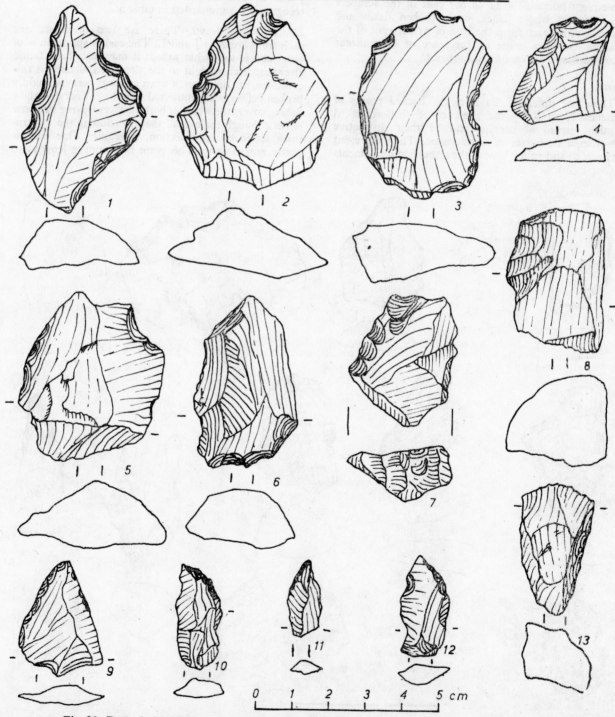

Fig. 90. Retouched implements from horizon K at Kalemba: 1–8—scrapers; 9–13—backed flakes.

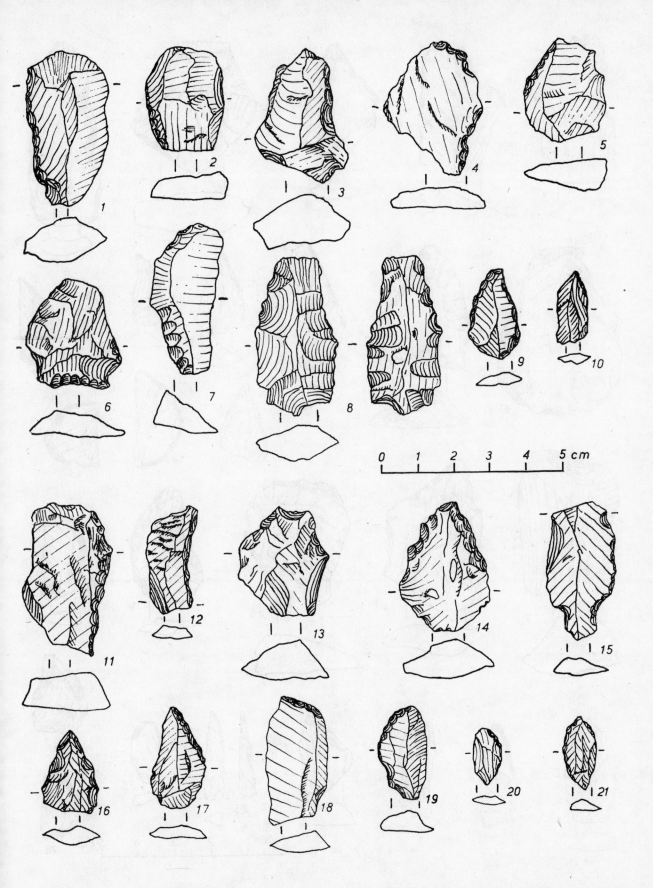

Fig. 91. Retouched implements from horizons L (1–10) and M (11–21) at Kalemba: 1–7—scrapers; 8—point; 9, 10—backed flakes; 11–13—scrapers; 14—point; 15—tanged flake; 16–18—backed flakes; 19–21—pointed lunates.

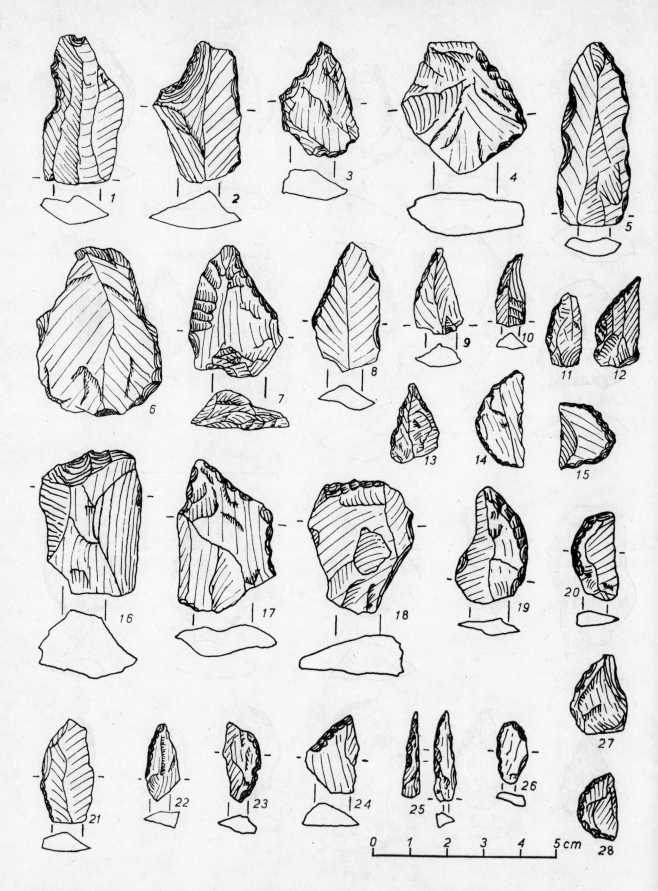

Fig. 92. Retouched implements from horizons N (1–15) and O (16–28) at Kalemba: 1–6—scrapers; 7—point; 8–13—backed flakes; 14—pointed lunate; 15—deep lunate; 16–18—scrapers; 19–27—backed flakes; 28—deep lunate.

its maximum surviving width is 23 mm. The example from horizon L is of quartz and bears fine shallow flaking over the whole of both surfaces leaving neatly denticulated edges. It has a symmetrical lenticular cross-section. The tip is broken, but the specimen survives to a length of 42 mm, its width and thickness being respectively 22 and 9 mm.

Bifacial ovate point. A single specimen from horizon J is of quartz, 28 by 18 by 11 mm, with a rounded tip and a thick untrimmed base. Apart from the basal areas the whole of both surfaces are covered by resolved flaking, producing a lenticular cross-section.

Unifacial sub-triangular points. This is by far the largest category, with twenty examples. Five are of chert, and the remainder of quartz. On seven examples the base is retouched to a roughly rounded form; on ten it is approximately straight and on two it has broken away. A large ovate chert flake trimmed to a triangular point at the distal end but with the remainder of its margin unmodified has also been subsumed into this category. Both round-based and straight-based types seem to occur throughout the time-span covered by the points as a whole. In size, the sub-triangular points

are likewise indistinguishable from the general class. Retouch is limited to the margins of the points, except on one example, from horizon G, where the flaking covers much of the dorsal surface of the implement. On one specimen (horizon K) the two sides are retouched from alternate surfaces. On a round-based example from horizon N the basal trimming is done from the dorsal surface. All the others are retouched from the ventral surface. The plan-shapes of the retouched edges show significant variation, and have been classed as straight, convex or concave, being distinguished left and right as when the implement is aligned with the ventral surface downwards and with the tip pointing upwards or away from the observer, in which position the points are here illustrated. The distribution of edge-plan shapes among the twenty sub-triangular points is as follows:

Left edge	Right edge	No. of specimens
Convex	Straight	9
Straight	Straight	4
Straight	Convex	3
Convex	Convex	2
Convex	Concave	1
Concave	Convex	1

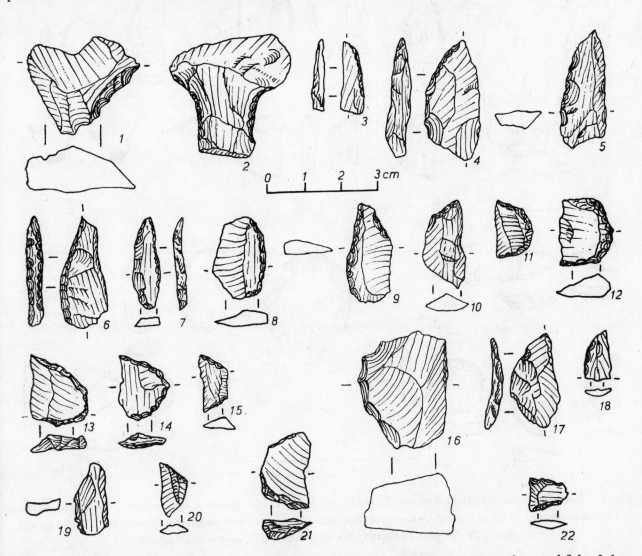

Fig. 93. *Retouched implements from horizons P (1–15) and Q (16–22) at Kalemba: 1—scraper; 2—tanged flake; 3–1 — backed flakes; 11, 12—deep lunates; 13—asymmetrical lunate; 14—triangular microlith; 15—trapezoidal microlith; 16—scraper; 17–20—backed flakes; 21—pointed lunate; 22—petit tranchet.*

Thus exactly half of the edges are classified as straight, 45 per cent as convex and 5 per cent as concave, but of the convex edges there are twice as many on the left side of the point as on the right. By far the most frequent form of sub-triangular point at Kalemba is one which is convex on the left side and straight on the right.

Unifacial foliate point. The single specimen is of quartz and comes from the lowest horizon, G; its length, breadth and thickness are 55, 31 and 10 mm respectively. Rough shallow flaking extends along the whole of both sides but is restricted to the edges.

Unifacial tanged point. A broken chert point from horizon G retains only the basal region. This is shaped by two opposed notches worked by near resolved flaking to produce a tang 13 mm long and 13 mm in maximum width.

Unifacial point of indeterminate shape. Horizon G yielded a fragment of the tip of a quartz unifacial point,

too small to allow the original overall shape to be ascertained.

Miscellaneous implements

The Kalemba excavations yielded only three retouched stone implements which cannot be subsumed into the categories described above, and which must perforce be described individually.

Shouldered flakes. The two examples come respectively from horizons H and M and measure 51 by 30 and 36 by 20 mm. In each case the striking platform is on the short end of the flake and has been partially removed by the production of a large notch to produce a neat tang and single shoulder, the remainder of the flake being unmodified.

Burin. The only convincing true burin recovered from Kalemba was found in horizon P. It is a simple single-blow burin produced, possibly accidentally, on a shatter-chunk measuring 22 by 13 by 7 mm.

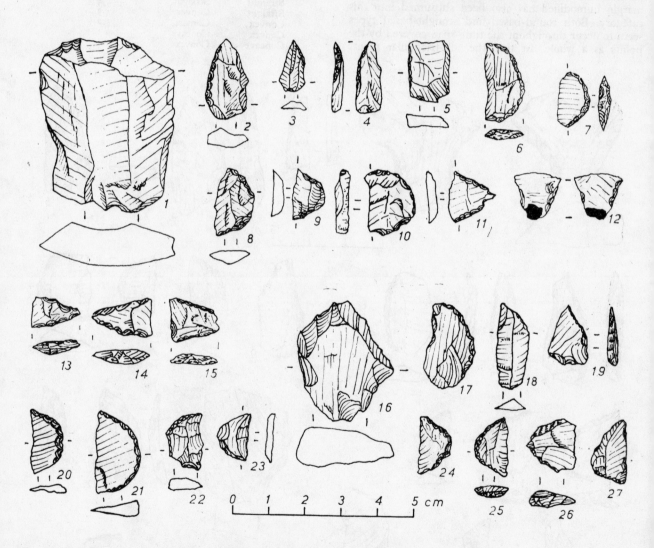

Fig. 94. *Retouched implements from horizons R (1–15) and S (16–27) at Kalemba: 1—scraper; 2–5—backed flakes; 6–9—pointed lunates; 10—deep lunate; 11–15—petits tranchets (no. 12 has mastic adhering); 16—scraper; 17–19—backed flakes; 20–25—pointed lunates; 26—deep lunate; 27—asymmetrical lunate.*

II. GROUND STONE ARTEFACTS

The Kalemba excavations yielded eleven ground stone axes or fragments thereof, two pestles, one linguate object, and four bored stones. The last objects are of particular interest as being the only specimens of their type so far recovered from an archaeological context in eastern Zambia. The stratigraphical distributions of the various ground stone artefact classes are summarized in table 47.

Bored stones

The four examples recovered are sufficiently heterogeneous to merit individual description (plate XV).

A complete specimen weighing only 46 gm comes from horizon L. It is made of a flat slab of soapstone 18 to 21 mm in thickness and oval, 44 by 35 mm, in plan (fig. 95:1). It is well rounded externally and this appears to have been largely the natural configuration of the slab before the perforation was produced. The perforation is circular and of 'hour glass' type, 12.5 mm in diameter at the centre, widening to a maximum of 15 mm at either end. Longitudinal striations on the sides of the perforation may be due to wear, subsequent to its manufacture.

Only a fourth part, also from horizon L, is preserved of the largest bored stone represented in the collection. It comes from the same grid square (H 10) as the complete example described above. Made of amphibolite, it appears originally to have been a flattened spheroid measuring some 120 by 130 mm and 80 to 90 mm in thickness, and shaped by thorough pounding and grinding. The 'hour glass' perforation was produced by pecking and was only partly smoothed; its maximum and minimum diameters are estimated to have been 42 and 25 to 30 mm respectively (fig. 95:2). The surviving fragment weighs 357 gm: the weight of the whole specimen was probably slightly in excess of four times this figure.

A small piece of chlorite-biotite schist (fig. 95:4) from horizon O, showing signs of pecking and grinding, is interpreted as a piece of a bored stone with an original external diameter of between 55 and 65 mm, and an 'hour glass' perforation 25 to 35 mm in diameter.

The fourth specimen, also from horizon O, is of soapstone and represents half, split down the middle, of a cylindrical bored stone, with its maximum dimension of 94 mm along the axis of perforation (fig. 95:3). The maximum external diameter was 58 mm, the outer surface being rather roughly shaped and retaining many striations from this process. The perforation, once again, is of 'hour glass' type, with its maximum diameter 32 mm and the minimum 18 mm. Deep gouge-striations are visible throughout the length of the hole except at the narrowest constriction, where subsequent wear has obliterated them. At each end of the perforation its walls have been carefully scraped latitudinally but in neither case does this penetrate for more than 15 mm along the perforation. The maximum thickness of the walls is only 21 mm. There are signs of wear after breakage. The specimen at present weighs 158 gm: the weight of the whole object before breakage must have been about 300 gm.

Axes

The larger of the two complete specimens, from horizon S, is made of siliceous chert. It is illustrated in fig. 95:6. The cutting edge had become detached, perhaps through use, but was found separately at the same level in the same grid square. The reassembled specimen weighs 294 gm and measures 95 by 60 mm by 38 mm in thickness. It appeares that the axe is a re-used specimen and that the original cutting-edge was at what is now the butt end. When this cutting-edge broke off, the axe was re-worked into its present form. The axe, as it now survives, has a fairly symmetrical, fat, lenticular cross-section. It was shaped primarily by bifacial flaking, but the curved cutting-edge was subsequently pecked and then neatly ground on both sides to an angle of approximately 45 degrees over an overall length of 38 mm. Flakes were removed from this edge, apparently through use, prior to its breaking off. After this break took place, flakes were struck from the fractured-end of the main body of the axe, as if in preparation for re-grinding, which was never undertaken.

The second complete axe (fig. 95:5), recovered from horizon R, measures 68 by 48 mm by 22 mm in thickness,

Table 47. Kalemba: distribution of ground stone artefacts, hammerstones, anvils, rubbing and grinding stones

Horizon	Bored stones*	Axes*	Pestles	Knapping hammers†	Pounding stones†	Anvils†	Rubbing stones†	Grindstones†
S	—	6	—	2	6	2	—	—
R	—	2	1	1	—	—	—	—
Q	—	—	—	4	1	—	1	1
P	—	1	1	2	1	—	—	—
O	2	2	—	4	1	2	1	—
N	—	—	—	5	—	—	—	—
M	—	—	—	3	—	—	—	—
L	2	—	—	3	1	—	1	—
K	—	—	—	7	1	—	4	—
J	—	—	—	4	—	—	—	—
I	—	—	—	2	—	—	—	—
H	—	—	—	—	—	—	—	—
G	—	—	—	—	1	—	—	—

*including fragments
†from sample area only

and weighs 105 gm. It too is made of siliceous chert and is similar in overall shape and technique of manufacture to the larger specimen. The cutting-edge, curved in plan, is straight in edge-view, like that of a true axe, and is ground from both sides to an angle of 45 degrees over a length of 36 mm. The entire periphery of the axe away from the cutting edge is, however, finely chipped. The ground cutting-edge shows scaled damage indicative of heavy use.

A roughout for an apparently similar implement in

chert came from horizon S and is illustrated in fig. 95:7. It is bifacially flaked all over to a symmetrical lenticular cross-section, and the edge is particularly carefully trimmed on both sides for three-quarters of the periphery. There is no sign of grinding or of use. The specimen measures 75 by 67 mm by 33 mm in thickness, and weighs 192 gm.

An object from horizon R (fig. 95:9) is interpreted as the broken cutting edge of a comparable axe made of fine-grained chert or mudstone. It is ground and finely

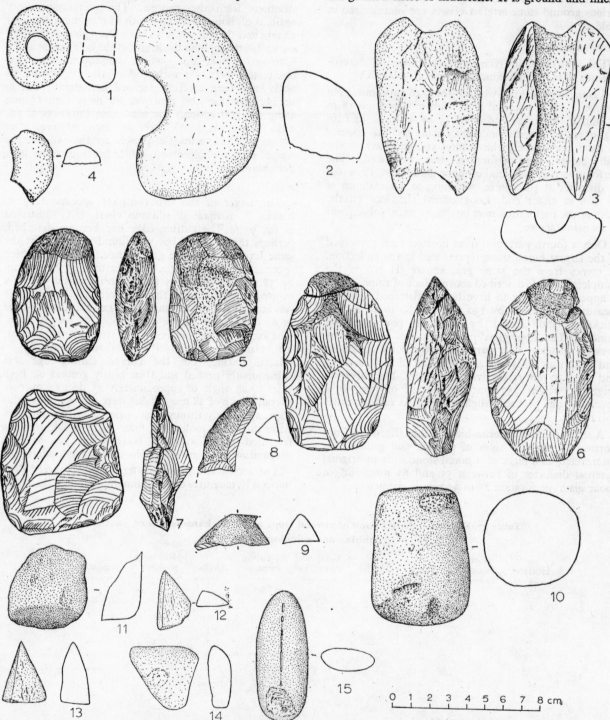

Fig. 95. Ground stone artefacts from Kalemba: 1—complete bored stone (horizon L); 2–4—fragments of bored stones from horizons L (2) and O (3, 4); 5, 6—complete axes from horizons R (5) and S (6); 7—rough-out for axe (horizon S); 8–9—axe fragments from horizons P (8) and R (9); 10—pestle (horizon P); 11—pestle fragment (horizon R); 12–14—ground 'points' of pigment (horizon L); 15—abraded linguate pebble (horizon P).

polished on both sides to an angle of approximately 65 degrees, but back from the edge are traces of pecked-over flake scars incompletely obliterated by grinding. The polished areas retain fine, multi-directional striations. The cutting edge, which is preserved to a length of 33 mm, shows only very slight signs of use.

A second broken cutting edge is made of a fine-grained igneous rock, perhaps diorite, and comes from horizon P. This is half of a longitudinally split linguate cutting edge, pecked and then ground to an angle of about 45 degrees, which survives to a length of 48 mm (fig. 95:8). Flaking from the cutting edge was caused by use, but was partly removed by subsequent re-grinding.

The remaining specimens are small flakes and chips which appear to come from ground stone axes similar to those described above. They come from horizon O—one quartzite flake and an unidentified chip; and horizon S—one flake of ophitic gabbro and three of granulite.

Pestles

These are represented by a complete granite specimen recovered from the rock fall excavated in horizon P and by a fragment of a somewhat larger specimen in an unidentified material from horizon R. The complete example (fig. 95:10) is cylindrical, weighs 370 gm, and measures 72 mm in length, 54 mm in diameter at one end and 48 mm at the other. The sides and the flattened larger end had been pecked to shape and the sides partly smoothed by grinding. The smaller end was ground completely smooth at right angles to the length of the cylinder. Microscopic examination of this surface revealed no trace of pigment. Red pigment was clearly preserved on the other pestle fragment (fig. 95:11), in rough areas adjacent to its smoothed central surface.

Linguate pebble

A natural linguate pebble (fig. 95:15) from horizon P, measuring 70 by 30 by 13 mm, shows signs of abrasion.

III. HAMMERSTONES, ANVILS, RUBBING AND GRINDING STONES

The following analysis and description are restricted to those specimens recovered from the sample-area defined in the section on the chipped stone artefacts.

Knapping hammers

There are thirty-seven examples (fig. 97:1–5) spread through the whole sequence except the two lowest horizons where their absence, in view of the small area of these deposits available for excavation, is probably fortuitous. The thirty-two unbroken specimens weigh from 15 to 250 gm apiece (mean 69 gm) and have maximum dimensions from 29 to 67 mm (mean 47 mm). The distribution of these measurements is shown in fig. 96. There is no significant change in preferred size or weight in different parts of the sequence, except that the five specimens weighing less than 30 gm all occur in horizons N to S, where the associated chipped stone implements are predominantly microlithic. Of the thirty-seven knapping hammers all but one are of quartz. As at Makwe, coarse granular quartz was generally not selected for this purpose. The exception is a haematite cobble from horizon O. The quartz examples are on artefacts (seven cores, eight shatter-chunks), rounded pebbles or cobbles (sixteen), or more irregular natural weathered fragments (five). Of all these types a strong preference was exercised for pieces of a flattened ovoid shape (fig. 97:1, 2) and, as has been shown, size and weight desiderata were also strictly observed. The fine massed pitting resulting from the use of the hammers is generally concentrated on one or both ends of the long axis and, on the more regular-shaped pieces, also along the periphery forming a continuous ring of utilisation following the largest diameter of the artefact.

Pounding stones

Of the twelve examples (fig. 97:6, 7), six are from horizon S; the remainder are distributed through all the earlier part of the sequence (table 47). Their maximum dimensions range from 68 to 118 mm with a mean of 87 mm, and their weights from 210 to 880 gm, the mean being 550 gm. Ten pounding stones are of coarse-grained quartzite—a material which was

avoided for the knapping hammers. Six of these are on cobbles and four on weathered angular fragments. There is one on a quartz cobble and one on an angular fragment apparently exfoliated from the rock-shelter wall. The pitting on these pounding stones is coarser and less localised than that observed on the knapping hammers. Three of the pounding stones had also been used as anvils.

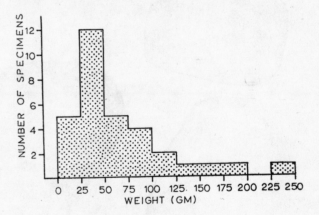

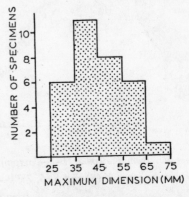

Fig. 96. Weights and maximum dimensions of knapping hammers from all levels at Kalemba.

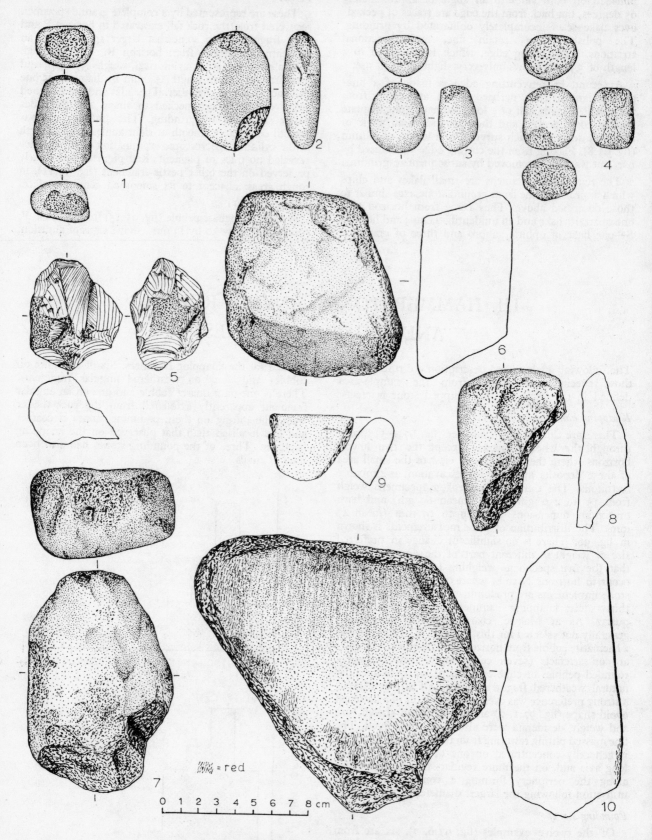

Fig. 97. Hammerstones etc. from Kalemba: 1–5—knapping hammers from horizons K (1, 2), L (3), M (4) and P (5); 6–8—pounding stones from horizons K (8) and S (6, 7); 9—rubbing stone from horizon K; 10—grindstone with red pigment from horizon Q.

Anvils

There are four anvils, two each being recovered from horizons O and S. Three of them are on quartz pounding stones (*e.g.* fig. 97:7) and one on a well-rounded chert cobble. Their weights range from 290 to 700 gm, and their maximum dimensions from 70 to 118 mm. Pitting is restricted to a well-defined central area of a flat surface lying roughly parallel to the long axis of the stone, and forms a regular depression between 12 and 35 mm across and 1 to 3 mm deep.

Rubbing stones

The seven specimens form a heterogeneous group. Four come from horizon K and the others from horizons L, O and Q. They are irregular slabs of feldspathic gneiss or coarse-grained granite on which part of the edge (on four examples), or an area of one of the flat or slightly concave sides, has been rubbed smooth without modifying the overall shape of the stone (fig. 97: 8, 9). The maximum dimensions of these artefacts range from 48 to 117 mm and their weights from 30 to 255 gm.

Grindstone

The single grindstone (fig. 97:10) was recovered from horizon Q. It is a large piece of a concave lower grindstone (*mphelo*) 67 mm thick and ground down to a maximum depth of 12 mm. The maximum dimension of this fragment is 170 mm and its weight 1820 gm. The fragment has evidently been used to a considerable extent since it became broken: its last use was clearly for the grinding of red pigment, abundant traces of which are preserved peripherally to the central grinding area.

IV. BONE ARTEFACTS

Bone artefacts, present in all but the three lowest horizons, only become common in horizons P to S (table 48). The most frequent forms are points, amongst which three distinct types are recognised.

Headed pins

There are three complete pins from horizon Q, one from horizon R, and a relatively crude fragment from horizon S. They were produced, apparently, from the long-bones of a large bird, with the epiphysis forming the head of the pin (fig. 98:1–4). On one example the epiphysis has been roughly carved to a spheroidal shape. The shafts are carefully trimmed and polished to a sharp point; on three examples this working extends right up to the head, on the other two it is restricted to the lowest third of the shaft. The complete examples are 50, 59, 77 and 125 mm in overall length. The cross-sections of the shafts are roughly circular in all cases. An example is illustrated in plate XV.

Bodkins

There are eight straight and two curved specimens (fig. 98:5–13) in this category. Of the former class, only one, from horizon P, is complete and measures 65 mm in length, tapering to a point at each end. Broken examples come from horizon L (two), O, P (three) and R. The bodkins are carefully worked over their whole surface. The cross-sections vary through time from sub-rectangular, through oval to circular; and this variation may be correlated with the stratigraphy.

Sub-rectangular specimens occur in horizons L (two), O and P; oval ones in P (two), Q and S; and circular ones in horizons P and R. It is noteworthy that the trend here is in the opposite direction to that observed at Makwe. The two curved bodkins are both represented only by fragments. One, from the surface dust, is a small sharpened rib, the other, from horizon P, is completely worked from an indeterminate bone (fig. 98:13).

Conical points

The conical points (fig. 98:14–16) are represented by two complete specimens from horizon S and one fragment from horizon Q. They are splinters of bone, varying in cross-section between 8 by 3 and 4 by 2 mm, sharpened to a point at one end only. The complete examples are 47 and 54 mm in length.

Needle

A single specimen, from horizon Q (fig. 98:17) survives to a length of 23 mm. It is the rounded butt end of a bone point with a circular cross-section. At the butt end is a small perforation, 1 mm in diameter, which is so weathered that its mode of manufacture cannot be determined; it is, however, unlikely to be entirely natural.

Carved bone tube

The single specimen of this type (fig. 98:18) comes from horizon S and is a split 21-mm length of a bird long-bone 6 mm in diameter. It originally formed a

Table 48. Kalemba: distribution of bone and shell artefacts

Horizon	Bone							Shell		
	Headed pins	Bodkins	Conical points	Needle	Tube	Pendant	Other	Beads	Pendant	Disc
S	1	1	2	—	1	—	—	8	—	1
R	—	1	—	—	—	—	—	3	1	—
Q	3	—	1	1	—	—	—	2	—	—
P	—	5	—	—	—	—	—	1	—	—
O	—	1	—	—	—	1	—	—	—	—
N	—	—	—	—	—	—	1	—	—	—
M	—	—	—	—	—	—	1	—	—	—
L	—	2	—	—	—	—	—	—	—	—
K	—	—	—	—	—	—	1	—	—	—
J	—	—	—	—	—	—	1	—	—	—

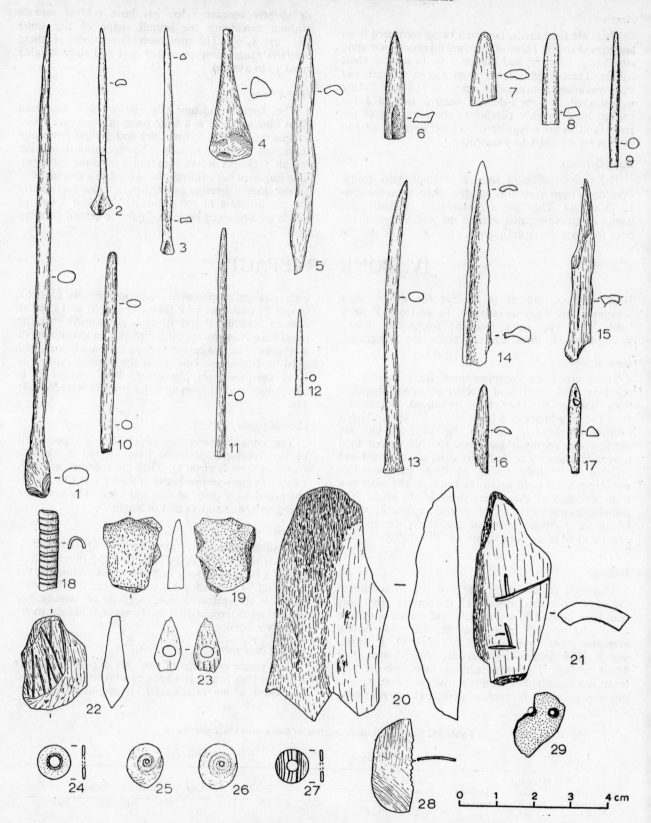

Fig. 98. Bone (1–23) and shell (24–29) artefacts from Kalemba: 1–4—headed pins from horizons Q (1, 2), R (3) and S (4); 5–12—bodkins from horizons L (6), O (7), P (5, 8–10), R (11) and S (12); 13—curved bodkin from horizon P; 14–16—conical points from horizons Q (16) and S (14, 15); 17—needle from horizon Q; 18—carved tube from horizon S; 19, 20—toothed fragments from horizons J (19) and K (20); 21, 22—engraved fragments from horizons M (21) and O (22); 23—pendant from horizon O; 24–27—disc beads from horizons R (24, 25) and S (26, 27); 28—disc from horizon S; 29—pendant from horizon R.

tube decorated with thirteen approximately equidistant carved grooves finely carved latitudinally around the diameter. A remarkably similar complete example was recovered from Makwe (q.v., p. 97).

Toothed bone fragments

Two fragments of bone, from horizons J and K, measuring respectively 19 by 15 and 61 by 30 mm, each bear two deep 'V'-shaped notches producing three pointed teeth (fig. 98:19, 20). These are on the end of the larger example and on the longer side of the smaller specimen. A comparable artefact came from horizon 2ii at Makwe. I am unable to suggest a purpose for which these objects could have been intended, since their age clearly precludes their use for decorating pottery.

Engraved bone fragments

A bone fragment from horizon M, measuring 50 by 22 mm, bears roughly incised marks, as shown in fig. 98:21. Another fragment, 25 by 18 mm, from horizon O (fig. 98:22) has, on one side, roughly parallel scratches which may be tool marks or may be the result of the bone having been gnawed by a rodent.

Bone pendant

This neatly worked bone fragment, found in horizon O, measures 14 by 7 mm by 1 mm in thickness. It is pointed at one end and pierced in the centre of the other, rounded, end by a hole 3 mm in diameter (fig. 98:23).

V. SHELL ARTEFACTS

The shell artefacts comprise fourteen disc beads, one pendant and one disc. Their stratigraphic occurrence (table 48) is restricted to the four uppermost horizons.

Beads

Horizons P, Q, R and S yielded one, two, three and eight beads respectively (fig. 98:24–27). One from horizon R and three from horizon S were made of Achatina shell; horizon S also yielded one specimen of water snail shell. The remaining nine beads, including all those from horizons P and Q, were made from the shell of a small undeterminable land snail (not Achatina). The Achatina specimens have finely ground edges and show little variation in size, being all 1 mm in thickness and 9 or 10 mm in diameter. The perforations have a diameter of 3 mm; two are of 'hour glass' type, produced by a conical drill, while two were produced by means of a similar instrument from one side only. The water snail shell bead is smaller (8.5 mm diameter) and thicker (1.5 mm); it is otherwise similar to the Achatina beads, with an 'hour glass' perforation. The land snail shell examples are all thin, trimmed discs made from the flat apex of the shell and between 9 and 12 mm in diameter. The perforations, 1 mm across, were punched at the thin centre of the spiral. The sequence shows a steady increase in the proportion of beads made of Achatina shell, which parallels a similar phenomenon observed at Makwe.

Shell disc

The broken half of an unpierced disc of water snail shell (fig. 98:28), 25 mm diameter, came from horizon S. Its edges are neatly ground and both sides are striated by grinding to expose a surface of mother-of-pearl.

Shell pendant

Horizon R yielded the burned remains of a pendant made of water snail shell (fig. 98:29). It is triangular, 18 mm in overall length, with a rounded end: it survives to a width of 12 mm. The edges were carefully ground. Two perforations at the rounded end were drilled from the concave side of the shell only. The specimen may have been lost or discarded before completion.

VI. PIGMENT

Material which had been used as pigment or which, although retaining no signs of use, may have been collected and brought to the rock-shelter for that purpose, was distributed throughout the Kalemba sequence with a single lacuna in horizons H to J.

The stratigraphical distribution of the material recovered is shown in table 49. The grindstone and pestle used for pigment preparation have been discussed above (p.153-5). The unmodified lumps of specularite and haematite range in weight from 10 to 380 gm and call for no special

Table 49. Kalemba: distribution of pigment

Horizon	Unmodified specularite	Unmodified haematite	Ground haematite	Ground points	Ochre discs	Pigment on grindstone	Painted exfoliation
S	—	—	—	—	—	—	7
R	—	—	—	—	—	—	5
Q	—	—	—	1	—	1	?1
P	—	1	1	—	—	—	—
O	—	1	—	—	—	—	—
N	2	—	1	—	—	—	—
M	—	1	—	—	—	—	—
L	—	2	—	3	3	—	—
K	—	—	2	—	—	—	—
J	—	—	—	—	—	—	—
I	—	—	—	—	—	—	—
H	—	—	—	—	—	—	—
G	—	1	—	—	—	—	—

comment. The haematite lumps classed as 'modified' (20 to 95 gm) each bear signs of rubbing, either smooth or striated, on one plane; this is interpreted as due either to use as a crayon or to grinding for the production of pigment.

Four specimens are classed as 'ground points' (fig. 95:12–14), but it is probable that they are not true implements, being merely the by-product of pigment-grinding. Three come from horizon L and one from horizon Q. The red-brown coloured materials are identified as haematite schist and magnetite. Their maximum dimensions range from 32 to 39 mm. All are triangular in overall shape and ground to two points either conical or semi-conical in cross-section. Two specimens are ground all over, the others only at the points. In materials such as these it is difficult to distinguish between grinding and wear due to use. In these circumstances, it is felt that the form of these artefacts may be coincidental to the grinding of the stones to produce lustrous powder, but their standardization is interesting.

Manufactured pigment cakes are represented by three specimens recovered from horizon L. Their yellow-brown material has been identified by the Geological Survey Department, Lusaka, as "earthy iron oxide with some flakes of specular haematite". It is almost certainly an artificial compound made by mixing crushed haematite and other colouring matter with a clay base and binding agent. The specimens comprise two discs 24 and 23 mm in diameter; on one both sides are rubbed smooth, on the other only one side is so modified. The third piece is an irregular lump, with a maximum dimension of 33 mm, on which several facets have been rubbed smooth. It may be significant, possibly indicating their use for mural decoration, that all three specimens were found within 1.5 m of the main wall of the rock-shelter; on the other hand it should be noted that this is the driest part of the cave and similar specimens deposited in damper surroundings may have disintegrated. Specimens are illustrated in plate XVIa.

Twelve or thirteen fragments of exfoliation bearing traces of paint were recovered from the excavated deposits; seven from horizon S, five from R and one (doubtful) from horizon Q. All were found within one metre of the main painted wall of the rock-shelter, in grid squares H 10 and I 10. Despite a careful examination of exfoliated fragments from lower levels, none were found on which any trace of paint was preserved. The paint on these thirteen specimens was exclusively red; none were noted which showed any trace of white paint such as was used for the majority of the rock paintings extant on the shelter wall today. The significance of these observations is further discussed in a later chapter.

VII. POTTERY

A total of 392 potsherds and three complete vessels was recovered during the Kalemba excavations. The sherds comprise one hundred decorated and/or rim sherds (25 per cent) and 292 undecorated body sherds. Of these specimens, 298 came from the twelve grid squares central to the excavation (H-I, 10–15) and, as this is the area where the stratigraphy of the upper levels is clearest, it is on this sample that table 50, which shows the stratigraphical distribution of the pottery, is based.

The single sherd from the top layer of horizon Q is best regarded as intrusive since it appears to come from the same vessel as a sherd from horizon R. With this single exception the Kalemba pottery is restricted to the two uppermost horizons. Within this area of the excavation, the only diagnostically Early Iron Age sherd comes from horizon R, while all the fifty-nine definitely later Iron Age specimens are from horizon S, where they increase markedly in frequency in the highest layer.

To utilise the largest possible sample, however, the following typological account of the Kalemba pottery is based on the three complete vessels (none of which came from the central area) and on all the one hundred decorated and/or rim sherds recovered. Of the latter, three sherds are clearly of Early Iron Age type and represent three different vessels, described below. Two other sherds, from a single vessel, may also be Early Iron Age. The remaining ninety-five decorated and/or rim sherds were of later Iron Age type. They were sorted initially for pairs and larger numbers of sherds representing the same vessel. The forty-two unpaired sherds which could be fitted into a square with 4-cm sides were then rejected. The remaining fifty-three later Iron Age sherds represent twenty vessels which,

together with the three complete specimens, are described below.

EARLY IRON AGE POTTERY

Type B2 variant. One necked vessel with an externally thickened rim and a rounded lip bears on the rim-band a horizontal band of diagonal comb-stamping, which is delineated on the lower margin by a row of impressions of a triangular stamp. In the concavity of the neck, which is separated from the rim by a sharp angle, are at least two parallel horizontal grooves (fig. 99:1).

Type C1. A vessel of undeterminable shape with a band of at least three parallel horizontal grooves is represented by the single body sherd shown in fig. 99:2.

Undecorated. One undecorated necked vessel (fig. 99:3) has an externally thickened rim and a lightly squared lip.

Table 50. Kalemba: stratigraphical distribution of pottery

Horizon	Layer	Undecorated body sherds	Early Iron Age types	Later Iron Age types	Total
S	1	125	—	49	174
	2	27	—	9	36
	3	9	—	1	10
R	4	9	1	—	10
	5	3	—	—	3
Q	6	1	—	—	1
	7	—	—	—	—
	8	—	—	—	—

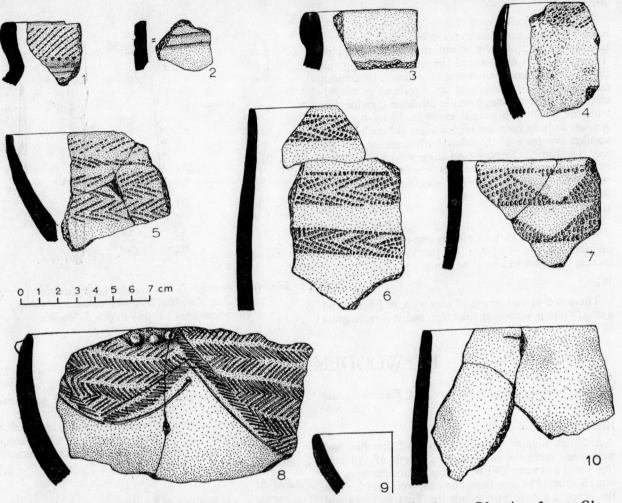

Fig. 99. Early Iron Age (1–3) and later Iron Age (4–10) pottery from Kalemba: 1—type B2 variant; 2—type C1; 3—undecorated; 4—type 1c(i); 5, 6—type 1d; 7—type 1e(i); 8—type 4; 9, 10—undecorated.

LATER IRON AGE POTTERY

(Except where stated, all these vessels have tapered rims and rounded lips.)

Type 1c(i). One open bowl (fig. 99:4) has, as its only decoration, a single horizontal band of diagonal comb-stamping, placed immediately below the lip.

Type 1d. Triple bands of herring-bone comb-stamping are found on three vessels. The bands are widely spaced on a beaker (fig. 99:6) and on one of undeterminable shape; they are adjacent to one another on an open bowl with tapered rim and squared lip (fig. 99:5).

Type 1e(i). This is represented by three vessels. One necked vessel bears, in the concavity of the neck, a band of upwards-pointing triangular blocks of comb-stamping. A globular pot with an undifferentiated rim and squared lip, is decorated with a row of rough diamond-shaped blocks of comb-stamping. A convergent-necked vessel with undifferentiated rim and squared lip bears a horizontal band of diagonal comb-stamping below the lip; below this band are two bands of upwards-pointing triangular blocks of comb-stamping (fig. 99:7).

Type 1g. One necked vessel and one of undeterminable shape are decorated with a broad band of massed comb-stamping. Two other vessels are represented by body sherds which bear traces of comb-stamped decoration.

Type 2c(i). A necked vessel, represented only by a single body sherd, bears horizontal bands of diagonal slashing, all in the same direction.

Type 4. One open bowl (fig. 99:8) is decorated with large segmental blocks of incised hatching, diagonal in alternate directions. This vessel also bears three small raised bosses immediately below the lip.

Undecorated. The ten undecorated vessels include one convergent-necked vessel with an undifferentiated rim and squared lip (fig. 99:10), one beaker, two necked vessels (plate XIII b) and two open bowls (fig. 99:9).

VIII. METAL OBJECTS

No slag, tuyeres or other evidence for the working of metal at the site was recovered from the Kalemba rock-shelter. Only four pieces of worked metal were found: all four are of iron and came from the uppermost 25 cm of the deposits, that is from the upper part of horizon S.

Arrowheads

Both have leaf-shaped heads (fig. 100:1,2). The more complete and better preserved specimen has a head 64 mm in length by 10 mm in maximum breadth. There are traces of a central rib on both sides, giving the head a maximum thickness of 3 mm. The tapering tang survives to a length of 33 mm, and is roughly circular in cross-section, 6 mm in diameter at its junction with the head. The second example, badly corroded, appears to have been broadly similar, although slightly smaller. No trace of the central rib remains; and the way the head has become bent suggests that no rib was ever present. The tang on this specimen has a sub-rectangular cross-section. The specimen is preserved to a maximum length of 83 mm.

Ring

Almost half of an iron ring is preserved, having an internal diameter of 25 mm (fig. 100:3). The band has a rectangular cross-section 5 by 4 mm.

Wire

There is a 34 mm length of iron wire, or fragment of a tang, 3 mm in maximum diameter, and sub-rectangular in cross-section.

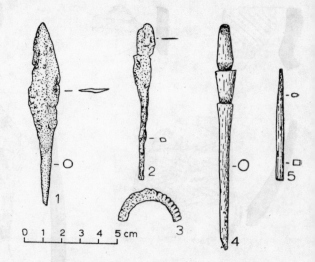

Fig. 100. *Iron (1-3) and wooden (4, 5) artefacts from horizon S at Kalemba; 1, 2—arrowheads; 3—ring; 4—arrow-point or link-shaft; 5—bodkin.*

IX. WOODEN ARTEFACTS

Both the wooden artefacts preserved at Kalemba come from horizon S.

Arrow-point or link-shaft

Although slightly damaged at one end, this fine and well made specimen survives to a length of 119 mm (fig. 100:4 and plate XVI b). Its maximum diameter (13 mm) is situated 25 mm from one end, from which place the object tapers to each extremity. Two neatly carved constrictions to a diameter of 8 mm occur at 24 and 40 mm from the thicker end; below the latter constriction the diameter tapers to only 4.5 mm at the broken end. The cross-section is circular throughout. The artefact's carved surface is well smoothed but retains striations from working: it is not possible to determine whether stone or a metal instrument was employed. This artefact was found embedded in the deposit immediately adjacent to and in the same level as the lean-to bamboo structure described above (p. 215 and fig. 75).

Bodkin

This is a thin sliver of bamboo 60 cm in length (fig. 100:5). It is of rough rectangular cross-section 4 by 4 mm for the first 28 mm of its length, then trimmed roughly to a round-sectioned point. The wood is torn as if worked by a scraping process rather than by cutting.

Chapter 17

Kalemba: Specialist Reports

I. FLORAL REMAINS

(*Identifications by* J. B. Gillett *and* C. H. S. Kabuye)

Floral remains in identifiable condition were recovered at Kalemba only from horizons R and S. They have been examined by Dr J. B. Gillett and Miss C. H. S. Kabuye, both of the East African Herbarium, Nairobi.

From the upper layer of horizon R, in grid square H 13, came a single raceme of *Sorghum arundinaceum* (Wild) Stapf. This is the common wild sorghum; and eastern Zambia is within the known area of its modern distribution (Doggett, 1970).

Horizon S in grid square H 11 yielded remains of *Eleusine coracana* (L.) Gaertn., a cultivated finger millet. The remains came from within the semicircular setting of posts described in chapter 15, which was interpreted as the remains of a lean-to structure. Miss Kabuye comments (*in litt.*, 15th January 1976) that "a single raceme appears to be the usual form, and the rest

an unusual form probably a result of introgression from *Eleusine indica* ssp. *africana*".

The beans contained in the pot buried from horizon S in grid squares L 16 and M 16, described above on p. 126, are probably *Canavalia virosa*, a wild African variety which is not infrequently cultivated. The pot contained some eight thousand beans. A sample was sent to the Mount Makulu Agricultural Research Station, Chilanga, Zambia for examination by the staff Entomologist and Pathologist. No evidence of insect damage or seed disease was detected.

Two fragments of maize cob (*Zea mays*), 15 and 18 mm in diameter, were also recovered from horizon S. In size, these compare with those from horizon 5 at Makwe, rather than with the larger examples from horizon 6.

II. FAUNAL REMAINS

(*Identifications by* John M. Harris)

Identifications of faunal remains from Kalemba were restricted to teeth, mandibular and maxillary material from the same sample-area as was utilised in the analysis of the chipped stone artefacts (p. 128, above). A total of 270 specimens was identified; these are summarised in table 51.

It may be assumed that virtually all the animal bones recovered from the Kalemba excavations represent the remains of creatures killed and brought to the site for meat or for obtaining other animal products such as skins. There is no evidence for the use of the site by animals. Furthermore, the fluctuations in the frequencies of faunal remains and of artefactual material (fig. 74, p. 124) parallel each other to a remarkable extent, indicating that the presence of animal bones in the deposits may be correlated with human activity.

Only eleven specimens were recovered from horizons G and H. Zebra (including undeterminable equids which, in fact, are almost certainly zebra) and wildebeest are each represented by three specimens. There are also five teeth of undeterminable bovids.

A comparable pattern continues into horizons I to K, where many more specimens were recovered. Of over 150 identified specimens from these three horizons, 34 per cent are equid. A further 23 per cent are of large bovids and 21 per cent of undeterminable bovids, mostly of large size. Bush-pig accounts for 8 per cent

and other suids 3 per cent. With the exception of a single fragmented elephant tooth from horizon K, the remainder of the assemblage from these three horizons represents a variety of small animals (baboon, ant bear, hyrax, small antelope, hare and porcupine), which together account for only 10 per cent of the identified specimens. Clearly, these small creatures were, in contrast with the zebra and large antelope, of relative insignificance to the site's inhabitants at this time.

From horizons L to N a much smaller sample, totalling only forty-five identified specimens, is available. Equids are still dominant, comprising 24 per cent of the total sample. Large bovids account for 16 per cent and undeterminable bovids for 27 per cent. Suids, at 13 per cent, are of importance comparable with that which they held in the lower levels; but wart-hog now predominates over bush-pig. Small creatures (hyrax, small antelope and porcupine) between them make up 16 per cent of the identified specimens.

A marked change is apparent in the faunal remains from horizons O to S. There are fifty-seven identified specimens. Equids here account for only 14 per cent of the total; and the large antelope (which come exclusively from horizon O and are thus entirely absent from the four most recent horizons) for only 4 per cent. Remains of small animals are much more varied and frequent than previously. They include galago, genet,

Table 51. Kalemba faunal remains

	HORIZON													Total
	S	R	Q	P	O	N	M	L	K	J	I	H	G	
GALAGIDAE														
Greater galago (*Galago crassicaudatus*)	—	—	1	—	—	—	—	—	—	—	—	—	—	1
CERCOPITHECIDAE														
Baboon (*Papio* sp.)	—	—	—	—	—	—	—	—	1	1	1	—	—	3
VIVERRIDAE														
Genet (*Genetta* sp.)	2	—	—	—	—	—	—	—	—	—	—	—	—	2
CARNIVORA														
Undeterminable	1	—	—	1	—	2	—	—	—	—	1	—	—	5
ORYCTEROPIDIDAE														
Ant bear (*Orycteropus* sp.)	—	—	—	—	—	—	—	—	—	1	2	—	—	3
ELEPHANTIDAE														
Elephant (*Loxodonta* sp.)	—	—	—	—	—	—	—	—	1	—	—	—	—	1
PROCAVIIDAE														
Hyrax (*Dendrohyrax* sp.)	1	1	2	3	1	2	—	1	3	—	—	—	—	14
EQUIDAE														
Burchell's zebra (*Equus burchelli*)	—	1	—	4	3	1	5	6	21	10	—	—	1	52
Undeterminable	1	1	—	1	—	2	—	3	5	8	1	1	—	23
SUIDAE														
Bush-pig (*Potamochoerus* sp.)	—	—	—	1	3	—	2	5	2	6	—	—	—	19
Wart-hog (*Phacochoerus* sp.)	—	—	—	—	1	—	—	1	2	—	2	—	—	6
Undeterminable	—	—	—	—	1	—	—	1	—	2	—	—	—	4
BOVIDAE														
Eland (*Taurotragus oryx*)	—	—	—	1	—	2	—	3	—	3	—	—	—	9
Kudu (*Tragelaphus strepsiceros*)	—	—	—	—	—	—	—	2	—	—	—	—	—	2
Bushbuck (*Tragelaphus scriptus*)	—	—	—	1	—	—	—	—	—	—	—	—	—	1
Wildebeest (*Connochaetes* sp.)	—	—	—	—	—	—	1	1	3	2	4	3	—	14
Waterbuck (*Kobus ellipsiprymnus*)	—	—	—	—	—	1	—	3	5	6	1	—	—	16
Reedbuck (*Redunca* sp.)	—	—	—	—	—	1	—	3	—	—	—	—	—	4
Sable antelope (*Hippotragus niger*)	—	—	—	—	—	1	—	—	1	—	—	—	—	2
Oribi (*Ourebia ourebia*)	—	—	—	—	—	1	—	—	1	—	1	—	—	3
?Thomson's gazelle (*Gazella thomsoni*)	—	—	—	—	?1	—	—	—	—	—	—	—	—	?1
Duiker (*Sylvicapra* sp./*Cephalophus* sp.)	—	—	2	—	—	—	—	2	—	1	1	—	—	6
Undeterminable	3	1	1	3	4	6	2	4	13	10	10	3	2	62
LAGOMORPHA														
Undeterminable	—	—	—	1	—	—	—	—	1	—	—	—	—	2
HYSTRICIDAE														
Porcupine (*Hystrix* sp.)	—	1	—	—	1	1	—	—	—	1	1	—	—	5
Undeterminable rodent	—	1	—	—	—	2	—	—	—	—	—	—	—	3
REPTILIA														
Monitor lizard (*Varanus* sp.)	—	—	2	—	1	—	—	—	—	—	—	—	—	3
Undeterminable lizard	—	1	3	—	—	—	—	—	—	—	—	—	—	4

hyrax, small antelope, hare, porcupine, rodents, monitor and other lizards which, between them, account for 49 per cent of the identified specimens.

The main trend which is apparent in the Kalemba faunal succession is thus one in which small animals steadily increase in frequency at the expense of the equids and larger antelope. Suids maintain a fairly steady occurrence throughout the sequence.

All the species represented in the collection have been present in the general area of the site during the recent past (Ansell, 1960; Wilson, 1975: 347–51), with the sole exception of Thomson's gazelle which Dr Harris has tentatively identified on the basis of a single tooth from horizon O. This species now occurs no nearer to the Kalemba area than central Tanzania. Although the specimen is indistinguishable from examples of Thomson's gazelle dentition housed in the collection of the National Museums of Kenya, its identification at Kalemba must be regarded as provisional.

It is difficult to distinguish between the effects of cultural (hunting preference) and environmental factors in the changing faunal patterns at Kalemba. Probably both were contributing causes. The high incidence of zebra and wildebeest in the lower horizons may indicate the existence of more open country in the vicinity of the site than has been the case in recent times. Under present climatic conditions, but before agricultural clearing took place, it is doubtful whether suitable habitats for these plains-loving species would have prevailed within 10 km of the site.

III. MOLLUSCS
(D.W.P.)

Shell fragments were abundantly preserved in the Kalemba deposits in horizons O to S, with occasional pieces from the lower levels. As in the case of the molluscs from Makwe, it has not proved possible to obtain a specialist's report on this material. Examination by the present writer reveals that the vast majority represents the large land snail *Achatina*.

Several specimens from horizons P to R show a systematic method of fracture (fig. 101) involving the perforation of the shell at intervals, presumably to drive the snail into the tip of the spiral shell. The tip was then detached. It appears probable that this was done to secure the snail for food. While *Achatina* is not eaten today in eastern Zambia, except in times of extreme hardship, it is regularly eaten in Nigeria (R. C. Soper, *personal communication*).

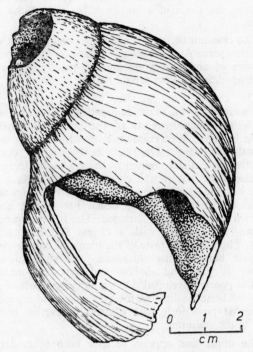

Fig. 101. Achatina shell from Kalemba, showing method of breakage to extract the meat.

IV. HUMAN SKELETAL MATERIAL
by Hertha de Villiers

The human skeletal material recovered from the Kalemba rock-shelter comes from four stratigraphic provenances; five individuals are represented.

SK 1

The earliest specimen is an isolated tooth recovered from horizon L in grid square I 17. It is the crown of a permanent lateral incisor, the root portion having been broken off.

SK 2, 3

The remains from the shallow grave dug from horizon O in grid square I 11 immediately to the east of the great fallen boulder, into the underlying horizon L, represent two individuals: the head and cervical vertebrae of a young adult female (Sk. 2), and the remains of an infant (Sk. 3).

SK 2

The cranium is represented by fractured and fragmented frontal, parietal and occipital bones; the mastoid, tympanic and petrous portions of the temporal bones; the right zygomatic bone and portion of the maxilla; the right zygoma and portion of the temporal squame; the basi-occipital; a portion of the greater wing of the right sphenoid bone; and fragments of the cranial base. The facial skeleton is incomplete—on the right side the superior and medial portion of the inferior orbital margins are present; on the left side the orbital margins are virtually complete as is the hard palate and alveolar margin of the maxilla. The cranial vault and facial skeleton have in part been reconstructed (plates XVII, XVIIIa).

The mandible is complete but for the condylar process and tip of the coronoid process on the right side. It had been fractured in the region of the symphysis menti and of the third molar on the right side (plate XVIIIb).

The extant maxillary teeth comprise the right canine, together with the roots of the broken incisors, premolars and first and second molars. Of the mandibular teeth, the right first and third molars are present as are the roots of the broken canine, premolars and second molar. On the left the first premolar and three molar teeth are *in situ*, as are the roots of the broken lateral incisor, canine and second premolar teeth. The sockets of the missing incisor teeth indicate that these teeth were present at the time of death. The first molar and premolar teeth show some wear with dentine exposure. The second and third molars show moderate to slight enamel wear with no dentine exposure.

The only postcranial remains are five fragments of cervical vertebrae.

The remains are those of a fully adult individual

probably in the second decade, as suggested by the molar pattern of attrition. Owing to the absence of the pelvis, it is not possible to assess the sex with any degree of accuracy. However, the lightly constructed cranial vault bones and mandible, the slight supramastoid crest and small mastoid process suggest that these remains are those of a female rather than those of a male.

The cranium corresponds in its general features with the southern African Negro female cranium but a number of divergences are present, mainly expressing themselves in the naso-orbital region.

The cranial vault appears to have been mesati-orthocranial. Owing to the damaged state of the cranium no reliable measurements of the cranial dimensions could be made. The cranium is ovoid and there is no frontal narrowing. The glabella is slightly curved and the superciliary eminences show a slight degree of development. The frontal chord-arc index is 84.4 per cent but the parietal curve is relatively flat (parietal chord arc index 90.6 per cent). The region above asterion is only slightly flattened. The mastoid process is small (22.5 mm) with a clearly defined mastoid crest. The tympanic plate of the temporal bone appears to have been slightly thickened. The supra-mastoid groove is wide and shallow and the supra-mastoid crest is poorly developed. On the inferior aspect of the temporal bone the digastric fossa is shallow and expanded somewhat posteriorly with a slight excavation of the base of the cranium.

The upper face appears to have been of moderate height with a slight degree of facial and subnasal projection. The orbits are of moderate height or mesoconch (estimated orbital index 80.9 per cent). The transverse axis is slightly oblique and the superior orbital margins are sharp and somewhat everted. The nasal bones lie in the same plane and the frontal processes of the maxilla are directed anteriorly. In these features of the orbits and nasal region a Khoisan influence may be detected. On the other hand, the interorbital region is of moderate width (estimated interorbital breadth 21 mm). The nose appears to have been platyrrhine and nasion is not depressed. The anterior nasal spine appears to have been moderately well developed. The inferior margin of the nasal aperture is formed by the fused spinal and turbinal crests, the lateral crest being separate. The subnasal alveolus appears to have been of moderate depth and the hard palate deep, sloping somewhat anteriorly.

When viewed from above, the mandible presents a somewhat U-shaped contour with divergences of the arms of the U behind the third molar. The alveolar arch itself is divergent U-shaped, the third molar slightly overhanging the internal contour of the body. The corpus mandibulae is of moderate height (m_2h 26 mm), the lateral surface tapers anteroposteriorly and is marked by a single mental foramen, directed superiorly and posteriorly, which lies below the apex of the second premolar, nearer the lower border of the corpus than the upper. Most of the internal surface of the symphyseal region can be seen from above. The genial region is marked by two small superior tubercles and a single median inferior tubercle. The digastric fossae are shallow and lie close to the lower border of the mandible. The ramus is narrow (rb' 32 mm), the mandibular notch moderately deep with little bony buttressing between the coronoid and condyloid processes. The coronoid process is triangular and hooked with an anterior convexity, its apex being directed upwards and

backwards. The condyle appears to have been small and oval, encroaching on the posterior aspect of the ramus. The ramus is set at an obtuse angle to the body ($M < 123°$). The angle of the mandible is slightly everted at the masseteric impression. The mental protuberance is moderately well developed and the mental tubercles are small; the resultant chin shape is pointed. (Table 52 sets out the measurements of the mandible).

In their general features the cranium and mandible are rather more Negroid than Khoisanoid. Thus in the main, these remains may be regarded as those of an individual showing Negroid and Khoisanoid characteristics.

SK 3

The remains comprise thirty fragments of the bones of the cranial vault; the right zygomatic bone; the crowns of the deciduous canine and second molar, two rib fragments and four fragments of vertebrae. The remains are those of an infant of about 12 months of age. It is not possible to assess the population group to which this infant belonged.

SK 4

This material was recovered from horizon O in grid square J 15. It consists of fractured and fragmented frontal, parietal and occipital bones; the mastoid and petrous portions of the right temporal bone, and the crown of a permanent upper central incisor tooth (the root portion had not yet been formed). The cranial vault has, in part, been reconstructed. The remains are those of a child of about seven or eight years of age. The apparent curvature of the cranial vault bones and the size of the incisor suggest that the remains are those of a child showing Negroid affinities.

SK 5

The remains from horizon Q (grid square K 10) are as follows:

Of the cranium there are preserved fractured and fragmented portions of the frontal, parietal and occipital bones (including the basi-occipital); the right mastoid, tympanic, petrous and squamous portions of the temporal bone; the right zygomatic bone; and portions of the body, greater wing and pterygoid plate of the left sphenoid bone. An isolated maxillary premolar shows wear with dentine exposure. The mandible is complete except for damage to the left condylar process and the right and left mandibular angles. The body of the mandible had been fractured in the region of the left canine. On the right side the second premolar and three molar teeth are present and on the left side the three molars are *in situ*. The remaining permanent teeth are missing, although from their sockets there is evidence that they were present at the time of death. The first molars show very unequal wear and appear also to have been carious. The right third molar shows evidence of caries. The remaining teeth show wearing with dentine exposure.

The postcranial remains consist of three fragments of vertebrae including the body and odontoid process of the axis; fourteen rib fragments; thirty-one fragments of os coxae; the distal end of the left ulna; a fragment of the shaft of the left femur; the distal extremity of a fibula; fragments of the shaft of a tibia; and one phalanx.

The remains are those of a fully adult individual probably in the third decade as judged by the pattern of

Table 52. Mandibular measurements (in mm unless otherwise indicated) of Sk2 and Sk 5 from Kalemba, compared with those of modern South African Negro males and females

| | Sk 2 | Sk 5 | South African Negro | | | |
| | | | Male | | Female | |
			Mean	Range	Mean	Range
cyl	—	19.2	19.9	16–25	18.3	14–24
rb'	32.0	39.4	35.2	26–44	33.1	27–39
m₂p₁	28.0	29.4	30.0	26–35	29.1	27–33
h₁	—	30.6	34.0	23–41	32.7	26–41
zz	41.0	39.5?	46.0	38–57	44.8	38–53
M∠	123°	118°?	120.6	103–135	125.0	115–138
cpl	73.0	76.0?	80.9	67–96	76.8	66–89
rl	54.0	59.0	57.6	45–69	51.9	42–62
gogo	90.0	—	91.3	74–110	84.2	70–98
crh	59.0	53.0	59.0	44–74	53.3	44–68
m₂h	26.0	27.0	26.5	19–35	25.0	20–33
Rameal Index	59.2	66.7	61.4	42.6–84.4	63.9	50.0–80.9

wear on the second and third molars. Owing to the fragmentary nature of the pelvis it is not possible to assess the sex accurately. However, the robust cranial vault bones and the eversion of the angles of the mandible suggest that these remains may be those of a male.

The cranium is too fragmentary to provide information useful to the assessment of the population group to which this individual belonged.

The mandible (plates XVIII c, d) is small. From above it presents a U-shaped contour with divergences of the arms of the U behind the third molar. The alveolar arch likewise is U-shaped. Most of the internal surface of the symphyseal region can be seen from above. The genial region is marked by a pit or depression. The digastric fossae are distinct and lie close to the inferior border of the mandible. The ramus is very broad (rb' 39.4 mm), the mandibular notch wide and shallow. The coronoid process is short and triangular, rather stout and hooked with an anterior convexity, its apex being directed upwards and slightly

backwards. The condyle is oval and large (19.2 mm). The angle of the mandible is everted at the masseteric impression. The mental protuberance is moderately well developed but the mental tubercles are virtually absent. The resultant chin shape is pointed. The corpus mandibulae is of moderate height (m₂h 27 mm) as is the symphysis menti (h₁ 30.6 mm). The lateral surface tapers anteroposteriorly and is marked by a single mental foramen which lies below the apex of the second premolar tooth nearer the lower border of the corpus than the upper. The foramen is directed superiorly and posteriorly. The mandibular measurements are listed in table 52.

The small size of the mandible, with the broad ramus and low cronoid, suggest a Khoisan, more particularly a San influence; on the other hand, the mandibular measurements fall within the ranges recorded for San and South African Negro mandibles (de Villiers, 1968; Drennan, 1938; Galloway, 1959; Schepers, 1941).

Chapter 18

The Kalemba Sequence

The evidence for human occupation of the Kalemba rock-shelter, which radiocarbon dates indicate covered a period in excess of 37,000 years, must first be examined to ascertain whether the habitation was continuous. A glance at the stratigraphical distribution of the thirteen age determinations (table 36, p. 127) strongly suggests that there were at least three hiatuses in the occupation, which may consequently be divided into four distinct periods.

It has been suggested in chapter 15 that dates GX-2767 and GX-2768, respectively from horizons L and M, do not represent the true age of those horizons, which are better dated to around 13,000 bc (as indicated by GX-2766 from horizon K and GX-2769 from horizon N). If this hypothesis is accepted, the remaining dates form a consistent series and suggest that the succession may be divided into the following principal periods of occupation:

Period (i), >35,000 bc, represented by horizon G;
Period (ii), c.25,000 – 21,000 bc, represented by horizons H to K;
Period (iii), c.15,000 – 11,000 bc, represented by horizons K to N; and
Period (iv), < 6,000 bc represented by horizons O to S.

Cessations in the accumulation of deposits are thus indicated at levels represented by the lower part of horizon H (where a marked decrease in the density of artefacts has already been noted on p. 124); by horizon K (which is marked by a massive rock-fall); and by the interface between horizons N and O (where attention has been drawn, on p. 122 above, to evidence for less intensive occupation). Of these, that in horizon K is of particular interest, since a rock-fall and apparent cessation of occupation at broadly the same time (c. 21,000 – 15,000 bc) has been noted at several other sites in south-central Africa (e.g. C.K. Cooke, 1973:3).

In the absence of any sterile levels separating different occupations, it is now necessary to examine the industrial succession to enquire whether or not this reveals any reflection of the breaks which are here postulated. The data presented are extracted from the relevant tables and figures of chapter 16.

Period (i)

The chipped stone industry of period (i) is differentiated from its successor by a markedly higher frequency of retouched implements. It is only in this horizon that unifacial points occur of other than sub-triangular type. Scrapers, which are the only other retouched implements recovered from horizon G, are characteristically made of whole flakes in preference to flake fragments or shatter-chunks. Artefacts of all types are somewhat larger than those in subsequent horizons. With the exception of a single pounding stone, no artefacts other than those of chipped stone were recovered.

Period (ii)

In period (ii) several developments may be discerned. Throughout this period the retouched implements represent only a tiny proportion (less than 0.2 per cent) of the chipped stone artefacts. The cores are predominantly radial. Backed tools, completely absent in period (i) and in horizon H, make their earliest appearance in horizon I in the form of convex-backed flakes of large size: the mean length of the eight examples from period (ii) deposits is 26.4 ± 5.0 mm. The only other backed specimen from this period is a single transverse-backed flake from horizon J. From 3.9 per cent of the retouched implements in horizon I, the backed flakes increase in frequency until they form 8.9 per cent of those from horizon K, at the end of period (ii). Points represent between 11 and 12 per cent of the implements in each of the horizons H to J. With the exception of two bifacial examples from horizon J, they are exclusively of the sub-triangular unifacial type. Scrapers, the most frequent implement type, show few changes from those of period (i), other than a slight but continuous reduction in size and a tendency to be made on broken rather than whole flakes.

Apart from the associated knapping hammers, the only artefacts not of chipped stone are two toothed bone fragments, one each from horizons J and K.

Period (iii)

In period (iii), the rate of change began to accelerate. Retouched implements as a whole continue to be of low frequency. Radial cores begin a steady decline in numbers, and tortoise cores completely disappear, their places being taken mainly by irregular types. Flakes in period (iii) deposits show a marked reduction in size over those of period (ii). At the beginning of period (iii), flakes with prepared striking platforms reach their greatest frequency, but decline markedly in horizon N.

Among the retouched implements, scrapers show a steady reduction both in size and in frequency: from over 80 per cent of specimens at the beginning of period (iii), they represent only 48 per cent of those from horizon N at its end. They are predominantly made on shatter-chunks and broken flakes: convex, concave and straight forms are of approximately equal frequency. The place of scrapers is progressively taken by backed tools, notably backed flakes which reach a peak of over 38 per cent of the retouched implements in horizon N. Convex-backed flakes are predominant: they are characteristically long (over 22 mm) and narrow. Straight- and transverse-backed flakes are present in small numbers throughout the period. Geometrics make their first appearance in the Kalemba sequence in horizon M, late in period (iii). Those of this period are exclusively of the pointed and deep lunate categories. Points are rare throughout the period.

In period (iii), artefacts other than those of chipped stone occur in significant numbers for the first time. There are two bored stones in horizon L, while knapping hammers, pounding stones and rubbing stones occur throughout the period. Bone bodkins make their first appearance, as does manufactured pigment in the form of discs and points.

Period (iv)

Period (iv), in contrast, presents a picture of an almost completely microlithic industry. The chipped stone artefacts show a continued reduction in size. Radial cores become progressively rarer, being replaced by single-platform and double-platform types. Bipolar cores appear for the first time. The change in core types is accompanied by a new emphasis on flakes with parallel (replacing convergent) dorsal scars, and on those with higher length-breadth ratios than those of the earlier period. There is a corresponding decrease in the frequency of flakes with prepared or pseudo-facetted striking platforms.

Retouched implements show a steady increase from 0.2 per cent of the chipped stone industry from horizon O at the beginning of period (iv) to 1.8 per cent near its end. Scrapers decrease markedly in frequency at the beginning of the period to only 25 per cent of the retouched implements from 48 per cent at the end of period (iii); and through period (iv) they decrease further, eventually reaching negligible proportions at the end of the site's occupation. In addition, there is a marked and sudden return to whole flakes as the preferred scraper base, an increase in the length of the scraper edge relative to the overall length of the implement, and a pronounced change from concave to convex as the dominant form of the scraper edge.

With the exception of the scrapers, and of a single point from the lowest level attributed to period (iv), all the retouched implements are backed. At the beginning of period (iv), geometrics overtake backed flakes as the most frequent class of retouched implement; and throughout the period there is a steady proliferation of the geometrics at the expense of the backed flakes. Backed points and miscellaneous backed pieces, which were first noted at the very end of period (iii), continue to form part of the assemblage from each horizon. Pointed and deep lunates, the two geometric types

which were represented in period (iii), both increase in frequency, the former showing a steady diminution in size. They are joined by asymmetrical lunates from horizon P onwards. Angled-backed geometrics make their first appearance, in the form of trapezoidal examples, in horizon O; triangular microliths and *petits tranchets* are first represented in horizon Q. The latter enjoy a marked but relatively brief vogue, disappearing again in the most recent horizon. The curved-backed flakes decreased steadily both in frequency and in size: they are also characteristically somewhat shorter and broader than those of period (iii). Transverse- and straight-backed examples also continue.

Artefacts of other materials show a further increase. Knapping hammers, pounding stones and rubbing stones occur throughout the period. There are two bored stones from horizon O at the very beginning of period (iv): in later times these objects are markedly absent. Ground stone axes first appear in horizon O, and continue to be represented thereafter, becoming more frequent in horizon S. Bone artefacts are common for the first time: bodkins, the only type of bone point represented in period (iii), continue in greater numbers than before, and are joined by headed pins and conical points from horizon Q onwards. Shell objects, which at Kalemba comprise exclusively beads and pendants, first occur in horizon P. Pigment is found at most levels, but is less frequent than it was in period (iii). Pestles and a grindstone used for its preparation are, however, represented.

In the upper two horizons pottery occurs. This is interpreted as representing contact with Iron Age peoples, to a consideration of which we shall return later in this chapter.

The Kalemba industrial succession may thus be regarded as conformable with the periodisation of the sequence which has been postulated on the basis of the radiocarbon dates. The distinction between the industries of the different periods is reflected most clearly in the relative frequencies of the main chipped stone retouched implement classes (fig. 102), and is confirmed by that of their sub-classes and that of the artefacts made from other materials.

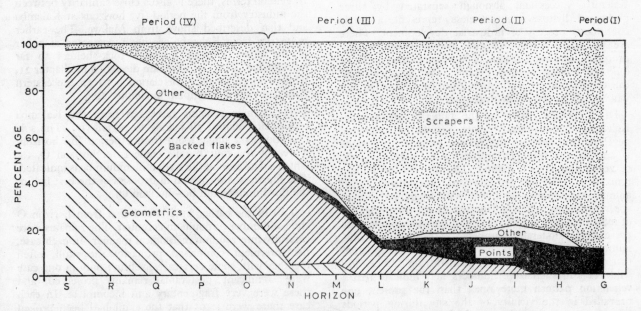

Fig. 102. Primary classes of retouched implements through the Kalemba sequence.

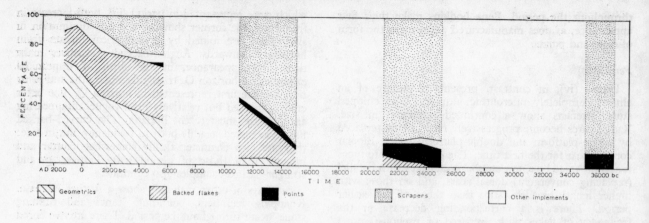

Fig. 103. Primary classes of retouched implements at Kalemba, set against a constant time-scale.

The general character of the succession appears to be as follows. The period (i) industry, for which a date before 35,000 bc is indicated, was of mode 3, its retouched implement assemblage being dominated by scrapers and unifacial points. Although flake-production was based on the use of radial cores, a significant number of elongated flakes, or 'flake-blades', was made. Period (ii), which had an unknown duration between c. 25,000 and c.21,000 bc, began with a second mode 3 industry comparable to the first but displaying an appreciably lower proportion of retouched implements. Later in period (ii) backed flakes make their appearance and steadily increase in numbers, heralding an industry apparently transitional between modes 3 and 5. At least 6,000 years separate period (ii) from period (iii), which was again of unknown duration within the time-bracket c.15,000 to c.11,000 bc. At this time the industry has a clear mode 5 aspect comparable, as will be shown in chapter 21 below, with that of contemporary material from elsewhere in eastern and central Africa. Period (iv) began about 6000 bc and lasted until recent times. It is associated with a second fully-fledged mode 5 industry, the makers of which, within the last two millennia, came into contact with Iron Age peoples.

Figs. 102 and 103 stress that the four periods of the Kalemba succession, although separated by three prolonged hiatuses, nevertheless represent a single continuous process of industrial development. There are no sharp breaks in the overall developmental processes; and most trends of industrial change can be followed through several periods. The significance of this observation for the eastern Zambian succession as a whole is discussed below in chapter 20.

Dr J. Harris' study of the faunal remains from Kalemba demonstrates further significant economic developments between the various periods. In periods i) and (ii) the specimens recovered are predominantly of zebra and large antelope. The absence of buffalo remains at Kalemba is, however, noteworthy. Small animals are represented by only a meagre number of specimens, and their contribution to the total quantity of meat obtained must have been miniscule. Suids were present in moderate numbers, with bush-pig outnumbering wart-hog. It has been suggested (p. 162) that the presence of the plains-loving zebra and wildebeest in such large numbers may indicate that a vegetation pattern more open than the present one prevailed in the vicinity of the site during periods (i) and (ii). Strong preference for the hunting of equids

and large bovids is, however, widely attested in southern Africa at this time-depth (Klein, 1974).

Period (iii) saw the start of the decrease in frequency of these large gregarious creatures and a corresponding increase in that of the small animals. Wart-hog replaced bush-pig as the dominant suid. These trends continue into period (iv), by which time the equids and large antelope have almost disappeared from the site, their place being taken by a variety of small animals which are almost exclusively of non-gregarious species. It is tempting to see this pronounced change as having been accompanied by the development of new methods of obtaining animal foods: trapping may have at least partly replaced more concerted hunting techniques. Such a development could have been a response to the establishment of denser vegetation in the Kalemba area, which would have resulted in the migration of the plains antelope and zebra out of the usual exploitation area of the site's inhabitants. The small creatures on which they now increasingly depended are all to be found in the immediate vicinity of the rock-shelter under present conditions.

The pattern of the faunal occurrences in period (iv) at Kalemba is concordant with that observed at Makwe. In general terms, there is also a close similarity between the industry from the period (iv) horizons at Kalemba and that described above from Makwe. The earlier industries from Kalemba are not represented at either of the other Eastern Province rock-shelters so far investigated. Their affinities are discussed in chapter 21, while a more detailed correlation between the eastern Zambian sites is attempted in chapter 20.

The human remains recovered from the Kalemba rock-shelter almost all belong to period (iv). The sole exception is a single tooth from a period (iii) horizon. Three of the four burials come from horizon O, for which a date around the sixth millennium bc is indicated. The fourth was recovered in deposits of the first half of the third millennium bc—horizon Q.

Two of the earlier burials and that from horizon Q show a number of points in common. The remains were carefully interred in a methodical manner. In each case, the interment comprised primarily the skull, often together with some cervical vertebrae: only in one case were significant postcranial remains preserved, and these were very fragmentary and incomplete. In each case there were signs that the skull had been broken before burial and the pieces separated. In one grave an adult, perhaps female, skull was associated with that of an infant about one year old.

There are thus strong indications that the dead were dismembered, and that only the heads—after being broken up—were buried at the site. The only deposit of postcranial remains, from horizon O, consisted of bones much fragmented, and burned. These discoveries, taken together, clearly indicate some ritual process of disposal of the dead: possibly cannibalism was involved.

Dr Hertha de Villiers has prepared detailed descriptions of the human skeletal material from Kalemba, in so far as it can be reconstructed. The conclusion reached is that the material falls within the known modern range of both Negroid and Khoisanoid individuals, but that characteristics of the former group are in most cases dominant. With reference to Sk 4 (a juvenile) and Sk 2 (an adult, possibly female), Dr de Villiers comments (*in litt.*, 13th December 1973): "the curvature of the cranial vault bones follows an even curve. The forehead is relatively flat and the occiput hemispherical. These are characteristics of the Negro cranium. The forehead in females is usually more vertical than in males. The marked angulation or bossing of the frontal, parietal and occipital bones, frontal narrowing, post-coronal flattening and supra-asterionic flattening described as characteristic of the Khoisan, particularly the San, crania are absent. Other Negroid, rather than San, characteristics are seen in the width between the orbits, the apparent depth of the palate, and the anterior slope of the palate. The cranial vault appears to have been short: this feature may reflect a San influence."

The Kalemba material thus supplements that from Thandwe in indicating that many physical features now found typically among modern Negroid populations may long predate the advent of the Iron Age to this region. The implications of the possible presence of a population sharing many physical characteristics of modern Negroids as long ago as the sixth millennium bc are discussed in chapter 21.

There is little evidence for contact between the inhabitants of the Kalemba rock-shelter and an Early Iron Age population, or for the use of the site by the Early Iron Age people themselves. Only three diagnostically Early Iron Age sherds were recovered. The stratigraphical provenances of these suggest that the time-span of the Early Iron Age is broadly represented in the depositional sequence by horizon R.

It must be concluded that the hilly country around Kalemba proved significantly less attractive to the Early Iron Age folk than did the more open fertile region to the west, where Makwe rock-shelter yielded evidence for a much more intensive Early Iron Age influence. This hypothesis receives some degree of support from the fact that a fairly intensive search of the plains around Mbangombe village (the only good agricultural or grazing land within easy reach of Kalemba) failed to locate any traces of Early Iron Age settlement, although several old village sites yielding Luangwa tradition pottery of the later Iron Age were discovered. Perhaps, as at Thandwe, the Early Iron Age advent to the Kalemba area was also of relatively late date; but the latter site provided no radiometric evidence for the age of the Early Iron Age contact, and the typological evidence is also inconclusive.

Later Iron Age material is restricted to the uppermost horizon, horizon S. The associated Luangwa tradition pottery is many times more prolific than that of the Early Iron Age. The mode 5 chipped stone industry continued without major modification through the greater part of horizon S, and only shows a significant reduction in quantity in the uppermost part of the horizon, where there is—for the first time—evidence for the actual occupation of the rock-shelter by Iron Age people. The structures associated with this occupation have been described above in chapter 15; and it is reasonable to interpret them as representing a place of retreat during one of the periods of Ngoni raids which took place in the nineteenth century. This is confirmed by local oral tradition, and by the discovery of a food-store apparently associated with the same phase of occupation.

The other extant manifestation of later Iron Age use of the rock-shelter is the extensive series of white rock paintings, which is described in chapter 19, below. Evidence is cited in that chapter which strongly suggests that most of the surviving paintings pre-date the nineteenth-century occupation, but that these may be but the last of a long succession of paintings. Exfoliated wall fragments bearing traces of red paint occurred in horizons R and S only: there are signs of red schematic paintings underlying the main series of white ones. Pieces of pigment, both natural and manufactured, were found in much earlier levels of the excavation; but of the uses to which they were put we have no knowledge.

Chapter 19

The Rock Paintings of Eastern Zambia

More than forty rock painting sites are now known in eastern Zambia: their location is shown on the map presented on p. 8 (fig. 2). As part of the research project here described, a detailed record was made of those paintings which were previously inadequately published. In this chapter, a gazetteer of all the known sites is presented, followed by an attempt to establish a stylistic sequence for the region as a whole. In a third section the dating and significance of the art is discussed.

I. GAZETTEER OF SITES

CHAFISI

Chafisi is a small rocky hill rising some 15 m above the plateau at 1100 m above sea level, at 13°58' south, 32°32' east. It lies 400 m south-east of the Chipata-Chadiza road at a point 48 km from Chipata. Manje Hill (q.v., below) is 1.5 km north-north-east of Chafisi. The main site, discovered by the present writer in 1965, is a shelter formed by a large westwards-facing rock slab resting at an angle of approximately 45°, situated near the north end of the hill, about half way up the slope. Between fallen rocks on the shelter floor is a very restricted habitable area littered with exfoliated fragments: no artefacts are visible here. At the back, the shelter roof forms a low cave only 60 to 90 cm high.

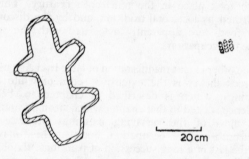

20 cm

Fig. 104. Rock paintings, in red, at Chafisi.

Two paintings are present (fig. 104): a red grid, 1.05 m above the floor, and a red outline zoomorph which is 2.15 m above the floor but only 1.0 m above the top of a fallen rock. The main rock surface is much stained by rain-wash which may have removed further paintings. Mode 5 quartz artefacts and later Iron Age sherds (chapter 5) occur on the surface below the shelter and in thin scatters elsewhere on the hill. A single sherd of Early Iron Age type was also found on the talus slope of the main shelter.

CHAINGO

This site is in Chipata District at 13°47' south, 32°12' east, and is reached by a path which runs for 1.5 km in a northerly direction from the north edge of Masinja village. The site is at ground level on the south side of a small rocky outcrop in flat forest country 1000 m above sea level. A slightly overhanging rock face, 11 m long, faces west-south-west. The floor area is limited to the western half of the shelter by a large boulder which comes within 75 cm of the main rock face at the latter's eastern end. A small illicit excavation,

made at some time between the visit of J. H. Chaplin in 1960 and that of the present writer in 1966, shows that the grey ashy deposit contained many large rocks and reached a depth of 50 cm. Later Iron Age pottery (see chapter 5) occurs, together with a quartz industry of mode 5 type.

The well-preserved paintings extend to within 60 cm of the ground and show a sequence of successive purple, red, and black and buff bichromatic schematic grids, overlain by an extensive series of white paintings (fig. 105; plate XIX). The latter include a large zoomorphic figure whose white outline has been filled with finger-dots in the same white paint, producing a design resembling a leopard skin. It is this painting which has given the site its name, Chaingo being the ChiNyanja for 'leopard'. The main motif is flanked by representations of hoes and axes, done in the same white paint. The Chaingo paintings have been described by Chaplin (1962:8) who also noted a group of three red grids at another site on the west side of the same rock outcrop.

CHALUMBE

Chalumbe Hill is situated in Chipata District at 13°28' south, 32°44' east (see map, fig. 19, p. 38). It rises some 18 m above the 1075-m plateau, 100 m south of the Chipata-Lundazi road and immediately to the west of the track to Chalumbe School which leaves the main road 400 m to the west of the Zawi Hill turn-off at Mabvundo. The site is on the south-east side of the hill, 6 m above the track to Chalumbe School. A large boulder provides two small shelters, facing north-east and south-east respectively. Both have floor areas of approximately 3.0 by 1.2 m and apparently shallow deposits displaying mode 5 quartz artefacts on the surface.

The paintings—a red grid and a yellowish-white grid overlying traces of a red motif (fig. 106)—occur in the north-east facing shelter approximately 1 m above the floor. Ant hills against the wall of this shelter may obscure further paintings. The south-east facing shelter has two rock slabs on the floor, each with a very smooth grinding hollow 7 to 10 cm in diameter. Zawi Hill (q.v. below) is clearly visible from the Chalumbe site, at a distance of 3 km, on a bearing of 153°.

CHIKANGA

Chikanga Hill rises to a maximum height of 1260 m and is situated at 14°08' south, 32°33' east, 7 km due east of Mbangombe village and a similar distance west of the Mwangazi river. The site, the position of which is shown

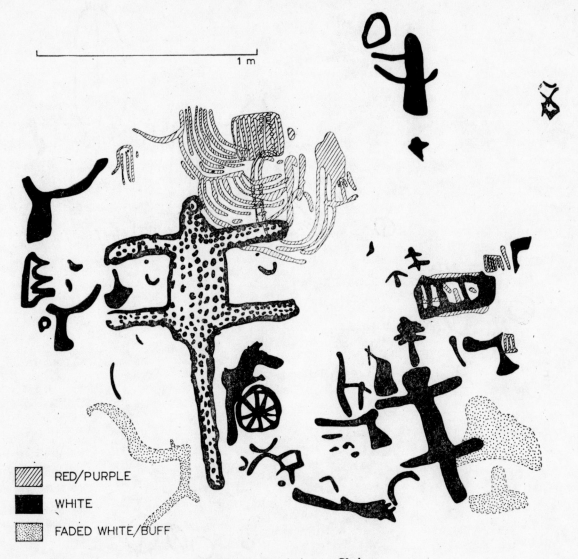

RED/PURPLE

WHITE

FADED WHITE/BUFF

Fig. 105. Rock paintings at Chaingo.

on fig. 68 (p. 120), lies at an altitude of approximately 1170 m, near the summit of a saddle lying to the south of the main peak. It consists of a rock overhang facing south-east. The site may be the same as one reported to the then Rhodes-Livingstone Museum in 1955 by Mr R. A. Hamilton who, however, gave the name of the hill as Mwinibanja. Hamilton described the paintings as "lines, ellipses and a figure in red", which agrees with those from the Chikanga site. Chikanga has not been visited by the present writer, and he is indebted to Mr M. S. Bisson for the sketch here reproduced (fig. 107). The paintings are exclusively red and include an outline zoomorphic figure, a comparable but limbless motif, various grids, circles and a set of parallel lines.

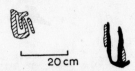

20 cm

Fig. 106. Rock paintings at Chalumbe, in red, the motif on the right being overpainted also in yellowish white (shown here as black).

CHIPANGALI

The Chipangali resettlement area (13°08′ to 13°14′ south, 32°46′ to 32°48′ east) lies in the extreme north of the region described in the present work, at a mean altitude of 1000 to 1050 m, some 20 km west of the Luangwa/Lake Malawi watershed. Five sites of rock paintings were reported by Mr P. Greening, and details of three of them have been published by Chaplin (1962:6–7). The paintings are all red schematic motifs, mainly grids, among which some elaborate chequer-board designs are noteworthy. They have not been visited by the present writer.

CHIPWETE

A large granite-domed mountain, reaching 1390 m above sea level, overlooks from the west the upper Chipwete valley 1.5 km north of Mbangombe village. On a saddle, about two-thirds of the way up the eastern face of the hill, is a small triangular rock-shelter (plate XXa), facing east-south-east, formed by two abutting boulders and capped by a third. Its location is shown in fig. 68 on p. 120. The flat ashy floor is 3.0 m wide at the shelter entrance and extends back, with reduced width,

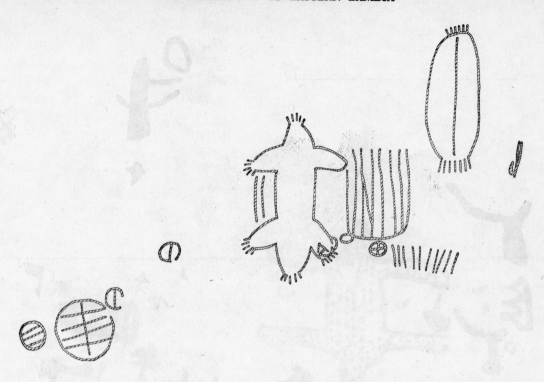

50 cm (approx.)

Fig. 107. Rock paintings, in red, at Chikanga (freehand sketch).

1 m

Fig. 108. Rock paintings, in white, at Chipwete.

for 6.0 m. Later Iron Age pottery occurs, but was not collected. There was no sign of Stone Age material.

Both of the two main boulders forming the shelter bear traces of paintings (fig. 108 and plate XXb), most of which are in white pigment. Both panels are superimposed on a blurred mass of pigment in which the original motifs can no longer be distinguished. The northern wall shows extensive traces of red designs (too faint to copy) underlying the white paintings. These are heavily flaked and there are indications that an attempt may have been made to remove them by hammering before the white motifs were added. Those of the white paintings which are decipherable include elaborate grid-like designs and a rectangular figure with a long neck and an animal head.

KALEMBA

The site has been described above in chapter 15, and the positions of the rock paintings are shown on the plan (fig. 69, p. 121). Two main groups of paintings are present. That in the main rock shelter faces north-west and extends for a maximum length of 12 m (plate XXIa). At the left end of the panel are faint traces of red schematic paintings, including three grids. Near the centre are several figures in buff paint, notably two crude animals and the head of a third. Both groups are overlain by the main series of white paintings. These include grids, circles, lines and many anthropomorphic figures showing varying degrees of stylisation (fig. 109). One human figure near the left end of the panel holds a circular object covered with dots (plate XXIb). Further to the right, a circle elaborated with dots and a cross (plate XXIIa) shows at least two periods of painting. Details of other interesting motifs are shown in plates XXIIb and XXIIIb.

Near the centre of the paintings is a clearly defined area, some 1.3 m across, where all trace of paint has been removed. Excavation demonstrated that this area precisely coincided with that of the lean-to structure described in chapter 15 above (see p. 125 and fig. 75). Since several motifs have been partly obliterated, it is clear that the paintings were not executed *around* the lean-to structure, but that paintings formerly present were removed after that structure was erected. It may be concluded, therefore, that most if not all of the Kalemba paintings were executed before the erection of the lean-to, for which event a nineteenth-century date has already been postulated (p. 169).

Fig. 111. Rock painting, in red, at Kamkomole.

The second group of paintings (fig. 110) faces south-west and has overall dimensions of 1.0 by 0.8 m. It comprises three whitish-buff anthropomorphic figures similar to those represented on the main panel.

KAMKOMOLE

Kamkomole Hill, Chadiza District, 14°07′ south, 32°26′ east, is a twin-peaked rocky hill lying 400 m to the west of the road which runs from Chadiza to Zingalume (see fig. 68 on p. 120). It is 6 km south of Chadiza and rises 90 m above the plateau, which is itself 1075 m above sea level. Robi village lies at the foot of the lower, southern, peak on the east side. The site is approximately half way up the east side of the northern peak of Kamkomole. A large overhanging slab faces south at 60° to the horizontal, at right angles to the general line of the hillside at this point. It has a narrow rocky floor fronted by a vertical drop and displays no traces of human use apart from faded red, highly schematised, linear anthropomorphic paintings (fig. 111) at a height of 1.2 to 1.5 m. A well defined shelter nearly at the top of the same slope has no paintings or deposit.

KATOLOLA

Katolola is a rocky ridge situated in Chipata District at 13°45′ south, 32°39′ east, some 1.0 km to the east of the Chipata-Chadiza road and 14 km from Chipata. It lies at 1215 m above sea level, immediately west of the headwaters of the Kafera stream, a southern tributary of the Lutembwe. The paintings from sites A and B have previously been noted by J. D. Clark (1959b: 170–1, 173), under the locality's earlier name of Rock-lands Farm.

Site A. Near the centre of the west side of the Katolola ridge a boulder, some 5 m high by 6 m wide, rests on the flat ground at the foot of the ridge. A large slab has exfoliated from the west side of the boulder, leaving a vertical scar 2.1 m high by 1.8 m wide, sheltered only by a 60 cm overhang and facing north-north-east. It is on this scar that first a red grid and then a large (1.90 m long) naturalistic figure, probably of an eland, were painted (fig. 112; plate XXIVa). This painting is of particular interest, not only for the fact that it is the first to be discovered in Zambia where there is a clear superimposition of a naturalistic painting over a schematic one, but also for the style in which the purple-brown eland is depicted. It is markedly dissimilar from naturalistic paintings in other regions of Zambia (D. W. Phillipson, 1972b: *passim*). The dewlap and mane are clearly indicated, but the legs are disproportionately small. Because of weathering, the head (if ever represented) is no longer visible. These paintings, and

Fig. 110. Paintings, in white, on the south-west-facign rock face at Kalemba.

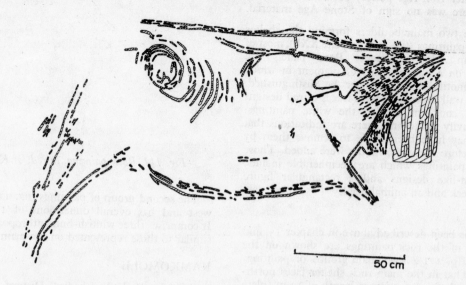

50 cm

Fig. 112. Rock paintings at Katolola A. A pale red grid is overlain by a purple-brown animal figure.

1 m

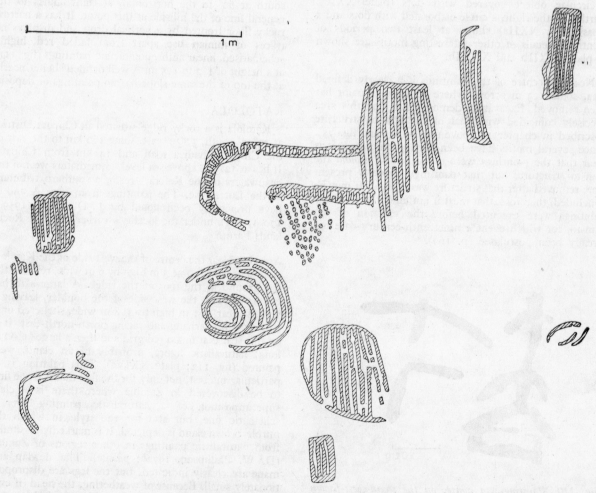

Fig. 113. Rock paintings, in red, at Katolola B.

also those at site B, are exposed to direct sunlight daily from noon onwards. The ground beneath the paintings is rocky with little sign of human occupation.

Site B. 40 m east-north-east of site A, and only 3 m above the foot of the west slope of the ridge, is an upright slab of rock 7.5 m high by 6.0 m wide, overhanging at 15° to the vertical and facing north-west. The south end of the rock face is fully exposed to rain and sun, but the north end, where the red schematic paintings are preserved, is protected by a boulder lying in front of the main rock slab. At the north end of the slab a small shelter floor 2.0 by 2.0 m contains traces of the excavation conducted by D. G. Lancaster in about 1938 (see p. 19, above). To the south of this there is only a narrow cleft between the main slab and the boulder. The paintings (fig. 113) are much washed out and blend into the patina of the rock. The lowest paintings are 60 cm above the floor of the cleft at a point where this itself is 30 cm above the shelter floor. The paintings comprise large and carefully executed groups of concentric circles and grids. From one grid emerge two horizontal ladder-like motifs below which are dots of red paint forming a design resembling rain falling from a cloud. The whole rock face is pitted with scars caused by stones being thrown at the paintings. Patination shows that these scars are not due to recent vandalism.

Site C. This site is reached by following the foot of the Katolola ridge southwards from site A for a distance of 250 m. It is on the south-south-east side of the ridge, about 10 m above the plain. A large boulder forms a small but very habitable shelter, facing due east. The flat floor, 3.0 by 2.5 m, has a grey ashy deposit, apparently of some depth, with mode 5 quartz artefacts visible on the surface. The whole shelter wall overhangs at 45° to the vertical and rises to a maximum height of 3 m. At 1.05 m above the floor is a single painting of a small arrow motif in white. The hill slope below this shelter displays large quantities of mode 5 stone artefacts.

A number of other sites and rock-shelters on Katolola ridge have surface indications of prehistoric occupation, but no sites were noted where there was evidence of deep deposits.

KAVUMO

Kavumo Hill, Chadiza District, 14°10' south, 32°28' east, lies 500 m south-east of Kachipande Village and is immediately south of the approach track to Nunda School, which turns eastwards from the Zingalume-to-Tafelansoni road 3 km south of Zingalume (see fig. 68 on p.120). The hill is 3 km east of this track and 1.5 km west of Nunda School. Kavumo Hill has two peaks separated by a saddle. The higher, northern, peak reaches an altitude of 1245 m above sea level, 120 m above the surrounding plain.

Site A is near the top of the smaller, southern, peak, on its north-north-east side, and faces east-north-east. Under a prominent horizontal rock slab (which does not form an integral part of the shelter) a rock surface 5 m wide overhangs for 3 m at about 40° from the vertical. The shelter floor, between rock falls, measures 2.5 by 2.0 m. Quartz artefacts of mode 5 and later Iron Age potsherds are visible on the surface of the apparently shallow deposits. Mode 5 artefacts are also present on the hill-slope below the shelter. The paintings (plate XXIVb) are red grids and extend to within 60 cm of the shelter floor.

Site B lies about half way down the hill, immediately below site A. A low rock overhang about 1 m high and 2 m in maximum width has been blocked by rough dry-stone walling, leaving only a narrow crack at the top through which three human skeletons and a group of later Iron Age pots can be seen lying on the shelter floor. Just under the overhang are faint traces of what may possibly be red paint.

Site C. This is situated on the south-west side of the higher, northern, peak of Kavumo Hill, at the level of the saddle, towards which it faces from the south-west. Site A is approximately 300 m distant on a bearing of about 110°. The shelter is formed by a rock slab, 10 m long, which overhangs at an angle of 40° from the vertical for a distance of some 5 m. The south-eastern third of the shelter is taken up by a large boulder, 3 m high, which supports the main slab. The shelter floor, which measures 6.0 by 4.5 m in maximum dimensions, is littered with slabs of exfoliated rock and disturbed by animal burrows. Mode 5 quartz artefacts, later Iron Age potsherds and a piece of worked iron occur on the surface of the deposit, which appears to be of no great depth. The paintings (plate XXVa) were done from the top of the boulder at the south-east end of the shelter. They consist of a red-outlined zoomorphic figure completely infilled with yellow-buff paint, similar to those from Thandwe and Manje (*q.q.v.*, below), and other buff-white grids apparently overlying the zoomorph. This in turn overlies red patches which are probably natural stains.

MAKWE

The Makwe site is described in detail in chapter 11, and the location of the paintings is shown in fig. 36 on p. 68. There are present red schematic paintings, white paintings, and charcoal drawings.

The largest panel of red schematic paintings, situated at the northern end of the main shelter wall, comprises a series of grid designs (fig. 114) partly obscured by a white encrustation. Below this panel, a large rock bears many faint traces of red, apparently schematic, paintings. These are too faint, through fading and encrustation, for individual motifs to be decipherable. Further to the south along the main shelter wall, between datum lines 9 and 10 of the excavation grid, is a faint red grid painting (fig. 115:1) at a height of 2.1 m above the 1966 floor level. Between datum lines 11 and 12, and at a similar height, is a group of red paintings (fig. 115:2) which includes three vaguely anthropomorphic motifs and a small grid. Near the southern end of the shelter are two red paintings situated high on the main overhang but easily reached from the tops of the fallen boulders. At datum line 14 of the excavation is the grid design illustrated in fig. 115:3. A further 5.5 m to the south are faint traces of another large grid (fig. 115:4). The last of the red schematic paintings at Makwe are outside the main shelter, at the right-hand side of a slight overhang on the western wall of the approach slope, some 3 m south of the entrance passage. They are much faded and comprise one motif of concentric ovals and the lower part only of a second, probably similar, design (fig. 115:5).

The only white paintings also occur outside the main shelter, in the centre of the small overhang noted above. Three motifs are represented (fig. 115:6): the paint of all is flaking and parts of the original designs are probably now missing. The largest is a possibly anthropomorphic design, while to the right is a delicate concentric circle

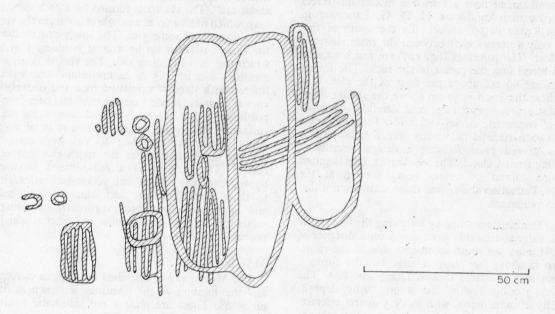

Fig. 114. The northernmost panel of rock paintings, in red, at Makwe.

motif. Below this are the badly flaked remains of what may have been a grid.

Near the centre of the main wall of the rock-shelter are two panels bearing drawings executed with a charcoal crayon. The clearer of the panels is here reproduced (fig. 116). The drawings represent rectangular or 'M'-shaped objects, frequently embellished at one end with a horned head, and at the other with a tail. Some also have two (*sic*) feet, close together and centrally positioned. These figures were readily identified by local residents as representations of men wearing masks associated with the ceremonies of the *Nyau* religious society. Further consideration of this attribution and its implications is presented in a later section of this chapter.

MANJE

Manje Hill is a prominent rocky feature 400 m to the south-east of the Chipata-Chadiza road 46 km from Chipata, at 13°57′ south, 32°32′ east. It rises some 100 m above the headwater *dambo* of the Chazombe stream to an altitude of about 1170 m above sea level. At the foot of the hill, beside the road, is the shop of Mr S. Z. Banda.

Site A. This site is on the west-north-west side of the hill, three-quarters of the way up. It is a fine large rock-shelter facing north-north-west (plate XXVb). The 12-m long back wall is slightly concave in plan, and

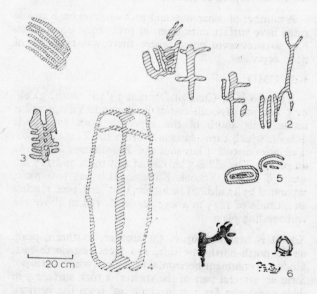

Fig. 115. Rock paintings at Makwe: nos. 1 to 5 are red, no. 6 is white.

the flat shelter floor extends in front of the wall for a maximum of 5.5 m. The overhang, which reaches 6 m above the floor, is formed by a rock, with a total

Fig. 116. Charcoal drawings at Makwe.

20 cm

height of 12 m, which extends for a maximum of 6 m from the back wall in a clear, smooth sweep from the vertical to within 30° of the horizontal. The floor slopes evenly down to the west, the total drop being about 1 m. The eastern half of the floor is largely obscured by fallen rocks and, in 1970, by a massive wooden porcupine trap. The western half has some fallen rocks but is mainly clear: later Iron Age potsherds, mode 5 quartz artefacts, debris of wood and bark rope left over from the manufacture of the porcupine trap, and several broken golf-ball-sized gourds of the type used for making dance-rattles were visible on the surface. In front of the shelter, at a height of about 2 m above the shelter floor, a flat rock surface extends for some 10 m.

The central section of the shelter wall is a mass of paintings extending from 30 cm above the floor to over 2 m. Especially in the lower part, the wall is such a mass of buff paint that recognition of individual motifs is virtually impossible. This effect appears to be due to the repeated re-painting of zoomorphic figures in red outline which were then filled with thick buff paint.

A trial trench 45 by 45 cm was excavated at the western end of the shelter floor, and reached rock at 60 cm. Mode 5 artefacts were encountered in small quantities throughout, but were not retained.

Site B. About 25 m south of site A, at the same elevation, is a roughly triangular rock-shelter formed by two rocks. That on the north is concave in section: that on the south is vertical. The shelter itself faces north-west; the painted (northern) side faces north-north-east. The flat open floor is about 5.5 m across at the opening and extends back for 3.5 m to a scree of large rocks which slopes upwards at 45° into the crack between the two rocks. At the front, the shelter is 6 m high.

Paintings cover an area about 1.5 m square and are a mass of indistinguishable superimpositions in buff and red. As with the similar paintings at site A, very few individual motifs can be deciphered.

The fine ashy soil of the shelter floor displays undecorated potsherds. A trial trench 45 cm square

excavated at the north side of the shelter entrance yielded traces of occupation by the makers of mode 5 artefacts, and reached solid rock at a depth of 45 cm. A group of fallen horizontal rock slabs in front of the painted surface has smooth grinding hollows, 7 to 10 cm in diameter, similar to those at Chalumbe, Mkoma and other sites. There is a sparse scatter of mode 5 quartz artefacts on the hill-slope below sites A and B.

Site C. This is a large rock-shelter on the north-east side of the hill, overlooking the Chazombe *dambo*. It appears as a horizontal crack, 40 to 50 m long, just below the top of Manje Hill, and is clearly visible from the Chipata road. The only access to the site is by negotiating smooth rock surfaces at an angle of 40° to 45°. The shelter is reported by the writer's less vertiginous emissaries to have a rock floor with no archaeological deposits. The paintings consist of one red outline zoomorphic motif filled with buff paint, and two red 'sunbursts'. No illustration is available.

MASINJA

Kamwani Hill is a rocky *kopje* located 300 m to the east of Masinja School in Chipata District at 13°49′ south, 32°12′ east. It is some 25 m high at 1050 m above sea level. Almost at the top of the south-west side is a slightly overhanging rock slab some 6 m high and 10 m long, facing almost due south. The sandy soil between the rocks at the foot of the slab was tested and found to have a maximum depth of 23 cm. Undecorated body sherds and mode 5 quartz artefacts occurred throughout. A painting of a red grid and a very faint red ladder design occur 1.8 m above the floor (fig. 118). They have previously been noted by Chaplin (1962: 8–10). On the north-west slopes of the *kopje* mode 5 artefacts and some probably mode 3 quartz flakes occur on the surface.

MBOZI

This site, located in the far east of the Chadiza District at 14°00′ south, 32°49′ east, has been described by Chaplin (1962:10–11), but has not been visited by the present writer. With one exception, the paintings in this extensive series are of the red schematic type. There is a

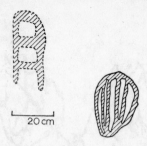

Fig. 118. Rock paintings, in red, at Masinja.

wide assortment of grids including elaborate chequer-board examples, and arrangements of concentric circles. Two of the grids are overlain by a single white star-like motif.

MITOO

This striking shelter is not easy to find, being largely obscured by bush on a gently sloping saddle, 1170 m above sea level, which separates the headwaters of the Mkandabwako from those of the Mkumbudzi, at 14°10′ south, 32°30′ east. It is 4 km due south of Kalemba (see fig. 68 on p. 120). The best approach is from Mbangombe village, 3 km to the north-west. The shelter faces south and occurs in an isolated pile of massive granite boulders some 10 to 12 m high. The main sheltered area, 8 m wide by 6 m deep, has a floor largely unimpeded by rocks but much eroded by water. A considerable quantity of archaeological deposit remains, however, and abundant mode 5 artefacts are exposed on the surface, together with occasional later Iron Age sherds. At the rear, the shelter area becomes much restricted, at first by a low roof less than 1.0 m above the floor, then laterally to produce two narrow steeply sloping tunnels some 60–80 cm in width. Several isolated red and white paintings (e.g. fig. 119) are, with difficulty, visible on the walls and roof of the main shelter and on the underside of the low roof at its rear.

Fig. 119. White rock painting at Mitoo.

MKOMA

Mkoma Farm, now owned by the Zambia Youth Service, lies in Katete District some 4 km north of the Great East Road, 32 km east of Katete. It takes its name from the 1435-m high Mkoma Hill, the summit of which forms the north-eastern boundary beacon of the farm. The Mkoma site lies at 13°54′ south, 32°12′ east, 3 km south-west of Mkoma Hill and 200 m north of the approach road to the Youth Service camp. The site is a large rock-shelter (plate XXVI) in the east side of an isolated rock outcrop rising some 18 m above the plain which at this point is at 1090 m above sea level. The shelter floor is some 7 m above the plain and is reached by a 40° slope littered with rocks. The shelter faces east-south-east and is 8.5 m in length. The fine domed over-hang curves from nearly vertical to within 20° of the horizontal and extends 6 m out from the wall. The floor has an area 8.5 m by 2.5 to 3.0 m and is relatively free of fallen rocks. Potsherds of later Iron Age type, mode 5 quartz artefacts, a fragment of a ground stone axe, pieces of iron slag and fragments of bone are all visible on the surface; and the deposit would appear to be of some depth. A boulder on the edge of the floor bears a smooth grinding hollow some 7.5 cm in diameter and 2.5 cm deep.

The paintings (fig. 120), previously described by Chaplin (1962: 10), comprise two distinct styles. High on the rock face (the lowest example being 3.0 m above the ground) is a series of schematic bichrome designs in dark reddish purple and yellowish white. They include grids, sets of parallel lines, a 'comet'–like motif and the elaborate 'knotted grid' illustrated in plate XXVII. Lower down, but much disfigured by broad vertical stripes where rainwater running down the rock face has removed all traces of paint, is an extensive series of white stylised designs including grids, anthropomorphs and representations of metal hoes and axes.

'MWALA WA MANJA'

Although it is situated approximately 1.0 km inside Malawi's Mchinji District, in an area where the water-shed boundary with Zambia is ill-defined, the site is noted here since it was located by the present writer in 1970 and full details have not hitherto been published (cf. Cole-King, 1973: 51–2). This 'rock of hands' is a large boulder with two overhangs, on the south side of a small rocky outcrop rising some 15 m above the sandy plateau which here has an altitude of some 1180 m. The co-ordinates are 13°33′ south, 32°50′ east: the location of the site is marked on fig. 19, p. 38. The floor of one overhang shows a slight scatter of mode 5 quartz artefacts: the westward-facing wall of the other bears the dark red paintings illustrated in fig. 121. The base of the painted area is 2.0 m above the present floor level. The site's name refers to the paintings, which consist of short lines, often in parallel groups of five, and which were clearly executed by means of fingers dipped in paint.

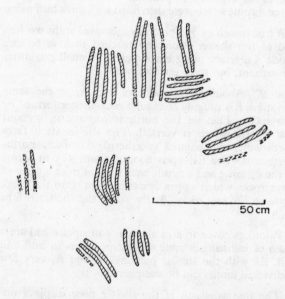

Fig. 121. Rock paintings, in red, at 'Mwala wa Manja'.

NJAZI

The rock-paintings at this site were located by Dr J. P. Bruwer in 1949. Subsequent attempts by J. H. Chaplin and by the present writer to relocate them have not been successful; and our information is thus derived solely from Bruwer's (1956) note. The site is located some 50 km north-west of Katete, at (very approximately) 13°53' south, 31°44' east, half way up a small hill adjacent to the main Njazi Hill, and faces south. The paintings are mainly red, with some motifs a creamy white. Bruwer reproduces sketches of twelve schematic motifs but does not indicate their individual colours.

RUKUZYE AREA

Six rock-painting sites have been located in an area beside the Rukuzye river and to the west of the Chipata-Lundazi road 50 km from Chipata. The area is in Chipata District between 13°21' and 13°22' south, 32°49' and 32°51' east. The thickly wooded country is flat or gently undulating at an altitude of 1050 to 1075 m above sea level, with frequent small rocky *kopjes*; it is drained by the north-westwards flowing-Rukuzye and its tributaries, including the Mapala.

Rukuzye A. This site is reached by turning north-west from the Chipata-Lundazi road at Chanje, 50 km from Chipata, onto the approach road to Rukuzye Dam. Five kilometres from the main road is a turning which runs west-south-west to the Development Area Training Centre, 1.0 km away on the eastern shore of the dam. In the angle north of that road, and west of the dam road, is a small rocky outcrop. On its west side is a westward-facing shelter formed by two large boulders which meet 2.0 m above the 4.5-m-square floor. The latter is of fine dust with later Iron Age potsherds on the surface. Similar sherds occurred elsewhere on the surface of the outcrop. Testing at one corner of the floor indicated that the ashy deposit was 25 to 30 cm thick, and that it contained a sparse mode 5 quartz industry. Paintings occur on the 45° overhang which forms the north side of the shelter. They consist of a red grid and, to the right, a red 'hairpin' motif, both badly obscured by smoke encrustation (fig. 122:1).

Rukuzye B. Three hundred metres past Rukuzye A is a similar but somewhat higher rock outcrop, 50 m to the north of the D.A.T.C. road. The D.A.T.C. offices and the dam shore are less than 400 m away to the south-west. A huge boulder resting upon another forms a large south-facing shelter with its roof at 30° to the horizontal. The main entrance to the shelter is on the east side: there is a smaller entrance on the west. The floor is largely covered with fallen rocks, between which are pockets of ashy deposit containing undecorated potsherds and mode 5 quartz artefacts. The paintings, which are low on the underside of the main overhang, are all executed in red. From left to right they are: an outline zoomorphic figure, a rectangle filled with finger dots, a grid, and a circle with a central dot (fig. 122:2-5).

Rukuzye C. One mile north from the Rukuzye Dam turn-off, on the Chipata-Lundazi road, is Tenje whence a track leads north-westwards following the Mapala/Rukuzye watershed. Five hundred metres from the main road this track passes 20 m to the south of a massive boulder surrounded by smaller rocks. A small overhang, not a true shelter, contains a single painting of a red grid (fig. 122:6).

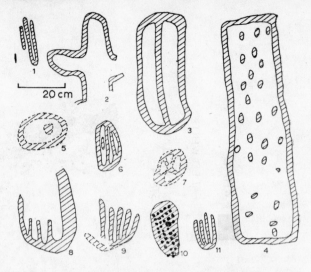

Fig. 122. Rock paintings from the Rukuzye area. All are red except no. 10, which is overlain with white dots (shown black).

Rukuzye D. This site, now destroyed, was described by J. H. Chaplin (1960: 47-8) under the name of Rukuzi Dam. It is presumed that the site was adjacent to the dam wall, but Chaplin's account is not very clear on this point. The paintings, in red, consisted of grids and a star-like design.

Rukuzye E. Two hundred metres past Rukuzye C, the Mapala road swings westwards around the north side of a rocky *kopje*. A small shelter three-quarters of the way up the south-west side faces west-south-west. Its 45° overhang is partly obscured by piles of fallen rocks which cover the whole floor. Later Iron Age potsherds were noted in cracks between these rocks, but there were no signs of Stone Age occupation. Similar sherds were found on the southern slopes of the *kopje*, but the bare rocky summit showed no signs of having been used as a refuge. The paintings, in red, are all faint and partly obscured by fallen rocks. They are low on the overhang and consist of a four-spoked wheel motif and a grid (fig. 122: 7, 8). The latter is partly destroyed by exfoliation. There are faint traces of other red paintings in the same shelter.

Rukuzye F. At a distance of 2.5 km past Rukuzye E (3.2 km from the main road) is a large pile of rocks lying 100 m south-west of the Mapala track. Low on the north-west side of the outcrop is a large west-facing shelter. The 2-m high overhang is at 30° to the horizontal and protects an extensive floor area much broken by rocks. The floor is further sheltered by two large fallen boulders on its west side. Sherds of later Iron Age pottery and mode 5 quartz artefacts were recovered from the talus slope to the north-west. Paintings, on the roof of the shelter, 1.8 to 2.0 m above the floor, can readily be reached from fallen rocks. From left to right they comprise a red open grid, a purple splodge overlain by finger dots done in fatty white paint, and a red closed grid (fig. 122:9-11).

SAKWE

An un-named outlier of Kamani Hill in Chadiza District, at 14°10' south, 32°27' east, rises 60 m above the Kavumo *dambo* to an altitude of 1140 m above sea

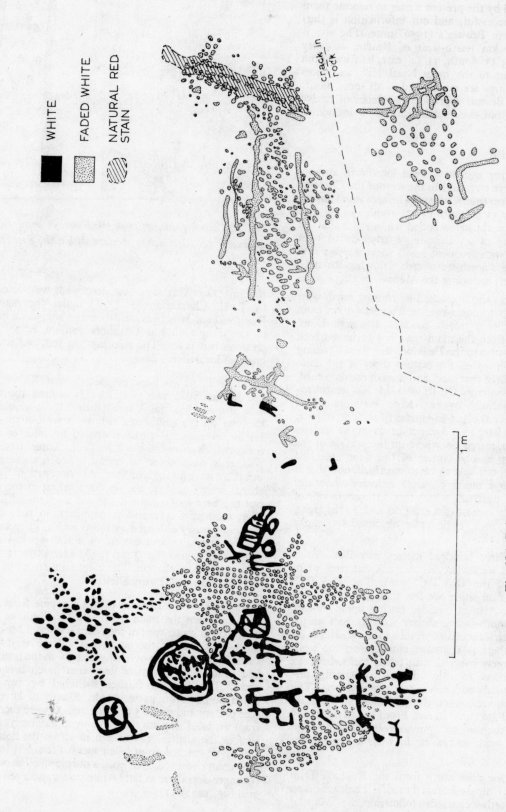

WHITE

FADED WHITE

NATURAL RED STAIN

crack in rock

1 m

Fig. 124. Paintings on the north-west-facing rock wall at Thandwe.

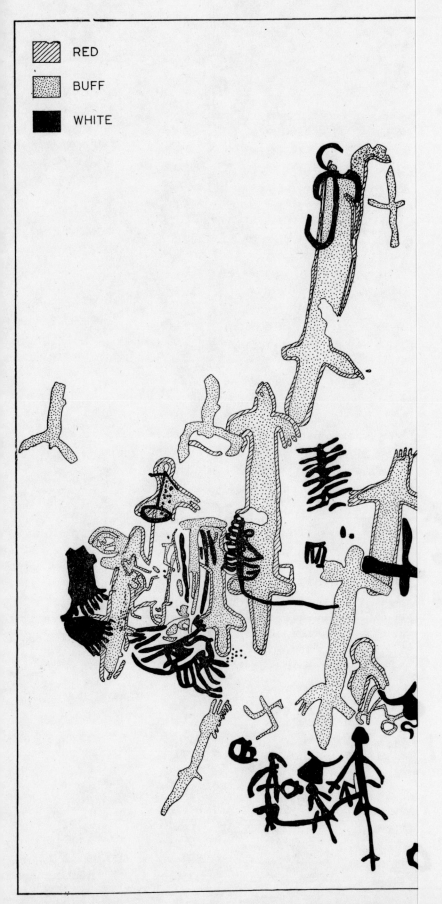

RED

BUFF

WHITE

Fig. 123. Paintings on the south

level (see fig. 68 on p. 120). Kamani Hill itself is 2 km east-north-east of the outlier and some 150 m higher. One of the sites in this group was investigated by Chaplin, who gave it the name of Sakwe, after a village 3 km to the north. The Sakwe sites are best reached from Kachipande village at the foot of Kavumo Hill on the track to Nunda School. They bear 335° from Kachipande, at a distance of 1.5 km.

Site A. This is situated two-thirds of the way up the hill on its north-east side. The paintings are on the south-east side of an alcove formed by the falling away of a triangular slab, which still lies at the foot of the parent rock, enclosing a small, 1.2 by 0.9 m, area at the foot of the painted panel, containing very little deposit and no artefacts. The painted surface is almost vertical and faces north-east. The paintings have been described by Chaplin (1962:11) and are here illustrated in plate XXVIII. A series of red schematic grids is overlain by zoomorphic motifs in red outline. These in turn are covered by further grids, some of which are unusually complex and angular. The outline zoomorphs show signs of having been repeatedly filled with thick, greasy pale buff-coloured paint.

Site B. Sixty yards to the south-south-west of site A, and slightly higher on the east side of the hill, is a 9-m long south-east-facing rock slab, about 6 m high and overhanging at 20° to the vertical. The 4.5 by 1.5 m floor area has shallow, somewhat disturbed deposits containing abundant mode 5 quartz artefacts. The shelter contains two groups of paintings (plate XXIXa): small white anthropomorphic figures near the floor, and diminutive red grids higher up and to the left.

Immediately to the south of site A, between sites A and B, a long low shelter, facing due east, has mode 5 quartz artefacts on the surface of a shallow root-disturbed deposit, but no paintings.

SEZAMANJA

Situated at 14°03′ south, 32°19′ east, close to the Nsadzu stream 16 km west of Chadiza, these paintings have been described and illustrated by Chaplin (1962: 11–12), to whose account the present writer has nothing

to add. The red paintings comprise several grids including an elaborate chequer-board example, a linear zoomorphic figure, and two circular motifs with complex internal subdivisions.

SIMBO

This site appears to be a westerly outlier of the main distribution of eastern Zambian rock paintings. Simbo Hill is situated some 16 km west of Petauke and 2 km north-west of Merwe Mission, at 14°07′ south, 31°12′ east. It rises from plateau country at 980 m above sea level. The site is a long shelter just below the summit of the hill on the south side. Both the shelter and the summit of the hill have yielded quantities of later Iron Age pottery, described in chapter 5. The paintings have been discussed by J. D. Clark (1959*b*:198). There are red grids overlain first by red and white bichrome motifs and then by white designs including grids, linear anthropomorphs and zoomorphs, and representations of metal tools. Local tradition states that some of the Simbo paintings were executed at the time when the hill was used as a refuge during the Ngoni raids in the nineteenth century.

THANDWE

A full description of Thandwe rock-shelter, together with a plan (fig. 26, p. 48) showing the location of the paintings, has been presented in chapter 7.

On the south-west-facing rock face, separated from that of the main rock-shelter, is a large panel of paintings (fig. 123) covering an area some 3.5 m square. The majority of these paintings are elongated zoomorphs in red outline filled in with thick buff paint: there is one comparable figure which lacks a red outline. This bichrome series is overlain by a number of white paintings, including various grids, pictures of metal hoes or axes, two enigmatic sub-rectangular objects with many projections from their lower surfaces,* and the unmistakable representation of a motor car.

---

*I have suggested elsewhere that these motifs may be representations of grain-bins (D. W. Phillipson, 1972*b*: 322).

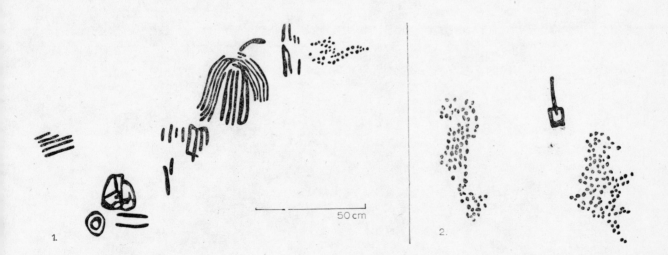

Fig. 125. White rock paintings at Thandwe: no. 1 is on the domed roof of the shelter, no. 2 is on a separate boulder.

50 cm

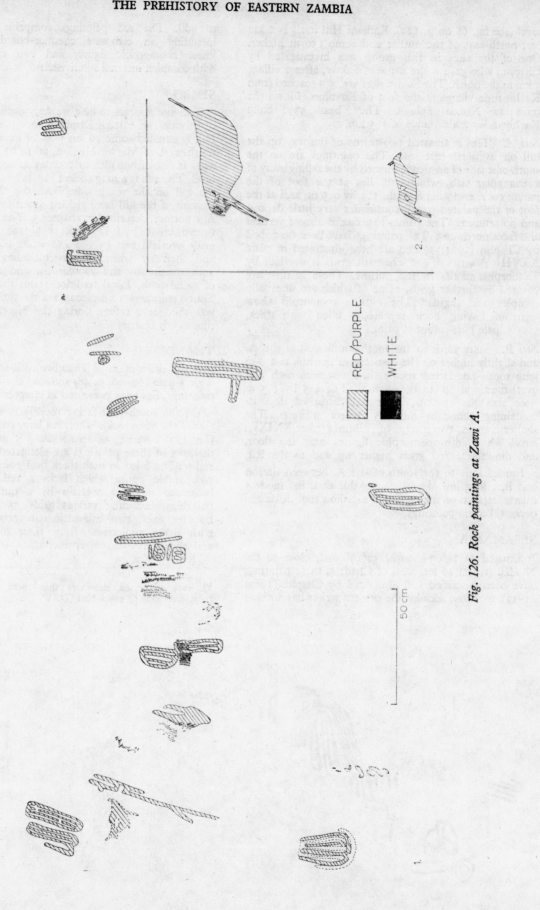

Fig. 126. Rock paintings at Zawi A.

The rear wall of the main rock-shelter, facing north-west, also bears paintings (fig. 124) for a length of 3.4 m: they extend to a maximum height of 1.8 m above the modern floor. On the right is a large zoomorphic figure composed entirely of whitish grey finger-dots and what may be interpreted as part of a second similar figure. These designs are overlain by a series of motifs in clearer white paint, comprising several linear anthropomorphic figures, three circular designs with internal sub-divisions, and a second picture of a motor car apparently being pushed by a stylised human figure (plate XXIXb). Further to the right are further paintings in whitish grey, comprising a linear zoomorph, and several designs of lines and dots, some of which overlie, and are aligned on, a natural reddish stain on the rock surface.

There are two smaller panels of paintings at Thandwe, both of which are reproduced in fig. 125. On the domed roof of the shelter, at the angle between the two over-hangs, is a series of whitish grey paintings much obscured by smoke-stains. They comprise dots, grids, concentric circles, parallel lines, and a subdivided circular motif comparable to those in the main shelter. On one of the boulders under the south-west overhang are further white paintings, badly faded through exposure to the weather. They comprise two areal designs of dots and what appears to be a representation of a hoe.

The Ngoni inhabitants of Kamukwamba village, adjacent to the rock-shelter, expressed to the writer (on several independent occasions) the belief that the white paintings at Thandwe were the work of Nsenga people and that they were done in conjunction with girls' puberty ceremonies. Again, quite independently and without prompting, Nsenga women now resident in Lusaka recognised copies of the subdivided circle motifs from the main rock-shelter and identified them as schematised 'diagrams' used for the sexual introduction of female initiates.

The reference to the Nsenga is both interesting and problematical, since the Thandwe Hills were, before the arrival of the Ngoni, presumably a Chewa area. As shown in chapter 2, the Ngoni had previously resided among the Nsenga; and it is possible that all their nineteenth-century contemporaries have been remembered as Nsenga. Alternatively, and more probably, the reference may be to Nsenga women who accompanied the male Ngoni to settle in their new area. Such women would doubtless initiate their daughters in their traditional way, just as they taught their children the ChiNsenga language.

ZAWI

Zawi Hill, Chipata District, 13°30′ south, 32°45′ east, is an isolated hill rising 100 m to an altitude of 1180 m above sea level between the Msandile river and its tributary the Kaulembe. The site rises immediately to the north-east of Kamkumwe village (plate XXXa), which is reached by turning east-south-east for 3.5 km from the Chipata-Lundazi road at Mabvundo, 29 km from Chipata.

Site A. The summit of Zawi Hill is formed by an enormous rock slab approximately 20 m high with an almost flat surface facing south-south-west and over-hanging by about 10° from the vertical. The surface is exfoliating and is much stained by rain-stripes, particularly towards the east. The foot of the slab is obscured by boulders, except at the west end where there is a small shelter whose 3.7 by 3.7 m floor is covered by a humic ashy deposit, apparently of no great depth, displaying undecorated potsherds on the surface. Mode 5 quartz artefacts are scattered on the hill slope, immediately below the shelter. The paintings from this site have previously been described and, in part, illustrated by J. D. Clark (1959b: 171, 173).

Red schematic paintings, mainly of lines and grids, occur on the shelter's north wall to a height of 2 m above the present floor (fig. 126:1). They are overlain by delicate designs in white, including rows of fine parallel lines, neat chequer-board grids and patterns of fine dots. There are also traces of a possible red naturalistic painting, but these are too badly faded for certainty. On its east side, the shelter is bounded by a steeply sloping boulder, 2.75 m high, which rests against the face of the main rock slab. Easily seen and reached from the top of this boulder, and near the middle of the main slab, are the two naturalistic paintings reproduced in fig. 126:2. The clearer of these is a small (31 cm), neat picture of an antelope, probably an eland. Its delicate and accurate outline is filled with a mass of lines so dense in the forepart as to give the initial impression of a solid block of colour. The head, horns and tail are neatly indicated, but the legs are somewhat under-emphasised (plate XXXb). The second naturalistic figure is more enigmatic. It is substantially larger than the eland, and has a chordate-shaped body which was probably originally sketched in fine lines, although fading is now so far advanced that one cannot be sure. Two hind, but no front, legs are shown; the figure has a long thin neck but there is no indication that a head was ever depicted. J. D. Clark (*op.cit.*: 171) has suggested that this painting may represent an ostrich;* but the present writer (D. W. Phillipson, 1972b: 17) has noted a close resemblance to quadrupedal figures represented at rock-painting sites in the Copperbelt region.

Fig. 127. Rock painting at Zawi C, in red-brown (shown hatched) overlain by yellow-buff (shown black).

Site B. Almost at the foot of the south-east side of Zawi Hill is a deep cleft formed by two boulders. Its rocky floor has no archaeological deposits. The western side of this cleft consists of an overhanging slab of rock some 7.5 m long by 5.5 m high, badly weathered and exfoliated, which retains very faint traces of red paintings. These are mainly vertical lines which may have been part of grids and possible traces of concentric circles. All these paintings were too faint and doubtful to be copied or photographed.

---

*The ostrich no longer survives in eastern Zambia, although archaeological finds described elsewhere in this volume indicate its survival into later Iron Age times.

Site C. This is situated about 25 m up the south-east side of Zawi Hill, some 50 m north-east of site B. An immense fallen boulder has formed shelters on both sides. That on the north-east is a narrow cleft with no signs of occupation. On the south side a low ceiling protects a floor area, 5.5 by 2.5 m, which is partly covered by fallen rocks. This shelter is enclosed on the south-east side by a low fallen boulder whose summit commands a wide view over the surrounding country. The ashy deposit on the shelter floor does not appear to be deep: and only later Iron Age potsherds are visible on its surface. There is, however, a scatter of mode 5 quartz artefacts on the hill slope between sites B and C. A bichrome grid of deep red brown and yellow-buff (fig. 127) is the only painting at site C. It occurs on the ceiling of the main shelter, at a point where this slopes at about 45°, and is only 1 m above the floor. Behind the main boulder is a large roofed passage-cave formed by several boulders, open at both ends: a single later Iron Age sherd was the only artefact recovered there.

II. THE STYLISTIC SEQUENCE

The rock paintings of central Africa have generally been divided into naturalistic and schematic styles, the former being regarded as the earlier (J. D. Clark, 1959*b*: 207–8). Such a division holds good for the majority of sites in most areas (D. W. Phillipson, 1972*b*), but in eastern Zambia two amendments are necessary. Firstly, as shown at Katolola site A, there was clearly some overlap between the period of execution of the naturalistic art and that of the schematic. Secondly, a place must be found in the sequence for the extensive series of stylised white paintings. In this section it will be convenient to discuss the stylistic sequence of the eastern Zambian rock paintings in reverse chronological order.

The most recent rock paintings in the region (excluding charcoal drawings such as those at Makwe) are those executed in white or buff-white paint, generally in a stylized, semi-naturalistic manner. This is abundantly clear from the study of superimpositions, notably at such sites as Chaingo, Chipwete, Kalemba, Kavumo C, Mbozi, Simbo, Thandwe and Zawi A. At all these sites, the white stylised paintings are superimposed on those of earlier periods; and no sites are known where these white paintings are covered by those of any other style. In several instances the subject matter of the white paintings is also indicative of their late date. At Chaingo, Mkoma, Simbo and Thandwe, the paintings of this group include clear representations of metal tools, notably hoes and axes. At Thandwe there are even two pictures of motor cars, thus incontrovertibly demonstrating that the execution of some white paintings has continued well into the present century. Further support for this dating is provided by the evidence which will be cited in the following section for the religious significance which the white paintings have, until recently, retained in the traditional societies of the modern inhabitants of eastern Zambia.

Within the area considered in the present volume, these white stylised paintings are known at Chaingo, Chipwete, Kalemba, Katolola C, Kavumo C, Makwe, Mbozi, Mitoo, Mkoma, Sakwe B, Simbo, Thandwe and Zawi A. In addition to the representations of metal tools to which reference has already been made, characteristic motifs are: zoomorphic designs, often filled with finger-dots to produce a leopard-skin-like effect, as at Chaingo and Thandwe; crude anthropomorphic designs, best seen at Mkoma and Kalemba; and schematic designs, notably series of parallel lines and grids. Such white stylised paintings are of frequent occurrence in central Malawi, but are rare in Zambia west of the Luangwa.

Closely related to the stylised white paintings is a series of bichrome designs in which thick white or pale buff paint, identical in appearance to that employed for the former group, is used in conjunction with red pigment. These red and white bichromes are found at Chaingo, Kavumo C, all three Manje sites, Mkoma, Rukuzye F, Sakwe A, Simbo, Thandwe and Zawi C. At three sites, Chaingo, Sakwe A and Thandwe, direct superimpositions occur in which bichrome motifs are overlain by white stylised paintings.

The most characteristic motif in the red and white bichrome series is an elongated zoomorphic design clearly related to the white 'leopard-skin' paintings of Thandwe and Chaingo. Here, a red outline delineates a long body and tail, four stumpy limbs often ending in (approximately) five 'fingers', and a head which shows no secondary features. The outline is filled in with pale buff paint. Characteristic examples of this type are to be seen at Kavumo C, the three Manje sites, Sakwe A and Thandwe. It is noteworthy that all these sites lie within a single 40-km stretch of country along the western edge of the high ground which borders the western margin of the Mwangazi valley. One of these bichrome figures at Thandwe shows that, in places, the red paint overlies the buff, while elsewhere on the same figure the converse is true, demonstrating that the figures were originally composed as true bichromes, and that they are not old red outlines that were only subsequently filled in with buff paint. Nevertheless, two of the Thandwe examples do show signs of several layers of buff paint; and Chaplin records his opinion that one of those at Sakwe A had received a coat of such paint only a short while before his visit there in 1958. The implications of these observations are discussed in the following section.

The other red and white bichrome paintings are schematic. They include a red oval splodge overlain by white finger-dots at Rukuzye F, the series of elaborate designs at Chaingo and Mkoma, and simpler grids such as that of Zawi C. They are best regarded as an elaboration of the large group of monochrome red schematic paintings, to a consideration of which we may now turn.

Red schematic paintings occur at Chafisi, Chaingo, Chalumbe, Chikanga, Chipangali, Kalemba (traces only), Kamkomole, Katolola sites A and B, Kavumo A, Makwe, Manje C, Masinja, Mbozi, Mitoo, 'Mwala wa Manja', Njazi, all six Rukuzye sites, Sakwe A and B, Sezamanja, Simbo and Zawi A and B. They are overlain in direct superimposition by red and white bichromes at Chaingo and Sakwe A, and by white stylised paintings at Mbozi, Kalemba, Simbo and Zawi A. Red schematic paintings are most often found at smaller sites then are those of the later series; large displays of these motifs on a single rock face are correspondingly rare.

One motif among those of the red schematic series deserves special mention. This is a red outline zoomorph almost identical to those found filled in with buff paint in the red and white bichrome series, but generally smaller and less elongated. Such paintings are known from Chafisi, Chikanga, and Rukuzye B. Only the last-named site falls far outside the restricted geographical distribution of the bichrome zoomorphs noted above. The remaining red schematic paintings form a heterogeneous series. Grids are the most frequent group, and they occur in considerable variety, from the simple rectangles with a single central bar, as at Makwe and Zawi A, to the elaborate chequer-board designs seen at Mbozi, Sakwe A and Chipangali. The large, unidirectionally barred grids with horizontal ladder-like projections, described from Katolola B, are also note-worthy. Other designs include: crude linear figures, possibly highly schematised anthropomorphs, as at Kamkomole and Makwe; concentric circles (Mbozi and Kalolola B); circles (Makwe); circle with pellet (Rukuzye B); and a rectangle filled with finger-dots (Rukuzye B).

Lastly, we come to the red naturalistic paintings, which are so far known only from Zawi A and Katolola

A. As noted above, they are believed to be the earliest series; but in the only direct superimposition, that at Katolola, a naturalistic painting occurs over a grid of the red schematic series. However, evidence from numerous sites in other parts of Zambia (D. W. Phillipson, 1972b) indicates that this situation is exceptional; and it is thus reasonable to interpret the Katolola superimposition as proof merely of some degree of chronological overlap between the naturalistic and schematic painting series. At Zawi, where paintings of both styles occur on the same rock face, their physical condition suggests that the naturalistic ones are the older.

The three recognisable naturalistic paintings consist of a life-size eland at Katolola, and a diminutive antelope, probably of the same species, at Zawi, associated with a second quadruped (or ostrich—see p. 183) of in-determinate type. All appear to have been drawn in a similar style—a neat outline filled in with finely sketched lines. On all, the legs are cursorily represented.

III. THE AGE AND SIGNIFICANCE OF THE PAINTINGS

In the previous section there has been demonstrated a stylistic sequence within the eastern Zambian rock paintings consisting of (in reverse chronological order): (iv) white stylised paintings; (iii) red and white bichromes, both stylised and schematic; (ii) red schematic paintings; overlapping with (i) naturalistic paintings. It has been shown that series (ii) to (iv) form a continuous development, being linked by the survival and adaptation of similar motifs. The stylistic break between series (i) and (ii) is much more clearly defined.

Evidence has already been cited for the relatively recent date of the latest series (iv), the white stylised paintings. This is shown most clearly by the representations of motor cars at Thandwe; but there are several independent lines of argument which support this conclusion.

At Thandwe, the significance of the white paintings is still remembered, and their execution is attributed to Nsenga women. As has been argued (p. 183), these Nsenga women were brought to the country surrounding the Thandwe Hills (previously occupied by Chewa) during the third quarter of the nineteenth century, so these paintings cannot pre-date c.1870. A nineteenth-century date is traditionally assigned to some of the paintings at Simbo.

On the other hand, at Kalemba there is evidence that the white paintings were obliterated at the time of the erection of a lean-to structure against the shelter wall; and the date of this event, which provides a *terminus ante quem* for the white paintings at that site, is placed in the same period of Ngoni raids and settlement as saw the arrival of the Nsenga at Thandwe. Further evidence, albeit negative, is provided by the exfoliated wall fragments recovered from the Kalemba excavations. Several of these, retaining traces of paintings, were recovered from horizons R and S, yet the paint which they bore was exclusively red. It may be concluded that at Kalemba the white paintings pre-date, but not by very long, the advent of the Ngoni. Some motifs included in the white stylised series at Kalemba strongly resemble those interpreted as sex-education diagrams at Thandwe.

Graffiti seen today in Chewa areas, notably on house walls in rural areas and those of bus shelters and bar

toilets in the towns, most frequently represent characters associated with the *Nyau* ceremonies. This matter is discussed in greater detail below; here attention is merely drawn to the fact that some of the motifs found among the white stylised paintings can also be associated with *Nyau*.

Some of the red and white bichrome paintings have also evidently retained their significance to local people into recent times. The clearest example of this is at Sakwe A, where Chaplin records that one of the zoomorphic figures received a new coat of clayey buff paint shortly before his 1958 visit. Since then, some of the paintings at this site have been scraped away by, according to local informants, people in search of medicine.

When we turn our attention to the red schematic paintings, reliance must be placed almost exclusively upon archaeological arguments. In discussing this problem elsewhere (D. W. Phillipson, 1972b; 323–5), I have pointed out that the conventional correlation between the red schematic paintings and microlithic industries of 'Nachikufan' type (e.g. J. D. Clark, 1959b: 210–11) is no longer tenable. There are far stronger reasons for attributing the red schematic art to Early Iron Age peoples. At least in so far as Zambia is concerned, Early Iron Age sites are known from all areas where red schematic rock-paintings occur; and the regional variants of the painting styles show a significant degree of correlation with those observed in the Early Iron Age industries.

There is a clear stylistic change between the naturalistic paintings and the red schematic ones, yet the chronological distinction between them is less well defined. At most central African sites where the two styles occur together, the naturalistic paintings are demonstrably earlier. That this was not invariably the case is shown by the superimposition of a naturalistic painting over a schematic grid at Katolola A. Other possible examples of naturalistic figures post-dating schematic motifs have been observed by the present writer at Mwela Rocks, near Kasama in the Northern Province of Zambia; and a comparable occurrence at Katzombo in Moçambique has been noted on p. 18, above. If the naturalistic paintings, like their counterparts south of the Zambezi, are to be attributed to the makers of the mode 5 stone industries, then the apparent contemporaneity of the two distinct artistic traditions is explained as the work of stone-tool-using and Early Iron Age people living synchronously in the same area.

This attribution to the Early Iron Age is in keeping with two pieces of archaeological evidence relating to the age of the red schematic paintings. At Nakapapula rock-shelter, in the Serenje District of Zambia's Central Province, it has been shown that paintings of this type post-date the third quarter of the first millennium ad, by which time Early Iron Age settlement is attested in the vicinity (D. W. Phillipson, 1969: 195). At Kalemba, exfoliation fragments bearing traces of red paint first appear in the archaeological deposits in horizon R, from which Early Iron Age pottery was also recovered, along with large quantities of mode 5 stone artefacts. Red schematic motifs are the earliest attested at Kalemba.

The evidence at present available thus suggests that the naturalistic and schematic traditions in eastern Zambian rock-paintings should be considered as the work of two distinct socio-economic groups. The generally earlier naturalistic representations were the work of stone-tool-using peoples. We have no knowledge of when their rock art tradition began. The paintings of their food-producing Iron Age contemporaries and successors took the form of a schematic tradition which has continued, in modified form, into very recent times.

Considering the intangible nature of the evidence, it is not surprising that most of our conclusions regarding the meaning and significance of the rock art refer to the more recent examples. There is little to be said in connection with the naturalistic paintings. The reader is referred to the literature dealing with this aspect of the far more abundant naturalistic art of southern Africa (e.g. Pager, 1975; Vinnicombe, 1976). Here it is appropriate only to point out that two of the three certain naturalistic paintings so far known from eastern Zambia are thought to represent eland; and it is now abundantly clear that, at least in the Natal Drakensberg, the eland occupied a special place in the religious and spiritual life of the later stone-tool-using societies.

With regard to the meaning of the schematic and later paintings, it is appropriate to begin with a discussion of the most recent examples of such art, and to enquire

Fig. 128. Drawings of Nyau characters on the wall of a bus shelter at Katete (nos. 1, 2, 4) and on a house wall at Yambani village, Chief Mlolo, Chadiza (no. 4). (Not to scale.)

how far the relevant data may be projected back in time.

Attention has already been drawn to the charcoal drawings at Makwe and to their identification as representations of *Nyau* characters wearing animal masks. There is a similar representation, in white paint, at Chipwete rock-shelter (fig. 128). Both show clear parallels with very recent pictures of *Nyau* characters to be seen today on house walls, and with the *graffiti* done by people waiting for buses. A link between the most recent paintings and *Nyau* having been established,* it is well to present a brief account of *Nyau* itself.

Matthew Schoffeleers (1973) has recently emphasised the traditional evidence for the relatively high antiquity of *Nyau*, which can be traced back with confidence at least to an early phase of the later Iron Age. This evidence is discussed in greater detail below (p. 195).

Before the achievement of Zambia's independence, *Nyau* had been for many years an illegal organisation in Northern Rhodesia. Most of the published information is therefore derived from neighbouring Chewa areas in Malawi. I. Linden (1975: 32) has summarised its position as follows: "The *Nyau* secret societies had been a central feature of Chewa culture for many centuries. They were societies of men whose identity was concealed during dance performances by the wearing of masks of ancestors and animals. Their participation was essential to the effective carrying through of the major rites of transition, whether of rebirth through initiation or of death. . . . For the Chewa *Nyau* . . . the essential activity is the performances at the major rites of the *chinamwali* girls' initiation and at the funerals of chiefs and headmen."

A brief published account of *chinamwali* in Zambia (Winterbottom and Lancaster, 1965) makes no specific mention of *Nyau* participation. (It deals with data recorded in the 1930's when *Nyau* was banned in the then Northern Rhodesia.) It does, however, record that "pictures are drawn on the ground where the women dance. . . . The pictures were set in a small circle of mud and were of low relief. These were a crocodile and a snake; and these are the most usual, though not the only, things represented. . . . The women dance all over these pictures, which are sometimes drawn with sand or maize flour." (*loc.cit.*, p. 348).

Apthorpe (1962) has drawn attention to the possibility that the spotted zoomorphic white paintings, such as that at Chaingo, may represent the genet cat, which is frequently depicted (albeit in a manner closely resembling a crocodile), on the ground or on a tree, at Nsenga puberty ceremonies. "The genet cat is a significant symbol in Nsenga puberty ceremonies. It represents the male principle, and potency" (Apthorpe, *loc.cit.*:13). As argued above, these spotted white figures are the last representatives of a long line of comparable motifs which can be traced back into the red schematic painting series. Their use in such ceremonies would explain the evidence, noted at several sites, for their frequent re-painting.

Apthorpe (*ibid.*) also illustrates a circular design made on the ground in white maize meal at an Nsenga puberty ceremony. It bears a striking resemblance to the 'diagrams' at Thandwe noted above. Werner's (1906: 97) note of "circles filled with geometrical patterns" may likewise refer to designs of this type. Comparable rock-paintings, also in white, occur at Kalemba; while red motifs at Sezamanja show a remarkable similarity.

Further afield, in the easterly areas of southern Malawi occupied by the Yao, comparable designs are made in connection with the initiation of boys (Stannus and Davey, 1913). Examples are illustrated by Stannus (1922). In the girls' *chisungu* ceremonies among the Bemba of northern Zambia, three-dimensional clay models serve a similar allegorical and instructive function (Richards, 1956).

We thus arrive back, by an independent route, at the association of the white paintings with female puberty ceremonies, which has already been demonstrated by oral traditions relating to the Thandwe site. Here, the circular motifs with internal subdivisions are interpreted as diagrams used in sexual instruction. They are associated with zoomorphic motifs executed with finger-dots. Both types of motif can be shown to be depicted, in various media, at puberty ceremonies over a wide area.

All the painted rock-shelters which have so far been excavated in Zambia have yielded Iron Age artefacts, particularly pottery, in the higher levels of their deposits, almost invariably intimately associated with stone industries of mode 5. It does not appear that Iron Age people have ever inhabited rock-shelters except for limited periods when they were used as refuges in times of war. Rock-shelters are, however, known to have been used temporarily by Iron Age peoples for initiation and other ceremonies. There is a considerable volume of evidence to associate many of the more recent rock paintings of eastern Zambia with such ceremonies, in particular with those connected with *Nyau*.

The only eastern Zambian site yielding archaeological evidence which throws any light on the possible ancient significance of the red schematic paintings is Katolola B, where stones were evidently thrown at paintings which strongly resemble rain falling from clouds. C. K. Cooke (1964) has described a site near Gwanda in Rhodesia where the throwing of stones at rock paintings forms a part of traditional rain-making ceremonies. In view of the design at Katolola it is tempting to suggest a similar explanation for the stone-throwing at that site also. Rain-making is known to be a practice which extends back at least to the earliest phases of the later Iron Age in eastern Zambia and Malawi (see below, p. 195).

Evidence has been cited above for attributing the earlier, red, schematic paintings to the Early Iron Age. Links in subject matter have been demonstrated between these red paintings and their later white counterparts: indeed, a continuous developmental process may be discerned running through the three series of schematic paintings. It is legitimate to conclude that the red schematic art may have had a significance to its Early Iron Age authors comparable to that held by the later white paintings in later Iron Age societies.

*An identical conclusion regarding paintings in Malawi has been reached, completely independently, by Dr Matthew Schoffeleers (*personal communication*).

Chapter 20

The Eastern Zambian Sequence

For the establishment of the industrial sequence of eastern Zambian prehistory, the results of four excavations are available. The chronological coverage of the four sites varies considerably (fig. 129). Kalemba, the site with by far the longest history of human use, was occupied intermittently from before 37,000 years ago into relatively recent times. At Makwe and Thandwe occupation seems to have begun respectively at some

date prior to the late fourth millennium bc,* and around—or shortly before—the beginning of the Christian era. Both sites can be shown to have continued in use until less than a century ago. Kamnama was

---

*But see below, p. 190, for a discussion of the date at which Makwe was first occupied.

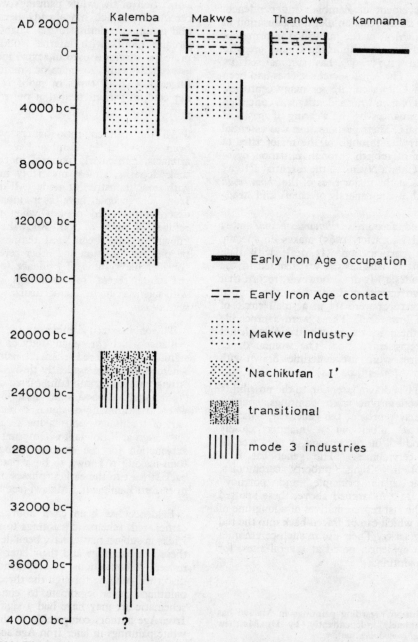

Fig. 129. Time-chart showing the periods of occupation of the four principal sites investigated in eastern Zambia.

occupied for a single fairly brief period around the fourth century ad.

It is now convenient very briefly to summarise the archaeological sequence of eastern Zambia as revealed by the excavations described in the foregoing chapters. To do this, it is appropriate to attach names to certain of the industries which have been recognised, primarily to those represented at more than one site. The justification for each of these attributions, and for the names chosen, is given in the respective sections. The wider affinities and connections of each industry are discussed in chapter 21.

I. MODE 3 INDUSTRIES

These are present, among the sites investigated, only at Kalemba. At this site, two phases are represented.

The mode 3 industry of Kalemba period (i), dated by a single radiocarbon analysis to before 35,000 bc, is known only from the very limited area of horizon G which it proved practicable to excavate. Its typological features have been summarised above in chapter 18. As no identity with any other known industry is proposed, it would be superfluous here to suggest a name for the horizon G industry, since no parameters for any such named entity could at this stage be put forward. The possibility of subsuming this material with an industry already defined from an adjacent region will be discussed in chapter 21.

The same points apply equally to the second mode 3 industry revealed at Kalemba; that recovered from horizon H and belonging to the earlier part of period (ii). The absolute age of this industry probably falls within the period 25,000 to 22,000 bc.

Although the two Kalemba mode 3 industries are separated by at least ten thousand years, they show remarkable similarity. The artefacts recovered are exclusively of chipped stone. The main difference revealed by analysis of the relatively small artefact samples yielded by the excavation is the much higher proportion of retouched implements in the earlier industry. There was, with time, a slight reduction in general artefact size between the two occupations. In both assemblages, the retouched implements consist exclusively of scrapers and points. The scrapers of the earlier industry are made for the most part on whole flakes, a preference which was less marked in the later industry. The points of both industries are all unifacial. Those from the earlier levels show a variety of forms, but only sub-triangular specimens are represented in the small sample attributed to the second mode 3 industry.

It is clear that a very considerable degree of industrial continuity pervades the mode 3 succession at Kalemba. The two assemblages which were recovered are best regarded as manifestations of a single industrial tradition. If reliance can be placed on the radiocarbon dates, this tradition must be regarded as having shown remarkable stability and lack of internal development through its duration of at least ten millennia.

The makers of these industries were hunters, concentrating on the exploitation of the larger gregarious bovids and zebra. The presence of herds of these animals within easy reach of Kalemba indicates a more open vegetation pattern than that which has prevailed in more recent times.

It has been suggested that the fluctuating frequency of exfoliation in cave and rock-shelter deposits may be linked, at least in part, with changing climatic conditions, notably rainfall and temperature. C. K. Cooke (1963:81–3) has shown that increases in the rate of exfoliation at Pomongwe Cave in the Matopo Hills of Rhodesia, if attributed to periods of increased rainfall, reveal a climatic sequence which correlates closely with that postulated by Bond (1957) on the basis of evidence of a completely different nature from the nearby site of Khami; and Bond's work has received further independent confirmation from the research of Brain (1969). It thus appears reasonable to link the low incidence of exfoliation in horizons H to J at Kalemba (fig. 74, p. 124) with a period of low rainfall, such as could have resulted in the more open vegetation indicated by the faunal remains.

II. MODE 5 INDUSTRIES

Backed microlithic implements, diagnostic of J.G.D. Clark's mode 5 industries, are first represented in the Kalemba sequence in horizon I. This belongs to a period for which radiocarbon dates indicate an age of around 23,000 to 22,000 bc. None of the other sites investigated in eastern Zambia have yielded evidence for occupation at this time. Such a date may be accepted as an approximate one for the start of a prolonged process of typological development which involved the gradual replacement of the scrapers and points of the preceding mode 3 industries by the backed microliths of mode 5. The chipped stone aggregates of Kalemba horizons I and J, together with that from the lower levels of horizon K, may best be interpreted as representing a process of transition leading up to the first appearance of a true mode 5 industry in the upper part of horizon K. Unfortunately, in view of the gap in the Kalemba sequence which is marked by the rock fall in horizon K, and which appears to indicate a cessation of some six millennia in the occupation of the site, the duration of this process cannot be estimated with any precision. The transitional industry is found through over 1.2 m of well compacted deposit, and it would be in keeping with the evidence of the radiocarbon dates to suggest that this accumulation represents some two millennia of occupation. How much of the succeeding period of some six thousand years, during which the site was not occupied, should also be attributed to this transitional process of industrial development is not clear. All that can be said on the basis of the evidence at present available is that by about 15,000 bc a fully microlithic mode 5 industry had been adopted by the inhabitants of Kalemba.

Typologically, the transitional industry is differentiated from its mode 3 predecessor by a general reduction in artefact dimensions and by the presence of convex-backed flakes of relatively large size. These steadily increase in frequency until, in horizon K, they account for almost 9 per cent of the retouched implements recovered. Two toothed bone fragments are the only artefacts not of chipped stone.

The faunal evidence indicates a continued reliance on large gregarious creatures as a source of food. Dry conditions, becoming progressively wetter through horizon J, are attested by the pedology of the Kalemba deposits. This process culminated in the rock fall in horizon K, which coincides with a long period when the Kalemba site was unoccupied. When use of the site was resumed, its inhabitants practised a fully developed mode 5 technology.

NACHIKUFAN I'

The earliest true mode 5 industry at Kalemba occurs in the uppermost levels of horizon K and continues through horizons L, M and N. Its duration cannot be estimated with precision, but probably covered most of the four thousand years beginning around 15,000 bc. Likewise, we do not know whether this industry's inception in eastern Zambia took place at this latter date or at some time during the previous several millennia.

The affinities of this industry, known in eastern Zambia only from Kalemba, are discussed at some length in chapter 21, below. There, it will be shown to belong to a widespread grouping of closely interrelated mode 5 industries which are attested, between the seventeenth and the eighth millennia bc, over a broad region of highland eastern Africa between Lake Victoria and the Zambezi. No satisfactory name for this complex of industries has yet been proposed: indeed, the only manifestation of it to have been analysed and described in detail is that found in northern and central Zambia, west of the Luangwa, where it is known as 'Nachikufan I' (J. D. Clark, 1950c; S. F. Miller, 1969; see also p. 14, above). For convenience, the same term is here applied informally to the corresponding eastern Zambian material.

This 'Nachikufan I' industry is differentiated from its predecessors at Kalemba by the relatively high frequency of backed flakes, among which long narrow examples with convex backs predominate. Geometrics, exclusively curved-backed, make their first appearance in the Kalemba sequence in horizon M, around the mid-point of the industry's period of florescence there. These backed microliths take the place of the points of the previous mode 3 and transitional industries, and steadily increase in numbers throughout this phase of the site's occupation until, in horizon N, the backed flakes and geometrics account for respectively 38 and 5 per cent of the retouched implements. Scrapers are now markedly less common than they were in earlier phases of the sequence. Other artefacts associated with the 'Nachikufan I' industry at Kalemba are bored stones, bone bodkins, manufactured pigment-cakes, pounding stones and rubbing stones. There is no evidence for the presence of ground stone axes.

Concomitant with these industrial developments were changes in economic practices which are illustrated by the faunal record. There was a marked decline in the numbers of large bovids and equids which were hunted. These were in large part replaced by a variety of smaller creatures. Wart-hog also came into prominence as a

dietary element at this time. It has been suggested above (p. 168) that this change may indicate the adoption of trapping as a means of obtaining animal foods, as well as the establishment of a vegetational pattern more closely resembling that which prevails at the present day.

THE MAKWE INDUSTRY

Throughout the deposits attributed to period (iv) at Kalemba, there is represented a distinctive mode 5 industry which differs in many marked respects from the 'Nachikufan I' industry of period (iii), although several developmental trends, both technological and economic, which began in the earlier period, were continued. This period (iv) industry bears an extremely close resemblance, both in general composition and in detailed metrical and stylistic characters, to that which is represented in a broadly contemporary context at Makwe. The Thandwe rock-shelter has also yielded an industry of this type, which may be compared with that of the later stages of the Makwe and Kalemba occupations. As will be demonstrated below (pp. 201–4), this industry is distinct from those which were in vogue in adjacent areas; and it is therefore proposed to designate it the Makwe Industry after the site at which it was first discovered and is best represented.

In our discussion of the Makwe Industry we are, for the first time in this survey, able to draw upon the evidence of more than one site. An idea of the extent of inter-site variation may thus be combined with one of temporal change to provide a view of the typological parameters of Makwe Industry aggregates. Before this is attempted, a re-examination of the chronological framework is necessary.

Period (iv) at Kalemba began, almost certainly, at some time during the sixth millennium bc. This dates the earliest manifestation of the Makwe Industry which has yet been located. The Stone Age industries of eastern Zambia during the five thousand years preceding this time are not known. We are thus unable to study the process of change by which the 'Nachikufan I' industry was replaced by, or evolved into, the Makwe Industry. It is clear that the makers of the Makwe Industry continued to occupy all three sites, Kalemba, Makwe and Thandwe, until well after the advent to eastern Zambia of the later Iron Age, early in the second millennium ad. Comparison with the longer Kalemba sequence enables an estimate to be made of the date of the initial (horizon 1) occupation of Makwe, for which no directly associated radiocarbon age determinations are available. Reference to figs. 63 (p. 114) and 102 (p. 167) shows the near identity of the composition of the retouched implement assemblage from the lowest levels at Makwe with those of horizons O and P at Kalemba, dated to the sixth and fifth millennia bc. There is no evidence for the presence at Makwe of a 'Nachikufan I' industry or of any manifestation of the Makwe Industry earlier than that at Kalemba (see fig. 129).

In contrast with those of 'Nachikufan I', Makwe Industry aggregates show a reduction in overall artefact size and a progressive abandonment of the radial-core technique of flake production in favour of techniques based on single- and double-platform cores and on bipolar cores. There is a corresponding change from flakes with predominantly convergent dorsal scar-patterns to those with parallel scars. Among the retouched implements backed microliths are now predominant, points having disappeared and scrapers being relatively infrequent. In the earliest Makwe Industry horizons backed flakes still outnumber the geometrics, but by about 3000 bc this position was reversed. Later trends at all the sites investigated include the increasing scarcity of scrapers and the progressively increasing frequency of geometrics at the expense of the backed flakes. Later in the third millennium, there appears in all the known Makwe Industry aggregates a substantial number of *petits tranchets*. This distinctive implement type remained in vogue for only a limited time, becoming rare again in levels dated to the first few centuries ad. A further continuing trend which prevails throughout the duration of the Makwe Industry at all the sites investigated is a steady increase in the frequency of retouched implements relative to the total chipped stone artefact aggregate (fig. 130).

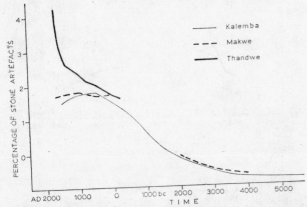

Fig. 130. Percentage of retouched implements in Makwe Industry aggregates from Kalemba, Makwe and Thandwe.

The three known sites of the Makwe Industry show remarkable similarity in the general composition of the chipped stone industry, in its metrical and stylistic characteristics, and in its temporal changes. The data on which this statement is based have been presented above in chapters 8, 12 and 16: they do not require detailed repetition here. Fig. 131 compares selected traits of the three site-sequences, set against a uniform time-scale.

Axes and pestles are the only ground stone implements which may be regarded as characteristic of the Makwe Industry as a whole. Bored stones, attested in the 'Nachikufan I' industry at Kalemba, continue into the lowest Makwe Industry horizon at that site, but are completely absent in the later horizons and at Makwe and Thandwe. At all three sites the grinding on the axes is largely restricted to the vicinity of their cutting edges. Preliminary shaping was by flaking, sometimes followed by pecking prior to the grinding process. Pestles are of cylindrical form at both Kalemba and Makwe: one example from the former site had been used for the preparation of red pigment.

In the non-lithic artefacts of the Makwe Industry greater inter-site variation is detected. Bone bodkins are represented at all three sites: apparently it was at some time early in the first millennium ad that they were joined by the more roughly made conical points which, in the upper levels of each rock-shelter, are the most frequent type of bone artefact encountered. In

detail, the bone points from the individual sites show significant differences. Curved bodkins and headed pins are represented only at Kalemba. At Makwe, the earlier bodkins have circular cross-sections and were replaced progressively by specimens of oval and sub-rectangular cross-section: at Thandwe the only bodkin, which is of late date, has a sub-rectangular section conformable with the contemporary Makwe specimens, but at Kalemba this trend is apparently inverted. The beads from Makwe show an interesting typological progression, the earliest specimens being all of bone, first discoid and then tubular in shape. After the hiatus in the site's occupation the beads are exclusively of shell, with imported glass beads appearing only at the very end of the sequence. No bone beads were recovered from Kalemba, and shell beads appear to have been made there at an earlier date than they were at Makwe. The latter site yielded an interesting series of shell pendants, but only a single comparable example came from Kalemba: these specimens date exclusively to the last two millennia.

The faunal remains from Makwe Industry deposits show a continuance of the trend, already established in 'Nachikufan I' times, towards small creatures as the principal source of meat and other animal products. At Kalemba, large bovids occur only in the earliest Makwe Industry horizon, and equids are comparatively rare throughout this phase of the occupation. At Makwe, the large gregarious animals are more frequently represented, as would be expected from a consideration of the two sites' respective environments; but they are nevertheless not so common as they were in the earlier horizons at Kalemba. Wart-hog was a particularly frequent item of diet at Makwe. The small faunal assemblage from Thandwe is conformable with those from the other two sites.

Evidence for vegetable diet is much less satisfactory. Only at Makwe were plant remains recovered from Makwe Industry levels which pre-date Iron Age contact, and there is no reason to believe that the few specimens preserved are representative of the range of species which was exploited. Rubbing stones, found at all three sites, may have been used in the preparation of vegetable foods, or for other purposes. The more formal grindstones from the upper levels are discussed below, in the context of contact between the rock-shelters' inhabitants and the Iron Age immigrants.

There is good evidence to associate some of the rock paintings of eastern Zambia with the makers of the Makwe Industry. In chapter 19 it was argued that the early naturalistic paintings, as represented in this region at Katolola and Zawi, were the work of a stone-tool-using population which partly pre-dated and was partly contemporary with the period of Early Iron Age settlement. The artists may thus be identified as the makers of the Makwe Industry. It is probable that the surviving naturalistic paintings of eastern Zambia date from the period of Early Iron Age contact or shortly before. There is no reason to doubt that the tradition of rock painting is not of considerably greater antiquity, but that its earlier manifestations have not survived.

Human skeletal remains, recovered from Makwe Industry contexts at Kalemba and Thandwe, have been studied by Dr Hertha de Villiers who considers that they show predominantly Negroid characteristics, less strongly developed Khoi-San features being detected in some individuals. The remains from both sites clearly pre-date the local inception of the Early Iron Age. The

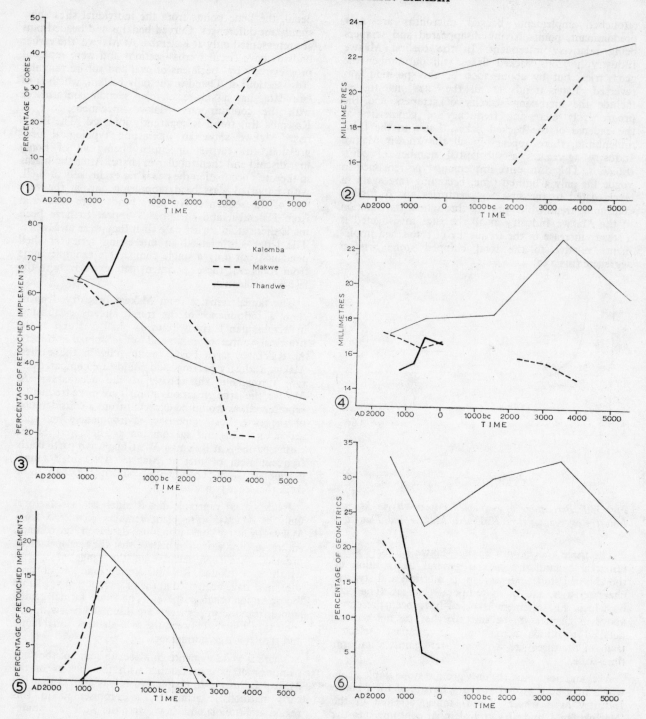

Fig. 131. Comparison of selected trends in chipped stone aggregates of the Makwe Industry at Kalemba, Makwe and Thandwe:
1. *Radial cores as a percentage of all cores*
2. *Mean length of whole flakes*
3. *Geometrics as a percentage of all retouched implements*
4. *Mean length of pointed lunates*
5. *Petits tranchets as a percentage of all retouched implements*
6. *Eared geometrics as a percentage of all geometrics.*

significance of this observation is discussed in its broader context in chapter 21, below.

Burial customs, although varied, show several points in common. The dead were evidently deposited with care, often in crevices between rocks or against the wall of the rock-shelter or a large boulder. In no case was a complete body interred. Those at Thandwe showed signs of having been partly dismembered prior to burial. At Kalemba, the burials were principally of heads and cervical vertebrae with virtually no other postcranial remains: the skulls generally showed signs of having been broken before they were interred. A deposit of burned and fragmented human postcranial bones was located elsewhere in a Makwe Industry horizon at Kalemba. Two burials, one of a fully adult male from Thandwe and one of a young adult female from Kalemba, were associated with the remains of infants: the former grave also contained two fragments of wart-hog skull, each retaining a pair of large tusks. No other finds can be interpreted as grave goods. One is left with the view that considerable importance was attached to the orderly disposal of the dead, but that burial was delayed until the corpses had become fragmented, whether by natural causes or by artificial means. It is hard to avoid the conclusion that the separate burial of fragmented heads at Kalemba may have been associated with some form of ritual dismemberment, perhaps involving the removal of the brain.

III. THE CONTINUITY OF STONE AGE DEVELOPMENT

One further point should be emphasised in connection with the Stone Age sequence before we turn our attention to the Iron Age industries. This is the remarkable degree of continuity which pervades the whole sequence from the first mode 3 industries of Kalemba to the latest phase of the Makwe Industry some forty thousand years later. Although there are several prolonged breaks in the sequence, there are apparently no major discontinuities in the overall process of industrial development.

Particular interest attaches to the inception of mode 5 technology. This is shown to have been a slow and gradual process. Occasional and poorly made backed flakes appear in the context of an otherwise mode 3 industry, and slowly develop in numbers, in quality and in variety. There is no indication that the appearance of this technology was due to introduction from some other area, or that it was other than a purely indigenous development.

IV. THE EARLY IRON AGE

All four excavated sites described in this volume yielded material which may be attributed with confidence to the Early Iron Age. Kamnama is the only Early Iron Age village site yet discovered in the region: it appears to have been occupied for a relatively brief period around the fourth century ad. At each of the three rock-shelter sites there is evidence that the makers of the Makwe Industry continued in occupation throughout the first millennium ad, during which period they established varying degrees of contact with the Early Iron Age folk. Such contact is attested at Makwe from some time within the first half of the first millennium ad: at Thandwe it does not appear to have taken place until several centuries later. The corresponding event at Kalemba cannot be dated within meaningful limits. These chronometric data are in keeping with the estimate recently proposed by the present writer (D. W. Phillipson, 1975: 333) of ad >310 to <1060 for the florescence of the Early Iron Age in the Malawi/eastern Zambia region.

Technologically, the Early Iron Age Industrial Complex (see pp. 14–17, above) presents a sharp break with the locally preceding Makwe Industry. Villages of *daga* structures make their appearance, as does abundant pottery and evidence for the practice of metallurgy. At Kamnama it appears that chipped stone artefacts were not produced or used by the Early Iron Age inhabitants.

Despite the small samples of Early Iron Age pottery which were recovered from Makwe and Thandwe, the assemblages from these two rock-shelters show some significant differences in composition from that obtained at Kamnama. In decoration (table 53) both Makwe and Thandwe present a lower relative frequency of types B1 and D1, counterbalanced by much higher numbers of types C1, C2 and D2. That these distinctions are not primarily due to selection at the rock-shelter sites of vessels having particular functions is demonstrated by counts of the various vessel shapes at each site (table 54), which show comparable representation of necked vessels relative to bowls, although pots with up-turned rims are represented only at Kamnama. Of these three assemblages of Early Iron Age pottery (that from Kalemba represents only three vessels and has been omitted from consideration here), only that from Kamnama can be attributed to a single phase of occupation. The material from Thandwe and Makwe is thought in each case to cover a substantial period of time; and it is reasonable to attribute the changes in composition, as regards decoration, to temporal change. These data provide the only indication yet available for

Table 53. Comparison of main decorative types (including variants) in the Early Iron Age pottery from Kamnama, Makwe and Thandwe

Decorative type	Kamnama	Makwe	Thandwe
A2	7%	2%	6%
B1	33%	17%	11%
C1	2%	31%	23%
C2	1%	14%	6%
D1	29%	9%	12%
D2	8%	23%	28%
F	3%	—	—
G	2%	2%	—
Undecorated	15%	2%	17%
Total sample	231	43	18

Table 54. Comparison of vessel shapes in the Early Iron Age pottery from Kamnama, Makwe and Thandwe

Vessel shape	Kamnama	Makwe	Thandwe
Open bowl	12%	17%	9%
In-turned bowl	10%	8%	9%
Necked vessel	67%	75%	82%
Pot with up-turned rim	10%	—	—
Carinated vessel	1%	—	—
Total sample	163	36	11

developmental trends within the Early Iron Age pottery tradition of eastern Zambia.

Evidence for the Early Iron Age economy has been recovered in disappointingly small quantites at the sites under review. At Kamnama, an extensive village with *daga* structures covered an area of some 5 ha. Such a large settlement is in itself strongly suggestive of a food-producing economy, but unfortunately no conclusive evidence for the practice of agriculture or for the herding of domestic animals was obtained from the Kamnama excavations. Only at Makwe were domestic animal bones recovered from contexts contemporary with the Early Iron Age presence, and it is noteworthy that they seem to occur for the first time at broadly the same stage in the sequence as does the Early Iron Age pottery. Although inconclusive when considered alone, therefore, the archaeological data from Early Iron Age contexts in eastern Zambia are in keeping with those obtained from other regions for the mixed farming economy of the eastern and southern African Early

Iron Age Industrial Complex as a whole (D. W. Phillipson, *in press*).

The red schematic rock paintings of eastern Zambia have been attributed (pp. 185–7, above) to the Early Iron Age people, and it was suggested that the execution of these motifs may have been connected in some way with initiations or other religious ceremonies. Such an interpretation would be in keeping with the evidence for use of rock-shelters by Iron Age peoples in south-central Africa. Despite the regular occurrence of Iron Age artefacts, particularly pottery, in the higher levels of the rock-shelter deposits, these are, in eastern Zambia, invariably intimately associated with Makwe Industry material, and it does not appear that Iron Age people ever inhabited rock-shelters except intermittently for religious purposes, for occasional shelter, or for refuge in time of war. Further consideration of the nature of the contact between Iron Age folk and the makers of the Makwe Industry is best postponed until after a summary has been presented of the later Iron Age of eastern Zambia.

V. THE LATER IRON AGE

The interface between the Early and later Iron Ages in eastern Zambia is not well documented by the excavations so far conducted. Typologically, the Luangwa tradition pottery of the later Iron Age represents a pronounced break with that of the Early Iron Age, and there is no suggestion of the pottery sequence of the region representing a developmental continuum. Chronologically, it appears possible that there may have been an overlap between the production of the two types of pottery, as is indicated by the graphs of their stratigraphical occurrence at Thandwe (fig. 34, p. 65) and Makwe (fig. 66, p. 117). Such an overlap, if indeed it occurred, must have been brief. This is indicated by calculations of the respective periods of florescence of the Early and later Iron Ages in the Malawi/eastern Zambia region, based on the intersextile ranges of the available radiocarbon dates (D. W. Phillipson, 1975: 333). The florescence of the Early Iron Age can be shown to have ended before ad 1060, while that of the later Iron Age began after ad 1080. It is probably safe to conclude, and also consistent with the limited data recovered from the excavations here described, that the change between the eastern Zambian Early Iron Age and the Luangwa tradition took place rapidly around the second half of the eleventh century ad.

The refuges and other nineteenth-century sites described in chapter 5 indicate that the Luangwa tradition was at that period widespread through eastern Zambia. No other later Iron Age pottery tradition is attested at any of the sites investigated.

The Luangwa tradition has continued into modern times, and is today the sole significant pottery tradition of eastern Zambia. Luangwa tradition pottery is, within this region, made by the Chewa, Nsenga and Ngoni as well as by the majority of the peripheral peoples of the Luangwa valley. The present writer (D. W. Phillipson, 1974) has presented elsewhere an account of the distribution and dominant typological features of the Luangwa tradition. The correlation between later Iron Age archaeology and traditional history is discussed in more detail below.

Economic data relating to the later Iron Age of eastern Zambia refer predominantly to its later phases. Since these data come almost exclusively from rock-shelter excavations where there is evidence for contact between later Iron Age people and the makers of the Makwe Industry, it is not possible to separate the economic activities of the two groups on other than a subjective basis. Iron-working was widespread throughout the second millennium ad; and the Thandwe rock-shelter, towards the end of the period of its occupation, was evidently used for this purpose. At Makwe, bones of domestic cattle are frequent throughout the horizons in which later Iron Age artefacts are represented: goats are also present, but in significantly smaller numbers. Here, and at Kalemba and Thandwe, wild animals are also represented in the faunal assemblages of the uppermost levels, and appear to indicate the continuation of the hunting practices of the later phases of the Makwe Industry. Various wild vegetable foods were gathered; of these the *mbula* nut, which occurs in large numbers at Makwe, was evidently favoured. For the first time traces of cultivated food-stuffs are found in the local archaeological record, but there is no reason to believe that any of these occurrences pre-date the last two centuries or so. The crops represented are finger millet, beans, pumpkin and maize. All are grown, in varying quantities, in eastern Zambia today. The last two crops are of New World origin, but their presence at Makwe in a probably eighteenth- or nineteenth-century context need occasion no surprise in view of the long history of Portuguese settlement in the Zambezi valley region only 150 km to the south. Maize was observed by de Lacerda to be grown widely in what is now eastern Zambia in 1798 (Burton, 1873). Finger millet and *Canavalia* beans are indigenous African crops (Harlan, 1971; J. B. Gillett, *personal communication*). The appearance of copper artefacts and glass beads at Makwe, in the same horizon as revealed the earliest occurrence of maize, is a further indication that the inhabitants of the region were establishing wider contacts. An eighteenth-century date for this process is fully in keeping with the historical evidence cited above in chapter 2 (see especially p. 11).

There is abundant evidence to attribute the most recent rock paintings of eastern Zambia—that is, the white stylised series—to the later Iron Age and to connect them with the conduct of initiation and other religious ceremonies, particularly with *Nyau*. This hypothesis receives further support and elaboration from a consideration of the inter-relationship between the archaeological and traditional historical evidence for the history of the local later Iron Age.

The oral traditions of the Chewa people, as outlined above in chapter 2, claim an origin connected with the migration of Kalonga from the Luba area of what is now Zaire at a date prior, but probably not more than two hundred years prior, to the beginning of the sixteenth century AD. There is no evidence for a significant break in the archaeological record at any date which could be accepted for this traditionally recalled event, the introduction of the Luangwa pottery tradition having taken place appreciably earlier.* In a recent evaluation of the Zambian later Iron Age, it was concluded that the historical traditions of the eastern half of Zambia may best be reconciled with the archaeological evidence in the following manner:

"A broadly homogeneous population [represented in the archaeological record by the Luangwa pottery tradition], probably lacking centralized political authorities, was established throughout the area early in the present millennium. This homogeneity is reflected in the wide dispersal of a common clan-system through the regions lying to the east of the Lualaba (Cunnison, 1959:62). Migration into the area from the Luangwa tradition's . . . homeland may or may not have been a continuing process through the succeeding centuries. Perhaps around the early sixteenth century if not before, small groups of people, tracing their origins to the centralised states or empires which had meantime arisen in what is now southern Zaire, began to move into the area and to establish themselves in political authority over parts of the indigenous population. Such groups included the ancestors of the Bena Ng'andu and the Bena Ng'ona, the ruling clans of the Bemba and Bisa respectively, and—later—the Lunda rulers who established the Kingdom of Kazembe. There is evidence that the foundation of Kalonga's Malawi [or Chewa] Kingdom predated those further west. It seems to have lacked the tightly-knit chain of authority characteristic of the later states. Although Undi's Kingdom traces its origin through that of Kalonga to pre-Kongolo Luba, its rulers and their system were probably derived thence before the development of the political organization was complete; it thus mirrors an earlier stage in that development. Of all the peoples in the Luangwa tradition area, the Nsenga probably retain most features of the earlier decentralized stage of development but, having been subject to Undi's Chewa for a considerable period, many of these features are partially submerged." (D. W. Phillipson, 1974: 18–19).

This conclusion has received substantial confirmation from the recent work of Schoffeleers (1973) who recognises a 'proto-Chewa' period predating the formation of the Maravi state systems. The latter event he dates to about AD 1400, citing traditional evidence supported by the unpublished excavation by J. D. Clark of an early Maravi shrine near Chapananga, dated by radiocarbon to early in the fifteenth century. A date in the late eleventh century, coinciding with that indicated archaeologically for the inception of the Luangwa tradition, would be perfectly acceptable for the beginning of Schoffeleers' 'proto-Chewa' period (cf. *ibid.*:48). It is clear that, while the Phiri clan came to the area between Lake Malawi and the Luangwa in about the fourteenth century, the Banda and Mbewe clans have a greater antiquity in the region (Hamilton, 1959: 220; Marwick, 1963: 378). The autochthones, such as the Banda, retained much ritual power, particularly in the field of rain-making, and were recognised as 'owners of the land', although the invading Phiri came to enjoy a near-monopoly of political authority.

Schoffeleers (1973:53–5) also cites convincing evidence that the *Nyau* brotherhoods date back to his 'proto-Chewa' period,† when they provided, *inter alia*, a means of solemnizing female puberty rites. *Nyau* appears to be linked in some way with the Banda clan. Assimilation of the religious authority of the Banda into the society dominated by the secular authority of the Phiri was apparently an extremely slow process.

The version of Chewa history here summarised is in full accord with the archaeological evidence for the eastern Zambian later Iron Age. In addition, it provides an indication of the antiquity of *Nyau*, with which many of the later rock paintings of the region appear to be associated, and suggests a possible historical context for the derivation of these paintings from the earlier red schematic series which is attributed to the Early Iron Age.

The manner in which the arrival of the Phiri and the formation of the Maravi state systems left little discernible trace in the archaeological record may be paralleled in the better documented process of Ngoni raiding and settlement which took place during the nineteenth century (p. 12, above). The numerous refuge

---

*J. C. Miller (1972) has argued that several of the traditions relating to the formation of states which claim a Luba or Lunda origin may refer to a significantly earlier period than has previously been supposed. Nevertheless, it is highly improbable that the events to which these traditions refer took place as early as the eleventh century.

†Schoffeleers (1973: 53) also argues, this time without supporting evidence, that the *Nyau* go "back in time to a hunting and food-gathering economy".

sites have yielded pottery, described in chapter 5, which may be taken as representative of that made by the indigenous population of the area at the time of the Ngoni arrival. Today, Ngoni women make Luangwa tradition pottery which is virtually indistinguishable from that of their Chewa neighbours; and likewise the ChiNgoni language is now almost extinct in Zambia. The reason for this is, presumably, that the Ngoni invasion was primarily of men: tradition is explicit on this point, as it is that women were one of the main commodities captured on the raids. Today, the

manufacture of Luangwa tradition pottery is exclusively the work of women, as is potting in the South African Nguni homelands (Lawton, 1967:30–80). It must be assumed that local women who were captured or otherwise assimilated into the Ngoni community continued to make pottery in their own traditional manner. Since children generally learn their mothers' language, a similar explanation may be offered for the local extinction of ChiNgoni (D. W. Phillipson, 1974: 21–2). The wider implications of these observations will be discussed in chapter 21.

VI. 'LATE STONE AGE'/IRON AGE CONTACTS AND INTERACTIONS

Iron Age people have been present in eastern Zambia since about the fourth century ad; yet there is considerable evidence that the makers of the Makwe Industry also continued to live in the area through all the eight centuries of the local Early Iron Age, and that they survived for several centuries the advent of the later Iron Age. The time of their final disappearance cannot be fixed with any precision, but the presence of an abundant stone industry in horizon 5 at Makwe, and in the levels immediately preceding the presumed nineteenth-century occupation of Kalemba, suggests that a date in about the seventeenth century is probable. So far in this chapter, the Makwe Industry's makers and the Iron Age societies have been considered separately. It remains, in view of the long chronological overlap between them, to discuss the evidence for the nature of the contacts and interactions which must have taken place.

It is clear that the two populations maintained, to a large extent, their separate identities throughout the period of their co-existence. At the Early Iron Age village site of Kamnama, as at the majority of comparable settlements in adjacent regions, no chipped stone artefacts were recovered. In the contemporary levels of all three excavated rock-shelters, on the other hand, such stone artefacts occur in substantial numbers associated with potsherds which are individual-ly identical in every way to those found at Kamnama. The obvious interpretation of these facts is that the Early Iron Age folk, an immigrant group, were the sole makers of this pottery, but that they did not make chipped stone artefacts. The indigenous population, the makers of the Makwe Industry, continued to practise their mode 5 stone-working technology, and obtained pottery from their Early Iron Age neighbours, the identity of the sherds from the rock-shelters with those from the villages being such as to preclude the possibility that the indigenes adopted the art of pottery manufacture themselves.

In the detailed analyses, which have been presented in previous chapters, of the later occurrences of the Makwe Industry at all three excavated rock-shelters, it is apparent that no major changes in the chipped stone industry accompanied the appearance of the Early Iron Age pottery. Indeed, both the general composition of the chipped stone aggregates and their metrical and stylistic characteristics continue the same gradual developmental trends as had been established long before, in pre-Iron Age times. It is legitimate to conclude that no major economic innovations were

adopted by the makers of the Makwe Industry during the period of their contact with Iron Age peoples.

That some form of contact between the two groups did in fact take place is indicated by the presence of Iron Age artefacts in the Makwe Industry sites. These artefacts comprise, primarily, pottery, metal objects, and grindstones. Significantly, however, Makwe Industry artefacts do not occur at the Early Iron Age village site of Kamnama. Iron Age material was found in varying quantities at the three excavated rock-shelters, being relatively frequent from an early date at Makwe, and to a rather lesser extent and later at Thandwe, but rare at Kalemba. These observations presumably reflect varying degrees and intensities of contact. Only at Makwe were bones of domestic animals found associated with Makwe Industry material of the period of Iron Age contact. There can be no doubt that domestic animals were introduced to eastern Zambia by Iron Age folk. Their occurrence at Makwe is thus in keeping with the hypothesis that inter-group contact was on a more substantial scale there than at the other sites.

There is also evidence for the use of rock-shelters by the Iron Age people themselves. Iron Age activities such as iron-working are attested; while schematic rock paintings, which may be shown to have been connected with Iron Age initiation and other religious ceremonies, demonstrate the physical presence of Iron Age people in the same sites as were still sometimes frequented by their Makwe Industry contemporaries.

The most satisfactory interpretation of Makwe Industry/Iron Age interaction during the fourteen or fifteen centuries of the two groups' contact with one another is that of a temporary client relationship. Such a situation may still be observed in several areas of southern Africa, notably in south-western Zambia where, on the arid plains between the Zambezi and Mashi rivers, small groups of Hukwe 'Bushmen' still continue, relatively unmodified, the wandering hunting existence of their 'Late Stone Age' ancestors. Hukwe do not themselves make pottery or smelt iron: they obtain both these commodities from their Lozi and Subiya Bantu-speaking neighbours in the Zambezi valley. Meat, skins and labour are the main items which the Hukwe exchange for the products of their neighbours. For much of the year, contact between the two groups is, in this sparsely populated region, rare. At certain seasons, however, groups of Hukwe emerge into the Zambezi valley and enter into a temporary client relationship with individual villages of

Subiya, where they render hunting and herding services in exchange for food and other village products. Through this process, some groups of Hukwe have recently begun to grow their own crops, or even to own a few head of cattle. Despite this increasing rate of acculturation, the wide cultural and social divergence between the two groups is recognised by both, and there is little integration.

Such a model provides an acceptable explanation of the archaeological data which are at present available from eastern Zambia. It is also in keeping with the oral traditions which appear to relate to the final remnants of the 'Late Stone Age' population of the region (see above, p. 10) and which emphasise the lack of contact between the two groups. Given their apparent self-sufficiency, why and how did the makers of the Makwe Industry disappear as a separate and viable entity?

The answer presumably lies in the expanding population of the later Iron Age, with its increased economic emphasis on the herding of domestic animals. With the passage of time, these factors would have restricted the ability of the Makwe Industry people to practise their traditional way of life; client relationships would have become more frequent and more permanent, resulting in the break-down of the social and economic divisions between the two groups. This in turn must have led to the absorbtion of the last of the Makwe Industry folk into the society of the now far more numerous later Iron Age farmers. Archaeology and oral tradition combine to place the final completion of this process around the seventeenth century AD.

Chapter 21

Eastern Zambia in African Prehistory

I. THE STONE AGE SUCCESSION FROM *c.* 40,000 BC

In this chapter it remains to discuss the prehistoric sequence of eastern Zambia in relation to those known from adjacent regions of eastern and southern Africa. This will be attempted in chronological order, beginning with the mode 3 industries.

MODE 3 INDUSTRIES

Dated, fully analysed and described mode 3 industries in south-central Africa are few and widely dispersed: the largest body of relevant data is from Rhodesia. Several caves in the Matopo Hills of Matabeleland have yielded mode 3 material which appears to be broadly contemporary with that from Kalemba. At Pomongwe and Tshangula, C. K. Cooke (1963) has investigated an industry named after the nearby site of Bambata, the retouched implements of which consist primarily of flake scrapers and unifacial points in approximately the same relative proportions as those in which the two types occur at Kalemba. At Pomongwe this Bambatan Industry is dated to around the thirty-fourth millennium bc. An apparently comparable aggregate, of which no detailed analysis has yet been published, comes from Redcliff some 250 km to the north-east, and is associated with four radiocarbon dates between the fortieth and the thirty-fourth millennia bc (Sampson, 1974: 206). These Rhodesian sites provide good general parallels for the contemporary mode 3 industries at Kalemba, that from Pomongwe being particularly close, perhaps largely because the poor quality quartz, of which many of the Bambatan Industry artefacts there were made, is similar in flaking properties to that used at the Zambian site.

Undated mode 3 material recovered from the Zambezi terraces in the vicinity of the Victoria Falls (J. D. Clark, 1950b; 1975) shares some features with the Bambatan Industry but, since no quantified analyses are available, and since the chalcedony raw material employed is so distinctive, detailed comparisons cannot be made with the aggregates from Pomongwe and Kalemba. The presence of bifacial points in the Victoria Falls region serves, however, to distinguish this western industry from those discussed above.

Further to the north, in central Zambia, are two sites which have yielded mode 3 material from excavated contexts, but which have so far been published only briefly. The first of these is at Twin Rivers, some 24 km south-west of Lusaka (J. D. Clark, 1971). There is evidence (Flint, 1959: 357–8) that the occupation of this hill-top site took place at a time when the local climate was somewhat drier than it is today. The two radiocarbon dates, respectively of prior to the thirty-fourth millennium and in the twenty-second or twenty-first millennia bc, while not placing the site's occupation between acceptably narrow limits, do serve to indicate its broad contemporaneity with the mode 3 industries at Kalemba. The evidence for relatively dry conditions would suggest a date after about 26,000 bc (van Zinderen Bakker and Coetzee, 1972). The artefacts from Twin Rivers are mainly of quartz: scrapers and points comparable with those from Kalemba are well represented, but there are also bifacial points and a number of heavy duty tools, notably core axes, which are not represented at the eastern Zambian site. The smaller artefacts at Twin Rivers may also be paralleled, as may those at Kalemba, in the collections recovered from the 'bone cave' at Broken Hill Mine, Kabwe, some 150 km north of Lusaka (Clark *et al.*, 1947). There are however, indications that the Broken Hill material may be very much earlier in date than that from the other sites here discussed (Klein, 1973).

In northern Malawi, Eggers has excavated an undated open site at Chaminade which, again, yielded an assemblage of points and flake scrapers such as would not be out of place in the Kalemba mode 3 industry, but which were associated with heavy duty tools such as picks, choppers, and core-axes (J. D. Clark, 1970a; Sampson, 1974; 229). The Chaminade material has been attributed to an industry variously described as Upper Sangoan and Lupemban; but its relationship to either entity, as known from other areas, appears to be somewhat distant.

From an initial consideration of these comparative data, one would be tempted to subsume the Kalemba mode 3 material within the Bambatan Industry, as this is known from south of the Zambezi. Such an attribution would, however, be premature. Kalemba shares one important non-typological feature with the Bambatan occurrences at Pomongwe and Redcliff: it is a cave site. There is thus the very real possibility that the absence of heavy duty tools, which is one of the most prominent features distinguishing these cave and rock-shelter assemblages from those recovered from the broadly contemporary open sites at Victoria Falls, Twin Rivers and Chaminade, may be due more to differing activities at the various sites than to any inate distinction of industrial tradition (cf. also J. D. Clark, 1971: 1231). The apparent similarity between the Kalemba and Rhodesian assemblages is increased by the fact that both are predominantly made of comparatively poor quality quartz. It may be concluded that, while the Kalemba mode 3 industry shows strong affinities with contemporary material from several other localities in south-central Africa, its attribution to any specific industrial entity would not be justified, since the parameters of the individual industries are at present neither well defined nor adequately understood.

The emphasis of the makers of the Kalemba mode 3 industry on the hunting of equids and larger antelope may be seen as characteristic of the practice at this period in southern Africa generally (Sampson, 1974: 211–6). The large numbers of small creatures represented in the faunal collection from the Bambatan Industry levels at Pomongwe provide an exception.

THE BEGINNINGS OF BACKED-MICROLITH MANUFACTURE

At several sites in Rhodesia the mode 3 Bambatan Industry is followed by one, characterised by the first local appearance of true backed microliths, which is known varyingly as Umguzan (Cooke, Summers and Robinson, 1966) or Tshangulan (C. K. Cooke, 1969). Umguzan assemblages are differentiated from those of the Bambatan Industry by a marked decrease in overall artefact size and by the appearance of convex-backed flakes and curved-backed geometrics. The development of the Umguzan Industry thus provides a close parallel for the appearance of the transitional industry represented in horizons I to K at Kalemba. Unfortunately, the date of this transition in Rhodesia cannot be fixed with any precision. The top of the Umguzan sequence at Pomongwe is dated to the first half of the fourteenth millennium bc, and its commencement is thus bracketed between this date and that of the thirty-fourth millennium for the underlying Bambatan Industry. The transition from mode 3 to mode 5 technology at Pomongwe could have been contemporary with that at Kalemba, but this cannot be demonstrated.

The development of techniques of backed microlith manufacture can be seen to have been a widespread phenomenon in the later mode 3 industries of southern Africa (Sampson, 1974: 231–57), and one that took place in various areas at different times within the broad period from about 40,000 to about 16,000 bc, and even much later in one or two areas. Several of the earlier of these occurrences, such as those at Klasies River Mouth and Skildergat on the south Cape coast, are overlain by industries which completely lack backed microliths and which resemble again fairly closely the underlying mode 3 industries. The most satisfactory explanation to place upon these observations is that some groups of the region's inhabitants, all of whom at one time practised a mode 3 technology, developed at various times the art of backed-microlith production, presumably in response to some economic need which at present remains poorly understood, but of which the identity will be discussed below. Other groups, however, retained their purely mode 3 technology into much more recent times. While it is possible that the two technologies were initially practised by the same populations to produce tools for different—perhaps seasonally determined—activities, it seems far more probable that they were, at least latterly, the work of distinct population groups. Certain sites in Rhodesia, notably Zombepata in the Sipolilo District of Mashonaland, and Bambata in the Matopo Hills, have also yielded evidence for successive occupation about forty thousand years ago by groups practising a conventional mode 3 technology and those whose artefacts included a high proportion of small parallel-sided flakes (Armstrong, 1931; C. K. Cooke, 1971). This may represent the initial stage of the process of technological differentiation which eventually led to the appearance of fully mode 5 industries.

A possible explanation for this development may be proposed from reference to the associated faunal remains. These, both at Pomongwe (Brain, cited by Sampson, 1974: 245) and Kalemba (p. 161, above) show a marked decrease in the numbers of large animals in the backed microlith horizons, relative to those found with the underlying mode 3 industries. Smaller prey calls for lighter hunting equipment, whether used for trapping or as projectile points or barbs. It is tempting to suggest that the appearance of backed microliths may be connected with changed hunting techniques, perhaps involving the development of the bow and arrow (cf. J. D. Clark, 1959a). Such a function for several forms of backed geometrics is in keeping with the evidence for the hafting and use of such artefacts cited in the appendix below.

In addition to the Rhodesian and South African regions already noted, several areas of south-central and eastern Africa have yielded evidence for the appearance of backed microliths in the context of the later mode 3 stone industries. Examples may be cited from Victoria Falls and Mumbwa Cave in southern Zambia, both of which are undated (J. D. Clark, 1950b; 1942); from Kalambo Falls where the relevant industry, named Polungu, has been dated to some period before the first half of the eighth millennium bc (J. D. Clark, 1974: 153–251); and from Kisese II, 65 km north of Kondoa Irangi in Tanzania (Inskeep, 1962), where occasional backed microliths are found associated with numerous scrapers as early as the thirtieth millennium bc. These developments may thus be seen to have been of wide geographical incidence, although they have little chronological integrity.

To the north of the Zambezi, this final mode 3 tradition continued to develop, as we shall see, into fully fledged mode 5 industries. To the south, however, no direct continuity can be demonstrated: indeed the microlithic sequence is interrupted by the florescence of a completely distinct stone-working tradition, to whose industries the name Oakhurst Complex has been given (Sampson, 1974: 258–91). This need not be discussed in detail here: suffice it to point out that assemblages of the Oakhurst Complex comprise varied large scrapers to the virtual exclusion of all other retouched implements. Such material is of widespread occurrence in South Africa, Rhodesia (where it overlies the Umguzan at Pomongwe) and Namibia. It dates from the period between 12,000 and 8000 bc.

In eastern Zambia, however, (as elsewhere north of the Zambezi) the development of the microlithic traditions shows no such interruption. The Kalemba sequence illustrates, in periods (ii) and (iii), a steady development from a mode 3 to a mode 5 technology, culminating in the achievement of a fully fledged mode 5 industry by about the fifteenth millennium bc. In its later stages, therefore, this developmental process took place more rapidly north of the Zambezi than it did in the south, for a fully microlithic industry flourished in eastern, central and northern Zambia some four millennia before the inception of the Oakhurst Complex in the latter region.

The Zambian site which has yielded a sequence providing the closest direct comparison with periods (ii) and (iii) of the Kalemba succession is Leopard's Hill Cave, situated some 55 km south-east of Lusaka (S. F. Miller, 1969). Both this site and Kalemba, although 450 km apart, share a similar environment, being situated in undulating Brachystegia-covered plateau country, at approximately 1200 m above sea level, near the lip of the northern slope of the Zambezi valley.

The lowest level at Leopard's Hill, securely dated to between the twenty-second and the twentieth millennia bc, has yielded an industry which has been dubbed 'proto-Late Stone Age' (J. D. Clark, 1970b: 241). The retouched implements consist of 13 per cent backed microliths which are predominantly convex-backed flakes with only one pointed lunate, 76 per cent scrapers of which the majority were made on chunks, and 4 per cent bifacial foliate points. Particular interest attaches to the presence of a large bored stone. There is clearly a very close resemblance between this industry and that recovered from Kalemba, especially in horizons K and L. There is, however, a significant difference in the cores which, at Leopard's Hill, are predominantly double-ended, used to produce small parallel-sided flakes or 'bladelets': only 10 per cent of the Leopard's Hill cores from this level are radial. The Leopard's Hill material is somewhat more evolved towards a mode 5 technology than is that of the Kalemba 'transitional' industry: it is likewise a little later in date, being in fact placed by the radiocarbon evidence in the early part of the hiatus between periods (ii) and (iii) at Kalemba.

The lowest horizon at Leopard's Hill was sealed by a layer of stalagmite which appears to represent a break of some five thousand years in the occupation of the site. When settlement was resumed, apparently during the first half of the fifteenth millennium bc, a fully fledged mode 5 industry was being produced. Curved-backed geometrics account for 21 per cent of the retouched implements, backed flakes for 40 per cent, and scrapers for 38 per cent. There are no angled-backed geometrics, and the backed flakes are predominantly of the narrow 'pointed backed bladelet' variety. This industry has correctly been subsumed within 'Nachikufan I' by S. F. Miller (1969; 1972), who demonstrates its identity with broadly contemporary material from other Zambian sites, notably Nachikufu, Chifubwa Stream and Mwela Rocks. The period (iii) industry at Kalemba falls well within the range of variation of these 'Nachikufan I' assemblages from west of the Luangwa (fig. 132).

THE ENVIRONMENTAL BACKGROUND

It is useful here to leave the industrial succession and briefly to discuss the climatic conditions which provided the physical environment for the development of the mode 5 industries. Evidence has been cited by van Zinderen Bakker and Coetzee (1972) to the effect that, prior to about 26,000 bc, the climate over most of eastern sub-equatorial Africa was somewhat warmer and wetter than at present. This 'Kalambo Interstadial' was followed by a relatively cool, drier period (the 'Mount Kenya Hypothermal') which lasted until about 12,000 bc and which, at least on the slopes of the East African mountains, was marked by temperatures some 5° to 8° centigrade cooler than those which prevail today.

If the correlation, proposed above (p. 189), between relatively high temperatures and rainfall on the one hand, and the rate of exfoliation from rock-shelter walls on the other, may be accepted, then the climatic fluctuations noted in the previous paragraph may be seen to be reflected in the Kalemba sequence. The pedological analysis of the deposits (pp. 124–5, above) drew attention to the high rate of exfoliation at the base of the deposit, in horizon G and the lower part of horizon H. It would be fully in keeping with the radiocarbon dates from Kalemba to link this part of the sequence with the warm, damp 'Kalambo Interstadial' of before 26,000 bc. The reduced level of exfoliation observed in horizons H to J, rising slowly to horizon N, would then correlate with the 'Mount Kenya Hypothermal' of 26,000 to 12,000 bc. The cooler, dryer conditions indicated for this time would have given rise to a more open vegetation than that which prevails today. At

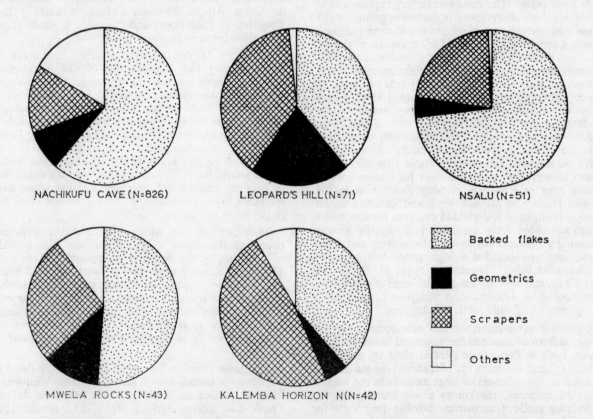

NACHIKUFU CAVE (N=826)　　　LEOPARD'S HILL (N=71)　　　NSALU (N=51)

MWELA ROCKS (N=43)　　　KALEMBA HORIZON N (N=42)

- Backed flakes
- Geometrics
- Scrapers
- Others

*Fig. 132. Composition of **retouched** implement assemblages from selected 'Nachikufan I' occurrences in Zambia. Data for Nachikufu, Leopard's Hill, Nsalu and Mwela Rocks are from S. F. Miller (1969).*

Kalemba, this is reflected in the abundance of equids and large gregarious bovids which were hunted during the early phases of the site's occupation.

At Kalemba, the development of a full mode 5 technology, as exemplified by 'Nachikufan I' and the Makwe Industry, was accompanied by a change in the associated faunal remains, which began to include a higher proportion of small creatures than had been hunted previously. This shift may tentatively be connected with the return of warmer, moister conditions during the millennia around 12,000 bc (van Zinderen Bakker and Coetzee, 1972), with the concomitant denser vegetation. Such a gradual climatic and vegetational change would have resulted in the migration of much of the large plains-loving gregarious fauna to drier regions such as those which lie further to the west.

A change in hunting techniques would have been a likely result of the altered availability of prey. Such a change is, as argued above, probably reflected in the archaeological record by the gradual appearance of backed microliths, several types of which will be shown below (appendix: pp. 215-8) probably to have served as points or barbs for arrows. Trapping of small creatures, particularly nocturnal species, may also be envisaged as a probable development at this time. These innovations resulted in the disappearance of the larger projectile points which were characteristic of many of the mode 3 industries.

The parallel between the development of microlithic technology and a shift in hunting emphasis is by no means restricted to eastern Zambia. A comparable phenomenon at Pomongwe has been noted above. In the southern Cape Province of South Africa a precisely similar situation prevailed, although both changes took place at a somewhat later date than they did at Kalemba: here, the disappearance of the gregarious plains antelope was largely brought about by the flooding of extensive coastal plains through the rise in sea level which followed the end of the last glaciation around the eighth millennium bc. On the coast, exploitation of marine food-resources partly replaced plains hunting (Klein, 1974). A shift to the hunting of smaller creatures is also attested in some inland regions of South Africa (H. Deacon, 1972). On an altogether different scale it is significant that substantial human occupation of the West African forest is not attested prior to the development of mode 5 technology in that region (Shaw, 1969).

REGIONAL MODE 5 INDUSTRIES

Returning now to the survey of the industrial succession of eastern and southern Africa, attention may be directed to evidence for regional mode 5 stone-working traditions. Particular emphasis will be placed on the elucidation of the chronology of their inception in different areas, and on their typological development.

It has become general to regard the succession of microlithic industries which continued to be made over much of northern and central Zambia from this period until comparatively recent times as comprising a 'Nachikufan Industrial Complex', following on from the original proposal for a 'Nachikufu Culture' (J. D. Clark, 1950c). The chronology and typology of the successive phases of this complex have been summarised in chapter 3 above (pp. 14-15) and need not be repeated here. Sampson (1974: 353), on the other hand, proposes to subsume virtually all the microlithic industries of southern Africa, including those named 'Nachikufan',

in a single 'Wilton Complex'. The usefulness and validity of both concepts must now be questioned.

'Nachikufan I' is now recognised as a manifestation of the earliest true microlithic industry so far known in sub-Saharan Africa, which is found in a broad belt of the eastern and south-central highlands stretching from Lake Victoria and southern Kenya, through Tanzania and northern Zambia, to the Zambezi (fig. 133). The characteristic tools in these assemblages are flake scrapers and small, narrow, convex-backed flakes, sometimes accompanied by small numbers of pointed lunates. In Zambia, bored stones are found to be an integral part of these industries, but the presence of ground stone axes is not firmly attested until later times. In addition to the Zambian sites already mentioned, comparable material comes from Kisese II rock-shelter in central Tanzania (Inskeep, 1962), where its beginning is dated to about 17,000 bc; from the Naisiusiu Beds at Olduvai Gorge (Leakey et al., 1972); from Munyama Cave on Buvuma Island in Lake Victoria (van Noten, 1971); and from Lukenya Hill near Nairobi (Gramly and Rightmire, 1973). At each of the last three sites radiocarbon dates of between the sixteenth and the thirteenth millennia bc have been obtained.

Around 8000 bc or shortly thereafter it appears that the early mode 5 industry of eastern Africa underwent a process of relatively rapid development, resulting in the appearance of a number of distinct regional industries. At the same time the general geographical distribution of the mode 5 industries was considerably extended by their inception in the greater part of the sub-continent lying to the south of the Zambezi, where they replaced the industries of the Oakhurst Complex. Examples of these regional mode 5 industries are the 'Upper Kenya Capsian' of the Rift Valley in southern Kenya, which is first attested early in the seventh millennium bc (L. S. B. Leakey, 1931; Sutton, 1972); the various industries which have been lumped together

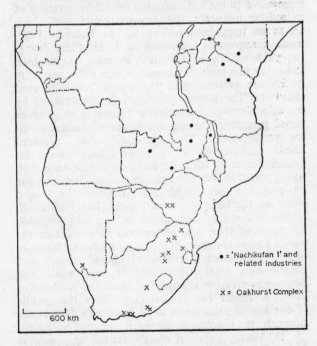

Fig. 133. Distribution of sites of 'Nachikufan I' and related industries compared with that of sites attributed to the Oakhurst Complex.

as the 'East African Wilton', such as those from the upper levels at Kisese II, at Nasera ('Apis Rock') in the Serengeti Plain (L. S. B. Leakey, 1936), and at Nsongezi on the Kagera river west of Lake Victoria (Pearce and Posnansky, 1963; Nelson and Posnansky, 1970). In Zambia, the equivalent industries in the regions between the Kafue and the Luangwa are 'Nachikufan IIA' and its successor 'Nachikufan IIB', noted above on pp. 14–15. In eastern Zambia this period saw the appearance of the distinctive Makwe Industry. In parts of southern and western Zambia it seems that a mode 3 technology continued for several thousands of years longer, until around the fourth millennium bc or even later.

In the regions south of the Zambezi formerly occupied by the practitioners of the Oakhurst Complex, this period saw the rapid inception of mode 5 technology. In most of Rhodesia it seems that the microlithic industries appeared in a fully fledged form sometime during the eighth or seventh millennia. Here, as possibly in more southerly regions, it is tempting to suggest that mode 5 technology may have been introduced from north of the Zambezi. This hypothesis is strengthened by the affinity which the mode 5 industry of much of Mashonaland, known as Pfupian (Robinson, 1952; Cooke, Summers and Robinson, 1966), has for 'Nachikufan IIA' with its large numbers of concave scrapers and bored stones. In the southern part of Rhodesia, Pomongwe Cave again provides the most intensively investigated sequence: here, the industry known as Matopan flourished from at least the seventh millennium bc until well after the advent of the Early Iron Age. It is characterised by the presence of large numbers of small convex scrapers; backed microliths are markedly less frequent, and among them backed flakes easily outnumber the geometrics (C. K. Cooke, 1963).

The last four millennia bc in northern Zambia are represented in the archaeological record by a variety of microlithic industries, the inter-relationships of which are as yet imperfectly understood. At Kalambo Falls, mode 5 aggregates attributed by J. D. Clark (1974: 107–52) to the Kaposwa Industry are made on mudstone and other fine-grained materials which differ markedly in fracture patterns from the quartz generally used elsewhere. The Kaposwa Industry is characterised by use of a developed microburin technique to produce varied geometrics, among which curved-backed forms are predominant. The aggregates from northern Zambia analysed by S. F. Miller (1969) show a far greater degree of inter-site variation at this time than was apparent in the earlier phases—so much so that she has proposed that 'Nachikufan III' should be defined solely on the basis of material from Nachikufu itself. There is a general diminution in size of microliths; the types of these and of scrapers recognised in the earlier phases continue, but with no particular forms in overall dominance. Grindstones, bored stones and ground axes were still in use at most sites. The heterogeneous group of aggregates classed as 'Nachikufan III' by Miller has yielded dates from the middle of the second millennium bc at Leopard's Hill to the fifteenth to nineteenth centuries ad at Nachikufu (S. F. Miller, 1971). A closely related aggregate at Nakapapula in the Serenje District (D. W. Phillipson, 1969) covers a similar time-span and has been described as sharing many features with 'Nachikufan III' at the type-site. The diversity of these industries is well illustrated in fig. 134, which summarises the relative frequencies of geometrics, backed flakes and scrapers in selected Zambian mode 5 assemblages. It is clear that these industries continued for over fifteen centuries after the arrival of Early Iron Age metallurgists and agriculturalists within their general area of distribution, although they were established well before that event.

It will be seen from the above outline that the industries classed as 'Nachikufan' cover a time-span of more than sixteen millennia. A consistent series of sequential phases has been demonstrated (but see Sampson and Southard, 1972), although the nature of the changes involved is not yet clear; in particular we do not know to what extent the sequence is an illusory compartmentalisation of a continuous typological evolution. Taking the Zambian sequence as a whole, it is now clear that 'Nachikufan I' is a representative of an early microlithic industry, characterised by the dominance of narrow, pointed, convex-backed flakes, which was widely distributed in the plateau areas of east-central Africa, and which was derived at least in substantial part from the final mode 3 industries of that region. Later phases were progressively localised and show increased inter-site variation. They may represent differential local developments from a 'Nachikufan I' common ancestor.

'NACHIKUFAN' AND 'WILTON'

Until recently it was usual to regard the microlithic industries of Zambia as divisible into two main geographical groups: 'Nachikufan' on the northern and central plateaux, and 'Wilton' in the south and west. The higher proportion of backed microliths, particularly curved-backed geometrics, in the 'Wilton' was held to represent a response to the more open country of the south, which favoured hunting with the bow and stone-tipped arrow; while the denser woodland of the northern regions resulted in the greater frequency of concave scrapers and other putative woodworking tools in the 'Nachikufan' industries. Recent research has provided some degree of support, but not conclusive proof, for these usages; and it may well be that the above is a valid explanation of what is indeed a general distinction between most of the mode 5 industries in the two areas. However, we do know that 'Nachikufan I' and 'IIA' predate the presence of microlithic 'Wilton' industries in the south, which are thus contemporary only with phases IIB and III in the north. Furthermore, it is these two latter phases which have most in common with the 'Wilton' industries, with which they share at least as great a typological similarity as they do with the earlier 'Nachikufan' phases. What was once seen as a largely geographical and environmental distinction may thus be regarded as based at least as firmly on chronological factors. It is indeed tempting to regard the 'Wilton' industries of Zambia as further examples of the regionally differentiated derivatives of the earlier 'Nachikufan' phases, marking a spread of mode 5 industries into new territories in which mode 3 technology had previously held sway long after the latter's replacement on the northern plateaux.

The clearest and most detailed picture of the 'Zambian Wilton' is that obtained from excavations at Gwisho Hotsprings on the southern edge of the Kafue Flats (Gabel, 1965; Fagan and van Noten, 1971), where occupation began shortly after 3000 bc and continued for some one and a half millennia. Backedflakes dominate the chipped stone industry, curved-backed geometrics occur in some quantity, but angled-backed geometrics are uncommon. Scrapers, generally small and convex, are relatively few; concave forms are virtually absent. Bored stones and ground axes are rare. The wealth of organic material preserved, including wooden artefacts, is an indication of the range of archaeological evidence which has perished on most other sites of this period.

At Mumbwa Cave, north of Gwisho on the opposite side of the Kafue Flats, 'Zambian Wilton' overlies mode 3 material in an as yet undated sequence (J. D. Clark, 1942), and appears to have lasted until after the beginning of the local Iron Age. Lack of evidence for a very prolonged 'Wilton' occupation or for typological change therein, together with the apparent similarity

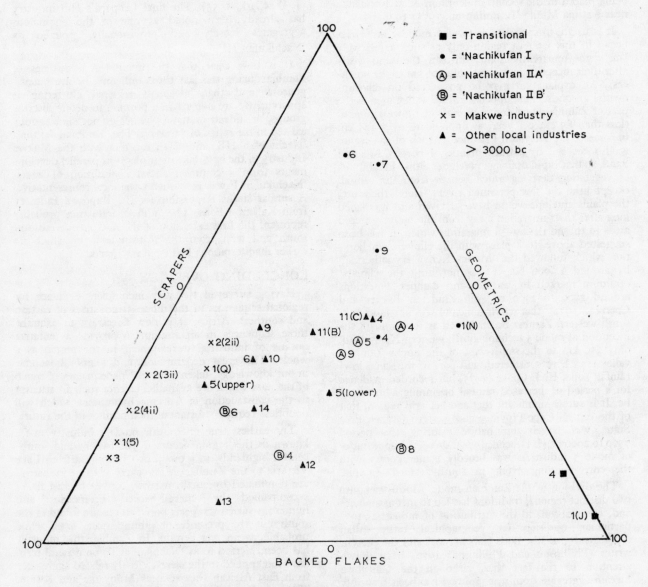

Fig. 134. Composition of retouched implement assemblages from selected Zambian mode 5 industries.
    Key to sites:
        1. *Kalemba (horizon indicated in brackets)*
        2. *Makwe (horizon indicated in brackets)*
        3. *Thandwe (all layers)*
        4. *Leopard's Hill (data from S. F. Miller, 1969)*
        5. *Nachikufu Shelter (data from S. F. Miller, 1969)*
        6. *Nachikufu Cave (data from S. F. Miller, 1969)*
        7. *Nsalu Cave (data from S. F. Miller, 1969)*
        8. *Bimbe wa Mpalabwe (data from S. F. Miller, 1969)*
        9. *Mwela Rocks (data from S. F. Miller, 1969)*
        10. *Kalambo Falls Kaposwa Industry (data from J. D. Clark, 1974)*
        11. *Gwisho Hotsprings B and C (as indicated) (data from Fagan and van Noten, 1971)*
        12. *Nakapapula (all levels) (data from D. W. Phillipson, 1969)*
        13. *Katombora Road, Livingstone (data from Inskeep, 1959)*
        14. *Chiwemupula (data from Phillipson and Phillipson, 1970)*

between the Mumbwa and Gwisho aggregates, makes it probable that the mode 5 industries of these two sites were broadly contemporary. Comparable industries in the Zambezi valley, likewise attributed to the 'Zambian Wilton', were first recognised in the Victoria Falls region (J. D. Clark, 1950b; 1975; see also Inskeep, 1959). In the upper Zambezi valley it is clear that the inception of mode 5 technology was an even later development than it was elsewhere in southern Zambia, being placed in the second millennium bc at Kandanda near Katima Mulilo (L. Phillipson, 1975; 1976).

It is useful to speculate as to why mode 5 industries began in this western region only at such a relatively late date—apparently some thirteen thousand years after their inception in regions only 500 km to the north-east. An explanation may be postulated on environmental grounds. This upper Zambezi valley area is the part of Zambia which today receives the lowest rainfall (less than 85 cm per year, as opposed to over 125 cm in some of the Northern Province). Much of the region is also covered by a thick mantle of porous Kalahari Sand, so that rapid drainage precludes either inhabitants or vegetation deriving much benefit from the rainfall except near the few perennial rivers. Here, therefore, the plains antelope would have survived and flourished long after their migration away from the better watered areas to the north-east—a migration which, it has been suggested above, took place with the climatic amelioration which followed the 'Mount Kenya Hypothermal' by around 12,000 bc. It was not until the climatic optimum marked by warmer and damper conditions around 2700 to 1300 bc (van Zinderen Bakker and Coetzee, 1972) that environmental circumstances in south-western Zambia became such as to stimulate the inception of mode 5 technology. In western Ngamiland, only 350 km to the south-west of the upper Zambezi valley sites here considered, and part of the same low-rainfall zone, H. J. Cooke (1975) has recorded evidence for a period of increased rainfall beginning about 2400 bc. It is surely significant that another arid region, that of the central Cape Province and western Orange Free State, was largely uninhabited during the period 7500 to 2600 bc (J. Deacon, 1974): there, the appearance of mode 5 industries was broadly contemporary with the corresponding event in south-western Zambia.

The division of the Zambian mode 5 industries into two distinct regional traditions has led to inconsistencies and, on occasion, to the attribution of industries to a particular tradition on geographical rather than typological grounds. Both Gabel (1967) and the present writer (Phillipson and Phillipson, 1970) have drawn attention to the fact that, although the Chifubwa Stream aggregate from near Solwezi has been plausibly subsumed into 'Nachikufan I' (J. D. Clark, 1958c; S. F. Miller, 1969), the microlithic industries of the Copperbelt region, which intervenes geographically between the latter site and the main concentration of 'Nachikufan' occurrences, show more features in common with the 'Wilton' industries of the south. The most detailed analysis so far undertaken of a Copperbelt microlithic aggregate is of that from Chiwemupula, in which curved-backed geometrics and convex-backed flakes form a majority of the intentionally retouched implements, angled-backed geometrics being rare. Scrapers were not common and were mainly convex (Phillipson and Phillipson, 1970). These Copperbelt industries, although no radiocarbon dates are yet available, may now be regarded as late and postdating the 'Nachikufan I' occurrences of the same

general area. 'Nachikufan I' industries are now seen to have a distribution wider than those of the later phases of the original 'Nachikufan' scheme, and the Copperbelt 'Wilton' is found to be one of the varied local industries which were contemporary parallel developments with the later 'Nachikufan' phases. Likewise, the final phase of occupation at Leopard's Hill yielded an industry akin to that from Chipongwe Cave, only 50 km to the west, which has sometimes been classed as 'Wilton' (J. D. Clark, 1955). The final Leopard's Hill industry has already been noted as one of the anomalous aggregates loosely and provisionally grouped as 'Nachikufan III'.

It is now clear that the microlithic industries of Zambia during the last three millennia bc are heterogeneous and that, although regional clustering is apparent, we are not yet in a position to define discrete groups, or indeed to state whether or not such groups existed in the range of variation. The 'Zambian Wilton', 'Nachikufan IIB' and 'III', together with the Makwe Industry of the east, take their places as parallel developments from a common ancestral tradition of which 'Nachikufan I' was presumably the local representative. A similar status is possible for the Kaposwa Industry from Kalambo Falls. The 'Wilton' industries probably represent the first extension of the microlithic tradition south and west from the plateau zone to which its earlier manifestations had been restricted.

CONCLUDING OVERVIEW

Having surveyed the very incomplete evidence for regional sequences in the mode 5 industries of eastern and southern Africa, it is now necessary to examine these sequences in an attempt to provide a tentative outline of industrial development in the region as a whole. The great geographical and temporal lacunae in our knowledge, taken with the inadequacies of much of the data which are available, restrict such an attempt to the construction of working hypotheses which will doubtless require substantial modification in the future.

The earliest true microlithic mode 5 industry so far known in this region occurs in the eastern and south-central highlands, in a broad belt stretching from Lake Victoria to the Zambezi. Aggregates of these industries are dominated by small, narrow, convex-backed flakes accompanied by curved-backed geometrics and numerous varied scrapers; bored stones are found in the south but the presence of ground stone axes, while probable, is not yet certain. In Zambia, this industry has been referred to as 'Nachikufan I'; no general term has been applied to the clearly closely related aggregates from East African sites such as Munyama and Kisese. These industries were widespread by the fifteenth millennium bc, although their typological antecedents may be traced back for at least a further seven millennia.

'Nachikufan I' and its related contemporaries represent what is probably one of the earliest fully microlithic mode 5 industries in the world (see Allchin, 1966; J. G. D. Clark, 1969). They may be seen to have developed from a mode 3 predecessor such as that investigated at Kalemba in eastern Zambia, where the slow and gradual process of the emergence of the mode 5 technology is clearly illustrated. It has been argued above (p. 200) that this development was, at least in part, a response to a process of climatic amelioration which resulted in changed faunal distribution. This in turn inspired developments in hunting techniques and in the related technology. There is thus no reason to attribute this development to any other process than indigenous technological innovation. Indeed, granted the primogeniture of these mode 5 industries, it is difficult to see how any other origin can be postulated.

Clearly, while these developments were taking place, other mode 3 industries were being continued, probably by distinct communities, virtually unmodified by these developments. These relict mode 3 industries tend to occur in what were then more open, arid environments. That diverse industrial traditions could, however, co-exist in relatively close proximity is demonstrated by the discoveries at Leopard's Hill and at Twin Rivers, situated within 80 km of each other on the Lusaka plateau, of 'transitional' and mode 3 aggregates respectively, both apparently dated to around the twenty-first millennium bc. Significantly, Leopard's Hill is situated in well wooded plateau country, while Twin Rivers is on the edge of the open Kafue Flats.

Regional differentiation in mode 3 industries leading to the development of techniques of blade-production and backing and, ultimately, of mode 5 technology, can be traced far back in the archaeological record to at least the fortieth millennium bc. The 'transitional' industry at Kalemba, which is seen as fairly directly ancestral to 'Nachikufan I', saw the beginnings of such technology around 22,000 bc, while industries elsewhere on the south-central African plataeau retained a mode 3 technology into much more recent times. The type of demographic situation here postulated would explain the periodic intrusions of aggregates with high blade-frequencies observed by C. K. Cooke (1971) in the mode 3 Bambatan successions at Zombepata and Redcliff in Mashonaland, at a time between 40,000 and 35,000 bc.

Parallel developments in the 'Middle Stone Age' of South Africa have been noted briefly above. Here, development of techniques for producing backed microliths took place earlier and with greater refinement than in the south-central African region; by 40,000 bc such industries were established in the Drakensberg area and on the south coast. The Umguzan industry of Rhodesia occupies a comparable position. These industries, however, do not seem to have proved directly ancestral to fully mode 5 industries. At some sites they were displaced by classic mode 3 aggregates; at others aggregates of the Oakhurst Complex intervened between them and the microlithic 'Wilton'; elsewhere long hiatuses in the occupation are evidenced and no continuity can be demonstrated.

The significance of the Oakhurst Complex is as yet imperfectly understood. Its aggregates comprise substantial numbers of large flake scrapers to the virtual exclusion of other tool-types; its distribution extends from the Matopo Hills of Rhodesia southwards to the south Cape coast and westwards to Namibia. Throughout this area the Oakhurst Complex is dated to between the twelfth and the eighth millennia bc. Comparable industries are known from further north but they are at least some twelve millennia older; they also occupy a stratigraphical position preceding the first local microlithic industry, but appear to antedate rather than postdate the development of microlith-production techniques within the milieu of the final mode 3 industries. Evidence is here quoted from eastern Zambia for a typological progression from the scraper-dominated aggregates of that region to the microlithic 'Nachikufan I'; no such continuity is indicated south of the Zambezi between industries of the Oakhurst Complex and their microlithic successors. These factors, considered in conjunction with the unspecialised nature of the relevant technology, indicate that it would be both unwise and unnecessary to attempt to derive the industries of the Oakhurst Complex from these northern counterparts; a fuller understanding of the former industries seems not to be attainable in the present limited state of our knowledge.

Throughout the area of its distribution, the Oakhurst Complex was replaced by microlithic mode 5 industries attributed to the Wilton Industrial Complex. The term 'Wilton' has in the past been applied somewhat injudiciously to microlithic aggregates in many parts of sub-Saharan Africa; now that the sequence from the type-site has been fully described (J. Deacon, 1972) it would be wise to restrict the use of the term to aggregates from the Cape Province and neighbouring areas which have a close and demonstrable affinity to those from Wilton itself: otherwise the term will become once again a meaningless abstraction (pace Sampson, 1974). These Wilton industries show parallel developmental stages over a considerable area, but their ancestry remains unknown. Their contrast with industries of the Oakhurst Complex is marked, yet no continuity has been demonstrated with the earlier microlithic industries such as the Howiesonspoort. North of the Zambezi, microlithic industries had been produced for over seven millennia before the appearance of the Wilton Complex in South Africa; however there is no sign of a geographical connection between the two areas either in Rhodesia—where mode 5 industries appear to have been introduced, perhaps from the north, at about the same time as the corresponding event in the Cape—or in the Transvaal. An early southwards spread of microlithic technology may possibly be demonstrated by future research in the currently unexplored areas of Moçambique or south-western Angola/Namibia, but for the present it appears advisable to regard the Wilton Complex as possibly an autochthonous South African development, the antecedents of which are unclear.

In Rhodesia and Zambia, as in other parts of eastern Africa, microlithic industries continued until the close of the Stone Age. They have been interpreted above as basically descended from the initial mode 5 industry of 'Nachikufan I' type and as showing increasing inter-regional differentiation. In these later industries, from about the eighth millennium bc onwards, curved- and angled-backed geometrics become dominant in place of the convex-backed flakes of the 'Nachikufan I' industries. Ground stone axes, the presence of which in 'Nachikufan I' remains uncertain, are clearly evidenced in northern and central Zambia from at least the eighth millennium. Such artefacts are extremely rare in southern Africa and also, at this time, in East Africa and the Congo basin; their appearance in Zambia in this context was very likely an independent development. Mode 5 industries do not appear to have spread to the Upper Zambezi area or to the interior plateau of South Africa until the last three millennia bc, when they replaced a late continuance of mode 3 technology in those areas. Their advent to these regions may be linked with the increased temperature and rainfall which is attested at this time.

The dominant lesson of this enquiry is emphasis on the ability of indigenous technological development to proceed on broadly parallel courses at different times, resulting on occasion in the presence of contemporary industries in adjacent areas at markedly contrasting stages of development. These parallel processes are not to be regarded as occurring *in vacuo*, without contact, inspiration and mutual influence; on the other hand the idiosyncracies and independence of many of the local successions are such that we can safely preclude the

Possibility of a common ancestor for the microlithic industries of sub-Saharan Africa, and state with some confidence that migration or even substantial population movement on other than a regional scale probably played a comparatively minor part in the dissemination of mode 5 technology through the sub-continent.

II. THE ANTIQUITY OF THE NEGROID PHYSICAL TYPE

The assumption has frequently been made in the past that the later stone-tool-using populations of south-central Africa were of Khoi-San physical stock, ancestral in general terms to that of the modern San and Khoikhoi. The Negroid stock, to which the modern Bantu-speaking population belongs, was thought to have been introduced through the same population movements as brought Iron Age culture to the region less than two thousand years ago (*e.g.* Hiernaux, 1974: 98; Oliver and Fagan, 1975: 94). In this volume, however, Dr Hertha de Villiers has presented detailed descriptions of pre-Iron Age human skeletal material from eastern Zambia which shows many physical features which are characteristic of recent South African Negroid populations. There are several possible interpretations for these observations, which must here be evaluated.

It is generally recognised that the Khoi-San and Negroid stocks share a common ancestry, although they may latterly have evolved in relative isolation, the former in the south-central and southern African savanna and the latter in the sudanic region and in West Africa (Brothwell, 1963; Tobias, 1966). In the Nigerian forest-belt, the Negroid stock is attested from the tenth millennium bc (Brothwell and Shaw, 1971). More recently, G. P. Rightmire (1974) has demonstrated that several of the skeletons recovered from associations with pre-Iron Age mode 5 industries in Kenya are metrically much closer to modern Negroid populations than to any other African physical type. The earliest of these East African Negroid-related individuals was recovered from Lukenya Hill near Nairobi, in a level containing an early mode 5 industry related to

'Nachikufan I' and dated as early as the sixteenth millennium bc (Gramly and Rightmire, 1973): it is thus significantly older than any of the apparently Negroid remains from eastern Zambia, all of which were associated with the Makwe Industry.

It would therefore be not unreasonable to suggest that the makers of many of the mode 5 industries of eastern Africa, at least as far south as the Zambezi, were—contrary to past belief—of a physical stock which shares much in common with that of the modern Negroids. Pre-Iron Age remains from even further south have also been suggested as related to the same population (Tobias, 1958).

There is, however, one important proviso which must be borne in mind. The comparative Negroid material which de Villiers (1968), Rightmire (1974; 1975) and others have used in their investigations is all modern, and mostly from South Africa. It is thus itself the result of a massive process of interbreeding between Iron Age and pre-Iron Age populations. The archaeological populations which appear to resemble modern Negroids may thus not be of true Negroid stock in the commonly accepted (although indefinable) sense of the term. Many physical traits which survive in the modern Negroid populations may in fact be basically pre-Negroid, later absorbed into the Negroid stock. At present, this is pure hypothesis, which cannot be proved or disproved until large, well dated collections of archaeological human skeletal material have been recovered from various regions and periods, thus relieving us of our present almost complete dependence upon exclusively modern comparative series.

III. THE EARLY IRON AGE

The inception of the Early Iron Age in south-central Africa represents the introduction of a culture which contrasts in a very pronounced manner with those which had gone before. The available archaeological evidence strongly indicates that the inhabitants of this region before the advent of the Early Iron Age were completely ignorant of food-production techniques, of pottery-manufacture and of metallurgy. They were hunters and gatherers, leading a generally mobile existence, living in small groups and basing themselves at caves or rock-shelters such as those excavated at Makwe and Kalemba in eastern Zambia, or at small, temporary, open-air camp-sites. In contrast, the Early Iron Age folk were farmers who herded domestic animals and who cultivated crops, who were accomplished potters and workers of iron and (in some areas) copper. They lived in substantial villages comprising houses built of puddled mud applied over a wooden framework. Economically, they introduced the way of life which has continued in rural areas of south-central Africa into modern times. The coming of the Early Iron Age may be said to have established the course of subsequent internal historical

developments throughout the region.

The fully evolved form in which these numerous cultural innovations suddenly appear in the archaeological record of south-central Africa indicates that they were not local developments, but that the Early Iron Age complex of which they form part was introduced into the region in a fully fledged form, its formative processes having taken place elsewhere. The evidence for the origin of the Early Iron Age industries will be discussed below.

The Early Iron Age in eastern, central and southern Africa is regarded as belonging to a single industrial complex both on account of its chronological integrity and because its pottery can be shown to represent a single clearly defined tradition (Soper, 1971). The geographical distribution of the known sites attributed to the Early Iron Age Industrial Complex is shown in fig. 135, which also indicates the several local groups which have been recognised largely on the basis of detailed studies of the pottery typology. It should be emphasised that several of the apparent lacunae in the Early Iron Age distribution are probably due primarily to the uneven coverage of research. This is almost certainly the reason for the apparent absence of sites in much of Angola and Mocambique; but it is clear nevertheless that the Early Iron Age Industrial Complex never penetrated far to the south of the Vaal into the greater part of the Cape Province, southern Namibia or the desert regions of Botswana. Its absence from much

of the Kenya highlands is also well attested. Two distinct streams may be recognised in the Early Iron Age Industrial Complex, as shown in fig. 135. These can now be demonstrated to be chronologically, as well as typologically, distinct (D. W. Phillipson, 1975).

The earliest known manifestation of the Early Iron Age Industrial Complex is recognised in the Lake Victoria region, where it is characterised by the

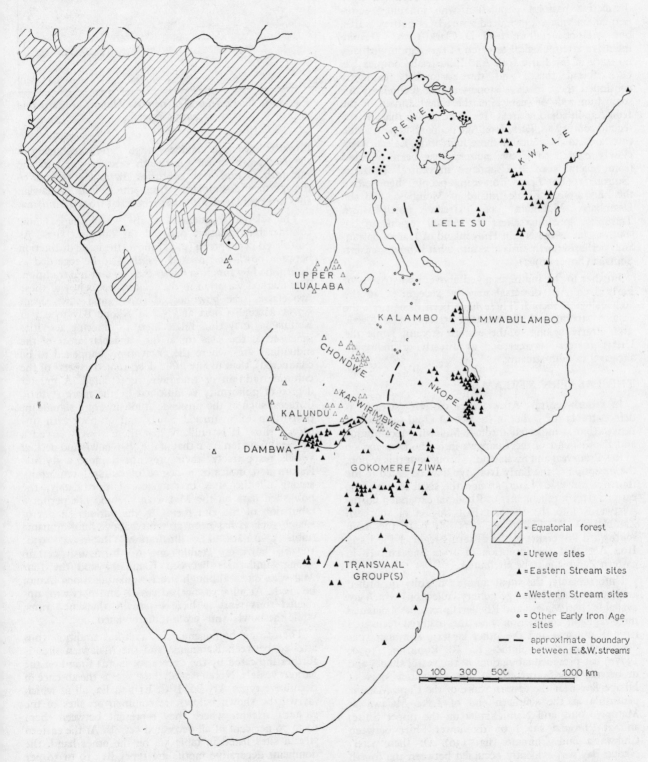

Fig. 135. Distribution map of Early Iron Age sites in sub-equatorial Africa, distinguishing the eastern and western streams as well as their component groups.

distinctive pottery known as Urewe ware. It was established in the regions of north-western Tanzania and Rwanda immediately south-west of the lake during the closing centuries of the last millennium bc. By about ad 200 the makers of Urewe ware had spread around the lake to southern Uganda and the Winam (Kavirondo) Gulf area of south-western Kenya (*ibid*.).

To the east of the Urewe ware zone lie the rift highlands of southern Kenya and northern Tanzania, which had for several centuries been occupied by a distinctive pastoral population who inhabited semi-permanent villages, produced a variety of pottery wares, but were not metallurgists (J. D. Clark, 1970*b*). Despite intensive archaeological research in this region, virtually no trace of the Early Iron Age Industrial Complex has been found there; and the pastoralists evidently continued their mode 5 stone-working technology for some hundreds of years after the establishment of the Iron Age in adjacent areas. It can be shown that, by the second century ad, Early Iron Age people had penetrated eastwards to the south of these highlands. Lelesu ware, closely related to Urewe pottery, has been reported from several sites in Usandawe in central Tanzania (Sutton, 1968). These iron-using people then settled the hills around Kwale, inland of Mombasa, and the Usambara Mountains of extreme north-eastern Tanzania, spreading along the coastal regions to the south as far as the Ngulu Hills inland of Dar es Salaam and, perhaps, northwards also into what is now southern Somalia (Soper, 1967).

Further to the south, as noted above, two streams of Early Iron Age dispersal may be recognised in the archaeological record. These have been designated the eastern stream and the western stream. The Kwale sites clearly belong to the eastern stream, while the Urewe material is regarded as directly or indirectly ancestral to both streams.

THE EASTERN STREAM

In south-central Africa the eastern stream is demonstrably the earlier of the two. A rapid southwards penetration is indicated through Malawi, Moçambique and Zambia east of the Luangwa into Rhodesia and on to the Transvaal and Swaziland. Throughout this region, the inception of the Early Iron Age may be dated to the fourth century ad. Later, around the sixth century, the eastern stream inhabitants of Rhodesia expanded north-westwards into the Victoria Falls region of southern Zambia (D. W. Phillipson, 1975). It is to the main southward dispersal of the eastern stream of the Early Iron Age that the inception of Iron Age culture in eastern Zambia is to be attributed.

Unfortunately, the small number of fully quantified analyses of Early Iron Age pottery collections which are available from Malawi and Rhodesia precludes a detailed inter-regional comparison with the material recovered from Kamnama and the other eastern Zambian sites described in this volume. K. R. Robinson (1970; 1973*a*) has provided tabulations of the vessel shapes and decorative motifs present at his excavated sites of Nkope Bay near the eastern shore of the Cape Maclear peninsula at the southern end of Lake Malawi, at Matope Court and Namichimba on the upper Shire, and at Phwadzi site I on the lower Shire between Chikwawa and Chiromo (fig. 136). Of these sites, Nkope Bay was evidently occupied between the fourth and the ninth centuries ad, and Matope Court around the seventh to ninth centuries, while Namichimba and

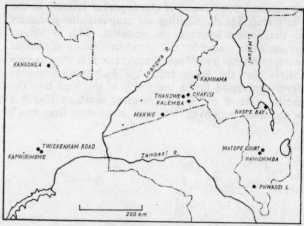

Fig. 136. *Early Iron Age sites in Malawi, eastern and central Zambia.*

Phwadzi have each yielded a single date, respectively in the late tenth to early eleventh centuries and in the mid-fifth to mid-sixth centuries. In tables 55 and 56 the pottery assemblages from these four Malawian sites are compared with that recovered from Kamnama.

The relative frequencies of the vessel shapes show considerable variation between the different sites. As postulated in chapter 4 (p. 21) above, the basic distinction between bowls and necked vessels is to be regarded as determined by function rather than by cultural tradition. The marked variation in the relative frequency of these two classes (the bowl/necked vessel ratio varies from 5.7 at Matope Court and 5.2 at Nkope Bay to 0.3 at Kamnama) may thus relate more to differing activities practised at the sites (or at the particular areas of the individual sites where the excavations happened to be conducted), than to any more deep-rooted aspects of the cultural tradition or traditions represented. A greater degree of uniformity is indicated by the more stylistic features, such as the presence at all sites of a significant proportion of in-turned bowls and of pots with up-turned rims. It is unlikely that these vessels served a different function from that of the open bowls and necked vessels respectively; their presence is more a stylistic feature and indicates a degree of cultural uniformity among all the sites investigated. Unfortunately, the published data on the Malawian sites do not permit a tabulation of the rim forms of the various shapes of vessel, such as has been presented above for Kamnama (table 3, p. 40). The illustrations (Robinson, 1970; 1973*a*), however, enable one to distinguish certain strong similarities between Kamnama and the four Malawian sites, although precise quantifications cannot be given. At all sites, necked vessels and pots with up-turned rims tend to have externally thickened rims, while the bowls' rims are undifferentiated.

The strong homogeneity of cultural tradition thus attested between Kamnama and the Malawian sites is further indicated by the decorative motifs found on the various vessels. Notable at all these sites is the absence of decorative types A1, B2, B/C, E1 and E2, all of which (as will be shown below) are common on sites of the western stream, where they represent between them 62 to 76 per cent of all decorated vessels. At the eastern stream sites listed in table 56, on the other hand, the dominant decorative motifs are types B1 (19 to 36 per cent), C1 (up to 37 per cent) and D1 (8 to 31 per cent).

The affinity between these five pottery assemblages,

Table 55. Comparison of vessel shapes of the Kamnama Early Iron Age pottery with those recorded at selected eastern stream sites in central and southern Malawi

Vessel shape	Kamnama	Nkope Bay	Matope Court	Namichimba	Phwadzi
Open bowl	14%	55%	41%	8%	14%
In-turned bowl	10%	28%	44%	40%	35%
Globular vessel	—	1%	—	3%	4%
Necked vessel	65%	6%	15%	41%	44%
Pot with up-turned rim	11%	10%	—	8%	3%
Total in sample	140	368	34	75	130

Table 56. Comparison of decorative motifs on the Kamnama Early Iron Age pottery with those recorded at selected eastern stream sites in central and southern Malawi

Decorative type	Kamnama	Nkope Bay	Matope Court	Namichimba	Phwadzi
A1	—	8%	2%	9%	16%
A2	7%	19%	33%	36%	22%
B1	33%	—	—	—	—
B2	—	—	—	—	1%
B3	—	—	—	—	4%
C1	2%	37%	16%	32%	24%
C2	1%	5%	—	2%	1%
B/C	—	—	—	—	19%
D1	29%	20%	31%	8%	—
D2	8%	4%	6%	—	—
E1	—	—	—	—	—
E2	—	—	—	—	—
F	3%	6%	6%	11%	1%
G	2%	1%	6%	—	—
Atypical	—	—	—	—	17%
Undecorated	15%	—	—	—	—
Total in sample	231	354	49	96	314

including that from Kamnama, is thus remarkably close, and there can be little doubt that all five sites, with other Early Iron Age occurrences in eastern Zambia and in central and southern Malawi, should be attributed to a single group, or regional industry. Robinson (1970; 1973a) has proposed the name Nkope ware for this type of Early Iron Age pottery: the name Nkope may thus appropriately be given to the group as a whole.

Robinson (1973b) has already provided a comparison between the pottery of the Nkope group and its eastern stream neighbours, Mwabulambo ware in northern Malawi and Gokomere/Ziwa ware in Rhodesia. In the absence of any fully quantified analyses for either of these neighbouring groups, only a generalised contrast may be made. As noted above, the distinction between Mwabulambo and Nkope wares is poorly defined, and there may eventually prove to be a typological progression from one to the other as one moves southwards through Malawi. Mwabulambo ware (Robinson and Sandelowsky, 1968) shares some characteristics with the pottery of the Kalambo group in northern Zambia (D. W. Phillipson, 1968a; J. D. Clark, 1974), and also with Kwale ware from further to the north. However, the Kwale affinities are stronger in Nkope than in Mwabulambo, notably in the forms of the in-turned bowls and in the fluted lips of some vessels. This has led to the suggestion (D. W. Phillipson, 1976a) that there may have been a distinct lowland facies of the eastern stream which dispersed southwards to the east of Lake Malawi and influenced the Nkope ceramic tradition at the south end of the lake. Significantly, these Kwale-like traits are not represented in Gokomere/Ziwa ware.

This latter material is widely distributed through eastern and south-eastern Rhodesia. Closely related Zhizo ware occurs in the south-western parts of the country, notably around Bulawayo (Robinson, 1966b; Huffman, 1974). Gokomere/Ziwa ware is best known from Mabveni in the Chibi District and from Gokomere, north of Fort Victoria (Robinson, 1961; 1963), as well as from sites in the Inyanga region further to the north-east (Summers, 1958). It is characterised by necked vessels bearing diagonal comb-stamped decoration (type B1) on their externally thickened rim bands, and by a variety of open bowls. Later developments which took place in this region around the sixth century included an expansion of settlement north-westwards to the Victoria Falls region and the establishment of contact with the western stream of the Early Iron Age, which arrived in central Zambia late in the fifth century and penetrated also south of the Zambezi into north-western Mashonaland (D. W. Phillipson, 1976a).

THE WESTERN STREAM

It is appropriate also to compare the Early Iron Age pottery of eastern Zambia with that recovered from regions lying to the west of the Luangwa river. In the latter area, the Early Iron Age is attributed to the western stream, and greater typological differences are apparent between it and the eastern Zambian material than were demonstrated between the latter and contemporary eastern stream wares from Malawi. The western stream material with which comparison will be made is that attributed to the Kapwirimbwe and Chondwe groups (D. W. Phillipson, 1968a), located respectively in the Lusaka area and on the Zambian

Copperbelt. The Kapwirimbwe group sites involved are Kapwirimbwe itself, dated to around the fifth century ad (D. W. Phillipson, 1968c; 1968d) and Twickenham Road, Lusaka, which appears to belong to the tenth and eleventh centuries (D. W. Phillipson, 1970). The Chondwe group is represented by the Kangonga site near Ndola, the occupation of which is probably not later than the eighth century (D. W. Phillipson, 1972a). The locations of these sites are indicated in fig. 136. Comparison has been facilitated by the fact that these assemblages were analysed by the present writer, using a system and terminology conformable with that employed above for the description of the eastern Zambian material.

Tables 57 and 58 provide details of the vessel shapes and decoration of the Kapwirimbwe and Chondwe group pottery contrasted with that from Kamnama: a comparison between the pottery styles of the two western groups has been presented elsewhere (D. W. Phillipson, 1972a: 119–20). It is seen that, while in-turned bowls are rare on western stream sites, their place is taken by open bowls with internally thickened rims which contrast with the undifferentiated rims that predominate on the open bowls from Kamnama. On the necked vessels, externally thickened rims are much more common at the eastern site. Fluted lips are not recorded on Kapwirimbwe and Chondwe group sites, and bevelled ones are represented only in the latter group, where they are rare. In decoration, the contrast is even more marked. False-relief chevron stamping is a highly characteristic feature of pottery of the Kapwirimbwe and Chondwe groups, where it frequently occurs either alone (type A1) or in combination with other designs. The relatively elaborate hatched designs E1 and E2 are also common at these western sites. All three types are, however, completely unrepresented in eastern Zambia. Comb-stamped designs are always rare in the west but, in the form of type B1, are the commonest decoration at Kamnama. It is clear that the eastern Zambian Early Iron Age pottery has much closer affinities with the Malawian Nkope ware than it does with the western stream material from central Zambia.

In order to account for the discontinuity in the Early Iron Age pottery traditions which is attested along the

Table 57. Comparison of vessel shapes and rim forms of the Kamnama Early Iron Age pottery with those recorded at western stream sites of the Kapwirimbwe and Chondwe groups

Vessel shape	Rim form	Kamnama	Kapwirimbwe	Twickenham Road	Kangonga
Open bowl	Undifferentiated	12%	7%	4%	39%
	Int. thickened	2%	27%	20%	17%
	Bil. thickened	—	1%	—	10%
	Ext. thickned	—	2%	4%	—
In-turned bowl	Undifferentiated	10%	1%	—	1%
	Bil. thickened	—	—	—	—
Globular vessel	Undifferentiated	—	3%	4%	—
	Int. thicknened	—	2%	1%	—
	Ext. thickened	—	2%	—	—
	Bil. thickened	—	—	—	—
Necked vessel	Undifferentiated	14%	26%	24%	1%
	Int. thickened	—	4%	12%	9%
	Ext. thickened	51%	23%	19%	2%
	Bil. thickened	—	—	—	17%
Pot with up-turned rim	Ext. thickened	11%	—	—	3%
Waisted	Undifferentiated	—	—	5%	—
	Int. thickened	—	1%	5%	—
Total in sample		140	158	84	88

Table 58. Comparison of decorative motifs on the Kamnama Early Iron Age pottery with those recorded at western stream sites of the Kapwirimbwe and Chondwe groups

Decorative type	Kamnama	Kapwirimbwe	Twickenham Road	Kangonga
A1	—	18%	41%	14%
A2	7%	4%	3%	2%
B1	33%	—	—	1%
B2	—	—	—	2%
B3	—	2%	3%	10%
C1	2%	4%	2%	5%
C2	1%	1%	—	10%
B/C	—	—	—	45%
D1	29%	16%	3%	1%
D2	8%	3%	6%	1%
E1	—	17%	19%	1%
E2	—	18%	13%	2%
F	3%	—	—	—
G	2%	—	—	—
Atypical	—	—	—	—
Undecorated	15%	3%	5%	7%
Total in sample	231	245	98	214

approximate line of the Luangwa valley, it is necessary to return to the general survey and to account for the presence of two distinct streams of Early Iron Age dispersal in south-central Africa. It was shown above how the eastern stream, ultimately derived from the Urewe settlements of the Lake Victoria region, had penetrated southwards down the eastern side of the sub-continent between the Luangwa valley and the Indian Ocean as far as the Vaal river by the fourth century ad. Further to the west, the picture is less clear because of the very incomplete geographical coverage of the archaeological research which has so far been under-

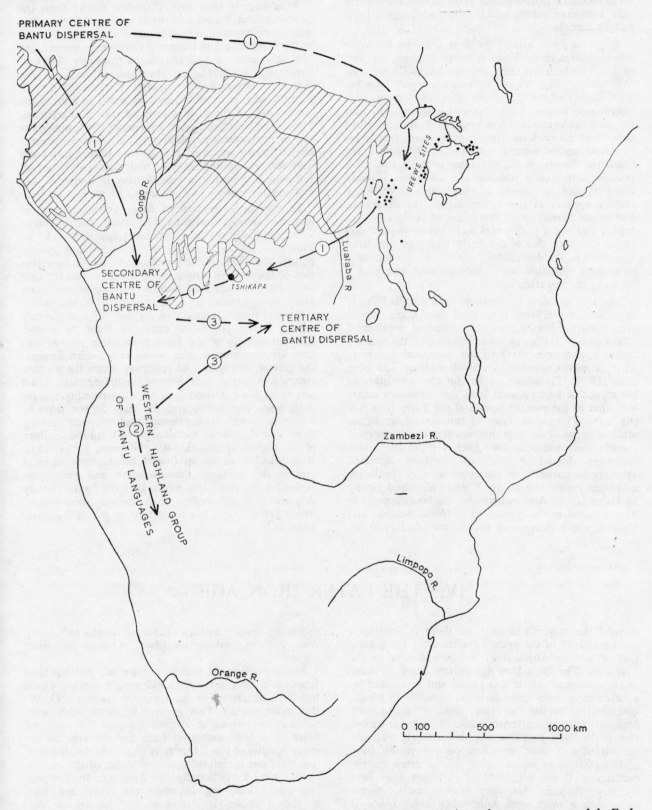

Fig. 137. *The three main stages in the dispersal of Bantu-speaking people which gave rise to the western stream of the Early Iron Age. The present area of the equatorial forest is shown hatched.*

taken. A general picture may, however, be proposed. It receives some degree of confirmation from linguistic evidence (Dalby, 1975), as has been suggested elsewhere by the present writer (D. W. Phillipson, 1976a). Discussion of the western stream of the Early Iron Age is of further relevance here because of the part which it can be shown to have played in the development of the later Iron Age culture which subsequently spread into eastern Zambia.

Attention must initially be drawn to the discovery near Tshikapa in the Kasai province of Zaire (fig. 137) of pottery which can fairly be regarded as Urewe ware (Nenquin, 1959), despite its location some 1300 km west-south-west of the main area of Urewe ware distribution around Lake Victoria. This material may be taken as evidence for a southward and westward spread of Early Iron Age people from the inter-lacustrine region around the southern fringes of the equatorial forests. A slightly later stage of this same process is probably indicated in the area between Kinshasa and the mouth of the Congo river. Here, pottery appears in the archaeological record around 200 bc (de Maret, 1975), but is not of Early Iron Age type. Later wares in this region, however, show strong similarities with that of the Early Iron Age Industrial Complex (e.g. Mortelmans, 1962). It is tempting to suggest that this latter material may represent a fusion of the two traditions.

The area of Zaire and north-western Angola lying to the south of the lower reaches of the Congo river is seen as having been a secondary centre of dispersal of Bantu speech (Dalby, 1975 and references), the primary centre having been north of the equatorial forests in what is now Cameroon. Detailed evidence has been cited (D. W. Phillipson, 1976a) for the correlation of the spread of Bantu speech from this secondary centre with that of the western stream of the Early Iron Age (fig. 137). The initial stages of this spread are better attested linguistically than they are in the archaeological record: there seems to have been a rapid southward expansion through Angola into northern Namibia, resulting linguistically in the appearance of the Bantu languages referred to as the Western Highland Group by Heine (1973). Archaeologically, this event appears to have resulted in the passage of domestic animals and knowledge of techniques of pottery-manufacture to the

Khoi-San-speaking stone-tool-using peoples of southern Namibia and the Cape Province of South Africa. The presence of both traits in the south-western Cape by at least the fourth century ad (Schweitzer, 1974) provides a provisional *terminus ante quem* for this southward spread of Iron Age culture.

At a slightly later date, a further spread from the north-western Angolan dispersal centre, this time in a general eastward direction, resulted in the introduction of the Early Iron Age Industrial Complex to western and central Zambia and to the Shaba (formerly Katanga) province of Zaire. The western stream of the Early Iron Age is well attested in the archaeological record of these regions, and its inception may be dated to around the second half of the fifth century ad (D. W. Phillipson, 1975). The map (fig. 135, p. 207) shows the approximate line of easternmost penetration of the western stream—the line along which its practitioners presumably came into contact, around ad 500, with the eastern stream folk who had settled in areas further to the south and east some one and a half centuries earlier.

In this area, the western Bantu expansion was, at least temporarily, contained. The known distribution of sites, especially on the Zambian Copperbelt (D. W. Phillipson, 1972a), suggests that a significantly greater density of Early Iron Age population soon built up in this part of the western stream's territory than was the case further to the east. This resulted in the apparently more rapid disappearance as a distinct entity of the earlier stone-tool-using population. Possible contributory factors to this population expansion were the greater inherent fertility of the Lusaka, southern plateau and Copperbelt regions in comparison with eastern Zambia, the greater variety of food resources which the western stream folk had at their disposal (including cattle and a variety of West African food crops), a possibly sparser indigenous population and the rich copper deposits which attracted wide-ranging trade-contacts during Early Iron Age times, including some from the territory of the eastern stream (D. W. Phillipson, 1972a: 121). It is possible to see in this archaeologically attested process of settlement, consolidation and population expansion the conditions which gave rise to the tertiary dispersal of Bantu-speakers from this very same region, which Dalby (1975) has recognised on purely linguistic grounds.

IV.   THE LATER IRON AGE

Around the eleventh century ad there is attested a sudden change in the pottery traditions of the greater part of eastern Africa from southern Kenya to the Transvaal. The Early Iron Age pottery ceases to occur in archaeological sites of this period and is replaced by a rather more heterogeneous series of wares in which, nevertheless, certain unifying features are readily apparent. The characteristic thickened or in-turned rims of the Early Iron Age become extremely rare, and the majority of later Iron Age pottery vessels have undifferentiated or tapered rims. Undecorated vessels, particularly at the beginning of the later Iron Age, are more frequent than they were in earlier times. Decoration is more areal, rather than banded, and is concentrated on the body of the vessel instead of on the rim. Comb-stamping is the characteristic decorative

technique from southern Tanzania southwards, with cord-rouletting taking its place in more northerly regions.

In this book we are primarily concerned with the later Iron Age pottery of northern and eastern Zambia, which has been attributed to the Luangwa tradition (D. W. Phillipson, 1974). This pottery is today made over virtually the whole of Zambia lying to the east and north of a line stretching from Lubumbashi to the lower reaches of the Kafue river (fig. 138). Its distribution does not therefore equate with that of the eastern stream of the Early Iron Age, for it includes the Copperbelt and Lusaka regions where the Early Iron Age, as shown above, is clearly of the western stream. Within Zambia, modern peoples who make Luangwa tradition pottery (see plate Ia) include the Chewa,

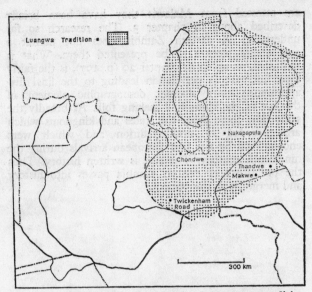

Fig. 138. The present distribution of Luangwa tradition pottery in Zambia, with sites which have provided dating evidence for its inception.

Nsenga, Ngoni, Tumbuka, Soli, Lala, Lamba, Bisa, Bemba, Lungu, Mambwe and the northern (Kazembe's) Lunda. It is also made in adjacent regions of Zaire, Malawi, Moçambique and Rhodesia.

Through the greater part of its area of distribution, the pottery of the Luangwa tradition makes a seemingly sudden appearance and presents a marked typological contrast with the preceding Early Iron Age wares. The date of this interface is securely placed around the second half of the eleventh century ad (D. W. Phillipson, 1975). The sequences investigated at Chondwe (Mills and Filmer, 1972) and Twickenham Road, Lusaka (D. W. Phillipson, 1970), emphasise the suddenness of the change from one pottery style to the other although, as argued above, there may have been a brief period of overlap between the two traditions in eastern Zambia. At Nakapapula rock-shelter (D. W. Phillipson, 1969), a comparable sequence is preserved, and a date of around the eleventh century is indicated for the inception of the Luangwa tradition. In all areas, the contrast between the Luangwa tradition pottery and that of the preceding Early Iron Age is pronounced, and there is no clear evidence for a transition or integration from one to the other. The suddenness of the break suggests that the Luangwa tradition may owe its introduction to the arrival of a new population element.

It is noteworthy that Luangwa tradition domestic pottery is today made exclusively by women. It has been argued (D. W. Phillipson, 1974) that potting in Early Iron Age times was done by men: the fact that the opposite sex was responsible for pottery manufacture among the later Iron Age immigrant groups would explain the remarkable clarity of the break between the two traditions and the complete lack of continuity of characteristic Early Iron Age traits into the Luangwa tradition.

Despite this marked contrast between the two types of pottery, it is apparent that the Early Iron Age ware which shows greatest affinity to the Luangwa tradition is that of the Chondwe group. Type B/C decoration, comprising blocks of comb-stamping delineated by grooves, is a characteristic feature of Early Iron Age pottery from the Copperbelt region, in which it becomes

progressively more frequent with the passage of time: this is also a major technique in the Luangwa tradition. In the Chondwe group also, exaggeratedly thickened rims are less frequent than in other Early Iron Age wares, and there is a greater incidence of undifferentiated rims which, with tapered forms, are the norm in Luangwa tradition pottery assemblages. It may be suggested that the currently unknown ancestor of the latter ware may prove to be more closely related to the Chondwe group pottery than to that of any other Early Iron Age group which is at present recognised. It may thus be suggested that the development of the Luangwa tradition out of an Early Iron Age predecessor may have taken place in an area not too far removed from the modern Copperbelt, perhaps to the north or west, from which it spread out eastwards during the eleventh century ad.

Such an origin in what is now the Shaba province of Zaire is in keeping with the evidence of several other cultural traits which, in south-eastern Africa, are associated with the later Iron Age. For example, flange-welded clapperless iron gongs have for many centuries been employed as "insignia of political leadership" (Vansina, 1969) in later Iron Age societies in this region, as at Great Zimbabwe (Garlake, 1973: 133-4) and Ingombe Ilede (Fagan, 1969: 92). The earliest archaeological occurrence of such objects, and the only one which appears to belong to the Early Iron Age, is in the great cemeteries of Sanga and Katoto on the upper Lualaba in Shaba, dated—probably—to the last quarter of the first millennium ad (Hiernaux, de Longrée and de Buyst, 1971; Hiernaux, Maquet and de Buyst, 1972). In so far as oral traditions relating to the early movements of later Iron Age peoples can be distinguished from those of their more recently arrived rulers, an origin in this region is compatible both with the clan histories themselves and with the relative ease with which later migrants from the same general region appear to have established themselves in political authority over the earlier arrivals (p. 195, above).

The hypothesis here proposed also receives support from linguistic studies. It has been recognised for some years that the Bantu languages on the eastern side of sub-equatorial Africa show a much greater degree of homogeneity than do those further to the west (Guthrie, 1962; Greenberg, 1972; Ehret, 1972). Bernd Heine (1973) has closely defined the area of this homogeneity and has named the languages involved the Eastern Highland Group. These languages are believed to have been derived from a common ancestor at a much more recent date than were the more diverse Bantu languages encountered further to the west. The geographical distribution of the Eastern Highland languages correlates much more precisely with that of the later Iron Age industries such as the Luangwa tradition than it does with that of the eastern stream of the Early Iron Age. It is fully in keeping with the linguistic material presented above to attribute the dispersal of the Eastern Highland Group of Bantu languages to the same movement of population as introduced to the same area the later Iron Age pottery industries. More detailed arguments in support of this correlation have been presented elsewhere (D. W. Phillipson, 1976b). Here it is sufficient to point out that Heine (1973), Ehret (1973) and Dalby (1975) all postulate that the Eastern Highland Bantu languages developed in the region of what is now south-eastern Zaire shown as the 'tertiary centre of

Bantu dispersal' on fig. 137 (p. 211). This is fully concordant with the arguments set out above for the area of origin of the Luangwa tradition. It is therefore permissible to conclude that the Luangwa tradition was brought to eastern Zambia by the same movement of population as led to the dispersal of the Eastern Highland languages.

Later developments in the archaeology of the later Iron Age in eastern Zambia and adjacent regions are not well attested. The Luangwa tradition pottery from Makwe (p. 104) shows some evidence for typological change with time, but this cannot be correlated with data from other sites. Regional later Iron Age industries are attested from Malawi: they have been briefly described above in chapter 3. The research so far undertaken in eastern Zambia does not permit a comparable picture to be presented there. What is indicated, as noted in chapter 20 (p. 197), is the fairly rapid increase in population leading to the final disappearance as a distinct demographic element of the last of the stone-tool-making folk. At broadly the same time there arose the states and kingdoms which are recorded in oral tradition and which were encountered by the first European arrivals during the nineteenth century. The rest is written history. Thus the prehistory of eastern Zambia passes into history and merges with the present.

Backed Microliths Retaining Hafting Mastic

The Makwe excavations yielded fifty-two chipped stone implements, and eight fragments of such implements, to which adhered varying quantities of a hard resinous substance. When excavated, this material was pale pink in colour, but after complete drying it became powdery and almost white. The fact that this substance adhered almost exclusively to the backed areas of microliths, and that in nine instances it formed a cast of a neatly cut groove-shaped cavity into which the microlith had evidently been hafted, demonstrated that this substance was the remains of a mastic used for cementing the microliths to handles or hafts.

Four samples of the mastic were submitted for comment to Dr Jean H. Langenheim of the University of California at Santa Cruz. Dr Langenheim reports (*in litt.*, 14th December 1970): "we can make no sense whatsoever out of the infrared spectra. I have never seen any resin or gum with comparable patterns; I wonder if perhaps it is some kind of a mixture."

Implements with mastic were found at Makwe in horizons 2ii (three specimens), 3i (sixteen), 3ii (twenty-seven), 4i (ten) and 4ii (four specimens). All but four came from the area of grid squares A to C, 10 to 13 (see fig. 36, p. 68): they were thus concentrated in the dryer and more protected area of the rock-shelter. Six comparable specimens came from horizons Q and R at Kalemba.

Mastic is found only on retouched implements and occurs almost exclusively on geometrics: it occurs on only one backed flake (a transverse-backed specimen), and there are no backed points or scrapers at either site which show traces of mastic.* The proportions of retouched implements of each type, from Makwe horizons 2ii to 4ii inclusive, which bear mastic are shown in table 59. Unless otherwise stated, the following discussion is based upon specimens from Makwe.

Casts of grooves into which geometrics were hafted are formed by the mastic adhering to two pointed lunates, two triangular microliths, two *petits tranchets* (one of which comes from Kalemba), one trapezoidal microlith and three fragments. These specimens indicate that the grooves were neatly cut, with smooth sides and rounded ends. They were made only slightly, if at all, wider than the thickness of the geometric which they were to house, and the microlith was thus a tight fit. One *petit tranchet* and one trapezoidal microlith each show an area of wear on a ridge adjacent to the edge of the mastic: this is presumably due to friction against the haft at a point where there was no intervening mastic. In plan, however, the grooves appear often to have been made substantially longer than the microlith which they were to house, and to bear little relationship to the shape of the geometric. A substantial quantity of mastic was necessary to fill the resultant gap and it is this, adhering to the backing of the microliths, which

preserves the cast of the hafting groove. None of the casts retains texture or grain reflecting surface features of the hafts themselves: there is thus no evidence whether the latter were of bone, horn, wood or some other material. The burin-like backed points would have been suitable instruments for cutting the grooves, whichever material was used.

Study of the remnant mastic enables a certain amount of information to be gleaned concerning the manner in which various geometric types were hafted, and this in turn suggests possible purposes for the hafted implements. The evidence for each type may now be discussed.

Pointed lunates. Mastic is restricted to the backing and adjacent areas of the flat surfaces (fig. 139:1–6; plate XXXI:1–3). The two specimens retaining groove-casts indicate that mastic was restricted to approximately half of the area of the lunate, the whole of the sharp edge being free of mastic but about two thirds of the back being encased in it. Mastic covered the back right up to one tip but stopped well short of the other. This indicates that the lunate was hafted diagonally, with the edge at an angle of about 45 degrees to the long axis of the haft. It is clear from another specimen that the hafting groove was cut back approximately at right angles to the intended line of the lunate edge, as shown in fig. 139:5, thus resulting in a large area to be filled with mastic. It is probable that this technique, by bringing mastic into contact with a larger area of the haft, resulted in improved adhesion. The postulated method of hafting a pointed lunate is shown in fig. 140:1. The other eight mastic-retaining pointed lunates (one of which comes from Kalemba) have only traces of mastic, but the positioning of these traces is in keeping with hafting in the manner here described. Four of these nine specimens are eared, and in each case the eared tip appears to be the one free of mastic: in other words it was not embedded in the haft.

Asymmetrical lunates. The four specimens which retain traces of mastic (*e.g.* fig. 139:17–19) seem to have been hafted in the same way as the pointed lunates, with the sharper tip free of the haft (fig. 140:2).

Deep lunates. Despite the fact that mastic is retained on fourteen deep lunates (*e.g.* fig. 139:7–16; plate XXXI:4-6), which is its highest incidence on any implement type, there is none showing the cast of a hafting groove. Thick blobs of mastic on the backs of four specimens do not show signs of the original external margin of the mastic, yet they are so large that one would expect them to bear part of a groove-cast had the deep lunates been hafted in narrow grooves in the same manner as the pointed and asymmetrical lunates described above. Furthermore, there is no indication of diagonal setting: four examples retain traces of mastic at intervals along the whole extent of the back. There are seven specimens with tiny pieces of mastic adhering to the main surfaces to within a few millimetres of the edge and tips. It is concluded that

---

*Both backed points and scrapers are, however, scarce in Makwe Industry assemblages (see tables 14 and 37, above).

Table 59. Makwe: backed microliths retaining traces of mastic

Implement type	Total specimens in horizons 2ii–4ii	Retaining mastic
Pointed lunates	413	9 (2.2%)
Deep lunates	144	14 (9.7%)
Asymmetrical lunates	68	4 (5.9%)
Total curved-backed geometrics	625	27 (4.3%)
Triangular microliths	159	10 (6.3%)
Trapezoidal microliths	98	3 (3.1%)
Petits tranchets	176	11 (6.2%)
Total angled-backed geometrics	433	24 (5.5%)
Convex-backed flakes	368	—
Straight-backed flakes	20	—
Transverse-backed flakes	88	1
Total backed flakes	476	1 (0.2%)

some, at any rate, of the deep lunates were hafted in a large lump of mastic, perhaps 'free riding' (fig. 140:3), that is not directly in contact with the haft itself, as described by H. Deacon (1966).

Triangular microliths. On all eleven examples (including one from Kalemba) mastic is restricted to the back and to the adjacent areas of the main surfaces, both tips and the edge being invariably clear (fig. 139:20–23; plate XXXI:7). Two specimens from Makwe retain casts of the groove into which the microlith and mastic were originally inserted. In both cases the neatly tapered edge of this groove lies approximately at right angles to the edge of the microlith. One of these specimens (fig. 139:23) is of particular interest: on one side the mastic retains a groove-cast, while on the other it bears the imprint of a second microlith which had evidently been hafted adjacent to this specimen and in the same groove. No clue can be gained as to whether or not this second microlith was also triangular. It appears that mastic originally covered approximately the rear two-thirds of each microlith. It may be that the asymmetrical triangles, those with one right-angled and one sharp tip, were mounted in pairs with the right angles adjacent (fig. 140:4) to form a continuous cutting edge or, less probably, with the sharp tips adjacent to form a two-edged point (fig. 140: 5). A pair of identical-sized triangles, 'left- and right-pointing' as shown in fig. 140:5, were found together in horizon 3i in grid square C 11. Both retain traces of mastic.

Trapezoidal microliths. There are only three examples (fig. 139:24–26) which retain signs of mastic. One (fig. 139:26) shows a groove-cast which is unusual in that the groove was evidently cut at 45 degrees to the intended angle of the microlith's edge, that is nearly parallel to the line of the backing (fig. 140:6). This microlith would thus have had a close fit in its haft. The other two specimens retain only slight traces of mastic adhering to the backing, and no further conclusions can be drawn.

Petits tranchets. Of fifteen examples (including four from Kalemba) which retain traces of mastic, two (one from each site) display groove-casts. On these, and on several other specimens, fragments of mastic extend over the rear two-thirds of the main surfaces (fig. 139: 27–31; plate XXXI:8–10). The tips and edge are invariably clear of mastic. To haft these implements in this manner, deep grooves would have been needed. That

they were generally cut fully deep enough is demonstrated by several specimens on which mastic extends backwards from the rearmost part of the back. For grooves of such depth to be cut longitudinally would require a haft of substantial thickness, say at least 25 mm, if it were not to be seriously weakened by the cutting of the groove. For this reason it is suggested that *petits tranchets* may have been hafted transversely in the ends of their handles (fig. 140:7).

Transverse-backed flake. The only backed flake to which mastic still adheres is a small specimen with a backed truncation at right angles to the edge (fig. 139:32). A small piece of mastic adheres to the bulb of percussion, indicating that the implement was hafted at the striking-platform end (fig. 140:8). The backed truncation may thus in this case be due to utilisation as a scraper rather than to intentional retouch.

It can be seen that traces of mastic are restricted, with a single exception, to the geometrics: in fact there occur mastic-bearing specimens of each of the six varieties of geometric recognised at Makwe. The survival of mastic over periods of up to five thousand years is clearly due to the occurrence of exceptionally favourable physical and chemical conditions which one must assume were associated at random with specimens of all tool types which were originally hafted by means of mastic. The distribution of mastic-bearing specimens through different types in the assemblage may therefore be taken as broadly indicative of the original proportional incidence of this method of hafting on microliths of different types.

It is remarkable that, although all whole flakes, broken flakes, cores and shatter-chunks from Makwe were carefully examined, not a single specimen was found to bear any trace of mastic. It has been recognised for some time that in many, if not all, central African 'Late Stone Age' assemblages utilised pieces of so-called 'waste' greatly outnumber formally retouched implements (*e.g.* D. W. Phillipson, 1969). Although the physical condition of the Makwe assemblage is not suitable for a detailed microscopic analysis of edge wear such as was conducted on the comparable artefacts from Chiwemupula on the Zambian Copperbelt (Phillipson and Phillipson, 1970; see also p. 25, above), it is clear that the Makwe material is no exception in this regard (p. 79, above). There is thus a strong indication that casual tools of this type were not hafted. The reason for this is not hard to find. Hafting,

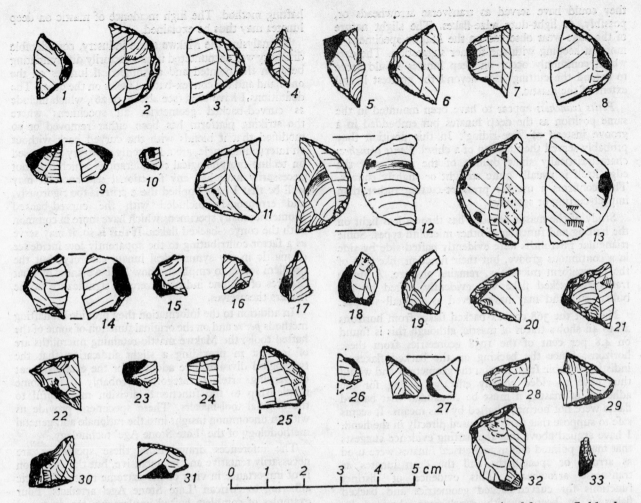

Fig. 139. Microliths from Makwe with mastic (shown here in solid black) adhering: 1–6—pointed lunates; 7–16—deep lunates; 17–19—asymmetrical lunates; 20–23—triangular micrcliths; 24–26—trapezoidal microliths; 27–31—petits tranchets; 32—transverse-backed flake; 33—backed fragment.

necessitating the shaping of a handle, cutting of a groove and preparation of mastic, must have been a time-consuming and laborious process compared with which the backing of a microlith would be rapid and straight-forward. Backing served not only as blunting to prevent the microlith, during use, from cutting through the mastic and splitting the handle, but also as keying to secure the better adhesion of the mastic. Backing in these cases should be regarded as an essential preparatory step to ensure secure and successful hafting. Similar blunting would, of course, be equally effective in protecting the fingers when an implement was used in the hand.

It is clear from the evidence discussed above that pointed and asymmetrical lunates were hafted in basically the same way, and that the exposure of a sharp tip and of the greater part of the sharp edges of the lunate was an important feature. The most probable function served by microliths mounted in this way is as spear- or arrow-barbs. The neatly worked ear found on one tip on four of these pointed lunates would increase the effectiveness and inextricability of such a barb.

Deep lunates were evidently mounted in a mass of mastic on the end of their handle. In such a manner

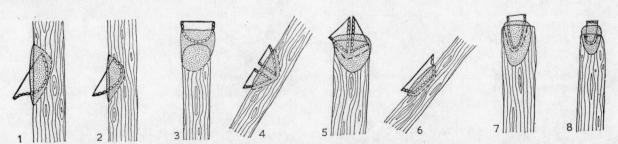

Fig. 140. Reconstructed hafting methods for backed microliths: 1—pointed lunate; 2—asymmetrical lunate; 3—deep lunate; 4, 5—triangular microliths; 6—trapezoidal microlith; 7—petit tranchet; 8—transverse-backed flake.

they could have served as transverse arrowheads or, possibly, as light-duty adze-flakes. The slight nature of the edge wear observed on the Makwe specimens is more in keeping with the former suggestion. The ears which commonly occur on deep lunates would serve to extend the cutting edge beyond the greatest lateral extent of the mastic.

Petits tranchets appear to have been mounted in the same position as the deep lunates but embedded in a groove instead of 'free-riding'. In this position they probably served the function of a chisel. *Petits tranchets* characteristically show dulling of the edge, and the edge itself is usually quite straight or slightly convex. This confirms a use for pressure-cutting rather than impact-cutting or scraping.

Study of the mastic remains has thrown less light on the hafting and function of other microlith types. Some triangular microliths were evidently hafted side by side in a continuous groove, but their function, like that of the trapeziform microliths, remains obscure. A single transverse-backed flake was evidently hafted by the bulbar end and may have served as a small scraper.

None of the 368 convex-backed flakes from horizons 2ii to 4ii shows traces of mastic, although this is found on 4.8 per cent of the 1058 geometrics from these horizons. Since the backing on the backed flakes is indistinguishable from that on the geometrics and would thus have provided equally effective keying for the adhesion of mastic, it must be concluded that backed flakes were not normally hafted by this means. It seems safe to suppose that they were used directly in the hand. I have argued above that the hafting evidence suggests that many pointed and asymmetrical lunates were used as arrow- or spear-barbs and the deep lunates as transverse arrowheads. This evidence of distinct functions for curved-backed geometrics and backed flakes is in keeping with conclusions obtained by microscopic analysis of the edge wear on artefacts from Chiwemupula (Phillipson and Phillipson, 1970), where it was demonstrated that on geometrics wear was concentrated along the edges, which were generally scaled and dulled, while heavy signs of wear on the backed flakes occurred most frequently on their points.

Similarly, backed points and scrapers do not appear to have been hafted.

Among the geometrics, mastic is most common on deep lunates (9.7 per cent) and least frequent on pointed lunates (only 2.2 per cent). It has been shown above that deep lunates were hafted in a manner different from the other types, and this 'free-riding' hafting necessitated the use of more mastic spread over a greater area of the implement than did the groove-hafting method. The high incidence of mastic on deep lunates may thus be explained.

In analysing the Makwe stone industry, considerable difficulty was encountered in satisfactorily differentiating between the pointed and asymmetrical lunates on the one hand and the convex-backed flakes on the other. The definitions I have used (see above, p. 26), which include as curved-backed geometrics all specimens where the striking platform has been either removed or so modified that it blends with the curved back without an intervening angle, are admittedly arbitrary and based on techno-morphological considerations which may not necessarily have had any functional relevance. It may well be that I have applied these criteria too rigorously, and erroneously included with the curved-backed geometrics many specimens which have more in common with the convex-backed flakes. If this is so, it may serve as a factor contributing to the apparently low incidence of mastic in my symmetrical lunate category; but the problem serves to emphasise how little we know of what features of a stone industry were of significance to the makers themselves.

In addition to the information they provide on hafting methods *per se* and on the original function of some of the hafted tools, the Makwe mastic-retaining microliths are of interest in providing a slight indication that the typological division here adopted for the establishment of varying artefact categories probably bears some relationship to the functional division meaningful to the original tool-makers. These specimens provide us with an uncommon insight into the rationale and general methodology of the 'Late Stone Age' technology.

The inferences drawn from these specimens are necessarily tentative and inconclusive, but the collection is of importance in view of the extreme rarity of mastic adhering to African 'Late Stone Age' artefacts. Four examples of complete hafted implements are described by J. D. Clark (1958a) and H. Deacon (1966) from sites in the Cape Province of South Africa, but these implements are all scrapers or adze-flakes, including specimens without intentional retouch. Remains of hafts without the stone inserts come from Melkhoutboom (Hewitt, 1931) and Matjes River Shelter (Dreyer, 1933), both also in the Cape. J. D. Clark (1968) and Langenheim (1968) have noted occurrences of resin from sites in Lunda, Angola, which they suggest may have been collected for use as mastic although none of the finds were found associated with artefacts. One specimen has been radiocarbon dated early in the first millennium bc. The Makwe collection is thus at present unique in sub-Saharan Africa, both for its size and for the range of information which it yields for the study of 'Late Stone Age' hafting methods.

Plate I

a. *Chewa women with Luangwa tradition pottery, near Chikuleni village, Chief Kathumba, 1966.*
b. Chimtunga, *a bored stone used by Chewa as a pot-boiler for heating beer. Overall length:* c. *25 cm.*

Plate II

a.   Early Iron Age pottery excavated by Carl Wiese from Chifumbaze in Moçambique. Scale: approx. 1/1. (Reproduced by courtesy of the Museum für Völkerkunde, Berlin.)

b.   The Kamnama Early Iron Age site.

Plate III

a.   Thandwe rock-shelter from the north.

b.   Excavation at Thandwe, from the south.

Plate IV

a. *Grave 1 at Thandwe, after removal of the covering slab. Scale in inches.*

b. *Little Makwe* kopje *seen from the summit of Big Makwe.*

Plate V

a.   The entrance to Makwe rock-shelter.

b.   View to the east from the front fallen boulder of Makwe rock-shelter.

Plate VI

a.   The interior of Makwe rock-shelter, from the north, before excavation. Scale in feet.

b.   The Makwe deposits: ash lenses in horizon 3. Scale in inches.

Plate VII

Artefacts from Makwe: top row: *knapping hammers (scale approx. 3/1):* centre: *detail of pounding stone (scale approx. 3/1);* bottom row: *bone artefacts (scale approx. 3/2).*

Plate VIII

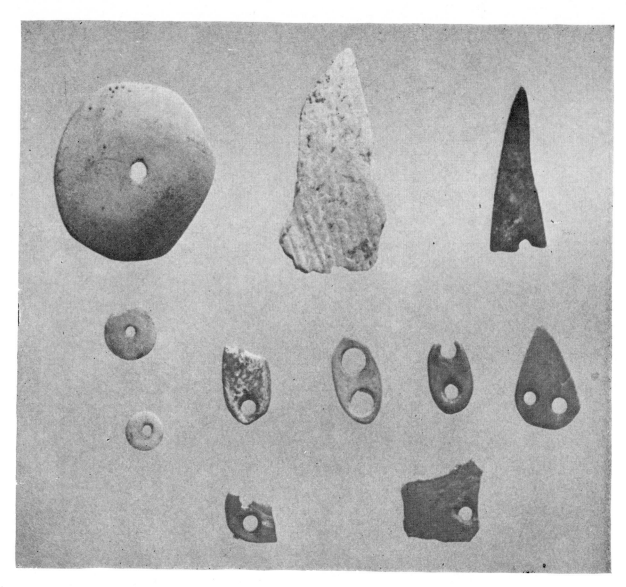

a. Shell artefacts from Makwe. Scale: approx. 2/1.

b. Fragments of mineralised twig from Makwe (see p. 107). Scale: approx. 3/2.

Plate IX

a.   Kalemba rock-shelter seen from across the Chipwete valley.

b.   View from Kalemba up the Chipwete valley to the Mbangombe plain.

Plate X

a.   Kalemba rock-shelter from the south-west, showing excavations in progress.

b.   The interior of Kalemba rock-shelter, from the north, before excavation. Scale in feet.

Plate XI

a.   The Kalemba excavation seen from the north-west. Scale in feet.

b.   The north-west excavation at Kalemba, from the south. Scale in feet.

c.   The north-west excavation at Kalemba from the south-east. Scale in feet.

Plate XII

Burial in horizon O, grid square I 11 at Kalemba:
a. with covering stones exposed, viewed from the south-west.
b. with covering stones removed, viewed from the north-east. Both scales in inches.

Plate XIII

a. The north-east face of the
    south-east excavation at
    Kalemba, showing displacement
    of the dividing boulder.

b. Kalemba: later Iron Age pot
    containing beans (see pp. 126-7).
    Scale in inches.

Plate XIV

Remains of pole- and bamboo-framed shelters preserved in horizon S at Kalemba. Scales in inches.
a. *From the north-west.*
b. *From the south-west.*

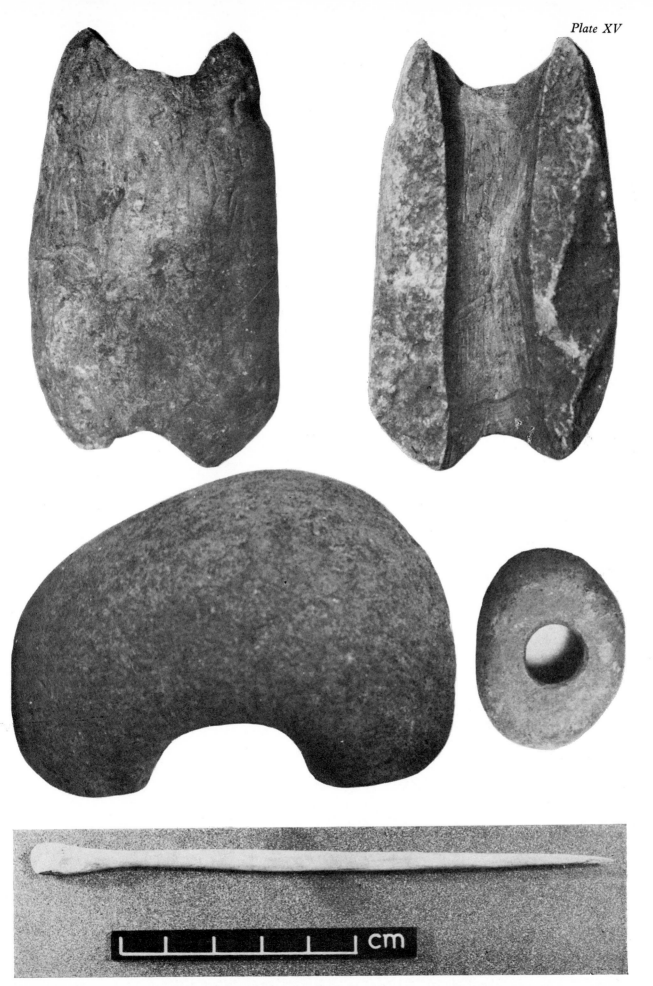

Plate XV

Artefacts from Kalemba: above: bored stones; below: headed bone pin.

Plate XVI

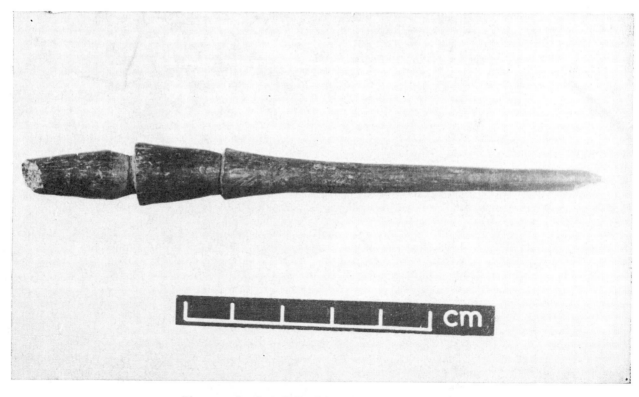

a. *Pigment cakes from Kalemba, horizon L.*
b. *Wooden arrowpoint or link-shaft from Kalemba, horizon S.*

Plate XVII

Kalemba skull Sk 2. Scales: 3/5 (top), 3/4 (below).

Plate XVIII

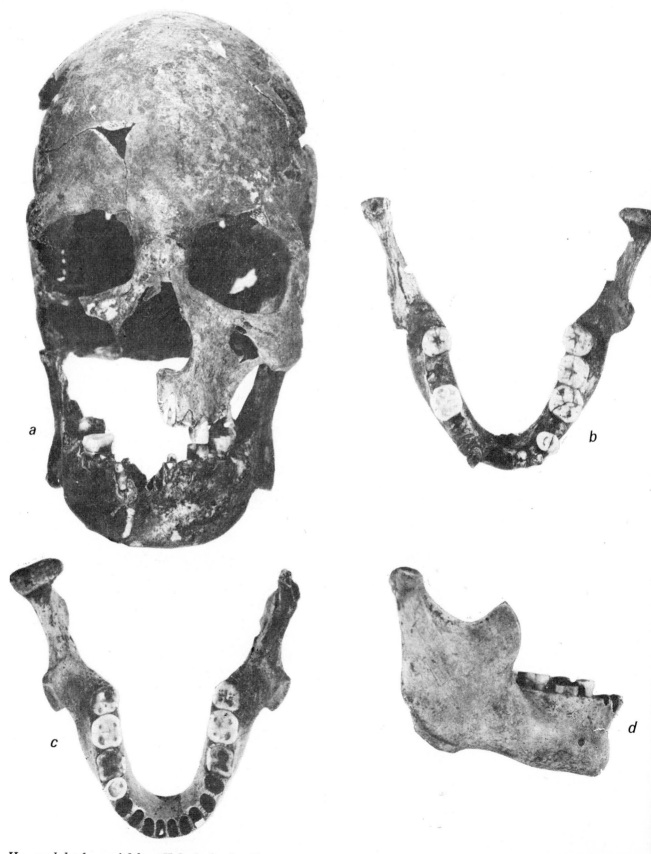

Human skeletal material from Kalemba (scale: 3/4):   a — skull Sk 2;   b — mandible Sk 2;   c, d — mandible Sk 5.

Plate XIX

Rock paintings at Chaingo. Width of illustrated area: 1.4 m.

Plate XX

a.   Chipwete rock-shelter viewed from the south-east.

b.   Rock painting at Chipwete. Width of illustrated area: 60 cm.

Plate XXI

a.   *General view of the main panel of rock paintings at Kalemba. Scale in feet.*

b.   *Detail of the north-eastern end of the main painted panel at Kalemba. Scale in feet.*

Plate XXII

a. Detail from the Kalemba paintings. Width of illustrated area: 40 cm.

b. Detail from the Kalemba paintings. Width of illustrated area: 60 cm.

Plate XXIII

a. The central portion of the main panel of rock paintings at Kalemba, showing obliterated area which was enclosed within a bamboo-framed structure in the nineteenth century. Scale in feet.

b. Detail from the Kalemba paintings. Width of illustrated area: 30 cm.

Plate *XXIV*

b. *Rock paintings at Kavumo A. Scale in inches.*

a. *Detail of rock painting at Katolola, showing schematic grid overlain by fore-part of naturalistic eland. Width of illustrated area: 50 cm.*

Plate XXV

a. Rock paintings at Kavumo C. Width of illustrated area: 3 m.

b. Manje site A, viewed from the south.

Plate XXVI

Mkoma rock-shelter, from the north.

Plate XXVII

Detail of the Mkoma rock paintings. Width of illustrated area: 65 cm.

Plate XXVIII

Rock paintings at Sakwe A. Width of illustrated area: 2.5 m.

Plate XXIX

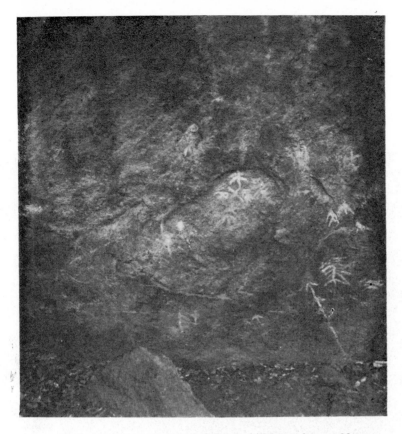

a.   Rock paintings at Sakwe B. Width of illustrated area: 90 cm.
b.   Detail of paintings on the north-west-facing panel at Thandwe. Width of illustrated area: 50 cm.

Plate XXX

a.   *Zawi Hill from Kamkumwe village.*
b.   *Rock painting at Zawi site A. Width of illustrated area: 45 cm.*

Plate XXXI

Makwe: backed microliths retaining hafting mastic. Scale: 3/1.
1-3—symmetrical lunates; 4-6—deep lunates; 7—triangular microlith; 8-10—petits tranchets; 11—backed fragment.

References

Allen, W. (1965) *The African Husbandman*. Edinburgh: Oliver and Boyd.

Allchin, B. (1966) *The Stone-Tipped Arrow*. London: Phoenix.

Alpers, E. (1968) 'The Mutapa and Malawi political systems to the time of the Ngoni invasions', pp. 1–28 *in* T. O. Ranger (ed.), *Aspects of Central African History*. London: Heinemann.

Angus, M. C. (1899) 'A trip to northern Angoniland', *Scottish Geographical Magazine*, XV: 74–9.

Anon. (1953) 'The first mine', *Northern Rhodesia Journal*, II, 2:81–2.

Ansell, W. F. H. (1960) *The Mammals of Northern Rhodesia*. Lusaka: Government Printer.

Apthorpe, R. (1960) 'Problems of African history: the Nsenga of Northern Rhodesia', *Rhodes-Livingstone Journal*, XXVIII: 47–67.

Apthorpe, R. (1962) 'A note on Nsenga girls' puberty designs', *South African Archaeological Bulletin*, XVII: 12–13.

Armstrong, A. L. (1931) 'Excavation in Bambata Cave and researches on prehistoric sites in Southern Rhodesia', *Journal of the Royal Anthropological Institute*, CXX: 239–76.

Baker, C. A. (1972) 'The development of the administration to 1897', pp. 323–43 *in* B. Pachai (ed.), *The Early History of Malawi*. London: Longman.

Barnes, J. A. (1948) *The Material Culture of the Fort Jameson Ngoni*. Livingstone: Rhodes-Livingstone Museum (Occasional Papers, no. I).

Barnes, J. A. (1951) 'The Fort Jameson Ngoni', pp.194–252 *in* E. Colson and M. Gluckman (eds.), *Seven Tribes of British Central Africa*. London: Oxford University Press.

Barnes, J. A. (1954) *Politics in a Changing Society*. London: Oxford University Press.

Barr, M. W. C. and A. R. Drysdall (1972) *The Geology of the Sasare Area: Explanation of Degree Sheet 1331, S. W. Quarter*. Lusaka: Zambia Geological Survey (Report no. 30).

Bishop, W. W. and J. D. Clark (eds.) (1967) *Background to Evolution in Africa*. Chicago: Chicago University Press.

Bond, G. (1957) 'The geology of the Khami Stone Age sites', *Occasional Papers of the National Museum of S. Rhodesia*, III, 21a: 44–55.

Brain, C. K. (1969) 'New evidence for climatic change during Middle and Late Stone Age times in Rhodesia', *South African Archaeological Bulletin*, XXIV: 127–43.

Brelsford, W. V. (1938) *Handbook to the David Livingstone Memorial Museum*. Livingstone: Rhodes-Livingstone Institute.

Brelsford, W. V. (1965) *The Tribes of Zambia*. Lusaka: Government Printer.

Broom, R. (1942) Appendix I: Note on the Mumbwa fauna, pp. 197–8 *in* J. D. Clark, 'Further Excavations (1939) at the Mumbwa Caves, Northern Rhodesia', *Transactions of the Royal Society of South Africa*, XXIX.

Brothwell, D. R. (1963) 'Evidence of early population change in central and southern Africa: doubts and problems', *Man*, LXIII: article 132.

Brothwell, D. R. and T. Shaw (1971) 'A late Upper Pleistocene proto-West African negro from Nigeria', *Man* (N.S.), VI: 221–7.

Bruwer, J. P. (1956) 'Note on the Njazi rockshelter site in the Eastern Province of Northern Rhodesia', *Northern Rhodesia Journal*, III, 1: 87–90.

Burton, R. F. (ed.) (1873) *The Lands of Kazembe*. London: Royal Geographical Society.

Chambers, E. G. (1958) *Statistical Calculation for Beginners*. Cambridge: University Press.

Chaplin, J. H. (1960) 'Some unpublished rock paintings of Northern Rhodesia', *South African Archaeological Bulletin*, XV: 45–9.

Chaplin, J. H. (1961a) 'A note on the forts of the Eastern Province', *Northern Rhodesia Journal*, IV, 5: 462–8.

Chaplin, J. H. (1961b) Unpublished tour report to Northern Rhodesia National Monuments Commission.

Chaplin, J. H. (1962) 'Further unpublished examples of rock art from Northern Rhodesia', *South African Archaeological Bulletin*, XVII: 5–13.

Clark, J. D. (1939) *Stone Age Sites in Northern Rhodesia and the Possibilities of Future Research*. (Supplement to *Museum Handbook*.) Livingstone: Rhodes-Livingstone Institute.

Clark, J. D. (1942) 'Further excavations (1939) at the Mumbwa Caves, Northern Rhodesia', *Transactions of the Royal Society of South Africa*, XXIX: 133–201.

Clark, J. D. (1950a) 'A note on the pre-Bantu inhabitants of Northern Rhodesia and Nyasaland', *South African Journal of Science;* XLVII: 80–5.

Clark, J. D. (1950b) *The Stone Age Cultures of Northern Rhodesia*. Cape Town: South African Archaeological Society.

Clark, J. D. (1950c) 'The newly-discovered Nachikufu Culture of Northern Rhodesia and the possible origin of certain elements of the South African Smithfield Culture', *South African Archaeological Bulletin*, V: 86–98.

Clark, J. D. (1954) 'Upper Sangoan Industries from Northern Nyasaland and the Luangwa Valley: a case of environmental differentiation?', *South African Journal of Science*, L:201–8.

Clark, J. D. (1955) 'Human skeletal and cultural material from a deep cave at Chipongwe, Northern Rhodesia', *South African Archaeological Bulletin*, X: 107–14.

Clark, J. D. (1956) 'Prehistory in Nyasaland', *Nyasaland Journal*, IX: 92–119.

Clark, J. D. (1958a) 'Some Stone Age woodworking tools in southern Africa', *South African Archaeological Bulletin*, XIII: 144–52.

Clark, J. D. (1958b) 'Schematic Art', *South African Archaeological Bulletin*, XIII: 72–4.

Clark, J. D. (1958c) 'The Chifubwa Stream rock shelter, Solwezi, Northern Rhodesia', *South African Archaeological Bulletin*, XIII: 21–4.

Clark, J. D. (1959a) *The Prehistory of Southern Africa*. Harmondsworth: Penguin Books.

Clark, J. D. (1959b) 'The rock paintings of Northern Rhodesia and Nyasaland', pp. 163–220 in R. Summers (ed.), *Prehistoric Rock Art of the Federation of Rhodesia and Nyasaland*. London: Chatto and Windus.

Clark, J. D. (1965) 'The Portuguese settlement at Feira', *Northern Rhodesia Journal*, VI: 275–92.

Clark, J. D. (1968) *Further Palaeo-anthropological Studies in Northern Lunda*. Lisboa: Companhia de Diamantes de Angola.

Clark, J. D. (ed.) (1969) *Kalambo Falls Prehistoric Site, Vol. I*. Cambridge: University Press.

Clark, J. D. (1970a) 'Interim report on the archaeology of the Malawi, Rungwe and southern Rukwa regions', *Quaternaria*, XIII: 305–54.

Clark, J. D. (1970b) *The Prehistory of Africa*. London: Thames and Hudson.

Clark, J. D. (1971) 'Human behavioural differences in southern Africa during the late Pleistocene', *American Anthropologist*, LXXIII: 1211–36.

Clark, J. D. (1972) 'Prehistoric origins', pp. 17–27 in B. Pachai (ed.), *The Early History of Malawi*. London: Longman.

Clark, J. D. (1973) 'Archaeological investigation of a painted rock shelter at Mwana wa Chencherere, north of Dedza, central Malawi', *Society of Malawi Journal*, XXVI.

Clark, J. D. (1974) *Kalambo Falls Prehistoric Site, Vol. II*. Cambridge: University Press.

Clark, J. D. (1975) 'Stone Age man at the Victoria Falls', pp. 28–47 in D. W. Phillipson (ed.), *Mosi-oa-Tunya: a Handbook to the Victoria Falls Region*. London: Longman.

Clark, J. D., K. P. Oakley, L. H. Wells and J. A. C. McClelland (1947) 'New studies on Rhodesian Man', *Journal of the Royal Anthropological Institute*, LXXVII: 7–32.

Clark, J. G. D. (1969) *World Prehistory: a New Outline*. Cambridge: University Press.

Cole-King, P. A. (1968) 'Mwala Wolemba on Mikolonge Hill', *Society of Malawi Journal*, XXI.

Cole-King, P. A. (1973) *Kukumba Mbiri mu Malawi: a Summary of Archaeological Research to March, 1973*. Zomba: Department of Antiquities (Publication XV).

Cole-King, P. A., J. E. Bushell and J. F. Bushell (1973) 'Zomba Range: an Early Iron Age site.' Zomba: Department of Antiquities (Publication XIV: 51–70).

Cooke, C. K. (1963) 'Report on excavations at Pomongwe and Tshangula caves, Matopo Hills, Southern Rhodesia', *South African Archaeological Bulletin*, XVIII: 73–151.

Cooke, C. K. (1964) 'An unusual burial in the Gwanda district of Southern Rhodesia', *South African Archaeological Bulletin*, XIX: 41–2.

Cooke, C. K. (1969) 'A re-examination of the "Middle Stone Age" industries of Rhodesia', *Arnoldia (Rhod.)*, IV, no. 7.

Cooke, C. K. (1971) 'Excavation in Zombepata cave, Sipolilo district, Mashonaland, Rhodesia', *South African Archaeological Bulletin*, XXVI: 104–27.

Cooke, C. K. (1973) 'The Middle Stone Age in Rhodesia and South Africa', *Arnoldia (Rhod)*, VI, no. 20.

Cooke, C. K. and K. R. Robinson (1954) 'Excavations at Amadzimba cave located in the Matopos Hills, Southern Rhodesia', *Occasional Papers of the National Museum of Southern Rhodesia*, II, 19: 699–728.

Cooke, C. K., R. Summers and K. R. Robinson (1966) 'Rhodesian prehistory re-examined: part I, Stone Age', *Arnoldia (Rhod.)*, II, no. 12.

Cooke, H. J. (1975) 'The palaeoclimatic significance of caves and adjacent land forms in western Ngamiland, Botswana', *Geographical Journal*, CXLI: 430–44.

Coxhead, J. C. C. (1914) *The Native Tribes of North-eastern Rhodesia*. London: Royal Anthropological Institute.

Cunnison, I. (1959) *The Luapula Peoples of Northern Rhodesia*. Manchester: University Press.

Cunnison, I. (trans.) (1960) *King Kazembe, and the Marave, Cheva, Bisa, Bemba, Lunda and other peoples of southern Africa, being the diary of the Portuguese expedition to that potentate in the years 1831 and 1832*. Lisboa: Junta de Investigações do Ultramar (Estudos de Ciências Politicas e Sociais, nos. 42, 43).

Dalby, D. (1975) 'The prehistorical implications of Guthrie's *Comparative Bantu*. I—Problems of internal relationship', *Journal of African History*, XVI: 481–501.

Dart, R. A. (1931): 'Rock engravings in southern Africa and some clues to their significance and age', *South African Journal of Science*, XXVIII 475–86.

Deacon, H. (1966) 'Note on the X-ray of two mounted implements from South Africa', *Man (N.S.)*, I: 87–90.

Deacon, H. (1972) 'A review of the post-Pleistocene in South Africa', *South African Archaeological Society, Goodwin Series*, II: 26–41.

Deacon, J. (1972) 'Wilton: an assessment after fifty years', *South African Archaeological Bulletin*, XXVII: 10–48.

Deacon, J. (1974) 'Patterning in the radiocarbon dates for the Wilton/Smithfield Complex in South Africa', *South African Archaeological Bulletin*, XXIX: 3–18.

Denbow, J. R. (1973) 'Malowa rock shelter: archaeological report'. Zomba: Department of Antiquities (Publication XIV: 5–49).

Dixey, F. (1939) 'The early Cretaceous valley-floor peneplain of the Lake Nyasa region and its relation to Tertiary Rift structures', *Quarterly Journal of the Geological Society*, XLV: 75–108.

Dixey, F. (1944) 'The geomorphology of Northern Rhodesia', *Transactions of the Geological Society of South Africa*, XLVII: 9–45.

Doggett, H. (1970) *Sorghum*. London: Longman.

Doran, J. E. and Hodson, F. R. (1975) *Mathematics and Computers in Archaeology*. Edinburgh: University Press.

Drennan, M. R. (1938) 'Archaeology of the Oakhurst shelter, George, Part III', *Transactions of the Royal Society of South Africa*, XXV: 259–93.

Dreyer, T. F. (1933) 'The archaeology of the Matjes River rock shelter', *Transactions of the Royal Society of South Africa*, XXI: 187–209.

Ehret, C. (1972) 'Bantu origins and history: critique and interpretation', *Transafrican Journal of History*, II: 1–19.

Ehret, C. (1973) 'Patterns of Bantu and Central Sudanic settlement in central and southern Africa', *Transafrican Journal of History*, III: 1–71.

Fagan, B. M. (1966) 'Radiocarbon dates for sub-Saharan Africa—IV', *Journal of African History*, VII: 495–500.

Fagan, B. M. (1967) *Iron Age Cultures in Zambia, Vol. I*. London: Chatto and Windus.

Fagan, B. M. (1969) 'Excavations at Ingombe Ilede 1960–2', pp. 55–184 in B. M. Fagan, D. W. Phillipson and S. G. H. Daniels, *Iron Age Cultures in Zambia, Vol. II*. London: Chatto and Windus.

Fagan, B. M. and F. van Noten (1971) *The Hunter-Gatherers of Gwisho*. Tervuren: Musée royal de l'Afrique centrale (Annales, no. 74).

Fagan, B. M. and D. W. Phillipson (1965) 'Sebanzi: the Iron Age sequence at Lochinvar, and the Tonga', *Journal of the Royal Anthropological Institute*, XCV: 253–94.

Flint, R. F. (1959) 'Pleistocene climates in eastern and southern Africa', *Bulletin of the Geological Society of America*, LXX: 343–74.

Fraser, R. H. (1945) 'Land settlement in the Eastern Province of Northern Rhodesia', *Rhodes-Livingstone Journal*, III: 45–9.

Gabel, C. (1965) *Stone Age Hunters of the Kafue*. Boston: University Press.

Gabel, C. (1967) 'Archaeology in the western Copperbelt', *South African Archaeological Bulletin*, XXII: 3–14.

Galloway, A. (1959) *The Skeletal Remains of Bambandyanalo*. Johannesburg: Witwatersrand University Press.

Gamitto, A. C. P. (1854) *O Muata Cazembe*. Lisboa.

Gann, L. H. (1964) *History of Northern Rhodesia*. London: Chatto and Windus.

Garlake, P. S. (1973) *Great Zimbabwe*. London: Thames and Hudson.

Goodwin, A. J. H. (1945) 'Some historical Bushman arrows', *South African Journal of Science*, XLI: 429–43.

Gouldsbury, C. and Sheane, H. (1911) *The Great Plateau of Northern Rhodesia*. London: Arnold.

Gramly, R. M. and G. P. Rightmire (1973) 'A fragmentary cranium and dated later Stone Age assemblage from Lukenya Hill, Kenya', *Man* (N.S.), VIII: 571–9.

Greenberg, J. (1972) 'Linguistic evidence regarding Bantu origins', *Journal of African History*, XIII: 189–216.

Guthrie, M. (1962) 'Some developments in the prehistory of the Bantu languages', *Journal of African History*, III: 273–82.

Hall, R. (1965) *Zambia*. London: Pall Mall Press.

Hamilton, R. A. (1959) 'Oral tradition: central Africa', p. 21 in D. H. Jones (ed.), *History and Archaeology in Africa*. London: School of Oriental and African Studies.

Hanna, A. J. (1956) *The Beginnings of Nyasaland and North-Eastern Rhodesia*. Oxford: Clarendon Press.

Harlan, J. R. (1971) 'Agricultural origins, centers and non-centers', *Science*, CLXXIV: 468–74.

Heine, B. (1973) 'Zür genetischen Gliederung der Bantu-Sprachen', *Afrika und Ubersee*, LVI: 164–85.

Hewitt, J. (1931) 'Artefacts from Melkhoutboom', *South African Journal of Science*, XXVIII: 540–8.

Hiernaux, J. (1974) *The People of Africa*. London: Weidenfeld and Nicolson.

Hiernaux, J., E. de Longrée and J. de Buyst (1971) *Fouilles archéologiques dans la vallée de Haut Lualaba, I—Sanga*. Tervuren: Musée royal de l'Afrique centrale (Annales, no. 73).

Hiernaux, J., E. Maquet and J. de Buyst (1972) 'Le cimetière protohistorique de Katoto (vallée du Lualaba, Congo-Kinshasa)', pp. 148–58 in H. J. Hugot (ed.), *Actes du VI Congrès Panafricain de Préhistoire*. Chambéry.

Hodgson, A. G. O. (1933) 'Notes on the Achewa and Angoni of the Dowa District of the Nyasaland Protectorate', *Journal of the Royal Anthropological Institute*, LXIII: 123–64.

Huffman, T. N. (1974) *The Leopard's Kopje Tradition*. Salisbury: National Museums of Rhodesia (Memoir no. 6).

Inskeep, R. R. (1959) 'A Late Stone Age camping-site in the upper Zambezi valley', *South African Archaeological Bulletin*, XIV: 91–6.

Inskeep, R. R. (1962) 'The date of the Kondoa rock paintings in the light of recent excavations at Kisese II rock shelter', pp. 249–56 in G. Mortelmans and J. Nenquin (eds.), *Actes du IV Congrès Panafricain de Préhistoire*. Tervuren: Musée royal de l'Afrique centrale (Annales, no. 40).

Inskeep, R. R. (1965) *Preliminary Investigation of the Proto-historic Cemetery at Nkudzi Bay, Malawi*. Livingstone: National Museums of Zambia.

Johnston, Sir H. H. (1897) *British Central Africa: an attempt to give some account of a portion of the territories under British influence north of the Zambezi*. London: Methuen.

Kay, G. (1965) *Changing Patterns of Settlement and Land Use in the Eastern Province of Northern Rhodesia*. Hull: University Press (Occasional Papers in Geography, no. 2).

Kay, G. (1967) *A Social Geography of Zambia*. London: University of London Press.

Klein, R. G. (1973) 'The geological antiquity of Rhodesian man', *Nature*, CCXLIV: 311–2.

Klein, R. G. (1974) 'Environment and subsistence of prehistoric man in the southern Cape Province, South Africa', *World Archaeology*, V: 249–84.

Kurashina, H. (1973) 'Archaeological investigations along the Nanyangu', Zomba: Department of Antiquities (Publication XIV: 71–89).

Lancaster, D. G. (1937) 'A tentative chronology of the Ngoni', *Journal of the Royal Anthropological Institute*, LXVII: 77–90.

Lane-Poole, E. H. (1931) 'An early Portuguese settlement in Northern Rhodesia', *Journal of the Royal African Society*, XXX: 164–8.

Lane-Poole, E. H. (1938) *The Native Tribes of the Eastern Province of Northern Rhodesia* (2nd ed.). Lusaka: Government Printer.

Langenheim, J. H. (1968) 'Infrared spectrophotometric study of resins from north-east Angola', pp. 151–4 *in* J. D. Clark, *Further Palaeo-anthropological Studies in Northern Lunda*. Lisboa: Companhia de Diamantes de Angola.

Langworthy, H. W. (1971) 'Swahili influence in the area between Lake Malawi and the Luangwa River', *African Historical Studies*, IV: 575–602.

Langworthy, H. W. (1972a) *Zambia before 1890: aspects of pre-colonial history*. London: Longman.

Langworthy, H. W. (1972b) 'Chewa or Malawi political organisation in the precolonial era', pp. 104–22 *in* B. Pachai (ed.), *The Early History of Malawi*. London: Longman.

Lawton, A. C (1967) 'Bantu pottery of southern Africa', *Annals of the South African Museum*, XLIX, 1.

Leakey, L. S. B. (1931) *Stone Age Cultures of Kenya Colony*. Cambridge: University Press.

Leakey, L. S. B. (1936) *Stone Age Africa*. Oxford: University Press.

Leakey, M. D., R. L. Hay, D. L. Thurber, R. Protsch and R. Berger (1972) 'Stratigraphy, archaeology, and age of the Ndutu and Naisiusiu Beds, Olduvai Gorge, Tanzania', *World Archaeology*, III: 328–41.

Lee, R. B. (1966) *The Subsistence Ecology of the !Kung Bushmen*. Ph.D. thesis, University of California, Berkeley.

Letcher, O. (1910) 'The rock paintings or inscriptions of Chifumbaze (Portuguese N. Zambezi)', *Rhodesia Journal*.

Linden, I. (1975) 'Chewa initiation rites and *Nyau* societies: the use of religious institutions in local politics at Mua', pp. 30–44 *in* T. O. Ranger and J. Weller (eds.), *Themes in the Christian History of Central Africa*. London: Heinemann.

Livingstone, D. (1874) *The Last Journals* (ed. H. Waller). London: Murray.

Macrae, F. B. (1926) 'The Stone Age in Northern Rhodesia', *Native Affairs Department Annual (Salisbury)*, IV: 67–8.

Macrae, F. B. and D. G. Lancaster (1937) 'Stone Age sites in Northern Rhodesia', *Man*, XXXVII: article 74.

de Maret, P. (1975) 'A carbon-14 date from Zaire', *Antiquity*, XLIX: 133–7.

Marwick, M. G. (1963) 'History and tradition in east-central Africa through the eyes of the Northern Rhodesian Cewa', *Journal of African History*, IV: 375–90.

Marwick, M. G. (1965) *Sorcery and its Social Setting: a study of the Northern Rhodesian Cewa*. Manchester: University Press.

McBurney, C. B. M. (1967) *The Haua Fteah (Cyrenaica) and the Stone Age of the South-East Mediterranean*. Cambridge: University Press.

Miller, J. C. (1972) 'The Imbangala and the chronology of early Central African history', *Journal of African History*, XIII: 549–74.

Miller, S. F. (1969) *The Nachikufan Industries of the Zambian Later Stone Age*. Ph.D. thesis, University of California, Berkeley.

Miller, S. F. (1971) 'The age of the Nachikufan industries in Zambia', *South African Archaeological Bulletin*, XXVI: 143–6.

Miller, S. F. (1972) 'The archaeological sequence of the Zambian Later Stone Age', pp. 565–72 *in* H. J. Hugot (ed.), *Actes du VI Congrès Panafricain de Préhistoire*. Chambéry.

Mills, E. A. C. and N. T. Filmer (1972) 'Chondwe Iron Age site, Ndola, Zambia', *Azania*, VII: 129–45.

Mortelmans, G. (1962) 'Archéologie des grottes Dimba et Ngovo (région de Thysville, Bas-Congo)', *in* G. Mortelmans and J. Nenquin (eds.), *Actes du IV Congrès Panafricain de Préhistoire*. Tervuren: Musée royal de l'Afrique centrale (Annales, no. 40).

Nelson, C. M. and M. Posnansky (1970) 'The stone tools from the re-excavation of Nsongezi rock shelter', *Azania*, V: 119–72.

Nenquin, J. (1959) 'Dimple-based pots from Kasai, Belgian Congo', *Man*, LIX: article 242.

Ntara, S. J. (1973) *The History of the Chewa*. Wiesbaden: F. Steiner.

van Noten, F. (1971) 'Excavations at Munyama Cave', *Antiquity*, XLV: 56–8.

de Oliveira, O. R. (1971a) 'The rock-art of Moçambique', pp. 4–6 *in* M. Schoonraad (ed.), *Rock Paintings of Southern Africa*. South African Association for Advancement of Science: Special Publication, 2.

de Oliveira, O. R. (1971b) 'A arte rupestre em Moçambique', *Monumenta*, VII: 49–79.

Oliver, R. (1952) *The Missionary Factor in East Africa*. London: Longman.

Oliver, R. (1957) *Sir Harry Johnston and the Scramble for Africa*. London: Macmillan.

Oliver, R. and B. M. Fagan (1975) *Africa in the Iron Age*. London: Cambridge University Press.

O'Mahoney, B. (1963a) 'Fort Young and Fort Patrick', *Northern Rhodesia Journal*, V: 296–8.

O'Mahoney, B. (1963b) 'Was Cinunda's the first Fort Jameson?', *Northern Rhodesia Journal*, V: 298–300.

Omer-Cooper, J. D. (1966) *The Zulu Aftermath*. London: Longman.

Pager, H. (1975) *Stone Age Myth and Magic*. Graz: Akademische Druck- und Verlagsanstalt.

Pearce, S. and M. Posnansky (1963) 'The re-excavation of Nsongezi rock-shelter, Ankole', *Uganda Journal*, XXVII: 85–94.

Phillips, K. A. (1960) *The Geology of the Sinda Area: an Explanation of Degree Sheet 1431, N.E. Quarter*. Lusaka: Northern Rhodesia Geological Survey (Report no. 9).

Phillips, K. A. (1963) *The Geology of the Lusandwa River Area: an Explanation of Degree Sheet 1331, S.E. Quarter*. Lusaka: Northern Rhodesia Geological Survey (Report no. 13).

Phillips, K. A. (1965) *The Geology of the Petauke and Mwanjawantu Areas: an Explanation of Degree Sheet 1431, N.W. Quarter and Part of S.W. Quarter*. Lusaka: Zambia Geological Survey (Report no. 15).

Phillipson, D. W. (1966) 'The Late Stone Age and Zambia's first artists', pp. 56–79 *in* B. M. Fagan (ed.), *A Short History of Zambia*. Nairobi: Oxford University Press.

Phillipson, D. W. (1968a) 'The Early Iron Age in Zambia—regional variants and some tentative conclusions', *Journal of African History*, IX: 191–211.

Phillipson, D. W. (1968b) 'Cewa, Leya and Lala iron-smelting furnaces', *South African Archaeological Bulletin*, XXIII: 102–13.

Phillipson, D. W. (1968c) 'The Early Iron Age site at Kapwirimbwe, Lusaka', *Azania*, III: 87–105.

Phillipson, D. W. (1968d) 'Finds from Kapwirimbwe, Lusaka', *Inventaria Archaeologica Africana*, series Z5. Tervuren: Panafrican Congress on Prehistory.

Phillipson, D. W. (1969) 'The prehistoric sequence at Nakapapula rockshelter, Zambia', *Proceedings of the Prehistoric Society*, XXXV: 172–202.

Phillipson, D. W. (1970) 'Excavations at Twickenham Road, Lusaka', *Azania*, V: 77–118.

Phillipson, D. W. (1972a) 'Early Iron Age sites on the Zambian Copperbelt', *Azania*, VII: 93–128.

Phillipson, D. W. (1972b) 'Zambian rock paintings', *World Archaeology*, III: 313–27.

Phillipson, D. W. (1974) 'Iron Age history and archaeology in Zambia', *Journal of African History*, XV: 1–25.

Phillipson, D. W. (1975) 'The chronology of the Iron Age in Bantu Africa', *Journal of African History*, XVI: 321–42.

Phillipson, D. W. (1976a) 'The Early Iron Age in eastern and southern Africa: a critical re-appraisal', *Azania*, XI.

Phillipson, D. W. (1976b) 'Archaeology and Bantu linguistics', *World Archaeology*. VII: 65–82.

Phillipson, D. W. (in press) *Later Prehistory of Eastern and Southern Africa*. London: Heinemann.

Phillipson, L. (1975) *A Survey of Upper Pleistocene and Holocene Industries in the Upper Zambezi Valley, Zambia*. Ph.D. thesis, University of California, Berkeley.

Phillipson, L. (1976) 'Survey of the Stone Age archaeology of the upper Zambezi valley, II: Excavations at Kandanda', *Azania*, XI.

Phillipson, L. and D. W. Phillipson (1970) 'Patterns of edge damage on the Late Stone Age industry from Chiwemupula, Zambia', *Zambia Museums Journal*, I: 40–75.

Rangeley, W. H. J. (1963) 'The earliest inhabitants of Nyasaland', *Nyasaland Journal*, XVI: 38–42.

Richards, A. I. (1956) *Chisungu*. London: Faber and Faber.

Rightmire, G. P. (1974) 'Problems in the study of later Pleistocene man in Africa', *American Anthropologist*, LXXVII: 28–52.

Rightmire, G. P. (1975) 'New studies of post-Pleistocene human skeletal remains from the Rift Valley, Kenya', *American Journal of Physical Anthropology*, XLII: 351–70.

Roberts, A. D. (1973) *A History of the Bemba*. London: Longman.

Robinson, K. R. (1952) 'Excavations in two rock-shelters near the Rusawi River, central Mashonaland', *South African Archaeological Bulletin*, VII: 108–29.

Robinson, K. R. (1961) 'An Early Iron Age site from the Chibi District, Southern Rhodesia', *South African Archaeological Bulletin*, XVI: 75–102.

Robinson, K. R. (1963) 'Further excavations in the Iron Age deposits at the Tunnel site, Gokomere Hill, Southern Rhodesia', *South African Archaeological Bulletin*, XVIII: 155–71.

Robinson, K. R. (1966a) 'A preliminary report on the recent archaeology of Ngonde, Northern Malawi', *Journal of African History*, VII: 169–88.

Robinson, K. R. (1966b) 'The Leopard's Kopje Culture: its position in the Iron Age of Southern Rhodesia', *South African Archaeological Bulletin*, XXI: 5–51.

Robinson, K. R. (1970) 'The Iron Age of the southern lake area of Malawi.' Zomba: Department of Antiquities (Publication VIII).

Robinson, K. R. (1973a) 'The Iron Age of the Upper and Lower Shire, Malawi.' Zomba: Department of Antiquities (Publication XIII).

Robinson, K. R. (1973b) 'The pottery sequence of Malawi briefly compared with that already established south of the Zambezi', *Arnoldia (Rhod.)*, VI, no. 18.

Robinson, K. R. and B. Sandelowsky (1968) 'The Iron Age of northern Malawi: recent work', *Azania*, III: 107–46.

Sampson, C. G. (1974) *The Stone Age Archaeology of Southern Africa*. New York and London: Academic Press.

Sampson, C. G. and M. D. Southard (1973) 'Variability and change in the Nachikufan Industry of Zambia', *South African Archaeological Bulletin*, XXVIII: 78–89.

Sandelowsky, B. and K. R. Robinson (1968) *Fingira: a preliminary report*, Zomba: Department of Antiquities (Publication III).

dos Santos, J. R. (Jnr.) (1938a) 'Pinturas rupestres de Chifumbazi', *Moçambique (Documentario Trimestral)*, XIII: 5–19.

dos Santos, J. R. (Jnr.) (1938b) 'Relatorio da Missao Antropológica à Africa do Sul e a Moçambique, 1a companha de trabalhos (1936)', *Trabalhos da Sociedade Portuguesa de Antropologia a Etnologia*, VIII: 257–308.

dos Santos, J. R. (Jnr.) (1940a) *Missao Antropológica de Moçambique, 2a campanha, Agosto de 1937 a Janeiro de 1938*. Lisboa: Agência das Colónias.

dos Santos, J. R. (Jnr.) (1940b) 'Prè-história de Moçambique', *Congressos do Mundo Português*, I, 1: 307–56.

dos Santos, J. R. (Jnr.) (1941) 'On the prehistory of Moçambique', *Moçambique (Documentario Trimestral)*, XXVIII: 23–75.

dos Santos, J. R. (Jnr.) (1955) 'Les peintures rupestres de Moçambique', pp. 747–58 in L. Balout (ed.), *Actes du II Congrès Panafricain de Préhistoire*, Paris: Arts et Métiers Graphiques.

dos Santos, J. R. (Jnr.) (1961) 'Pré-história de Moçambique: o que està feito, o que pode e deve fazer-se', *Congrès Nacional de Arqueologia*, I: 449–60.

Schepers, G. W. H. (1941) 'The mandible of the Transvaal fossil human skeleton from Springbok Flats', *Annals of the Transvaal Museum*, XX: 253–73.

Schoffeleers, M. (1973) 'Towards the identification of a proto-Chewa culture: a preliminary contribution', *Malawi Journal of Social Science*, II: 47–60.

Schweitzer, F. (1974) 'Archaeological evidence for sheep at the Cape', *South African Archaeological Bulletin*, XXIX: 75–82.

Shaw, T. (1969) 'The Late Stone Age in the Nigerian forest', pp. 364–73 *in* J. P. Lebeuf (ed.), *Actes du I Colloque International d'Archéologie Africaine*. Fort Lamy.

Soper, R. C. (1967) 'Kwale: an Early Iron Age site in south-eastern Kenya', *Azania*, II: 1–17.

Soper, R. C. (1971) 'A general review of the Early Iron Age of the southern half of Africa', *Azania*, VI: 5–37.

Stannus, H. S. (1922) 'The WaYao of Nyasaland', *Harvard African Studies*, III: 229–372.

Stannus, H. S. and J. B. Davey (1913) 'The initiation ceremony for boys among the Yao of Nyasaland', *Journal of the Royal Anthropological Institute*, XLIII: 119–23.

Staudinger, H. (1910) 'Funde und Abbildungen von Felszeichnungen aus den alten Goldgebieten von Portugiesichsüdostafrika', *Zeitschrift für Ethnologie*, XLII: 141–44.

Stefaniszyn, B. (1964a) *Social and Ritual Life of the Ambo of Northern Rhodesia*. London: Oxford University Press.

Stefaniszyn, B. (1964b) *The Material Culture of the Ambo of Northern Rhodesia*. Livingstone: Rhodes-Livingstone Museum. (Occasional Papers, no. XVI).

Summers, R. (1958) *Inyanga*. Cambridge: University Press.

Sutherland-Harris, N. (1970) 'Zambian trade with Zumbo in the eighteenth century', pp. 231–42 *in* R. Gray and D. Birmingham (eds.), *Pre-Colonial African Trade*. London: Oxford University Press.

Sutton, J. E. G. (1968) 'Archaeological sites in Usandawe', *Azania*, III: 167–74.

Sutton, J. E. G. (1972) 'New radiocarbon dates for eastern and southern Africa', *Journal of African History*, XIII: 1–24.

Tobias, P. V. (1958) 'Skeletal remains from Inyanga', pp. 159–72 *in* R. Summers, *Inyanga*. Cambridge: University Press.

Tobias, P. V. (1966) 'The peoples of Africa south of the Sahara', pp. 112–200 *in* P. T. Baker and J. S. Weiner, *The Biology of Human Adaptability*. Oxford: University Press.

Trapnell, C. G. (1943) *Soils, Vegetation and Agriculture of North-Eastern Rhodesia*. Lusaka: Government Printer.

Trapnell, C. G. (1962) *Vegetation-soil Map of Northern Rhodesia*. Lusaka: Department of Surveys.

Trotter, M. and G. C. Gleser, (1952) 'Estimation of stature from long bones of American Whites and Negroes', *American Journal of Physical Anthropology*, X: 453–514.

Vansina, J. (1969) 'The bells of kings', *Journal of African History*, 187–97.

de Villiers, H. (1968) *The Skull of the South African Negro*. Johannesburg: Witwatersrand University Press.

Vinnicombe, P. (1976) *People of the Eland*. Pietermaritzburg: University of Natal Press.

Weidenreich, F. (1936) 'The mandible of *Sinanthropus pekinensis:* a comparative study', *Palaeontologica Sinica*, Series D, VII: 1–162.

Werner, A. (1906) *The Native Races of the British Empire: British Central Africa*. London: Constable.

Werner, A. (1907) 'Bushman painting', *Journal of the Royal African Society*, VII: 387–93.

Wiese, C. (1891–2) 'Expediçao portugueza a M'Pesene', *Boletim da Sociedade de Geographia de Lisboa*, X (1891): 235–73, 331–430, 465–97; XI (1892): 373–599.

Wilson, V. J. (1975) 'Game and tsetse fly in eastern Zambia', *Occasional Papers of the National Museum of Rhodesia*, B, V (6): 339–404.

Winterbottom, J. M. and D. G. Lancaster (1965) 'The Chewa female initiation ceremony', *Northern Rhodesia Journal*, VI: 347–50.

Zambia Survey Department (1967) *Soils Map of the Republic of Zambia* (Zambia Atlas, sheet 12). Lusaka: Government Printer.

van Zinderen Bakker, E. M. and J. A. Coetzee (1972) 'A re-appraisal of late Quaternary climatic evidence from tropical Africa', pp. 151–81 *in* E. M. van Zinderen Bakker (ed.). *Palaeoecology of Africa*, *VII*. Cape Town: Balkema.

Index

The research described in this book, involving three major rock-shelter excavations and the investigation of numerous minor sites, has revealed an archaeological sequence covering at least the past thirty-five thousand years. The greater part of this period covers the later phases of the local 'Middle Stone Age' and the whole of the inception and development of the 'Late Stone Age'. A detailed picture was obtained of the technology and economy of the region's inhabitants through this long period of development: this is here discussed in relation both to the changing environmental conditions of eastern Zambia, and to contemporary events in other regions of sub-Saharan Africa. One of the most important results of the work here described has been the demonstration that the 'Late Stone Age' industries of eastern Zambia and, by implication, those of a much wider area of south-central and eastern Africa, were an essentially local development which owed little to inspiration or cultural contact from the inhabitants of more distant regions.

Also investigated were the Early and later Iron Ages of eastern Zambia, which mark the arrival of agricultural societies in the region. The long period of chronological overlap between these peoples and the stone-tool-using hunter/gatherers is here discussed in detail, and the extent of contact and acculturation between the two groups is evaluated. Both the Early and later Iron Age societies are considered with regard to their place in the general picture which is now emerging, from both archaeological and linguistic studies, of the spread of Bantu-speaking agriculturalists into sub-equatorial Africa. In the case of the later Iron Age, comparison is also made between the archaeological record and the historical evidence provided by the oral traditions of the present inhabitants of eastern Zambia.

Finally, a detailed description is presented of the over forty rock painting sites which have now been discovered in the region. A stylistic sequence is established which may be correlated with the archaeological succession. Within the chronological framework thus provided, it has proved possible to ascertain the probable significance which the rock paintings held in the lives of the artists.

The author, D. W. Phillipson, is now Assistant Director of the British Institute in Eastern Africa. He was Secretary/Inspector of the Zambia National Monuments Commission from 1964 until 1973.

£9.50 (K. Shs. 140; U.S $17.50)

ISBN 0 500 97003 3